COURTAULDS

AN ECONOMIC AND SOCIAL HISTORY

Sir John Hanbury-Williams (*circa* 1956)

D. C. COLEMAN

COURTAULDS

AN ECONOMIC AND SOCIAL HISTORY

III

CRISIS AND CHANGE
1940–1965

CLARENDON PRESS · OXFORD
1980

Oxford University Press, Walton Street, Oxford OX2 6DP

OXFORD LONDON GLASGOW
NEW YORK TORONTO MELBOURNE WELLINGTON
KUALA LUMPUR SINGAPORE JAKARTA HONG KONG TOKYO
DELHI BOMBAY CALCUTTA MADRAS KARACHI
NAIROBI DAR ES SALAAM CAPE TOWN

Published in the United States by
Oxford University Press, New York

British Library Cataloguing in Publication Data

Coleman, Donald Cuthbert
Courtaulds.
Vol. 3: Crisis and change, 1940–65
1. Courtaulds (*Firm*) – History
338.7'67'700941 HD9861.9.C68 79-41133

ISBN 0-19-920111-0

Printed in Great Britain
by W & J Mackay Limited, Chatham

INTRODUCTION AND ACKNOWLEDGEMENTS

THE agreement by which I undertook to write a history of Courtaulds was signed in January 1962. Some weeks earlier Imperial Chemical Industries had made their celebrated take-over bid for Courtaulds. Discussions about the proposed history had started in the summer of 1961, at which time there was no knowledge of such an impending bid. When the agreement was signed, however, it was not clear that Courtaulds would survive as an independent company. It did, and in the course of the next few years a new group of men rose to power within the Board and came to dominate the company's policies. In 1969, when the two volumes which were the outcome of the 1962 contract were published,[1] I agreed to collect material for a third volume and in 1974 contracted to write it. It was agreed that it should cover the quarter-century 1940–65, thus including the I.C.I. bid and its immediate aftermath.

History, as is well known, is commonly written by victors, not losers. The vindication of the revolution of 1688 was written by Whigs, not Tories. It is the victors' version which achieves the status of orthodoxy until, in time, it is challenged—unless State or Church effectively forbid such heretical acts. When I undertook in 1974 to write about the years 1940–65 in Courtaulds' history I recognized that the commission carried with it an implication even more potentially hazardous than that normally attaching to a commissioned business history. Would I not find myself writing—and certainly be accused of writing—a vindication, a eulogy even, of those who had come to power in the early 1960s after having led the opposition to the I.C.I. bid and apparently overthrown the policies of their predecessors? The uncharitable, though hardly preposterous, thought occurred to me that that was just what I was being asked to write. I hope it will be evident to readers that the result is not of that nature; and that my uncharitable thought was indeed unjustified. What I have tried to do is to examine the changing composition and outlook of a body of about eighteen men, comprising the Board of Courtaulds, and the ways in which it perceived and grappled with the problems besetting the company. A recent reviewer of a business history spoke of it as providing a 'boardroom

[1] *Courtaulds. An Economic and Social History*, Vol. I, *The Nineteenth Century: Silk and Crape;* Vol. II, *Rayon* (Oxford, 1969).

view', the 'view from the bridge'.[1] Whatever the justification of those comments in that context, it could, I think, be reasonably claimed that I have tried to provide not so much a view *from* the boardroom as a view *of* the Board. In so doing I have necessarily looked at the conflicts and shifting alignments which developed within it; at the clash of attitudes and personalities; at its changing social and educational composition; and at its varying perception of the surrounding economic environment. What I have specifically tried to avoid is any attempt to evaluate actions of which the major consequences could be seen to be evident only after 1965. In so far as consequences can reasonably be attributed to particular policies, within the period up to 1965, I have exercised my right to comment and criticize.

The approach has necessarily meant that this volume contains fewer statistical tables, graphs, and analyses of technology than its predecessors; and rather more about the actions and attitudes of mind of certain persons. It also necessarily implies a larger element of subjective judgement on my part. As when writing the previous volumes I have had complete and unrestricted access to all of the company's records during the period of the history. Whenever possible I have quoted letters or memoranda, thus to allow the actors to speak in their own words. I have tried not to use oral evidence unsupported by written evidence in arriving at an opinion or account of an episode. But this has not, of course, always been possible. Not all pieces of evidence, written or oral, have been in mutual accord; some oral expressions of opinion—despite confident assertions by their propounders that they were matters of fact—have been simply contradictory. On various issues I have therefore had to try to reconcile conflicting statements or impressions. Because this volume deals with very recent history many of those who participated in the developments here examined are still alive. To some who were thus involved my account will probably seem biased; to others it may seem to offer a reasonable approximation to reality. However it may appear, it remains a product of my own attempts to arrive at a balanced view of evidence which, like so much with which historians are faced, is sometimes inconsistent and, in certain areas, defective. In so far as the laws of libel permit and with an unwillingness to cause gratuitous offence, I have commented and quoted with total freedom. The resulting book, it must be emphasized, should be seen as reflecting my personal judgement on the topics with which it deals. In no sense whatever

[1] *The Times* 13 February 1978: review by David Wainwright of T. C. Barker, *The Glassmakers: Pilkington, the rise of an international company, 1826–1976.*

does it represent (any more than did the previous volumes) an 'official' Courtaulds viewpoint. Some of my judgements may not be very agreeable to some people. In comparison with accounts of recent political in-fighting, however, they seem to me to be mild indeed. And business history will fail, and be seen to fail, in its tasks if it wraps business leaders in cloaks not available to political leaders.

Much of what I wrote in the way of acknowledgements in the Preface to Volume I applies, *mutatis mutandis*, to the present volume. I have continued to incur sundry debts of gratitude to many persons, both inside and outside of Courtaulds, in the differing worlds of business and university, who have aided me in various ways: by giving technical advice, by allowing themselves to be interviewed (for a list, see the Note on Sources on pp. 323–4). by providing hints and help of all sorts. I thank them all. To four persons I owe especial debts.

To Lord Kearton, Chairman of Courtaulds both when I was collecting material for this volume and when I contracted to write it, I am very grateful for his having sanctioned this extension of the original volumes. To Sir Arthur Knight, Chairman since 1975, I am particularly indebted for his close personal interest in the work—as in business history generally—and for his friendly and unfailing support. I would like, once again, to give my special thanks to Miss Bernardine Gregory, research assistant and secretary for this volume as for its predecessors. Her knowledge of the company, its ways, its records, and its staff, and her willingness to go to endless trouble in assembling historical material has been of inestimable benefit ever since I first started work on this project some seventeen years ago. Finally, I wish to record a very personal debt to my wife for enduring, living with, listening to, and commenting upon, drafts of every chapter in all three volumes.

1979 D.C.C.

CONTENTS

VOLUME III

LIST OF GRAPHS

LIST OF PLATES

LIST OF TABLES IN THE TEXT

ABBREVIATIONS

A.G.M. Annual General Meeting (of Courtaulds)

A.K.U. Algemeene Kunstzijde Unie

A.V.C. American Viscose Corporation

B.N.S. British Nylon Spinners Ltd.

C.P.A. Calico Printers Association Ltd.

C.T.A. Comptoir des Textiles Artificiels (later part of Rhône-Poulenc)

Du Pont E. I. du Pont de Nemours & Co. (Inc.)

E.H.Q. Engineering Headquarters (of Courtaulds)

Feinstein C. H. Feinstein, *National Income, Expenditure and Output of the U.K., 1855–1965* (Cambridge, 1972)

F.N.F. F.N.F. Ltd. (Fly Needle Frame)

F.S.D. Fine Spinners & Doublers Ltd.

I.C.I. Imperial Chemical Industries Ltd.

I.N.A.C.S.A. Industrias del Acetato de Celulosa, S.A.

I.R.C. Industrial Rayon Corporation

L.C.C. Lancashire Cotton Corporation Ltd.

M.C. Monopolies Commission

M.C. *Man-made cellulosic fibres* Monopolies Commission, *Man-made cellulosic fibres. A Report on the supply of man-made cellulosic fibres* (HMSO, 1968)

Reader, II W. J. Reader, *Imperial Chemical Industries*, Vol. II (Oxford, 1975)

Saiccor South African Industrial Cellulose Corporation Ltd.

Snia Snia Viscosa (Societa Nazionale Industria Applicazioni Viscosa)

T.C.F. T.C.F. of Canada Ltd. (Transparent Cellulose Film)

V.G.F. Vereinigte Glanzstoff Fabriken (later part of A.K.U.)

Worswick & Ady (eds.) G. D. N. Worswick and P. H. Ady (eds.), *The British Economy in the 1950s* (Oxford, 1962)

PART I

THE WAR AND ITS AFTERMATH, 1940–54

CHAPTER I

The War Years

I

ONE event of the war years towered above all others in the force of its impact upon the development of Courtaulds Ltd. and upon the minds of those in charge of the company: the forced sale of its subsidiary, American Viscose Corporation. Although it did not happen until March 1941, the whole episode has already been examined in Vol. II of this history, because, for reasons explained there, it seemed best comprehended if viewed in the context of previous relations between Courtaulds and A.V.C. and the United States government. The sale marked the end of one era in the company's history; its aftermath marks the beginning of another. Its effect in stimulating an obsessive urge in the minds of some directors to secure the re-establishment of Courtaulds in the United States will be examined later.[1] Meanwhile, however, for all the anger and indignation of Samuel Courtauld and John Hanbury-Williams and for all the £27 million compensation awarded to Courtaulds by the British government in July 1942, the war went on, bringing its own frustrations and interruptions and ensuring that business was far from being 'as usual'.

Physical damage to the company's assets was relatively slight. The notorious German air raid on Coventry which devastated the centre of the city in 1940 had no drastic or long-lasting effect on production either in the main works or at Little Heath; and although there were more bombs on both the Coventry and Nuneaton plants in 1941 which did cause damage—Coventry losing about one-half of its productive capacity—total output was not seriously impaired simply by high explosives. If the *Luftwaffe* did not greatly damage the company's British factories, the Royal Air Force wreaked no bigger havoc on the Glanzstoff–Courtaulds plant at Cologne. Much greater destructive success, however, blessed the achievements of the Allied air forces at Calais where an air-raid in May 1942 put the company's French subsidiary, Les Filés de Calais, then under Vichy control, out of action for some time. The irony was doubly unhappy because Courtaulds

[1] See below, pp. 86–96.

had supplied the aerial photographs of the factory and generally helped in bringing about the desired damage to enemy rayon output. Seven years later only a half of a war-damage claim of about £330,000 had been met by the French government. But even after adding the indirect losses to Courtaulds consequent upon their investment in Snia Viscosa and some war damage to Italian plants, the total of losses arising from the destructive damage of the belligerents in Europe was trivial compared with the price of American generosity, paid by Courtaulds and the British taxpayer.

Shortages of labour and raw materials were commoner causes of interrupted workings. They periodically affected the operation of the Italian plants and of Cologne—otherwise busily contributing much rayon staple fibre to the German war effort—and towards the end of the war occupation by the advancing allied forces combined with shortages to bring production to a halt. In Britain most plants kept going, though generally well below capacity; some, however, were wholly or partially diverted to quite other activities. The engineering shops, for example, were turned over to making sundry parts for guns and aircraft; workers in other factories produced incendiary bombs, parts of rockets, and like contributions to the waging of war; and the company took over and ran with its own staff, for the Ministry of Supply, an Ordnance factory near Wolverhampton. Although the rayon industry came within the schedule of 'reserved occupations', labour of all sorts and ranks went off to the war or to contribute specialized technical knowledge to its scientific underpinning. In raw-material supplies, dependence upon North American sources of wood-pulp, as well as upon the allocations determined by the government controllers of paper and rayon, soon became complete. The situation grew particularly difficult in 1941–2, with a lessened flow of pulp supplies from Canada, and the necessary acceptance of some cotton linters as a substitute. It was hoped to secure cheaper Indian cotton but wartime shipping arrangements made it easier to obtain the dearer American cotton. By the spring of 1942 wood-pulp stocks at the factories were very low and production was dependent on shipping arrivals. If these were commonly subject to the hazards of enemy attack so they were occasionally to those of domestic bureaucracy, as in March 1942 when one arm of government removed wood pulp, temporarily, from the priority shipping-list just when another arm wanted more 'utility' fabrics made from rayon. However, co-operation and planning at home and successes against submarines in the Atlantic, brought relief in the course of 1942–3; an allocation, for the whole rayon industry, of 40,000 tons of wood pulp and 8,000 tons of cotton permitted the production programme (albeit with a 15 per cent. cut in textile yarn output) to be maintained; and by the end of 1943 it was the quantity and quality of available labour rather than of raw materials which were providing the most effective brakes on production.

Government contracts of one sort or another formed the major sources of demand which kept plants in operation. In the textile mills at Halstead, Braintree, Leigh, and Halifax, in 1944, for example, over 60 per cent. of the looms and 52 per cent. of the employees were directly engaged on production for war purposes; and of the remaining looms 30 per cent. were turning out Board of Trade 'utility' fabrics. All the nylon-yarn output of the small plants set up by British Nylon Spinners, the joint undertaking of Courtaulds and I.C.I., incorporated in January 1940, was destined for war purposes, chiefly for parachutes. Negotiations with the Ministry of Aircraft Production had started in 1940 and production on a small scale began in Coventry in 1941; but air raids brought damage and, after some convoluted negotiations with the Ministries of Supply and of Aircraft Production, an additional small plant at Stowmarket in Suffolk began producing in December 1942.[1] In viscose-yarn output a very important element was the Ministry of Supply contracts for tyre cord, replacing scarce cotton in tyre manufacture. This did not come into full operation until 1943, as British military authorities had previously refused to use rayon tyre cord, a lack of faith not shared by their American counterparts who used it extensively. In 1943, however, a government tyre-yarn programme demanding up to 260,000 lb. per week from Courtaulds was under way, with consequent strains upon labour supply and the designation of the Wolverhampton factory as a producer of a 'vital store'. As Table 1 shows, industrial yarn (predominantly tyre yarn) was the only product of the company's yarn mills to register an increase during the war years.

However, even this very high rate of increase in tyre-yarn output did not enable production to reach the tyre-yarn target by the time that the war ended. The gigantic pre-war increase in the production of staple fibre in Germany, Italy, and Japan[2] not only went unmatched in Britain but continued so even after the war brought scarcities of natural fibres. In June 1940 Samuel Courtauld, in the course of providing estimates of the cost of making Army service dress with mixtures of wool and staple fibre, was complaining to Lord Catto, then at the Ministry of Supply, that the British government had totally failed to understand the possibilities of

[1] See below, Chapter IV. [2] See Vol. II, pp. 174–6, 186.

TABLE I

Output of Courtaulds' yarn mills, 1939–45, by type of yarn

'000 lb.

	Viscose textile yarn	*Viscose industrial (tyre) yarn*	*Viscose staple fibre*	*Acetate yarn, staple, and tow*	*Total*
1939*	46,200	100	58,300	7,500	112,100
1940*	55,900	100	55,800	6,400	118,200
1941	34,700	200	53,700	4,400	93,000
1942	29,500	400	46,100	3,900	79,900
1943	26,000	3,100	50,400	3,500	83,000
1944	26,700	8,000	53,000	3,300	91,300
1945	27,700	11,300	52,100	4,300	95,400

* The figures given for these years are slightly different from those in Vol. II, Table 70, p. 322.

synthetic fibres. Perhaps as a legacy from Churchill's budget of 1925 rayon was still evidently regarded in such quarters as just another sort of silk and therefore a luxury.[1] 'Whitehall', observed Courtauld in a 1940 memorandum, 'is constantly throwing silk stockings in our teeth.' That curious procedure ended, staple fibre found its way into sundry fabrics and, as the figures show, its output was nearly maintained from 1940 to 1945 (apart from the grim year 1942) whilst that of ordinary textile yarn halved over the same period.

II

After that grim year of 1942—grim not simply for one British firm but for the people of Britain, for the country's economy, armed forces, and prestige—the light at the end of the tunnel of war began to look just a little larger and brighter. As allied successes against Germany in the Mediterranean, in Russia, and in north-western Europe in the course of 1943–4 began to bring nearer the hopes of peace, so, in sundry boardrooms and government offices, plans were prepared for economic recovery, for the repair to battered, run-down, and over-strained British industry.

As early as October 1942, Samuel Courtauld told his Board that systematic study of the various problems likely to confront them in the years immediately after the war should start forthwith. To that end a network

[1] Vol. II, pp. 259–61.

of committees was set up to examine 'the problems of post-war reconstruction'. Because of wartime difficulties the pre-war structure of working committees had been effectively, though not formally, abandoned. The new committees were to be separate, investigatory devices; and, as the chairman was careful to explain, 'reconstruction' was to mean not only physical replacements, but also 'the re-building, where necessary, of our methods'. In November an 'Advisory Council' (identical in name, but not in membership, to its predecessor in the 1930s[1]) of seven directors was established to co-ordinate the work of five committees: on Research, Foreign Affairs, Finance, Labour, and the resoundingly entitled Central Development Committee. The committees were all directorial in composition, but each committee was to appoint subcommittees on which 'suitable members of the staff should be called upon to serve'. By April 1943 the familiar procreative processes of administrative life had led to the birth of seventeen committees and subcommittees, including the Advisory Council but excluding two subcommittees the personnel of which had yet to be recruited. Some 55 persons were involved though multiple and interlocking membership was such that the total nominal membership of this great probe of the future was no less than 138.

In the difficult circumstances of wartime, it is not perhaps surprising that the company secretary was soon having to remind laggards to start their deliberations; and that the first meeting of the Central Development Committee did not happen until September 1943. However, in the course of 1943–4 sundry meetings took place, many reports were written, and some ideas generated. The more important of these concerned the company's organization, the provision of improved research facilities, the use of the substantial accumulation of gilt-edged funds, and the physical reconstruction or enlargement of plants, especially the yarn mills. But the discussions of the committees and subcommittees were soon caught up by the race of events as the war ground to an end, as directors and managers returned or new men were appointed, and as the state intervened to influence post-war decisions. New and different committees were formed in 1945, but in 1946 the whole apparatus of wartime planning was formally abolished. The state's intentions, meanwhile, had been made clear as early as 1943, for in the course of that year the company's thoughts on where new factories might be sited—thoughts which were not wholly ignorant of 'development area' policies and had already led to an investigation of Northern Ireland—were jogged into particular directions by intervention

[1] See Vol. II, pp. 235–6.

in the person of Hugh Dalton, then President of the Board of Trade. In a letter of August 1943, addressed to 'Samuel Courtauld, D.Litt.', he expressed the hope that 'important undertakings such as your own would give a lead to Industry by setting up factories in places where there was otherwise a likelihood of severe and persistent unemployment'. He offered as possibilities Merthyr Tydfil, Caerphilly, Dundee, or Glasgow. To them were shortly added two R. O. F.s (Royal Ordnance Factories) at Drigg and Sellafield in West Cumberland about which the company had already made some tentative enquiries in March 1943. So began a long sequence of negotiations and investigations, plans and counter-plans, complicated by the company's wish to extend the Greenfield plant in order to effect a large increase in the output of staple fibre.

These developments will be examined in Chapter III. Meanwhile, in the light on subsequent events, it is perhaps worth looking at the ideas which the company entertained during the war years of the likely size of the post-war market for its products. On the basis of sundry enquiries amongst trade customers carried out during the war, various estimates of likely sales and necessary output were put together in 1943–4. A consolidated production programme submitted in 1945 by H. L. Johnson, the then managing director in charge of the yarn mills, and used by the Board for making a decision about a proposed new factory, may be taken as the authorized version. It is compared in Table 2 with the 1945 output, and with average actual output in 1951–2, the approximate end of the planning period.

TABLE 2

Planned and actual rayon output, 1945–52

	1945 output		*1945 planned output in 5–7 years*		*actual output 1951–2 (annual average)*	
	mn. lb.	%	*mn. lb.*	%	*mn. lb.*	%
Viscose textile yarn	27·7	29	85·7	28	53·6	21
Viscose tyre yarn	11·3	12	32·5	11	33·7	14
Viscose staple fibre	52·1	54	150·0	49	149·2	59
Acetate (all types)	4·3	5	37·5	12	14·7	6
Total	95·4	100	305·7	100	251·2	100

The average for 1951–2 includes the sharply depressed year of 1952; if 1951 output were taken alone a total of 274·7 would make the plans of 1945 look slightly less over-optimistic. The most important deviations from the wartime hopes were obviously in viscose textile yarn and acetate rayon. These too-high hopes largely rested on pre-war evaluations of the merits of competing textile fibres and took inadequate regard for recent developments, especially that of nylon. The viscose yarn mills, fount of Courtaulds' wealth and the darlings of the Coventry bosses, had the maximum attention lavished upon them in these plans. The intention to more than treble yarn output was based on an estimate put forward by the managing director in charge of yarn sales, P. S. Rendall, which foresaw possible post-war sales reaching the figure, splendid both in size and precision, of 92,899,000 lb. It was a long way from any reality ever achieved, as ordinary rayon yarn slipped further down the scale of relative importance in the company's output. In contrast, staple fibre not only continued the growth started just before the war, however belatedly in Britain, but effectively achieved planned output. The desirability of major post-war expansion in this branch of production was strongly emphasized as early as February 1943 by P. J. Gratwick, the managing director on the textile side. He foresaw home demand calling for a trebling of capacity in the years immediately after the war and for a five-fold increase in five years' time. Events proved him right, though it was not until the early 1960s that Courtaulds' output of staple fibre was indeed five times what it had been in the early 1940s.

The financial results of the production and sale of rayon during the war years did not contribute much to the resources available for post-war expansion. Prices were the subject of much discussion and negotiation between sundry bodies with sundry names: on the government side, the Board of Trade and, notably, the Central Price Regulation Committee; on the side of the rayon industry, the British Viscose Association, the Central Rayon Office, and the Rayon Producers Committee (later to become the Man-Made Fibres Producers Committee). Capitalism it may have been but it was all a very long way from free enterprise. Early in 1940 when the export trade was being favoured as a vital method of obtaining foreign exchange, the rayon producers, with the approval of the Board of Trade, devised a scheme whereby a levy on yarn sold in the home market (which raised domestic prices by 3*d.* per lb.) was used to provide rebates to exporters of rayon fabrics. The advent of Lease-Lend in 1941 as well as the general course of the war drastically curtailed exports; and the introduction of the utility-clothing scheme, also in 1941, caused the Board of Trade to inquire into production costs in rayon manufacture. Wood-pulp supply difficulties and the enforced use of cotton linters certainly caused these to rise in 1942–3. By 1944, however, these problems had been surmounted. In the words of a letter from a future Chancellor of the Exchequer, Hugh Gaitskell, then an official of the Board of Trade, the time had come to reduce the price of continuous filament yarn and to 'discontinue or materially reduce the levy of 3*d*. per lb. which is still being paid'. In May 1945 the levy was abolished and prices reduced. It was coupled with increasing pressure upon the government, from Courtaulds and other producers, to remove the excise duty—another post-war target. Meanwhile, Courtaulds on their own account had initiated a reduction in staple-fibre prices after the rise which had been permitted in 1942, again as a consequence of increases in production costs. The proposal for reduction was made in December 1943, with a view to maintaining a cheap supply of staple to spinners and securing consequent effects on the selling price of utility clothing. Discussions with both the Board of Trade and the Director General of Civilian Clothing led to the reduction, 3*d*. per lb. becoming effective in March 1944. The Courtaulds Board was doubtless gratified to hear that it had been 'very well received in the trade'—as doubtless it was intended to be.

The effect of all this, together with the very high levels of taxation introduced by the advent of Excess Profits Tax, was to ensure that net profits were small. The method of assessing E.P.T., using 'standard' pre-war years, meant that Courtaulds were ill-placed because of their poor profit record just before the war. Rayon prices seem to have gone up slightly less than wholesale prices generally. Despite the reduction in costs consequent upon the new Preston plant coming into operation at the beginning of the war, under-capacity working effectively raised wartime costs. In the seven-year period 1932–8 pre-tax profits (excluding investment income) totalled £18·2 million; in the seven-year period 1939–45 they rose to £24·2 million (+33 per cent.) But in the latter period taxation rose a great deal more, from £4·9 million to £15·5 million (+216 per cent.); and the wholesale and retail price index rose by about 63 per cent. and 45 per cent. respectively. So, even though those indexes may be only a rough and ready guide to Courtaulds' problems, it seems likely that gross money profits during the war years failed to hold their real value; and net retained profits cannot possibly have been adequate to provide for necessary replacement of assets, the prices of capital goods rising far more than those of consumer goods. Subsequent reiterated complaints by Courtaulds' chairmen about this state of affairs were not without justification.

Nevertheless, in its wartime plans for recovery and expansion, the company was not seriously hampered by fears of a cash shortage. Indeed, the very opposite problem presented itself, for the result of the A.V.C. compensation together with accumulated pre-war reserves meant that by the end of 1945 Courtaulds were sitting on nearly £40 million of government stock and gilt-edged securities. How precisely these should best be spent was what exercised the Board over the next twelve years and more; and the decisions, right and wrong, made at that time proved crucial for the future pattern of events. Amongst the innumerable plans of wartime there were of course some elaborate schedules of possible capital investment. Out of sundry calculations prepared by the Engineering department at Coventry in its efforts to cost schemes authorized, proposed, considered, or just mooted by the Board or individual directors, a consolidated version of February 1945 envisaged a total expenditure, at home and overseas, over the next ten years, of £68,660,000 which had been raised to £77,489,000 by December of that year. This latter estimate may be taken as a final reflection of hopes and intentions generated during the war years. Within the same seven-year planning period, as used in Table 2, i.e. to 1952, the total estimated capital expenditure was rather over £64 million. Leaving aside substantial sums intended for repairs, replacements of obsolescent machinery, and extensions in existing plants, nearly £22 million out of this £64 million was the expected cost of completely new factories proposed for the manufacture of rayon of all types; over £5 million was allowed for similar spending overseas, including rayon plants in both Australia and India; and £3 million was scheduled for a plant to manufacture wood pulp. Outside rayon, allowances were much smaller: £3·5 million for the whole textile side; £3·5 million on nylon with British Nylon Spinners; £1·3 million on the casein fibre 'Lanital' just being developed in the late 1930s; £2 million for chemicals and plastics; and £1,350,000 for all research and development including the building of a new 'Fundamental Research Laboratory'.

The reality was to be rather different; some of the plans were fulfilled; many were not. What happened depended in part upon future developments outside Courtaulds' control and which few within the company foresaw, in part upon the decisions made by those in command. It is time to look at them, to see who and what sort of men they were and what they did in matters of central organization and policy.

CHAPTER II

The Board and the Company

I

At the beginning of the war Courtaulds' Board consisted of eighteen directors, including full- and part-time members. Table 3 sets out the membership, in order of appointment to the Board, and by age.

TABLE 3

The Board, 1939

Date of appointment	*Name*	*Age in 1939*	
1913	S. A. Courtauld	74	
1913	F. J. Nettlefold	72	
1915	S. Courtauld	63	Chairman
1920	S. Bourne	63	Deputy chairman
1922	J. S. Addison	58	Managing director
1924	F. Johnson	61	
1929	J. C. Hanbury-Williams	47	Managing director
1933	H. L. Johnson	35	Managing director
1935	P. J. Gratwick	54	Managing director
1935	J. E. Pedder	37	
1935	F. J. Rodd	44	
1935	A. H. Kilner	62	
1937	P. S. Rendall	44	
1937	W. H. Glover	56	
1937	F. T. Davies	33	
1938	G. Courtauld	36	
1938	W. P. Courtauld	29	
1939	R. A. Kinnes	46	

With a median age of 54 it could hardly be described as unusually elderly for a ruling body in British industry. Moreover, the two survivors of the original 1913 flotation of Courtaulds Ltd. had long ceased effectively to guide the destinies of the firm, if indeed they had ever done so; and practical power rested with a small group of younger men—Gratwick,

Hanbury-Williams, H. L. Johnson, and Addison, together with the dominant figure of the chairman, Samuel Courtauld.

The war years soon brought change and difficulties. In 1942, Nettlefold retired and Bourne died. The latter had played a diminishing part in the leadership of the company, and in easier times the loss would hardly have been irreparable. A more serious blow was the death of Addison in December 1943, not long after he had succeeded Bourne as deputy chairman. Although not as close to the chairman as some other directors, he was a highly respected and experienced member of the Board, and had come to occupy an increasingly important position in the company. War-service meant that the three youngest full-time directors were more or less continuously absent from the Board for most of the war. Peter Courtauld,[1] effectively Addison's understudy on the textile side of the business, went into the Army at the beginning of the war; so also did F. T. Davies who, along with George Courtauld, became part of that curious enterprise S.O.E. (Special Operations Executive). This characteristically English venture—half-amateur, half-professional—for the pursuit of unorthodox warfare, espionage, and counter-espionage, with its offices in Baker Street and its concealment within the administration of the Ministry of Economic Warfare, had a plentiful sprinkling, in its initial organization and leadership, of City men of a recognizable social class. Courtaulds was particularly well represented, for in addition to George Courtauld and Davies from the Board, it also provided several non-directorial recruits into S.O.E.[2] Davies's absence from the company left Hanbury-Williams to deal with all the overseas side of the business. As already indicated,[3] he had been much involved in the negotiations concerned with the forced sale of A.V.C.; his part-time directorship of the Bank of England had brought extra demands on his time, particularly at the beginning of the war; and he, too, had a temporary involvement with what lurked within the Ministry of Economic Warfare, for during a period of absence in 1942 he wrote a report on the administration of S.O.E. Not only were these full-time directors away or exceptionally occupied, but in addition the most

[1] Walter Pierre Courtauld.

[2] They included Bickham Sweet-Escott who had recently joined the company, and who subsequently wrote about his experiences in a book appropriately entitled *Baker Street Irregular*. For further details of the businessmen in this non-business enterprise, see *Baker Street Irregular* (London, 1965); the official history by M. R. D. Foot, *S.O.E. in France: an account of the work of the British Special Operations Executive in France, 1940–44* (2nd ed. London, 1968); and E. H. Cookridge, *Inside S.O.E.* (London, 1966).

[3] Vol. II, pp. 465–78.

important of the company's outside directors, Francis Rodd (who in 1941 had succeeded his father as Lord Rennell) was also away on war service. Moreover, although he returned to England in 1944 he resigned from Courtaulds' Board in June of the same year. The ostensible reason was inability to give enough time to Courtaulds' affairs; the more immediately practical reason was that as a partner in Morgan Grenfell, he had been put in an embarrassing position by the fact that Morgan Greenfell had absorbed Cull & Co., who were the financial advisers to Courtaulds' rivals, not to say adversaries, British Celanese.

The net result of all these absences and extraneous demands was that the functioning members of the Board were extremely hard-pressed. So much so that Samuel Courtauld made a number of representations to various members of the government seeking to secure the release from the Army of his two cousins and of Davies. He wrote first in December 1943, after the death of Addison, telling the then President of the Board of Trade, Hugh Dalton, that the company's 'headquarters staff' were 'stretched to breaking point', and asking specifically for the release of George and Peter Courtauld. The former did indeed return in February 1944; but in September of that year further pleas for the release of Peter Courtauld and Davies brought no successful response. Copies of the letters were sent to the Chancellor of the Exchequer (Sir John Anderson) and Lord Catto at the Bank of England. Not wholly surprisingly, Dalton observed in reply that it was not easy to 'justify the release out of their turn and before the end of the war in Europe, of men now serving in the Army'. In the cause of securing Davies's release more letters flowed: to Lord Selborne[1] and Oliver Lyttleton.[2] By February 1945 Hanbury-Williams was ill; the various ambitious plans for post-war recovery and expansion, at home and abroad, had been formulated; and Samuel Courtauld, himself not in good health, was getting desperate. After consultation with his son-in-law, R. A. Butler, he sent a long memorandum to that curious protégé of Churchill's, Brendan Bracken,[3] whom Courtauld knew but could hardly have much liked, asking him to draw to the Prime Minister's attention the cases of Davies and Peter Courtauld. Some amiable irrelevancies were sent in reply. But the end of the war eventually brought what sundry talks and many letters had not achieved. The General Election of July 1945 set its unex-

[1] Minister of Economic Warfare.

[2] Later Lord Chandos, then Minister of Production.

[3] Minister of Information. See A. Boyle, *Poor, dear Brendan: the quest for Brendan Bracken* (London, 1974).

pected political seal on Britain's domestic, post-war scene and by the end of the year Courtaulds had not only regained their directors from the embrace of the War Office but had made four new appointments, one of which was to be of major consequence for the future of the company.

Before considering those appointments, it is pertinent to stress that at that time Courtaulds' Board was still much as it had been before the war, not only in membership but in attitude.[1] The gulf, alike in personnel and approach, between 'Coventry' and 'London' had not been bridged; the weaknesses in organization, perceived and commented on by the chairman and Hanbury-Williams in 1937–8, had grown rather than diminished. So also had the Board's corporate reliance on its chairman to initiate decisions which would precipitate change. Samuel Courtauld's intention—not always matched by action—to bring about needed reforms, and especially to introduce new men and a new spirit in the company's scientific research and development, had in no way abated. The circumstances of the war had stimulated his idealism about improvement in industry and society. Despite his boardroom problems, between 1941 and 1945 he made various speeches up and down the country, published sundry articles, and wrote numerous letters to *The Times*. Three themes recurred: the importance of scientific research; the improvement of employer/employee relations; and the need for more government participation in industry. Although in retrospect much of it now seems rather platitudinous, the last, and most strongly emphasized of these themes, made a sound far from comforting to many businessmen (not excluding some on his own Board). The publication which, more than any other, brought his views to a wide audience had its origins in a suggestion made by R. A. Butler. Samuel Courtauld's only daughter, Sydney, had married Richard Austen Butler (now Lord Butler of Saffron Walden) in 1925; and the latter's climb up the ladder of politics had brought him in 1941, at the age of 39, to the Presidency of the Board of Education. He had also become chairman of the Conservative Party's committee on post-war problems; and it was for that body that Samuel Courtauld wrote in November 1941 a piece called 'The Relations between Government and Industry'. His friendship with Maynard Keynes then resulted in a modified version appearing in April 1942 in the *Economic Journal* under the title 'An Industrialist's Reflection on the future relations of Government and Industry'; and at the same time this was published as a separate pamphlet called *Government and Industry: their future relations.*[2] The resulting publicity found Courtauld (described by one paper as 'shy,

[1] See Vol. II, pp. 210–43. [2] Macmillan, 1942.

arty, philanthropic rayon millionaire') branded as a Fascist by the Left and as a Socialist by the Right. But the reality was a considerable influence exercised by Samuel Courtauld through his son-in-law on the Conservative Party's moderate wing,[1] and conversely a reinforced determination by Courtaulds' chairman to effect changes within his own company.

The earliest of the new appointments to the Board brought no change of significance: in 1944 C. M. Whittaker was put on the Board primarily as a recognition of his long service in charge of dyeing operations and his position as an expert on dyes. Already 66, he did not play an important part in the Board's deliberations and he retired in 1950. Of much greater consequence was the appointment in April 1945 of Sir Wilfrid Freeman. Air Chief Marshall Sir Wilfrid Rhodes Freeman, Bart., G.C.B., D.S.O., M.C., had had a distinguished career in the R.A.F., and had been one of the great successes of the war in the organization of aircraft production.[2] First approached in January, he accepted in March 1945, despite pressure on him to become deputy chairman of A.E.I. He came with, initially, something of a roving brief to investigate Courtaulds' whole organization. The result, whatever it did for the company, is an historian's delight, for he wrote numerous pungent and uninhibited memoranda about what he saw. Whether, in the longer run his remarkable talents brought any major tangible achievements for Courtaulds is questionable; for although he became a deputy chairman in 1949 and looked like coming to exercise considerable power, he died in 1953 at the age of 64. But while he was active, he was probably the only really outstanding man of experience and proven administrative ability on the Board; and his critical forthrightness can hardly have been anything but beneficial to an organization which, as he described it in December 1946, was like 'a big Empire on the decline'.

When the Conservatives were swept out of office, it was more or less inevitable that Samuel Courtauld should consider getting his son-in-law on the Board. Since 1929 Butler had sat for the Essex constituency of Saffron Walden which incorporated within its boundaries much Courtauld land and property; there was sympathy and understanding between the two men; and he had useful personal contacts with members of the new Labour government. The election result was announced on 26 July. On 29 July Samuel Courtauld wrote to Hanbury-Williams: 'Seeing that

[1] Sundry letters and papers in Samuel Courtauld's files, including correspondence with both Butler and Henry Brooke (later Lord Brooke) supplement and amplify the brief account in Lord Butler's own memoirs, *The Art of the Possible* (1971), esp. Chap. 7.

[2] He was Chief Executive, Ministry of Aircraft Production, from 1942 to 1945.

R.A.B. is out of his job, could you possibly sound the managing directors and others about his coming on our board . . . Personally I think it would be an excellent thing for the company, in view of his reputation in education, his experience . . . at the ministry of labour, and his good relations with leading Labour ministers.' Hanbury-Williams enquired amongst the 'London directors' and got H. L. Johnson to speak to those whom Hanbury-Williams revealingly described as the 'Mill Directors'. The result was a foregone conclusion, though the appropriate expressions of approval were notably deficient in enthusiasm. No significant consequences seem to have flowed from the appointment; Butler's real interests lay elsewhere. In any event, his part-time stay was relatively short; he resigned in October 1951 on the return of the Conservatives to power and on his appointment as Chancellor of the Exchequer.

By far the most striking of the new appointments of 1945 was that of A. H. (later Sir Alan) Wilson. The direct outcome of the chairman's concern with science, it precipitated a head-on collision between 'London' and 'Coventry'; and it marked a turning-point in the slowly changing composition of the Board, away from the Courtauld family, the 'rayon men', and the whole pre-war structure.[1] It was a big portent for the future. Both at A.V.C. and in Britain, Courtaulds' research and development arrangements had been very largely concentrated on empirical matters emanating from factory and production problems; fundamental research was almost non-existent; and the intellectual quality of the research staff was generally not of the highest. The programme of reform, set in motion at A.V.C. before its loss to Courtaulds, had no counterpart in the British end of the business where, moreover, war demands brought to a halt all but the most urgent work. The contrast can be seen in the research and development staff at the two companies:

	A.V.C.	*Courtaulds*
1939	64 (Jan.)	146 (June)
1941	254 (Sept.)	125 (Sept.)

The company's former chief chemist, W. H. Glover, who had been appointed to the Board in 1937 as a reward for services rendered, was much identified with the limited nature of the research programme; he did not 'direct' research in any meaningful sense; he simply 'represented research on the Board'. In the course of 1942–3, at the bidding of the chairman he

[1] See below, Chapter VII, especially pp. 132–40.

wrote a report on work at the company's laboratories and participated in the work of the new committee on research. Much discussion went on about where a planned new laboratory for fundamental research might be situated; and in the course of 1943 soundings were made of certain professors of chemistry at Cambridge University to ascertain their willingness to act as research advisers to the company. The radical decision was made to import a new scientist to head the company's research organization. In suggesting possible candidates, or advisers about candidates, Davies played an active role, despite his absence from the firm. His wartime work had put him into touch with some scientists, specifically with D. M. Newitt, Professor of Chemical Engineering at London University, who had also been with S.O.E. Scientists evidently impressed him; and the names of sundry Fellows of the Royal Society (many subsequently very well known —Todd,[1] Goodeve,[2] Linstead,[3] for example) were bandied about with optimistic gusto. George Courtauld, as the director in charge of recruitment and personnel, also took a hand. So in addition to Newitt himself various eminent university scientists were consulted—Sir Alfred Egerton at London, Professor Hinshelwood and Sir Henry Tizard at Oxford, Professor Norrish at Cambridge[4]—on a suitable head of Courtaulds' research and development. George Courtauld in a letter written to Hanbury-Williams after he had seen Hinshelwood urged speedy action and added the refreshingly realistic comment that he was less sanguine than some of his colleagues that 'we shall be able, when we do at last decide to make a move, to pick, for the asking and a high salary, the best brain in the country'. In November 1944 the new job was offered to Goodeve; he turned it down. Shortly afterwards Davies brought to lunch with the other directors A. H. Wilson, F.R.S.—a mathematical physicist of distinction, then 39 years of age, who had made important scientific contributions; he had worked on radio communications and atomic energy during the war; and was currently a Fellow of Trinity College, Cambridge, and

[1] Subsequently Lord Todd; then Professor of Organic Chemistry at Cambridge University.

[2] Later Sir Charles Goodeve; then Reader in Physical Chemistry at University College, London.

[3] Later Sir Reginald Linstead and Rector of Imperial College, London; then Deputy Director of Scientific Research at the Ministry of Supply.

[4] All, like Newitt, F.R.S.; Egerton was then Professor of Chemical Technology at Imperial College; Hinshelwood, Professor of Chemistry at Oxford; and Tizard, who had played a very active role in scientific/military matters during the war, was then President of Magdalen College, Oxford; Norrish was Professor of Physical Chemistry at Cambridge.

a university lecturer in mathematics. In January he paid a visit to the laboratories at Coventry and Bocking, talked to Glover, and wrote a lucid but gloomy report on what he found. Nevertheless, in February he accepted the offer of the job, director in charge of research and development, to take up his duties formally in September 1945. Then the storm broke.

In July one of Glover's staff, a long-serving chemist in charge of the research and development laboratory at Coventry, sent a long, impassioned, and indignant memorandum to the chairman and Hanbury-Williams; the gist of it was that it was outrageous that a 'purely theoretical scientist—a mathematician' should come to direct Courtaulds' research. He secured the support of Glover and other older members of the Coventry staff; between them they proceeded to refuse all co-operation with Wilson. Matters got gradually worse. In October Davies, feeling a 'moral responsibility' for Wilson, expressed to Hanbury-Williams his 'profound disapproval of the manner in which he has been treated at Coventry' and urged action against Glover. In November, Wilson sent two documents to the chairman. One was a detailed account of an acrimonious conversation that he had with Glover, the main burden of which was that as Wilson was not a chemist Glover considered it a waste of time talking about research matters to him. The other was an ultimatum: either Glover, the offended chemist, and other 'subversive elements' all went or he resigned and returned to Cambridge where, as he put it, 'the Plummer Chair of Physics is still vacant . . . and the whole academic world would be very relieved if I were to return to fill the post'. The London directors rallied behind their man, even though some believed Wilson had been rather less forceful than he might have been in dealing with the Coventry malcontents. Glover resigned; and Samuel Courtauld himself drafted and dispatched to the disgruntled chemist a letter somewhat reluctantly requiring the latter's resignation. He went—though by no means immediately and not without substantial compensation.

The decision about Wilson had important consequences for Courtaulds, both immediate and distant. The appointment itself, and indeed the explorations leading up to it, also had a wider significance in that it was an indirect result of the links between scientists, businessmen, and the government forged by the war. Although it may reasonably be assumed that in the absence of the war Courtaulds would have taken steps to improve their capacity in scientific research, the circumstances of the war put some of their non-scientific directors into contact with scientists engaged on war work—and all those mentioned above had been variously so engaged—in a way which otherwise might not have occurred. Within the company the decision brought on to the Board, for the first time, a director of research and development who was a scientist of real distinction, with a first-class intellect. Wilson in turn brought to the company younger scientists, to help in the rebuilding of Courtaulds' research effort. Amongst them, lured from I.C.I. in July 1946 and appointed to head the chemical engineering research department, was a 35-year-old expert who had already made a name for himself working on the U.K. atomic-energy project during the war: C. F. Kearton. Six years later he joined Courtaulds' Board. Thereby was lit a fuse which was ultimately to detonate Wilson's resignation in 1962 and Kearton's succession to the chairmanship in 1964. Immediately, however, the decision to appoint Wilson represented a major victory by the London directors, in pursuit of change, over the Coventry men, intent on the *status quo*. Moreover, that victory had not been obstructed by Samuel Courtauld's long-persisting tendency to find some middle path which would avoid upsetting those who were the inheritors of the original Coventry pioneers—which, in this case, meant the beneficiaries of the system of patronage established by H. L. Johnson's father, Harry Johnson, who had died in 1938.[1]

Directors new to the company were soon apprised of the system. Some of Freeman's earliest comments after his appointment are revealing. In 1946, after visiting the yarn mills, he noted, for example, that at Flint (where the manager was one of Harry Johnson's men) the welcome was unfriendly; and the managers were, he observed, 'second-rate'. The atmosphere in the textile mills, by contrast, was better. The friction between Coventry and London, he observed, was something 'which everyone recognizes, everyone ignores and which will certainly grow if it is not forcibly tackled and speedily stamped out'. The trouble was caused not so much by the directors as by their managerial subordinates, remnants of Harry Johnson's praetorian cohorts. H. L. Johnson's technical expertise was immense; but his loyalty to the firm could not always coincide with his loyalty to the memory of his father; so he remained chronically indecisive. In the Wilson decision Freeman's support was accompanied by a telling rider: 'If it is true that Henry Johnson and Glover have been run by their staff instead of running their staffs, then great as may be the temporary loss caused to the company by the resignation of the

[1] Vol. II, pp. 234–5, 443.

former, I find it difficult to believe that it is irreparable.' In the event, Johnson did not resign, but three years later, in indifferent health, he relinquished his managing directorship, and became a part-time director. The 'Coventry spirit' did not, of course, disappear with the appointment of Wilson. How it seemed to him, when he first encountered it, is best delineated in his own words in a letter about a possible appointment at Coventry, written to the chairman in 1951:

> When I came to Coventry in 1945 I was immediately faced with the 'old Coventry spirit' which is the most unpleasant phenomenon I have ever met in my life. It was dealt with by actions which need not be detailed again, but as a result two appointments were made . . . which were major blunders. Amongst other things the whole of my energies were immobilised for about three years in counteracting the effects of those appointments . . .
>
> A major task since 1945 has been the neutralising of the 'old Coventry spirit', in which P.S.R. [P. S. Rendall] has taken a leading part and which I have helped. The spirit is not dead yet unfortunately but at least it is under control.

II

In addition to these new appointments and to the momentous consequences flowing from that of Wilson, one other major change transformed Courtaulds' Board just as post-war reconstruction got under way. Early in May 1946, Samuel Courtauld suffered a severe attack of pneumonia; as soon as he was fit to do so he made it clear to his colleagues that he would have to resign as chairman. Two possible candidates for the succession existed: Gratwick and Hanbury-Williams. The former, then aged 61, had long textile experience, much shrewdness, and some enthusiasm for the bottle. The latter, at 54, but with six years longer experience on the Board, had presence, diplomatic skills, and splendid manners. A draft in Samuel Courtauld's hand and dated 25 May makes it clear that Hanbury-Williams was his choice; and a letter of 8 July, recording a talk he had had with Gratwick, expresses his conviction that the latter did not want to be chairman. George Courtauld organized support from amongst the remaining directors and before July was out the choice was made, though the formal hand-over did not take place until 24 October 1946. Samuel Courtauld remained on the Board, but his stay there was not long for in December 1947 he died, aged 71.

Even before his illness, plans were being made for a Board reconstruction pending Samuel Courtauld's likely retirement. To this end Kinnes, director and chief accountant, had been asked to give his views on the structure of the Board, senior management, and general organization. He took the opportunity, in a memorandum sent to the chairman in February 1946, to make some penetrating but far from complimentary observations. Much of his memorandum was taken up with his pet scheme for decentralization;[1] but some of it voiced his opinions about the Board and potential recruits thereto. Noting the age-structure of the Board, he observed the absence of 'experienced men between 45 and 60' and viewing those under 50 (and excluding Wilson whom he regarded as 'at present very much of a specialist') he doubted whether future 'leaders of the company' would be found amongst them.[2] He proved to be right: they were not so found. Amongst the managerial staff there was no possible candidate on the yarn side of the business; and only W. H. Nankivell, of the textile branch, did he think to be of Board calibre. His views were confirmed: Nankivell alone was promoted to the Board, becoming a director in 1947. Amongst the Head Office staff he could think only of C. W. Sheldon, the then Secretary, as potential Board material. So he was, joining the Board in 1948. Not until 1952 were any other promotions made to the Board from the existing management structure. These events testified more to the inadequacies of pre-war recruitment than to Kinnes's influence, for he was not a popular or especially powerful member of the Board. The object of his especial approval was Freeman whom he wanted to see made a deputy chairman. His particular disapprobation was reserved for Henry Johnson whom he wished to see superseded for he was 'incapable of leadership and has no abilities in the fields of organisation and administration'. Moreover, should he remain a managing director he might at some time become a deputy chairman 'with a reversion . . . to the chairmanship at some later date'—a development which Kinnes, not surprisingly, regarded as 'quite disastrous'. Amongst Kinnes's other proposals for redistribution of Board responsibilities was one which was frequently to occur in Courtaulds' Board deliberations: the wish to find some distinguished outsider, not an expert in any of Courtaulds' technical concerns but a man of wisdom and character who would put matters right and somehow solve all the problems. It was to occur again later; despite the forceful activity of Freeman the results rarely lived up to expectations. And, despite all the talk, at this particular time the only outsider in this category to come on the Board was

[1] See below, pp. 31–3.

[2] The men he thus doubted were Pedder, George and Peter Courtauld, H. L. Johnson, and Davies.

Sir William Stanier, a distinguished and elderly engineer[1] who was brought on as a part-time specialist director on the retirement in 1947 of the company's equally elderly but quite undistinguished engineering director, Frederick Johnson. Stanier's appointment was followed by that of a new engineering director, G. T. Verrall, also brought in from outside Courtaulds, in 1949. Over the next four years the only other changes were the appointment of Freeman and Rendall as deputy chairmen in 1949 and 1950 respectively; the retirement in 1950 of Kinnes as a full-time director, though continuing in a part-time capacity; also in 1950 the retirement of Whittaker; and, finally, in 1951, the retirement of the long-enduring Samuel Augustine Courtauld, at the formidable age of 86. The median age of 54 in 1939 fell to 52 in 1947 and to 50 at the end of 1951.

The man who succeeded to the chairmanship and who, nominally at least, steered Courtaulds through the greater part of the stormy years covered by this volume differed in many respects from his predecessor. John Coldbrook Hanbury-Williams—offspring of the union of a Major-General and a daughter of Emil Reiss of the merchant family of Reiss Brothers—was a snob, liked titles, married a Byzantine Princess, and relished Court appointments. Samuel Courtauld—scion of the last of the Unitarians in his family—turned down a barony, disliked the society of the merely rich, collected Impressionist paintings, was a patron of music, and had the remnants of a Victorian Nonconformist conscience. Courtauld had learnt a great deal about textiles and rayon, knew the company needed better scientific personnel, and was idealistically attracted by the problems of the relationship between capital and labour. Hanbury-Williams knew little or nothing about production technology, despised technical men, remained ignorant of science, and wholly indifferent to industrial relations. Yet Hanbury-Williams was Samuel Courtauld's personal choice; he was, indeed, the last of the firm's chairmen to be the family's nominee. Was it Rugby calling Wellington? Or the not always tactful Courtauld impressed by the Hanbury-Williams courtesy, presence, and suavity? Or was there no real alternative?

The choice was in fact wholly consistent with the nature of Courtaulds' Board and the then existing and recognized channels of recruitment thereto. In 1952, six years after his succession to the chairmanship, Hanbury-Williams summarized his conception of that Board in the course of a

[1] He was aged 71 at the time of his appointment From 1932 to 1944 he had been Chief Mechanical Engineer to the then London Midland and Scottish Railway. Like the scientists mentioned earlier (p. 18), he too had had an advisory role to a ministry during the war.

memorandum on the company's organization which he circulated to four of the senior directors:[1]

For a long time there has been no fundamental change in the constitution of the Board of Courtaulds Limited. The Executive Directors have directed and managed, and on the whole they have been successful. There has been a Gentlemen's Club atmosphere in the Board Room, and I believe it is true to say that over the years this has spread to all the Departments of our business. It is in fact part of the goodwill of the Company which we must safeguard. On the other hand great care must be taken to avoid inefficiency.

Hanbury-Williams came on to the Board in 1929. So at the time he wrote these words, he had been there for 23 years, a longer experience than that of any of his colleagues. Though not thus articulated by anyone else at an earlier date—or at least not in surviving records—the conception could equally have been formulated in the 1930s. In 1938, of the 17 members of the Board, 14 had been at Public Schools; and of the 7 who attended Universities, 6 had been at Oxford or Cambridge. There were two sorts of directors: firstly, 'Gentlemen', who knew the same people, spoke the same language, and/or were members of the same family; and secondly, 'Players'—honorary gentlemen, so to speak[2]—whose technical expertise and achievements for the company had been sufficient to earn membership of the club. In one or two cases, the categorization was blurred but most directors fell clearly into one or the other of the two groups. This is not in the least to say that those in the former category were necessarily less efficient, less imaginative, or less enlightened than those in the latter category. Indeed the very opposite was sometimes true. It is simply to point to what had become the conventional channels of directorial recruitment, in Courtaulds as in many other British firms, and were recognized as such. In 1946, Hanbury-Williams clearly came into one category, Gratwick in another. That, in itself, was not enough. What mattered was that Gratwick was not seen to have sufficiently outstanding qualities as a 'Player' director to offset his 'honorary' status and become chairman. Samuel Courtauld, however much he had differed in character and interests from Hanbury-Williams, could have been in his own way just as much a signatory to the 'Gentlemen's Club' convention. And, after all, in 1946, the Board briefly embraced the largest representation ever of the extended Courtauld

[1] Gratwick, Rendall, Freeman, Kinnes.

[2] For some elaboration of this concept, historically, see my article, 'Gentlemen and Players', *Economic History Review*, 2nd ser. XXVI (1973).

family on the Board of Courtaulds Ltd., with six out of the seventeen directors.[1] The choice that he made, and which was so readily supported in the Board, was at once a symbol of continuity and a testimony to a crucial belief inherent in the concept of the gentleman: that gentlemen are likely to be the better leaders. And that is precisely what this particular choice failed to demonstrate.

It seems quite clear that in leading the Board of Courtaulds Ltd. Hanbury-Williams followed the well-known principle of 'divide and rule'. Evidence of this comes not simply from the verbal testimony of many of his former colleagues but from the existence, of which many of them were unaware, of his private files of personal correspondence replete with letters from directors criticizing the doings or attitudes of other directors. Such letters were evidently encouraged. They did not lead to positive action; when replies survive they are naturally non-committal. But they served as a vital flow of intelligence which facilitated rule by the division and diffusion of power. Hanbury-Williams was not the simple and straightforward soldier that behaviour and background suggested to some observers. The front was all urbanity, charm, good manners. He was handsome; he had presence. If to one director of British Nylon Spinners, he was to appear as 'a superb stuffed shirt',[2] some of his own Board stood in considerable awe of him. But behind the front was a devious and complicated personality. He seems to have enjoyed setting people against each other; and as one former colleague put it, he 'imposed the more unpleasant parts of his personality on the Board', and was 'not a nice man'. But some at least who have subsequently abused him were once undoubtedly frightened of him; and only too probably toadied to him when he commanded power and the granting of favours. Promoted 'Players' with practical experience, like Nankivell, he ignored; he was contemptuous or patronizing to those he could refer to as 'technical persons'—an attitude which was to have appalling results when applied to men of the calibre of Wilson and Kearton. Social position and Court appointments—Gentleman Usher to George V, Edward VIII, and George VI, and Extra Gentleman Usher to George VI and Elizabeth II—vied with his directorship of the Bank of England in shaping his concern with prestige.

Prestige was, indeed, the consideration which loomed largest in his notion of a policy for Courtaulds Ltd. The Bank of England signified

[1] S. A. Courtauld, S. Courtauld, W. P. Courtauld, G. Courtauld, R. A. Butler (son-in-law), and J. E. Pedder (cousin).

[2] Quoted Reader, II, p. 374.

prestige to him, and it was wholly characteristic of Hanbury-Williams that on Samuel Courtauld's retirement from the chairmanship he should have proposed for him the honorific title of 'Governor' of Courtaulds Ltd. The analogue of the Governor of the Bank of England was so obvious that Hanbury-Williams felt it necessary to consult the then Governor (Lord Catto) and Deputy Governor (Cameron Cobbold)[1] of the Bank. Not surprisingly, both Samuel Courtauld himself as well as Catto and Cobbold turned down the idea. A far more important example of his concern with the prestige of Courtaulds was his obsession with the need to re-establish the company in America. As already indicated,[2] the circumstances of the loss of A.V.C. particularly incensed him; and his subsequent determination to recommence operations in the U.S.A. constituted one of the very few items of positive policy in his post-war activities as chairman —a policy in which to him profitability counted less than prestige. His upbringing and previous experience in overseas matters bequeathed to him a latter-day 'imperialist' outlook. So the expansionist mode was not confined to the U.S.A. It was under his aegis that Courtaulds started rayon production in Australia, began forestry and wood-pulp manufacture in South Africa, devoted more time and energy to enterprise in Canada, as well as continuing their not always rewarding involvements in continental Europe.

In many of these expansive and prestige-seeking acts, Hanbury-Williams relied heavily on F. T. Davies. Closest of all the directors to the new chairman, both personally and in social status, Davies also possessed a remarkably similar family background. Hanbury-Williams's father was Major-General Sir John Hanbury-Williams, G.C.V.O., K.C.B., C.M.G.; Davies's father was General Sir Francis Davies, K.C.B., K.C.M.G., K.C.V.O. Although Davies was fourteen years younger than Hanbury-Williams, their military fathers were almost exact contemporaries: Hanbury-Williams, senior, lived from 1859 to 1946; Davies, senior, from 1864 to 1948. The families came from the same area of Britain and would have occupied the same stratum of 'county society'. The Hanbury-Williams were a landed family long settled in the Herefordshire–Monmouthshire region; the Davies lived at Elmley Castle, near Pershore, the family hailing from the Worcestershire–Herefordshire area. Neither son followed his father into the Army; both went into business and later

[1] Later Lord Cobbold and from 1949 to 1961 Governor of the Bank. See also below, p. 144.

[2] Vol. II, Chapter XV, *passim*.

served in wartime. Hanbury-Williams left Wellington to work for his mother's family business, the London and Manchester-based firm of Eastern merchants, Reiss Brothers; Davies, after leaving Eton for some brief business experience in Britain and Germany, went to Courtaulds at the end of 1929 and then at the age of 31 joined Hanbury-Williams on Courtaulds' Board in 1937. Hanbury-Williams served in World War I with a commission in the 10th Royal Hussars; Davies became a Colonel in the Grenadier Guards in World War II; and, incidentally, alone of the post-war Board, retained in business the use of his wartime rank. Hanbury-Williams married Princess Zenaida Cantacuzene; Davies married a daughter of the fourth Lord Brougham and Vaux.

Similar outlooks do not *have* to spring from similar social backgrounds and life-styles. But it is hardly to espouse a belief in crude social determinism to suggest that so notable a set of parallels cannot have been totally irrelevant in bringing together Hanbury-Williams and Davies as the prime movers in Courtaulds' 'imperial' phase of policy in the years between 1946 and Davies's departure from the company in 1954.

At home, meanwhile, such policy as Hanbury-Williams had was essentially one of containment and restoration. So long as post-war reconstruction dominated the company's minds and energies, and a tolerable equilibrium could be maintained by his divide-and-rule policies amongst potentially conflicting elements within the Board, his chairmanship was reasonably, if negatively, effective. In retrospect, it is easy to observe that he did not understand the changed position of Britain and the new needs of British industry in the post-war years. But he was far from being alone in that. His tactical ability to rule in a small and fairly homogeneous group, and to give suitably beneficent and urbane nods to the doings of the executive directors, allowed dignity to masquerade as leadership. But this activity, or inactivity, totally lacked strategy and ideas—about higher profits, improved productivity, new fibres, new processes, more efficient organization. Indeed, his voluminous surviving correspondence is notable for one striking quality, apart from its length: his own letters hardly ever say anything. Only too often they simply repeat in slightly different words just what a correspondent has already said. There is no evidence that Hanbury-Williams had any innovative ideas whatever. For these he had to rely on others. By the later 1950s—when the absorption of British Celanese had created an entity too big for him properly to grasp; when the impact of the new scientist-technologists, Wilson and Kearton, was making itself vigorously felt; and when losses and difficulties were the fruits of the overseas expansion to which he had set his heart—by then Hanbury-Williams's chairmanship was beginning to verge on the disastrous.

III

Among the post-war reconstruction problems to which this Board turned its collective mind that of the company's organization figured prominently. It was a survival from pre-war debates. In 1937–8 the leading directors had been expressing concern over the weakness of Courtaulds' organization, holding that members of the Board were too much concerned with detailed administration and that there were too few managers of the requisite quality to whom matters of policy could be devolved.[1] The shelving of such questions on the outbreak of war was followed by their reconsideration as the war began to move into a more hopeful phase. Two main and related courses of action were proposed as remedies for the diseases which were diagnosed and much subsequent argument turned upon these two remedies. They were the establishment of what were called 'management committees'; and a form of devolution in the basic organization of the company normally referred to in the Board's discussions as 'hiving-off'. Before examining what was done and not done in both these two directions, it would be well to examine the nature and course of the internal criticism of the company's organization.

It inevitably acquired a new vigour and a more caustic mode of expression on the arrival of Freeman—that, to a large extent, was what he was there to provide. But it preceded him. The pre-war worries of Hanbury-Williams and Samuel Courtauld were echoed, with an insistent frequency, by Kinnes. In his memorandum of February 1946 (and apart from his comments on the abilities of certain of his colleagues), he underlined the same two major defects: the Board's excessive involvement in departmental or local management matters at the expense of 'general lines of policy and high administration'; and the difficulty in implementing any plans for delegation because of the 'lack of men of suitable calibre' amongst the existing managers. He stressed, then and later, that the company was facing a very serious organizational crisis. At other times over the next few years other directors added their quota of complaints. Davies complained that the preoccupation of the directors with day-to-day work meant that the allocation of funds to extensions or new enterprises was done in a hap-

[1] Vol. II, pp. 232–8.

hazard manner. Butler observed—and his colleagues agreed—that very inadequate information was given to the Board before being asked to decide on sundry proposals. Wilson told the chairman in 1951 that he did not believe that 'the Board, *as a collective body*, functions properly'. But all this paled into polite apologetics in comparison with the bombardment of scathing commentary which fell upon Hanbury-Williams and his colleagues from Freeman. As early as October 1945, he reported to Samuel Courtauld that there was not 'one man of outstanding ability amongst the managers' of the yarn factories; and threw in for good measure the observation that the working conditions in the company's factories were below those he had hitherto found in industry. He, too, complained of Board procedure, specifically of time wasted over trivia and of 'ill-digested and badly presented papers and memoranda'. Above all he complained that the Board failed to decentralize its operations, and that directors did not know how to delegate their responsibilities. His gloomy but only too pertinent aphorism already quoted, that the company was like 'a big Empire on the decline', he amended in the light of post-war exertions to the observation that Courtaulds was like 'a sick man who requires his health to be built up but whom we are pressing to play squash rackets'. Hanbury-Williams showed no sign of being amused by either metaphor, and contented himself by replying that he did not agree that the company was like a big Empire on the decline, but felt that it was inadequately staffed to carry out the expansion programme. That exchange was in December 1946. Three years later Freeman remained unimpressed by the progress made. 'Years of "easy money"', he wrote to Gratwick in December 1949, 'have made the company somewhat spineless and slack. Faults and mistakes tend to be covered up rather than exposed and punished.' The company was astonishingly easy-going; and far too many of its members put their own interests and convenience before those of the company. Too much detail was still dealt with at Board level to the detriment of the consideration of major problems. There was an unhealthy 'resistance-to-change mentality' in the company. And as for staff, this had increased to the point that the company was probably overstaffed.[1] 'Courtaulds', he told Butler, was too ready to 'suggest jobs to be done by a man rather than to say what the job was and then nominate the man to do it'. These few examples, expressed in letters and memoranda, typify a frustration so incompletely relieved that in January 1951 he summed much of it up in the

[1] Weekly and monthly-paid staff had indeed grown from 3,070 in 1946 to 5,559 in 1950. See below, Chap. XIII, esp. pp. 294–5.

outburst that the company remained 'over-centralized, constipated, and stagnant'.

Of the two remedies, the setting-up of the management committees was much the milder purgative. Proposals for their establishment arose out of discussions held in 1943 about the possibilities of company reorganization. The more drastic forms of reorganization would obviously take some time to implement, even if agreement about them could be reached; meanwhile, the management committees were to be a beginning. Samuel Courtauld was apparently responsible for their invention. Amongst their purposes, they would, in words characteristic of Hanbury-Williams's thinking and expressed by him in a memorandum of December 1943, 'give extra status, prestige and encouragement to selected members of our staff'. They were to be different from some similar pre-war committees in that more power was to be given to non-Board members. By a decision of 1944 four were set up, corresponding to what were called the four 'divisions' of the company: Rayon Yarn, Rayon Staple fibre, Textiles, and Chemicals. Their shortcomings did not elude Freeman's snapping jaws. They had become, he told Rendall and Hanbury-Williams in 1947, 'little more than technical debating societies' instead of the 'Local Boards' originally envisaged. Nevertheless, more were set up, with more powers over purchasing, price-fixing, factory management, and recruitment. The original four grew to eight.[1] The Board chairmen of the management committees were exhorted by Hanbury-Williams to delegate authority wherever possible; the committees were entrusted with more information on costs; and in June 1950 their non-Board members were treated to a speech by the chairman replete with pious references to 'Mr. Sam'. Still more amendments were made to their names, numbers, and constitution, the eight of 1947 being reduced to seven in 1950.[2] Denounced by Freeman as a failure, they nevertheless survived to undergo sundry mutations, until finally replaced by different structures. Meanwhile, the bigger remedy of hiving-off took precedence in the Board's deliberations.

The possibility of breaking down Courtaulds Ltd. into a number of subsidiary operating companies, linked together by a holding company to control policy and finance, had been discussed by various directors in 1938–9. It was raised again by Kinnes in 1943 and the eminent firm of

[1] Viscose Rayon, Acetate Rayon and Staple, Viscose Staple, Processing, Engineers, Plastics, Chemicals, Textiles.

[2] Viscose Rayon, Acetate Rayon and Staple, Viscose Staple, Processing, Engineers, Textile, and Arrow and Westcroft Mills.

accountants and auditors, Price Waterhouse & Co., were asked to prepare a report on the proposition. This they did in November 1943, reporting in favourable terms. Put aside again, and with the management committee remedy introduced to provide a palliative for observed symptoms, the bigger pill was once more paraded for inspection by Kinnes in 1946–7. His was now the strongest voice urging this particular change. Courtaulds, he told Hanbury-Williams (who didn't much like him), needed drastic reorganization; fewer directors, not more, concentrated in a holding company; the assets of the company should then lie in its shareholdings of the subsidiary, operating companies; thereby, not only would better overall policy direction be facilitated but opportunities for management to exercise directorial functions in the subsidiary companies would be created. It was very much an accountant's scheme and it was one generally favoured in British industry for dealing with the problems created by increased size. Not everyone on Courtaulds' Board approved of the idea as became evident at a special meeting held in January 1947.

At this important meeting Hanbury-Williams came out against the scheme, using the familiar formula that the 'time was not ripe', and urging that the management committees should be given time to prove their worth. Gratwick and Rendall also spoke against it. The result was that nothing particularly new was done. The temporary wartime planning committees[1] having been wound-up, the management committees and various internal Board committees constituted the basic structure of organization and control together with the various subsidiary and overseas companies on the periphery. The setting-up of separate 'divisions' within the company was endorsed, at least in name, and certain directors specified to be in charge of certain divisions. But the powers and degrees of separateness of those divisions were left blurred. The major sop to those pressing the need to strengthen the company's organization was the expressed intention of seeking the appointment of 'one or two additional directors from outside the Company's organization'. In June of the same year, a Finance Committee and a General Purposes Committee of the Board were newly constituted and specified; and to the former was added a newly appointed chief accountant who was not, however, a director.

Nevertheless, the idea of hiving-off did not disappear from the Board's collective mind, for a new and different reason was added to mere inefficiency as a possible justification for splitting up the company into legally separate entities: the nationalization programme of the Labour

[1] See above, pp. 6–7.

government. The bringing into public ownership of what came to be called the 'commanding heights' of the economy was part of the Labour Party platform. Their advent to power in 1945 soon brought some reality of nationalization, for example, the coal industry and public air transport; the Monopolies and Restrictive Practices Act of 1948; and much embittered controversy, especially that surrounding the iron and steel industry. For Courtaulds, with a monopoly of viscose staple fibre and a dominating position, though not a monopoly, in the rayon industry as a whole, the nationalization programme appeared to all the Board as a threat, not immediate but not to be ignored. In the course of 1948 the directors, discussing this threat, pondered upon the possibility of legally separating the rayon side of the business from the rest of the company; and the chairman included an eulogy of 'Free Enterprise' in his speech to shareholders in 1949. It was precisely in this connection that the term 'hiving-off' became commonly used at this time, in Courtaulds as elsewhere, as a legal process for avoiding nationalization. In the event, the return of Labour to power in 1950 with only a very small majority followed by the arrival of a Conservative government in 1951 removed this particular justification for splitting up the Courtaulds organization. But it again revealed that the formula did not command general assent in the Board.

Something more, however, still had to be done about over-centralization and all its much lamented consequences. So early in 1950 it was at last decided to do a trial run of separation, by splitting off the chemicals branch as though it were a separate company but without formal legal separation. A divisional board was set up, with Wilson as chairman; and it was hoped that if success attended the experiment, similar arrangements would be made with other branches of the business. In the autumn of 1950, Freeman was advocating the rapid adoption of a similar procedure with 'Fibro' (viscose rayon staple fibre). This soon precipitated a full-scale row between London and Coventry, providing Freeman thereby with ample scope for more home truths about his fellow directors. Pedder and Henry Johnson, predictably, informed the chairman that they objected to the idea: viscose yarn and staple fibre, they said, were so intertwined that they should not be divorced. Freeman then told the chairman and his deputies what he thought of them:

Mr. Johnson is a reactionary . . . [who] likes to pretend that the present organisation of the yarn side is the result of a carefully planned scheme rather than what it is—a hotch-potch grafted on to an antiquated system. He has been consistently lobbied and persuaded by Mr. Pedder . . . [who] has lobbied steadily and energetically against the 'hiving-off' of any Division for the sole reason that he deprecates any curtailment of his 'empire'. He has kept all authority to himself, has avoided so far as possible any delegation of responsibility, and steadfastly refused to bring forward his juniors, since he cannot tolerate any possible future rival.

Wilson, indicating some of the staff problems he had encountered in running the newly autonomous Chemicals Division, was likewise given a bad report by Freeman: 'Mr. Wilson has made a mess of the Chemical Division and, therefore, wishes everyone to believe that the business of 'hiving-off' gave rise to insurmountable difficulties. He has been faced with resignations but lacked the moral courage to accept one and so avoid all the others.' A few months later, with the whole business still on the boil Wilson dispatched to Hanbury-Williams a long carefully argued critique of the Board as well as a set of reasons why he did not approve of any more hiving-off. Despite the shortcomings of the Board he concluded that the present system of running the company as a whole, a product of trial and error, worked reasonably well, adding characteristically, 'if we are going to have something more rational it is worthwhile seeing that it is practical as well, and that more anomalies are not introduced than those eradicated'. Hanbury-Williams promptly showed the letter to Freeman and Gratwick; and Freeman took the opportunity to send Hanbury-Williams a riposte to Wilson which included the comment that Wilson devoted 'too much time to those interests of the Company which concern him least and too little to those which concern him most'.

These joustings on company organization were continued, and indeed brought to a head, in 1952. Kinnes returned to the attack with another long memorandum on his favourite proposals, adding some more pertinent but unendearing comments about the Board. Davies expressed doubts on more hiving-off but wondered whether another outside expert should be asked for an opinion. Johnson thought it was all too much too soon. Sundry directors worried about the likely damage to the undertaking as a whole and what was nebulously described as its 'family spirit'. Hanbury-Williams produced his 'Gentlemen's Club' memorandum, of which the crucial paragraph has already been quoted,[1] but nevertheless committed himself to a belief in some degree of hiving-off into separate legal companies. A detailed internal report was obtained, setting out the mechanics and implications of various schemes of decentralization. The upshot of all this was that the proposal for full hiving-off into legally separate subsidiaries

[1] See above, p. 24.

was dropped. The chairman and his three deputies (Hanbury-Williams, Gratwick, Freeman, and Rendall) advocated instead the re-grouping into divisions in the manner of the Chemicals Division. The recommendation was accepted, and plans were set on foot for the creation of a Textile Division on the same lines as the Chemicals Division. The sharp economic recession of 1952 began to bite and the Board got on with other matters, not the least of which was an economy campaign.

So, as in some of its related pre-war discussions, Courtaulds' Board had read memoranda, secured reports, debated, wrangled, been swayed by powerful interests within the company, and had finally taken the cautious road. Specifically, it had taken a small, but only a very small, step towards the type of multi-divisional structure pioneered by some of the biggest and most successful firms in the U.S.A. during the 1920s and 1930s, notably Du Pont, Standard Oil of New Jersey, Sears Roebuck, and General Motors. The adoption of this form—characterized by the existence of a decentralized structure of autonomous operating divisions, based on product rather than function, but controlled by a general office concerned solely with long-term policy decisions—was proceeding rapidly in America in the 1940s and 1950s, so that by 1960 it had become the accepted form of organization in most large industrial enterprises.[1] Not so in Britain. Although very large concerns, such as Unilever and I.C.I. had perforce developed patterns of organization suited to wide variation in product or geographic spread of interests, the older functional form of organization—with a hierarchy of specialized functions topped by the chairman or managing director—remained far more common well into the 1950s and 1960s.[2]

The divisions and the management committees in Courtaulds were still some way from those of the American-type multi-divisional structure, or indeed from those of I.C.I. The newly developed Chemical and Textile Divisions of the early 1950s represented the farthest distance the Board was then willing to go. Moreover, chemicals and textiles then represented two of the less important contributors to profits. Only Freeman seems to have had any real awareness of other organizations, specifically mentioning I.C.I. and Unilever in this country and Standard Oil in the U.S.A. The Board itself undoubtedly continued to spend too much of its time on detail. Whatever the demerits of the decentralization scheme which Kinnes was advocating—and it is far from clear that it would have been the right

[1] Alfred D. Chandler, *Strategy and Structure* (Cambridge, Mass., 1962), p. 49.

[2] Derek F. Channon, *The Strategy and Structure of British Enterprise* (London, 1973).

answer—it at least provided for the possibility that the Board of the proposed central holding company should concentrate on strategic policy. However tactless Freeman may have been in trying to hurry the Board on to more decentralization, he, too, was trying to achieve the same end. But the slow and cautious methods prevailed. Why? For all the pressure of vested interests as represented by the Coventry directors and for all Hanbury-Williams's lack of positive policy perhaps ultimately what ensured caution was that nobody on the Board could really imagine whom they would trust to carry out those strategic functions. Despite the considerable expertise on technical matters and genuine concern for the company manifested by individual directors, the Board, as a decision-making body on high policy, lacked courage and self-confidence. Hanbury-Williams's coda to his encomium of the 'Gentlemen's Club' atmosphere—'On the other hand, great care must be taken to avoid inefficiency'—is as revealing as the encomium itself. For its tacit assumption, in the context in which it was written, was that although business efficiency might indeed not be compatible with that 'atmosphere', it was the latter which had at all costs to be preserved. As for drastic change as an adaptation to changed circumstances—of Britain, of Courtaulds, of a tried system—it would have seemed not only unnecessary but simply otiose.

IV

This, then was the Board which ruled Courtaulds Ltd. and controlled its shareholders' £32 million (nominal) of paid-up capital during the immediate post-war years of recovery. The broad areas of responsibility of the Board at the beginning of 1952 are shown in Table 4. In addition to these main-Board directorships, many or most of those on the Board were also directors of subsidiaries or associated companies, for example, at various times, Rendall, Gratwick, and Wilson of British Nylon Spinners; Hanbury-Williams, Gratwick, and Davies of British Cellophane; Freeman, H. L. Johnson, and Davies of Courtaulds (Canada); Sheldon and Davies of both Courtaulds (Australia) and Les Filés de Calais; Hanbury-Williams and Davies of Snia Viscosa.

The problem of recruiting to the Board (which, with sixteen members, was two short of its customary number) continued to press. The wise outsiders failed to materialize. By 1950–1 search for possible candidates amongst the more promising layers of the younger management began to

TABLE 4

The Board and its responsibilities, December 1951

Chairman	Sir John Hanbury-Williams.*	
Deputy chairmen	Sir Wilfrid Freeman, Bart.	Administration and new projects
	P. J. Gratwick	Textiles
	P. S. Rendall	Rayon
Full-time directors	J. E. Pedder	Yarn
	W. H. Nankivell, O.B.E.	Textiles
	A. H. Wilson, F.R.S.	Chemicals and Research
	G. T. Verrall	Engineering
	F. T. Davies }	Overseas Subsidiaries and Investments
	C. W. Sheldon }	
	W. P. Courtauld	Use-development
	G. Courtauld	Personnel
Part-time directors	R. A. Butler	
	R. A. Kinnes	
	H. L. Johnson	
	Sir William Stanier, F.R.S.	

* Knighted in 1950.

look potentially rewarding. The contrast of attitude between the old and the new directors, however, soon revealed themselves here as in other matters. Johnson wrote to Hanbury-Williams proposing a candidate from amongst the old Coventry hands largely on the familiar grounds of experience and as a reward for past achievements. Wilson countered it by emphasizing the need to look ahead to the consequences of such appointments. This proposal simply represented a gamble on this particular man 'changing sides'. If he did not then all the work of changing 'the spirit at Coventry' would be wasted. The logical course of action was to retire the 'old sweats' and then promote the more promising younger men. He named a younger candidate. Johnson wrote to say that 'we should be exceedingly careful before appointing a younger man'. The ritual ended; neither was appointed.

Freeman, as usual, was the most uninhibited in his comments on potential directors. In December 1950 he wrote to Hanbury-Williams summarizing his views on three candidates—none of them remotely associated with the 'old Coventry spirit'—recently considered by the Board. One of them was not in fact appointed until 1958 and so can be considered later.[1]

[1] See below, pp. 137–8.

Of one of the other two, J. G. Smith, then the chief yarn salesman, Freeman observed that despite his conscientiousness and his grasp of the staple-fibre side of the business, he was unlikely to 'contribute much at Board level' and that 'if he could do so I doubt if anyone would listen to him'.[1] A year later as the time approached for a decision, Wilson, in his mild, unforceful, rational language, again raised the pertinent issues:

What we are really looking for is reserves for Gratwick and Rendall, both of whom are much more than salesmen. Granted that J. G. Smith is a first-class salesman, is he a top-ranking commercial man in the widest sense? E.g. are we to look to him to succeed Rendall on the Rayon Producers Committee and to deal with Government Departments at the highest level? Unless we are reasonably clear as to where we are aiming I feel we may fill the little gaps and leave the large ones wide open.

All to no avail. Smith was appointed as from March 1952. And Freeman was proved right: in the ten years he remained on the Board, for all his effectiveness at persuading customers to buy staple fibre, he contributed nothing of consequence to the higher policy of the company.

To match this undistinguished appointment another was made at the same time. In an opposite direction, it also demonstrated the prescience of Freeman's observations:

Very able, quick thinking and probably quick tempered. Immense ability for hard work, constructive thought, and is rapidly obtaining a very extensive knowledge of the Company's business. He thinks clearly and can express himself well on paper and in speech.

I don't think he will tolerate fools and may be over-ambitious. He is probably apt to jump to conclusions on subjects on which he is ill-informed without taking the trouble to ascertain the facts. His judgment is not therefore always sound.

I think he could be made a member of the Board in 1951, for I believe his worst failings will disappear when he finds his opinions subjected to critical analysis at Board level.

And so, in March 1952 in fact, C. F. Kearton became a director of Courtaulds. Earlier, in October 1951, Butler had resigned on becoming

[1] In his covering note, Freeman suggested to Hanbury-Williams that this letter—of which he made no copy, which was sent from his private address, and which also contained some unflattering personal comments about Smith—should be destroyed. It was not; it took its place, along with the other observations on other directors, in Hanbury-Williams's private intelligence file.

Chancellor of the Exchequer in the new Conservative administration; and in May 1953 Freeman died suddenly. With these and subsequent changes in 1954–5, one phase both in the composition of Courtaulds' Board and the policy which it pursued was brought to an end, and a new one begun.

What, meanwhile, had the post-war administration achieved, at home and overseas?

CHAPTER III

Recovery at Home

I

BEFORE the loss of A.V.C., Courtaulds' profits depended substantially upon the performance of its American subsidiary: from 1929 to 1939, A.V.C. contributed a proportion, varying from 19 to 63 per cent. but averaging nearly 40 per cent., of the total gross income of Courtaulds Ltd.[1] So the company's financial results could not be presented in the context simply of its activities in Britain. In the phase of post-war recovery, however, the remitted contribution of its overseas production or investment income was trivial: during the five-year period 1950–4, for example, it accounted on average for only about 3 per cent. of gross income before tax and depreciation.[2] Consequently the general financial results given in Table 5 depended overwhelmingly on the sale, in home or export markets, of production in Britain.

During the period covered by Table 5, prices rose. Taking averages of 1940–2 and 1952–4, the retail prices index rose by about 78 per cent.;[3] over the same period Courtaulds' pre-tax profits rose by 308 per cent. So there was genuine recovery, well above the rate of inflation, although most of it was concentrated in the period from 1950 onwards. Moreover, the return on assets showed a surge, in the boom of 1950–2, to rates not seen since the 1920s.

Just as these revived profits depended on home manufacturing, so they still rested very largely on the production and sale of viscose rayon in one form or another. The profit and loss accounts of Courtaulds Ltd. in this period show 'mill profits' as contributing about 80 per cent. of total pre-tax gross income, i.e. before deduction of research and development costs,

[1] See Vol. II, Table 68, p. 315.

[2] Even this figure includes interest on loans to subsidiaries such as Courtaulds (Canada). If the overseas contributions are considered as part of group profits, rather than as remitted dividends and interest, the overseas proportion of pre-tax group profits rises to about 10 per cent. for 1952–4.

[3] Feinstein, Table 65.

TABLE 5

Financial results, 1940–54, Courtaulds Ltd. and Courtaulds Group

	(a) *Profit and interest before tax**	(b) *Tax*	(c) *Dividends less tax*	(d) *Retained profits*	(e) *Total net assets*	(f) *(a) as percentage of (e)*
	£ mn.	£ mn.	£ mn.	£ mn.	£ mn.	%
Courtaulds Ltd.						
1940	3·3	1·8	1·3	0·2	41·1	8·0
1941	4·2	2·9	1·1	0·2	52·4†	8·0
1942	4·0	2·7	1·1	0·2	52·5	7·6
1943	3·7	2·6	1·1	—	52·5	7·0
1944	3·2	2·3	1·1	−0·2	52·3	6·1
1945	3·2	2·2	1·2	−0·2	52·1	6·1
1946–7‡	3·7	1·6	1·5	0·6	52·7	7·0
Courtaulds Group						
1947–8	5·5	3·8	1·2	0·5	60·2	9·1
1948–9	6·6	3·5	1·2	1·9	62·9	10·5
1949–50	8·0	3·8	1·2	3·0	67·5	11·9
1950–1	16·8	9·0	1·7	6·0	77·7	21·6
1951–2	18·5	10·3	1·6	6·4	86·1	21·5
1952–3	9·8	5·3	1·7	2·8	92·2	10·6
1953–4	18·2	11·4	2·3	4·5	111·7	16·3

* But *after* deduction of debenture and/or loan interest.

† Adjustments made as a consequence of the sale of A.V.C. resulted in a capital surplus of £11·1 million.

‡ The company's financial year was changed from 31 December to 31 March at this time, so this row of figures relate to the 15 months ended 31 March 1947. The accounts after this date refer to what then came to be called Courtaulds Group instead of Courtaulds Ltd.

replacement of fixed assets, sundry head office expenses, and the like. Table 6 shows the percentage contributions, to those mill profits, of the main production lines. These are necessarily only approximate guides, for reasons explained in the notes to the Table, but the general orders of magnitude and trends shown by the figures are not likely to be far wrong. Two lines of profit showed relative decline, after the immediate post-war re-stocking boom: viscose textile yarn and woven and knitted fabrics. Conversely viscose industrial yarn and viscose staple fibre, acetate yarn and

TABLE 6

Sources of mill profits, 1945–54

	Total mill profits	*Viscose textile yarn*	*Viscose industrial (tyre) yarn*	*Viscose staple fibre*	*Acetate yarn and staple fibre*	*Textiles and knitting*	*Chemicals*
	£000	%	%	%	%	%	%
1945 . .	2,392	53	6	28	—	15	2
1946–7 (15 months)	3,742	45	12	34	1	7	1
1947–8 . .	3,825	44	11	29	—	15	2
1948–9 . .	4,718	54	13	19	6	15	3
1949–50 . .	7,565	31	11	34	5	9	3
1950–1 . .	13,320	34	12	39	10	8	4
1951–2 . .	13,643	28	21	31	12	6	5
1952–3 . .	9,262	13	28	46	12	4	6
1953–4 . .	17,685	22	23	43	7	3	6

Note: The Total mill-profit figures are net of deduction for common central services, e.g. Coventry Central Department, etc.; but the figure from which the percentages are calculated are gross of the deductions. Consequently, as will be readily seen, the percentages normally add up to rather more than 100, except in 1949–50 when an accounting adjustment introduced a discrepancy in the opposite direction. However, these discrepancies are not large enough significantly to alter the *general* proportions and trends indicated by these figures.

staple, and chemicals all increased their shares, with viscose staple fibre and tyre yarn emerging as the biggest contributors to the company's profits. These trends broadly, though not precisely, fit in with the differences between planned and actual output, as already indicated in Chapter I;[1] and with the course of change in output as shown in Fig. 1. As the curves in the graph show, output recovered at roughly the same rate for all products up to 1948 but thereafter the weakening of viscose textile yarn and the strengthening of industrial yarn and staple fibre became evident, even before the recession of 1951–2. The implementation of recovery at home, however, was even more complex than the figures might suggest.

In the task of turning plans into reality, with all the enforced adaptation to the unforeseen involved therein, three particular factors complicated Courtaulds' programmes for post-war recovery and expansion in viscose rayon. They were: government policy on factory location; the company's

[1] See above, Table 2, p. 8.

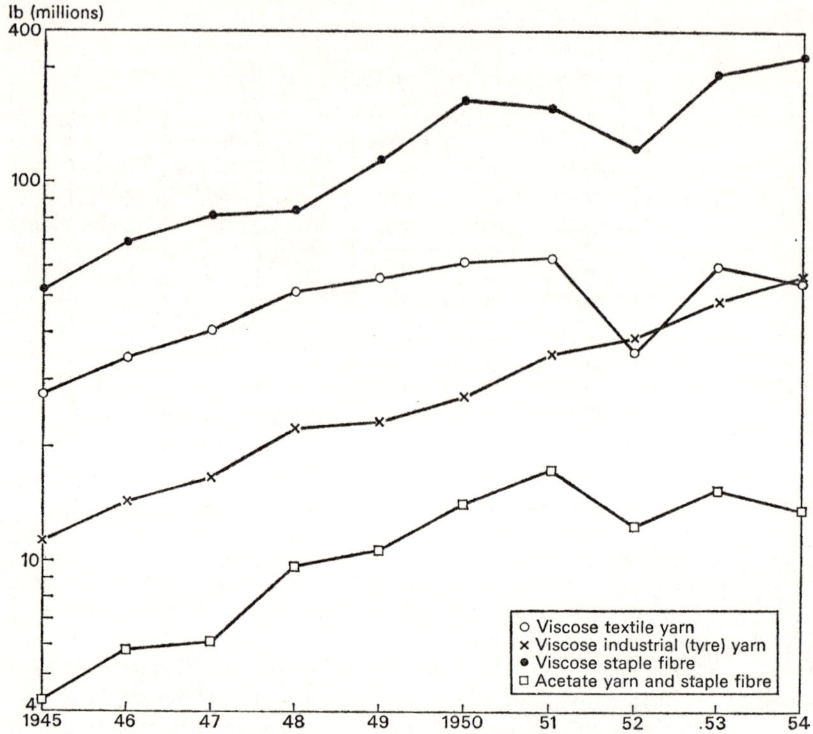

FIG. 1. *Courtaulds, U.K.: rayon output, 1945–54*

Source: M.C. *Man-made cellulosic fibres*

comparative backwardness in research and development; and the varying pattern of demand, itself partially influenced by changes in government policy.

II

Tentative probings into the possibilities of Northern Ireland and government signposts to various 'development areas'[1] were followed up in the course of 1943–4. Sir Basil Brooke,[2] Prime Minister of Northern Ireland, lunched at 16 St. Martin's-le-Grand[3] and dangled such inducements as abundance of labour in the hope of attracting Courtaulds' employment-creating investment. Various possible sites for a staple fibre plant in Northern Ireland were examined in the course of 1944 and one at Carrickfergus looked the most promising. This factory was at that time

[1] See above, p. 7. [2] Later (1952) Lord Brookeborough.

[3] The then Head Office, since 1926 (see Vol. II, p. 249).

expected to provide capacity for staple fibre in addition to the intended expansion of the existing plant at Greenfield (North Wales) by the building of a third production line. Samuel Courtauld had indeed made a particular point of this in a letter to Hugh Dalton at the Board of Trade in 1944; extolling the virtues of 'Fibro' both for export and for the rehabilitation of Lancashire, he had asked for priority in going ahead with putting up the extra unit at Greenfield. Greenfield was not, however, in a Development Area. So after some negotiation, Dalton agreed to this request on the undertaking that Courtaulds would also site one of their intended new factories in a Development Area. After investigations into various possible sites proffered by the Board of Trade, two mainland coastal sites in Development Areas emerged as serious contenders for rayon factories: Dundee and Sellafield, as well as a site for engineering and processing activities at Accrington.[1]

Meanwhile, the Northern Ireland project had been treated as a separate exercise. Northern Ireland's different political status put it outside the government's main Development Area policy; and amongst Brooke's inducements was the possibility of local labour and materials being available so that Courtaulds could start building work there earlier than elsewhere, indeed before the end of the war. This was in fact the prime reason for going there. Building costs were reckoned to be rather higher than in Britain; and, despite earlier hopes about local demand, it soon came to be appreciated that the local market would prove too small in itself to justify a separate unit. As investigations proceeded however, it became evident that an early start would not be possible; so the Northern Ireland scheme began to appear simply as one of the various sites for possible expansion. Nevertheless, after further Board discussion it was eventually decided to honour the promises made to Brooke and to go ahead; the site at Carrickfergus was bought early in 1945.

Although it was initially intended that the Carrickfergus plant should be used for staple fibre, it increasingly became a matter of argument how the various products should be allocated or re-allocated amongst new and existing factories. Should the proposed Dundee factory be for staple fibre or for tyre yarn? Was it not desirable to build new plant for tyre yarn on the land available by the existing Preston factory? In June 1945 it was decided to put Carrickfergus on viscose textile yarn, not on staple fibre. The Sellafield plant was to have been for acetate yarn. But then it turned out that the costs of the Dundee plant would be rather high because of

[1] See below, p. 194, on the fate of the Accrington project.

problems of effluent disposal; and visits both to America and Germany suggested that techniques inadequately heeded by Coventry could increase staple-fibre productivity at Greenfield, without a new plant.[1] So, because the government was not keen to give priority for building at Preston, why not switch Sellafield to tyre yarn, and allocate the acetate unit to Preston and keep Dundee in reserve for a staple-fibre plant when the siting problems there could be solved? A letter containing recommendations on these lines was sent to Stafford Cripps—who had taken over from Dalton at the Board of Trade—in November 1945. It received his blessings. With the additional expectation that a viscose-textile-yarn plant as well as a tyre-yarn plant might eventually be built at Sellafield, this pattern of allocation became agreed policy early in 1946, with government approval.

None of it ever happened. The central snag was Sellafield. The history of this episode is worth examining in some detail because it provides a splendid little example of the wholly unintended consequences of state planning.

The designation of the economically run-down region of West Cumberland—centering on the old coal and iron working district in the hinterland of Whitehaven and Workington—as a Development Area was a logical enough move in the Labour government's industrial location policy. But behind that particular special area lay a very different sort of special area—the Lake District. So as soon as it was announced that Courtaulds were to take over the former Royal Ordnance Factory at Sellafield and to draw their water supply from Ennerdale Water by a scheme which would involve raising the level of that lake 6 feet and removing a famous lakeside inn, the Anglers' Hotel, various preservationist voices were quickly audible. The Council for the Preservation of Rural England, the Standing Committee on National Parks, and the Friends of the Lake District were joined by the then Chairman of the National Trust, the Earl of Crawford and Balcarres, who, being also a personal friend of Samuel Courtauld, acted as an intermediary. Dr. C. E. M. Joad, popular broadcaster and pseudo-intellectual, joined in with a letter to *The Times*. Amongst other characteristic inaccuracies, he stated that the purpose of the 'artificial silk factory at Sellafield' was to 'provide silk stockings for the women of England'. The very use of the term 'artificial silk' in 1945 together with the easy assumption that its function was to make women's stockings embodied an ignorance far from being confined to this particular radio pundit. At about the same time Stafford Cripps was assuring Samuel

[1] See below, pp. 49–50.

Courtauld that he was 'attaching a great deal of importance to your Sellafield project as contributing to solve the unemployment problem in that part of West Cumberland'; and the authorities of the Borough of Whitehaven, who had long drawn water from Ennerdale and who were responsible for the scheme to raise the level of the lake, announced their determination to push on with the scheme 'despite any opposition there might be'. A paper war of words developed.

There was, however, another term in the bargaining equation: the excise duty on rayon yarn. The circumstances of the imposition of the rayon duties in 1925 have been described in Volume II.[1] Despite their subsequent reduction, the abolition of the duty on staple fibre in 1935, and the granting of drawbacks on export, all pre-war attempts to persuade the government to remove what was obviously a misconceived excise in the first place had received nothing but the usual Treasury refusal. So post-war attempts by the Labour government to persuade the rayon industry to put its new factories in particular areas was soon met with a demand for a particular quid pro quo. In December 1944 the British Rayon Federation had submitted a memorandum to the then Chancellor of the Exchequer[2] arguing the case for the abolition of what had become simply an arbitrary tax on an industrial raw material; and the pressure was renewed with the coming of Dalton to that post in July 1945. But the Budget of April 1946 disappointed the rayon and textile interests by containing no reference to the desired abolition.

Now it so happened that the Budget Speech and Courtaulds' Annual General Meeting neatly coincided. So in his speech to shareholders Samuel Courtauld took the opportunity publicly to warn that failure to abolish the excise duty on rayon might cause the company to reconsider its plans for the Sellafield plant. At the Board meeting on the following day, discussion of this very issue was interrupted by the receipt of a message from Dalton to the chairman to the effect that he had read the speech and would like to discuss the matter. It worked—or nearly so—for in June the Chancellor of the Exchequer undertook to give a rebate of the duty on rayon used for tyre yarn. In the course of a speech during the debate on the Finance Bill, Dalton, in his customarily florid and patronizing fashion, referred to 'Mr. Samuel Courtauld . . . [whom] I regard not only as a personal friend, but as one of the most valuable figures in British Industry', and stated that Courtauld had 'definitely undertaken to go ahead' with the transformation of the old Sellafield Ordnance factory into a new tyre-yarn plant. The

[1] See Vol. II, pp. 259–63, 327–8, 343, 362–3. [2] Sir John Anderson.

bargain was completed on the government side by the final abolition of the rayon excise in April 1947. Meanwhile plans went ahead with the clearing of the site and for the construction of a factory estimated to cost some £11 million. Although Whitehaven Borough Council and the local amenity societies continued in conflict, in December 1946 the Ministry of Health approved the scheme for taking water from Ennerdale Lake, subject to various modifications and requirements designed to safeguard the beauty of Ennerdale. But now another twist to the whole exercise came with Courtaulds' reassessment of the market for rayon yarn. A sales estimate in December 1946 put the estimated annual sales of viscose textile yarn at approximately 13 per cent. lower than the previous estimate made in April 1945; the drop was attributed largely to falling demand in export markets. So a committee was urgently convened in January 1947 to reconsider the expansion plans. After a series of internal reports had been written and digested, the Board in March 1947 decided to reduce the textile-yarn-spinning capacity to be installed at Carrickfergus; to drop the new building at Preston and use the existing factory there for tyre yarn together with a reduced capacity for textile yarn; to postpone any building operations at Dundee for at least two years; and to scrap the tyre-yarn project for Sellafield. That was to be replaced by an acetate plant, hitherto destined for the new building at Preston, but which, of course, represented the original notion of what was to be done at Sellafield. A letter embodying all this was sent to both Dalton and Cripps.

Having thus spent about three years gyrating around sundry schemes and making various revisions to one particular government-chosen location, this whole exercise was brought to an abrupt halt in June 1947 by the announcement that the Ministry of Supply proposed to erect an atomic plant at Drigg, five miles south of Sellafield. Following some investigations by Freeman, Hanbury-Williams quickly wrote to Cripps saying that Courtaulds now felt at liberty to withdraw from the project, as labour for the rapid building of two factories there would clearly not be forthcoming and production could hardly begin before 1953 which, he observed, was 'a dismal prospect'. After much high-level talking, the government made up its mind and the decision was conveyed to Courtaulds in a letter from Cripps to Hanbury-Williams: as Courtaulds wished to withdraw, the Ministry of Supply would take over Sellafield again and build the atomic plant there instead of it at Drigg (which was the less satisfactory site). So Courtaulds never went to Sellafield and the Windscale atomic energy plant was built instead.

By the external delays and oscillations contingent upon the planning decisions of the state, Courtaulds had thus been accidentally rescued from the consequences of their own mistaken planning decisions. For in the autumn of 1947 sales and output estimates for both viscose textile yarn and all types of acetate were again reduced. As even the reduced viscose-textile-yarn estimates were in fact never attained and the acetate output reached only after the acquisition of British Celanese in 1957, Courtaulds were thereby spared a large amount of quite unnecessary capital expenditure. In September 1947 Board votes for some £12 million of capital expenditure at Sellafield and Preston were cancelled. Although in his speech to shareholders at the 1948 Annual General Meeting the chairman spoke of projects modified or cancelled in 1947 because of 'economic conditions outside our control', and of government requests for retrenchment in the difficult circumstances of the time, a letter from Freeman to Hanbury-Williams of August 1947 reveals only too clearly Courtaulds' awareness of the awkward position the company was in:

I had some talk with R.A.B. [i.e. R. A. Butler] on . . . the avoidance of undertaking large building schemes at the present time. R.A.B. was advising me that we would have to be very careful how we went about the business of explaining to the Government why we were not carrying out our big expansion scheme and were leaving Sellafield unreplaced by a new site, and allowing Dundee to lapse for a year.

I am well aware that we are on thin ice . . .

We should wait for the Government to approach us, and then I think our line should be: first, the grave shortage of raw materials; secondly, that Sellafield was to have been an acetate factory and that we cannot get the raw materials in this factory until the Standard Oil Refinery scheme is through;[1] and thirdly, that technical developments since 1939 have shown that we can produce far more yarn from our existing mills than we thought possible in the past.

In time, it was all sorted out. The existing acetate plant at Little Heath, Coventry, was adapted for increased output and continued to be responsible for all the company's acetate production until 1957. The existing viscose-yarn mills—Coventry, Aber, Castle, Wolverhampton, and Preston—continued to produce between them all the viscose-textile-yarn output until they were joined by Carrickfergus in 1950. By the end of the post-war decade average production for 1953–4 was distributed thus:

[1] See below, p. 52.

'000 lb.

Coventry	*Aber*	*Castle*	*Wolverhampton*	*Preston*	*Carrickfergus*
3,400	9,500	10,900	12,700	11,100	9,600

The output of tyre yarn was spread over Coventry, Wolverhampton, and Preston until the early 1950s when Wolverhampton ceased production and Preston rapidly increased its output, supplemented by smaller quantities from Coventry and Carrickfergus. Greenfield was expanded to produce all the considerably increased quantities of staple fibre; the Dundee project was abandoned; and it was not until 1954 that a new site was picked for another staple-fibre plant, at Grimsby, which finally came into full operation in 1958.

III

Behind these fluctuating plans lay a complex of needs for technical change, often postponed by wartime stringencies. In the production of viscose textile yarn the main pending innovation was the introduction of the continuous spinning process instead of the box-spinning commonly used before the war. For Courtaulds this meant the purchase of the patent rights to the process which had been invented by the Industrial Rayon Corporation and brought into operation at their Ohio plant in 1939.[1] Pre-war negotiations for the purchase were resumed in 1945 and in October of that year Courtaulds bought for $5 million the patent rights for the U.K. and various other countries,[2] a parcel of 'know-how', and a ten-year technical and patent-exchange agreement. Courtaulds recouped the $5 million by granting licences to a number of companies in other countries.[3] But the equipment and re-equipment of the yarn factories, new and old, proceeded for some time with the box-spinning machinery. Before they could be installed the new machines had to be made, tested, and then produced in appropriate numbers—tasks entrusted to Courtaulds' Engineering department (or Division as it subsequently became). Post-war

[1] See Vol. II, p. 414, n. 1.

[2] Belgium, Denmark, Finland, France, Italy, Netherlands, Norway, Spain, Sweden, and Switzerland, as well as Canada and Australia.

[3] Italy (Snia Viscosa), Switzerland (Viscose Suisse), Holland (Nyma), Belgium (Fabelta), Spain (S.N.I.A.C.E.), and Sweden (Svenska Rayon), as well as Les Filés de Calais which in turn granted sub-licences to C.T.A. and Société Lyonnaise. The total received was £1,193,277 and 54,545 Snia Viscosa ordinary shares, together with £184,027 received by the Calais subsidiary.

shortages of raw materials, as well as difficulties both in space and staff,[1] found the Engineering department under considerable pressure; and the manufacture and installation of the continuous spinning equipment proved to be slower than had been expected. Ultimately—and, again, more by accident than intent—this proved to be beneficial. For despite the high hopes, the continuous-spinning process turned out to be far less satisfactory in practical working, partly because of high maintenance costs. Carrickfergus was indeed the only Courtaulds' factory to use the process for textile yarn, all the others continuing to use modified and improved box-spinning. Moreover, the failure of the viscose textile yarn market to show the hoped-for buoyancy, and its declining profitability, made such investment less and less worthwhile. In reality the main beneficiary of the purchase of the I.R.C. patents was tyre-yarn production. From the experience with the new machinery Courtaulds' own research and engineering efforts gradually developed new continuous-spinning machinery for tyre yarn which was brought into operation at Preston in 1950 and Carrickfergus in 1953.[2]

In the more promising area of staple-fibre production Courtaulds had again to make their immediately post-war advances by borrowing from elsewhere. With both Glanzstoff-Courtaulds and A.V.C. Courtaulds had agreements for the exchange of technical information; the agreement with A.V.C. continued in being after the 1941 sale. In practice, however, technical exchange with A.V.C. was inoperative during the war although Courtaulds did send a representative on a factory visit in 1943; whilst that with Cologne was, of course, entirely suspended. As soon as hostilities ceased Courtaulds sent visiting parties in 1945 to their overseas interests. They soon discovered that there was something to be learned from American and German practice, particularly in viscose preparation, in tyre-yarn spinning, and above all in staple-fibre production. The performance of Glanzstoff-Courtaulds and A.V.C. in staple fibre contrasted sharply with that of Courtaulds in Britain. Whilst home output had fluctuated around 50 million lb., with a slightly falling trend,[3] Cologne output more than doubled between 1939 and 1944, reaching nearly 20 million lb. at the latter date; and A.V.C.'s output rose from 28 million lb. in 1939 to over 100 million lb. in 1945. It was to these visits that Johnson referred when he told the Board in October 1945 that the whole programme for the development of Greenfield had been revised as a consequence of visits to staple-fibre plants in Germany and the U.S.A. Investment

[1] See below, p. 194. [2] See below, Fig. 2, p. 53. [3] See Table 1, above, p. 6.

in improvements made more effective use of existing capacity, and, along with the third unit at Greenfield, rendered unnecessary any new staple-fibre plants whilst permitting output to multiply four-fold in the decade after 1945.[1]

Although some part of the lag in British performance may well have been due to shortages of raw materials and similar wartime and immediately post-war difficulties, there can be little doubt that, in this as in other matters, Courtaulds were reaping the harvest of Coventry's complacency and wholly inadequate pre-war research effort. When the Canadian company started putting in a staple fibre production line in 1947, it drew heavily on A.V.C. advice and methods, as it did on other technical matters. A visit there in 1948 by one of the Coventry 'old sweats' produced shocked disapproval of the Canadian management not having consulted Coventry; and his report concluded with the chauvinistic observation that there was 'a tendency to encourage a drift from anything British, and to counter this, more frequent visits from both sides should be arranged'. It predictably drew a fierce blast from Freeman:

> To assume that Coventry are always right and that any idea emanating from A.V.C. is wrong is dangerous and somewhat typical of our company. If it had not been for A.V.C. and Wilson's insistence that we should follow their Fibro practice, Greenfield would have stood where it did 4 years ago and we should have erected a wholly unnecessary plant outside Dundee at a prodigious cost.

Two years earlier, in June 1946, Freeman had himself visited the A.V.C. plants and had written then from New York:

> I find it difficult to understand how Pedder, having seen the continuous spinning of tyre yarn, did not immediately take steps to have this method introduced into our factories. He had all the drawings and information that was required. The same applies to the 'Fibro' set up which has enabled Front Royal to increase their output . . . at negligible capital cost . . . I can only suppose that Pedder did in fact tell Henry Johnson what he had seen, but the latter ignored what he was told until he could see it for himself . . . Generally speaking, I should say that A.V.C. had out-stripped us technically.

And in 1952 when Courtaulds were preparing to re-enter the American production scene with a plant to produce staple fibre there, Freeman was still lamenting Coventry's inadequacies: 'It has always been a matter of grave concern to me to think that the factory being installed in America contains so little Courtauld equipment.' What was achieved after the war

[1] See Fig. 1, above, p. 42.

1. Sir Alan Wilson (in 1961)

2. Continuous spinning plant for rayon yarn, Carrickfergus, 1952

certainly owed much to Wilson; and it was he who not only insisted on more research but, in 1950, called for the erection of an experimental staple-fibre pilot plant at Coventry to facilitate further improvements.

In the production of acetate rayon the technical difficulties in the way of low-cost expansion were of a wholly different nature. They also appeared to be of less consequence if only because Courtaulds did not occupy the dominant position which they had in viscose rayon. They remained in second place to British Celanese. Responsible for only 19 per cent. of total acetate yarn and fibre output just before the war,[1] Courtaulds' share had risen to only about 25 per cent. in 1955. The very high increase in output planned so optimistically in 1945 (from 4·3 million lb. to 37·5 million in 1950–2)[2] never looked like being achieved; and the rate of increase which was in fact obtained over the decade 1945–54 was lower than viscose staple fibre or tyre yarn and only slightly better than viscose textile yarn.[3] Its increased contribution to profits in the early 1950s, as shown in Table 6, owed much to the weakening role of viscose textile yarn. In so far as acetate's mediocre performance was affected by technical problems of supply, rather than of changes in demand, it depended not on Courtaulds' need to rectify shortcomings in production processes, but on the cost of certain crucial raw materials. These were chemicals quite different from those used in the viscose process. They demand attention because the attempts to solve these problems of supply reveal the way in which Courtaulds began to find themselves increasingly involved in industrial chemistry, an involvement which in the next phase (considered in Part II) almost pushed the company into the chemical rather than the textile industry.

The crucial chemicals were acetic anhydride and acetone. There were various ways in which they could be secured. Courtaulds bought them from the Distillers Company—who made them from ethyl alcohol obtained by the distillation of imported molasses—or from the Shawinigan Company of Canada who made them by a different process. In the U.S.A., they were got from propylene, a by-product of the 'cracking' of oil hydrocarbons; this was a much cheaper method which was responsible for a good part of the lower costs and higher profits of A.V.C.'s acetate production at its Meadville plant than that at Courtaulds' Little Heath plant, *circa* 1938–41.[4] British Celanese had made them themselves from ethyl alcohol purchased from the Distillers Company, but in 1942 brought into operation at their Spondon factory an oil-cracking plant of their own

[1] See Vol. II, p. 351. [2] Table 2, above, p. 8.
[3] See Fig. 1, above, p. 42. [4] See Vol. II, p. 418.

for this purpose—the first of its kind in the U.K. to make chemical raw materials. So, once again, Courtaulds seemed to be technically backward; some part of that lag, however, reflected both a general British technical lag and a specific awareness within Courtaulds that a move into this sort of chemical production might be a hazardous business, or at any rate only potentially justifiable if their scale of acetate output and sales were substantially enlarged. Moreover it might also, in chemical and commercial logic, suggest their moving into the wider field of plastics. Between 1943 and 1946 discussion and negotiations designed to solve this problem took various forms. There were talks about oil-cracking with Trinidad Leaseholds Ltd. and with Manchester Oil Refinery Ltd., and, of course, with the Distillers Company; with Standard Oil of New Jersey and its subsidiary Anglo-American Oil, and with Shell. 'Courtaulds', wrote F. T. Davies in a memorandum of June 1945, complaining that there was too much talking and not enough detailed examination of the costs and possible profits, 'must decide *now* whether they wish to enter the chemical engineering industry'. Most of these lines of enquiry soon proved abortive; protracted negotiations, largely conducted by Freeman, with Standard Oil for the setting up of a joint company also finally came to nothing. The main outcome of all these enquiries was the acquisition of the rights to a process for the conversion of acetone into acetic anhydride; a plant for this was eventually set up at Little Heath and brought some cost-reduction, acetone itself continuing to be bought from the Distillers Company. It did not result, during this first post-war decade, in Courtaulds entering 'the chemical engineering industry' to any notable extent; but it did result in a considerable access of strength and experience in research and development in this area. It did so largely because of the nature of the chemistry of acetate production; it led almost unavoidably, as the chemically simpler viscose process did not, to a different world of chemical engineering. The main pay-off was to come later,[1] and was far more than the slight increase in the profits for the sale of chemicals shown in Table 6.

Notwithstanding these various technical obstacles, Courtaulds did achieve productivity gains in all their main lines of rayon output during the post-war decade of recovery. Fig. 2 exhibits these in the form of indexes of output-per-man-hour for viscose textile yarn, industrial (tyre) yarn, and staple fibre, and for all acetate products (chiefly acetate yarn[2]).

[1] See below, pp. 152–3.

[2] Marketed by Courtaulds as 'Seraceta' (see Vol. II, pp. 183, 271, 309, 418); the trade marks 'Dicel' and 'Tricel' (for diacetate and triacetate yarns) came from British Celanese

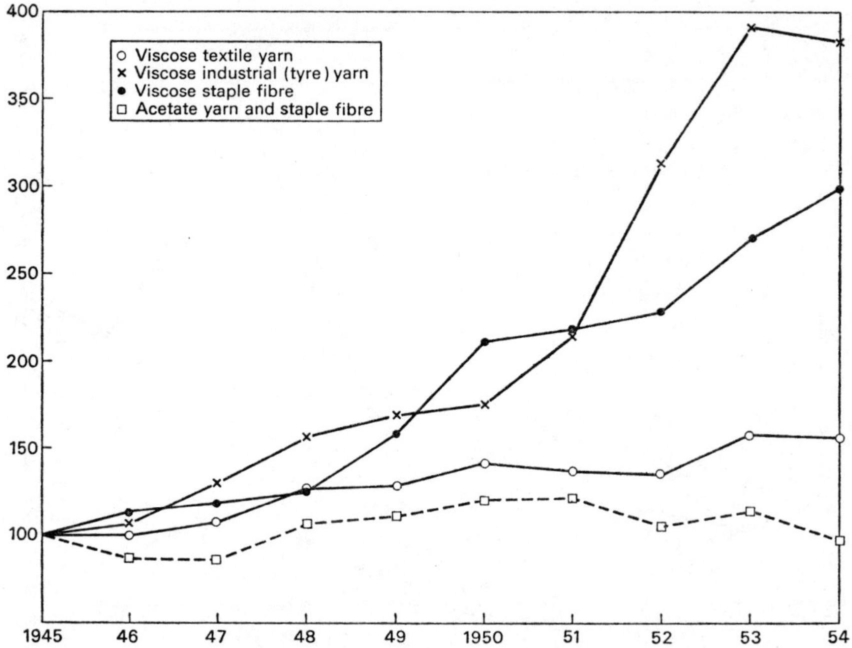

FIG. 2. *Courtaulds, U.K.: index of output per man-hour, rayon, 1945–54 (1945 = 100)*

The introduction of continuous spinning for tyre yarn is evident in the sharp increase after 1951.

Fig. 3 exhibits, in the same way, the movement of total factory cost (pence/lb.) for the same products, compared with an index of average labour earnings in viscose spinning over the same period.[1] The much more impressive gains in staple fibre and industrial yarns show clearly in Fig. 2; on the other hand, the greater impact of the 1951–2 recession on textile yarn and staple fibre shows up in Fig. 3 in the sharp rise in costs consequent upon greater idle capacity. The choice of 1945 as a base year will tend to exaggerate the gains, but the relative changes are clear enough; and the average rise in money costs over all products from 1945–6 to 1953–4 (20 per cent.) was far less than that in average spinning earnings (95 per cent.) or in the general index of wholesale prices for materials and fuel used in manufacturing (81 per cent.).[2]

and were thus used by Courtaulds Group only after the merger with British Celanese in 1957.

[1] These are averages of wages paid (not wage rates) for viscose spinning at all the yarn plants. On wages and earnings, see below Chapter XIII.

[2] *The British Economy: Key Statistics, 1900–66* (London and Cambridge Economic Service, 1966), Table E, p. 8.

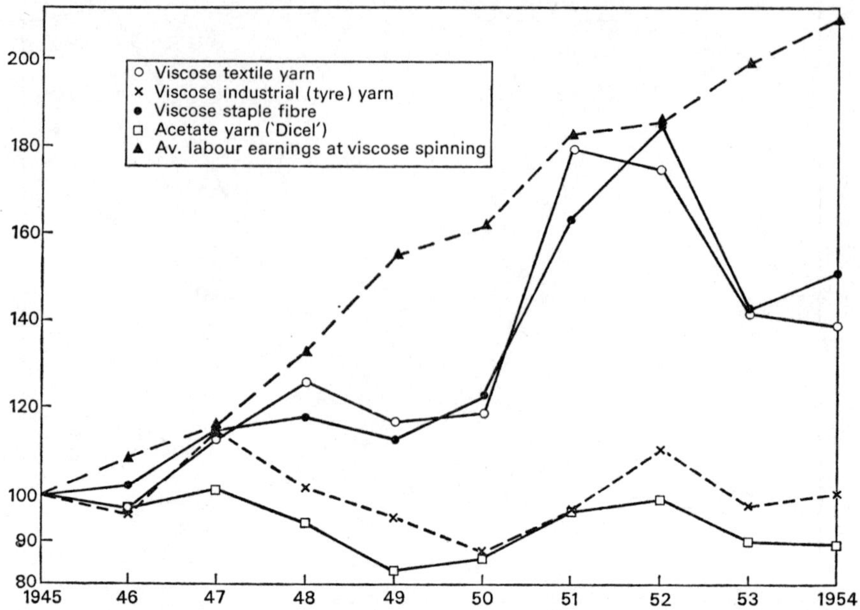

FIG. 3. *Courtaulds, U.K.: index of total factory costs and average labour earnings, rayon, 1945–54 (1945 = 100)*

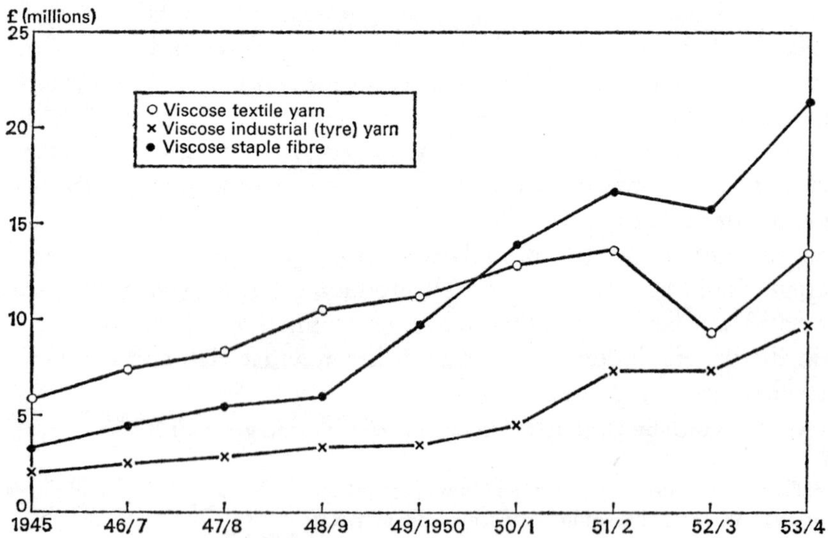

FIG. 4. *Courtaulds, U.K.: rayon sales, 1945–1953/4*

IV

As is evident from Fig. 4 the post-war recovery decade falls into two clearly marked periods: virtually uninterrupted expansion until 1950–1; and then recession and/or retardation until 1953–4. But behind the general trends lay a complex of demand influences of which the three most important were: the prices of substitute yarns and fibres; changes in overseas competition; and government policy in relation to post-war economic controls as it affected the home market.

In the period of immediately post-war expansion rayon was relatively well-poised for recovery, a situation which no doubt helped to stimulate Courtaulds' over-optimistic sales forecasts made in 1944–5. Despite its advances in U.S.A., nylon was not yet being produced in the U.K. in quantities sufficient to make more than a small dent in total sales.[1] The

TABLE 7

Yarn and fibre prices: rayon, cotton, and wool, 1939–54

d./lb.

	Yarn		*Fibre*		
	Viscose textile filament (150 den.)	*Cotton* 60s	*Viscose staple*	*Cotton American middling*	*Wool* 46s
1939	30·8	18·7	10·2	5·9	14·5
1940	36·5		11·5		
1941	44·5		12·7		
1942	47·5		16·8		
1943	47·5		17·0		
1944	47·5		14·5		
1945	45·8		14·0		
1946	45·0	40·0	14·0	14·0	23·5
1947	42·3	47·6	14·6	20·5	29·6
1948	43·0	64·1	16·5	22·8	30·2
1949	43·0	62·3	17·8	24·9	36·8
1950	44·2	83·1	18·8	38·8	87·8
1951	54·0	120·8	25·0	46·5	119·0
1952	54·0	87·2	26·8	39·3	62·9
1953	54·0	73·6	25·5	31·8	71·8
1954	54·0	85·3	24·0	33·0	73·8

Sources: rayon: M.C. *Man-made cellulosic fibres,* Appendix 3, supplemented by internal sources; cotton and wool: D. C. Hague, *The Economics of Man-made Fibres* (London, 1957), pp. 36–7.

[1] See below, Table 14, p. 79.

prices and the output of natural fibres had been far more adversely affected by the war than those of what was still the only man-made fibre in significant production. As Table 7 shows, neither textile yarn nor staple fibre advanced in price to anything like the same extent as cotton and wool. By 1947 the pre-war relative positions of rayon and cotton prices had been reversed, and by 1951 the price gap in favour of rayon had widened substantially.

In addition to these price advantages, the British government's wartime utility-clothing scheme favoured rayon, not simply by its prescribed use for sundry utility fabrics, but by the post-war continuance of the scheme until 1952, together with the termination, meanwhile, of clothes rationing in 1949. Utility fabrics were free of purchase tax; non-utility fabrics paid a 66⅔ per cent. tax. So the end-uses to which textile rayon (viscose and acetate, yarn and staple fibre, but excluding tyre yarn) was put were affected by the continuance of these arrangements in the post-war, and post-clothes rationing, re-stocking boom. In 1949 approximately 40 per cent. of total U.K. consumption of textile rayon went into dress fabrics, as compared with only 25 per cent. before the war; it was estimated that rayon provided about 80 per cent. of all fibres used in women's dresses and blouses. Some indication of this clothing demand can be seen, for textile yarn only, in the figures in column (a) of Table 8. They show the consumption by the chief outlets for Courtaulds' production.

TABLE 8

Post-war outlets for rayon textile yarn

	(*a*) *1948/9–1949/50*	(*b*) *1953/4–1954/5*	*Percentage change*
	'000 lb.	'000 lb.	
Weaving			
Dress fabrics	7,322	5,049	−45
Linings	8,152	12,366	+52
Yarn for crêpe	4,738	904	−81
Furnishing draperies	1,222	4,115	+237
Knitting			
Stockings	5,215	1,707	−67
Circular knitting	3,074	4,957	+61
Warp knitting	2,169	2,351	+8
Elastic web and braid	2,767	3,800	+37
Lace trades	1,584	800	−49

Despite its unexpectedly large use in dress fabrics, staple fibre, because of the particular nature of the schedules in the utility scheme, was employed much less than had been expected in certain other uses, specifically those which did not fall within the scheme and thereby qualify for remission of purchase tax.

As these influences combined to give a particular short-term twist to the pattern of home demand, the overseas market was likewise given a short-term boost by the temporary elimination of certain competitors, notably Germany, Italy, and Japan. As Table 9 shows, exports of textile filament

TABLE 9

Courtaulds' exports of viscose textile yarn and staple fibre, 1939–54

mn. lb.

	Viscose textile yarn	*Viscose staple fibre*
1939	4·9	31·3
1940	10·6	11·9
1941	12·4	15·9
1942	8·2	6·1
1943	7·7	6·3
1944	8·6	6·6
1945	8·3	15·3
1946	8·8	16·6
1947	7·7	12·3
1948	12·4	20·7
1949	9·8	16·2
1950–1*	15·7* (12·6)	25·2–(20·2)
1951–2	7·5	14·3
1952–3	5·5	19·4
1953–4	11·2	15·6

* 15 months January 1950–March 1951. Adjusted annual rates in parentheses.

yarn rose to 1950–1, reaching a level higher than before the war. Although exports of staple fibre did not reach the 1939 level, they too rose to 1948, but then fell and fluctuated around a figure which represented a much lower proportion of total sales (approximately 16 per cent. in 1947–51) than in 1937–9 (approximately 40 per cent.).[1] Increased home demand was undoubtedly reflected in this falling export proportion, and there were quite substantial imports between 1948 and 1951, falling off thereafter.[2]

[1] Vol. II, Table 81, p. 365.

[2] See Hague, op. cit., p. 72. They were particularly marked in 1951 as a consequence of the temporary remission of the import duty consequent upon a world shortage of fibres, a situation associated with the Korean War.

The growing home demand saw a rising proportion of rayon going into the cotton-weaving trades; and a substantial increase in exports of textile piece-goods likewise contributed to Courtaulds' post-war recovery. All this did not, however, prevent Courtaulds from being worried about the resurgence of ex-enemy competition as plans went ahead to restore the Japanese and German economies. During the course of 1947 correspondence and meetings at the Board of Trade between Hanbury-Williams, Sir Stafford Cripps, and his successor there, Harold Wilson, showed much apprehension on Courtaulds' part about what Hanbury-Williams called 'the disastrous effect that an excessive concentration of the German and Japanese export drive on rayon would have on British export trade'. Cripps's rejoinder, a sharpish lecture, included an admirably terse piece of realism: 'our ability to forestall future competition by making use of any opportunity provided by military victory is illusory'.

During the first phase of recovery to 1950 both the government and the trade association—the British Viscose Association[1]—nominally influenced prices. Official price control, instituted during the war, remained until 1950; and Courtaulds signed a further five-year agreement with the B.V.A. in 1945. The agreement did not set quotas and was primarily a price-notification scheme. In practice it had little effect and prices continued to be set through the complex of committees active during the war. The agreement was not renewed in 1950; but a good deal of consultation on prices remained, with Courtaulds continuing to act as price-leader in viscose just as British Celanese were in acetate.

The second phase, 1950–4, saw not only changes in the course of recovery, but considerable variation in the experience of the different branches of production—a statement true both of Courtaulds Ltd. and of the economy as a whole. To the balance of payments crisis of 1951–2 was added a recession in production and exports which, though mild in general, affected the sales of consumer durables such as footwear, furniture, and textiles more than the capital-goods industries.[2] The clearest reflection in Courtaulds' output and sales was the triumphant advance of tyre yarn, virtually unaffected whilst the textile yarns and staple fibre experienced sharp cutbacks. The latter were particularly severe, though brief, because of panic reductions in stocks after a considerable building-up of stocks during the boom. For Courtaulds a further complication to the whole conjuncture of 1950–2 was provided by two different crises in the supply of raw materials. A world shortage, with consequent rising prices, of

[1] Vol. II, p. 345. [2] Worswick & Ady (eds.), pp. 20–1.

wood-pulp developed in 1950–1; and at the same time a sulphur shortage arose, largely as a consequence of U.S. policy in relation to the Korean War. Though overcome by various routes,[1] both had effects on production and prices. And the subsequent course of recovery from the recession was probably not much helped by the continuance of a government purchase-tax scheme between 1952 and 1955 designed to provide a transitional phase after the ending of utility clothing in 1952.[2]

But to such particular short-term forces at work in the recession have to be added the long-term developments coming to a head at this time. In the early 1950s nylon became available in rapidly growing quantities;[3] the old rayon stocking was on its way out. This particular loss was not of any great significance to Courtaulds; in 1948–9 stockings accounted for less than 10 per cent. of viscose-textile-yarn output. But there were also sharp declines in the demand for viscose yarn for crêpe, for dress fabrics, and for the lace trades, to some extent counterbalanced by increases in its use in furnishing fabrics, linings, and knitting. The counterbalancing demands, however, proved inadequate: 1951–2 turned out to be a high point in the production and sale of viscose textile yarn from Courtaulds' factories. Thereafter it has gradually declined, save only for an occasional good year.[4] The relative movement of prices went into reverse, as is evident from Table 7, after the peak in natural-fibre prices in 1951, narrowing the gap though still leaving rayon cheaper. A world-wide promotion campaign pushed the sales of cotton fabrics, aided by the introduction of various 'easy-care' finishes. The export boom in U.K. textile exports slackened off, as former enemy countries were rehabilitated. Staple fibre did find compensating markets; as its use in dress fabrics declined it was increasingly employed in curtains, upholstery, and carpets, though the real boom in the last of these did not come until the later 1950s and thereafter. It was, however, tyre yarn which at this period showed the greatest resilience in recovery. Not only was it given improved strength, but its price, relative to that of the long-staple Egyptian cotton otherwise used in making tyre cord (see Table 10), remained very advantageous, even after the crisis of 1951. Not until later did nylon- and steel-cord

[1] To alleviate the sulphur shortages, Courtaulds embarked on a joint venture to make sulphuric acid from anhydride as well as equipping a new unit to make it from pyrites. For the steps taken to deal with wood-pulp supplies, see below, pp. 113–6.

[2] It was much criticized by Courtaulds. For details, see Worswick & Ady, pp. 21, 437.

[3] See below, p. 79.

[4] In 1964, production which included the then recently absorbed plant of British Enka marginally exceeded that of 1951.

TABLE 10

An index of tyre yarn and cotton prices, 1945–54

1939 = 100	*Rayon tyre yarn*	*Egyptian cotton*
1945	149	205
1946	147	243
1947	134	307
1948	126	626
1949	126	597
1950	130	676
1951	161	1,118
1952	162	989
1953	162	609
1954	162	678

emerge as serious competitors to rayon for this use.

Perception of these developments as they happened, or were gradually foreseen, left its mark upon the deliberations of Courtaulds' Board and the policy decisions which it took. In October 1952 Freeman was demanding of Johnson, and of various research chemists, to know what was being done to improve the physical qualities of textile yarn. An important Board meeting of February 1953 considered a report on the 'Development of Man-Made Fibres over the next 10 years in relation to Courtaulds U.K. interests', made by one of the staff[1] after visits to the U.S.A., Canada, and continental Europe. During the discussion Rendall agreed that Courtaulds should be concerned to try to produce an acrylic fibre. Research work on acrylics had in fact been under way since early in 1951 in Courtaulds' own laboratories as well as discussions with an American company about a possible co-operative effort. In the course of 1951–3 reports on the technical qualities and on the patent position had been obtained on various synthetic fibres, especially polyamides (e.g. nylon), polyesters (e.g. 'Terylene') and acrylics (e.g. 'Orlon'). The growing production and diverse uses of such fibres in the U.S.A. was examined with apprehension. These developments will be considered in detail later.[2] For the moment suffice to note that it was in 1953 that policy decisions on these issues were being forced upon the company by the increasingly obvious fact that rayon textile yarn, which had made Courtaulds big money in the past, had had its day. The return on the capital invested in producing it was significantly lower than that invested in producing staple fibre or tyre yarn. Production costs in all

[1] E. H. Boas. [2] See Chapter IX below.

sections had been lowered by research effort. Where should research effort be directed in the future? How should it be fitted in with pricing policy? Should textile yarn be supported or allowed to drift further downhill? Should the maximum effort be put to developing new fibres? What were Courtaulds' long-term plans in such matters? These and other questions were posed by Wilson and Freeman in their very different ways, to a harassed Rendall and to a complacent and not always comprehending Hanbury-Williams.

V

By the side of rayon, few of the other sources of Courtaulds' income were of sufficient consequence at this time to demand detailed consideration. To indicate something of their relative contribution Table 11 is a counterpart to Table 6, both being derived from the profit and loss account of Courtaulds Ltd. (*not* Courtaulds Group). It shows the percentage contribution to all pre-tax, gross incomes other than mill profits (totals of the latter are brought forward from Table 6 and included for comparative purposes).

Columns (a) and (b) in Table 11 embody the results of liquidating the greater part of the massive holding of government securities received in compensation for the loss of A.V.C., and the corresponding growth in holdings of short-dated paper or the like. Even in 1954, however, Courtaulds still had nearly £18 million of government stock. The rise and decline of the dividends paid by Lustre Fibres Ltd. (column (d)), Courtaulds' rayon exporting subsidiary, mirrors the boom and slump in the overseas trade in rayon already discussed. The significance of the dividends from British Nylon Spinners (column (e)) and the complex and troubled story which lay behind them forms the subject of Chapter IV; and Courtaulds' overseas involvements, some of which resulted in the fluctuating share of earnings listed in column (f), will be examined in Chapter V. The profit contribution of Courtaulds' investment in the Anglo-French British Cellophane Ltd.,[1] remained small though comfortingly growing over the period. The significance of this interest in the packaging industry will be discussed in Part II in the context of the policies of diversification which came to the fore in the later 1950s.[2]

The one remaining field of the company's activities which does demand

[1] For its foundation, see Vol. II, pp. 372–4.
[2] See below, Chapter VIII.

TABLE 11

Sources of 'other income', Courtaulds Ltd., 1945–54

Percentage 'other income' contributed by

	Total mill profits	Total other income	(a) Government securities	(b) Treasury bills, bank deposits, tax reserve certs., etc.	(c) British Cellophane (dividend and loan interest)	(d) Lustre Fibres	(e) B.N.S.	(f) All overseas investments	(g) All other
	£000	£000	%	%	%	%	%	%	%
1945	2,392	1,318	80	3	1	—	—	11	5
1946–7 (15 mths)	3,742	1,449	74	5	1	—	—	6	14
1947–8	3,825	1,405	42	1	6	36	—	5	10
1948–9	4,718	1,989	19	1	4	50	—	15	11
1949–50	7,565	1,437	16	3	5	42	—	14	20
1950–1	13,320	2,390	16	2	5	17	33	15	12
1951–2	13,643	2,667	10	2	6	21	22	20*	19
1952–3	9,262	1,955	7	6	4	5	41	27	10
1953–4	17,685	2,149	12	10	8	16	37	3	14

Notes: See notes to Tables 5 and 6 above.

* Excludes £370,000 of arrears on dividends from Snia Viscosa received and credited in 1951–2.

attention now is that old but neglected pasture, the company's homeland: textiles. As Table 6 showed, the textile mills, including the knitting branch, never contributed more than 15 per cent. of mill profits during the post-war recovery decade; and that achievement was concentrated in the years 1945–9, when the average share was 13 per cent. compared with a mere 6 per cent. in 1950–4. In Table 11, lurking in the 'all other' category (column (g)), are a few very small dividends from Samuel Courtauld & Co., at that time the textile equivalent to Lustre Fibres Ltd., and even some tinier and sporadic contributions from Luvisca., Morton Sundour Fabrics Ltd., and F.N.F. Ltd.[1]

Neither from their own knitting branch nor from their investment in the development of Sir James Morton's invention, the Fly Needle Frame (F.N.F.), did Courtaulds gain much profit. The stronger growth in warp knitting than in weft knitting in the post-war decade was mainly based upon fibres other than viscose rayon. Despite some early proposals by Gratwick that the company should find a new factory in the Nottingham area for its knitting activities, in fact they continued to be housed unsatisfactorily in the Wolverhampton factory, with an experimental knitting plant at an old Courtaulds location, Earls Colne in Essex. After making a loss in 1946–7 gross mill profits therefrom averaged only £142,000 per annum over the seven-year period 1948–54. A successful prototype of the F.N.F. machine was developed and installed at Braintree in 1942. After the war a factory was leased at Burton-on-Trent for the commercial manufacture of the machines. A substantial number were made and sold[2] but, for various reasons, they did not ultimately prove to be economically and technically satisfactory; moreover, their production and development had been supported by a continuous input of large sums of money from Courtaulds and accompanied by a corresponding output of increasingly acrimonious relations with Morton Sundour, their partners in the venture. F.N.F. was eventually sold, in 1958. As for Morton Sundour Fabrics, despite (or because of) the high quality of their fabrics and the originality of their design, the arrears on the second preference dividends were not cleared off until 1942 and no payments of the ordinary dividend were made until 1950. By 1956, Courtaulds were considering whether to dispose

[1] For the origins of all these concerns, see Vol. II, pp. 370–2. Samuel Courtauld & Co. later ceased to be concerned simply with textile exporting and in 1959 assumed responsibility for much of the weaving activities of the group. See below, p. 171.

[2] According to Jocelyn Morton, *Three Generations in a Textile Firm* (1971), p. 361, about 1,600 were still running at the time when he wrote.

of their share, for in the 21 years since the original investment the total net dividends received amounted to some £134,000 on an investment of £460,500.[1]

In Courtaulds' own textile mills the most pressing need at the end of the war was modernization. A number of national reports between 1944 and 1949[2] had emphasized the absence of automatic looms in the cotton and rayon sectors of the U.K. weaving industry. In 1944 Samuel Courtauld was furiously attacking the *Report of the Cotton Board Committee* for what he considered to be Lancashire's complacent and old-fashioned attitude; he sent a long and detailed memorandum on the subject to Hugh Dalton at the Board of Trade, documenting it with statistics which showed, *inter alia*, that in 1936 Britain had the lowest percentage of automatic looms (3 per cent.) of all the main textile producing countries in the world. In Courtaulds, a report was prepared in 1945 on the age and nature of all the machinery in all their textile mills. The report provides a remarkable insight into the age of the machinery in these particular British textile mills just after World War II. Table 12 is based upon the total number of machines of all sorts listed in the report in each of the company's five textile mills then operative—Halstead, Braintree, Brook Mill and Bedford Mill, both at Leigh, and Halifax. All told 5,731 pieces of machinery were listed: looms, dobbies, warping machines, pirn winders, sizing machines, drawing frames, throwing mills, and so on.

TABLE 12

Age-distribution of machinery in Courtaulds' textile mills, 1945 (percentages)

	1900 and earlier	*1901–10*	*1911–20*	*1921–30*	*1931–40*	*1941 and later*	
Looms . . .	7	18	24	33	18	–	100
Dobbies and jacquards	3	13	23	52	6	3	100
Preparatory machinery (warping, winding, twisting, throwing, sizing, etc.) . .	–	14	31	31	22	2	100
All machines . .	4	15	24	41	14	2	100

[1] See below, p. 278, for Courtaulds' acquisition of Morton Sundour.

[2] e.g. *Report of the Cotton Board Committee* (1944); Board of Trade Working Party Reports: *Cotton* (1946); *A Survey of Machinery in the Weaving Section of the Cotton Industry* (Cotton Board, 1949).

Because this method implicitly assumes homogeneity of the whole 5,731 items, it obviously does not represent the age-distribution of monetary investment in the mills. But the broad similarity in the distribution of the three categories suggest that the general pattern is not greatly distorted. Although 41 per cent. of the machinery had been installed in the 1920s, 43 per cent. dated from the first two decades of the century or earlier.

The number of looms listed in the report and their distribution by age and mill is shown in Table 13. Out of the total of 2,499 looms, nearly a half dated from 1920 and earlier and only 388 (15·5 per cent.) were reasonably modern automatic looms; the 440 automatic looms at Bedford Mill were obsolete single-shuttle Northrop looms dating from 1914–19. The report recommended capital expenditure of over £2·2 million on the mills; and proposed expenditure on the dyehouses at Bocking and Droylsden brought the total to approximately £3 million.

The result was an initially vigorous campaign of re-equipment which soon slowed down in the face of difficulties in securing the required machinery; of the indifference of the more powerful lobbies within the

TABLE 13

Age-distribution and location of looms, 1945

	1900 and earlier	*1901–10*	*1911–20*	*1921–30*	*1931–40*	*1941 and later*
Halstead . .	152	417	59	244	84(72A)	—
Braintree . .	—	—	—	234	—	—
Brook Mill, Leigh .	24	25	50	242	—	—
Bedford Mill, Leigh	—	—	440(A)	—	316(A)	—
Halifax . .	—	—	42	106	64	—
Total . . .	176	442	591	826	464	—

Note: (A) = automatic looms.

company which pushed interest and investment into other directions; and of the harsher economic climate for textile sales in the early 1950s. The attempts to get automatic looms ran into import-control difficulties and precipitated a series of negotiations between 1945 and 1949 first with the American firm of Crompton & Knowles and later with Sulzer Bros. of Switzerland about the possibilities of setting up a joint firm with Courtaulds for the production of automatic looms in Britain. Nothing came of the negotiations. Courtaulds complained about the inability of British loom makers to make high-quality automatic looms, and eventually imported, new or second-hand, a substantial number of foreign looms. A policy of concentration and limited improvement emerged. For experimental work on the development of staple fibre fabrics a new mill was bought in 1946—Bull Royd Mill, near Bradford. Brook Mill, Leigh—the least suitable for modernization of all the company's textile mills—was sold in 1953; many of the old looms at Halstead were scrapped; but, even by 1954, the Board was still being asked to 'consider proposals for completing' the re-equipment of Halstead with automatic looms. A new policy for textiles had yet to emerge.

CHAPTER IV

I.C.I. and B.N.S.

I

ALTHOUGH the war impeded the development of the newly formed British Nylon Spinners and restricted its small output to the requirements of the Ministry of Supply, it did not impede the rapid growth of acrimonious relations between the parents of this promising child. Whilst Courtaulds and I.C.I. had kept out of each other's territories in accordance with the agreement of 1928, their dealings had been limited, harmonious, and purely commercial.[1] Once they came together to co-operate in the exploitation of I.C.I.'s licence from Du Pont for nylon,[2] harmony vanished and discord took its place. As Dr. Reader has observed, the two firms having thus married, 'some twenty-five years later, after one of the noisiest corporate quarrels in the history of British business, the marriage ended in divorce'.[3] That divorce constituted a mutually acceptable solution to the problems created by the abortive I.C.I. take-over bid of 1961 which was indeed a noisy corporate quarrel. Both quarrel and divorce are the subject of detailed analysis in Chapters X and XI below. The route thereto was long and complex; and it began with the troubled relationships which followed the setting up of B.N.S. in 1940.

At one level of explanation, the developing relationship between the two companies was a logical outcome of the evolution of truly synthetic fibres, as distinct from cellulosic fibres, which had the effect of increasing the emphasis upon the chemical side, as distinct from the textile side, of the business of making and selling them. Courtaulds Ltd. had emerged as a textile/chemical firm from the profits of rayon and from the experience of textiles; I.C.I. Ltd. had emerged as a chemical firm from the fusion of constituent companies which, however diverse, had all been primarily concerned with chemicals. To I.C.I. nylon was a possible new source of profit in chemicals; to Courtaulds it was a potential rival to rayon. Courtaulds quickly appreciated that it was not a rival to be beaten but to be joined; I.C.I. knew that they had to acquire expertise in making and selling textile fibres. So the logic of co-operative effort between the two

[1] See Vol. II, pp. 263–5. [2] See Vol. II, p. 374. [3] Reader, II, p. 372.

companies seemed indisputable. At another level of explanation, however, the specific course of worsening relations between the two companies in the lifetime of B.N.S. as a joint company, i.e. 1940–64, was a product of conflicting personalities; of divergent styles of direction and management; of varying patterns of internal organization; and of differing business experiences. Thus contrastingly equipped the two companies had successfully operated in their separate fields. Put together, however, and the result was the rapid generation of mutual suspicion and mistrust. Totally different ways of looking at issues were revealed; divergent aims were brought out into the open; relative strengths and weaknesses were exploited, to the disregard of mutual tolerance.

Intertwined with the main theme constituted by B.N.S. were three lesser, but important, contributory causes of ultimate disharmony. In chronological order of appearance they were: Courtaulds' refusal to co-operate over I.C.I.'s protein fibre 'Ardil'; the failure of a proposed general agreement between the two companies; and a quarrel about 'Terylene'. To simplify the analysis of a highly complex pattern of developing relationships, these lesser contributions will be considered first.

II

The research which produced nylon was by no means the only work on potential man-made fibres proceeding in the 1930s. It was merely the most successful. Amongst other lines of enquiry, investigation into the possibility of producing fibres from protein stimulated the interest of both Courtaulds and I.C.I. As already mentioned,[1] in 1937 Courtaulds had bought the rights from Snia Viscosa to the patents taken out by Antonio Ferretti for the manufacture of fibres from casein, the protein of milk. I.C.I., meanwhile, had taken up the suggestion, made in 1935 by W. S. Astbury and A. C. Chibnall, of making fibres from vegetable protein; and had experimented specifically with groundnuts. These were otherwise used for the manufacture of margarine, and much protein remained after the extraction of the oil. So when the two companies came together over nylon in 1939 each company had its experimental protein fibre, each of which was regarded as a potential substitute for wool. Courtaulds had not, however, pursued their research with any great speed. Although Snia Viscosa's exploitation of the Ferretti patents had already led to the production and sale of 'Lanital', Courtaulds' work on what they later came to call 'Fibro-

[1] Vol. II, p. 379, n. 1.

lane' had barely left the laboratory stage. Despite Board approval in 1939, and again in February 1940, of recommendations to build a plant at Little Heath to make casein fibre, the war postponed any such work. But I.C.I. had already christened their fibre 'Ardil', named after their Explosives Division's factory at Ardeer in Scotland where it was developed, and were becoming enthusiastic about the possibilities of commercial production.

It was against this background that discussions took place in 1940 on the suggestion made by I.C.I. that the two companies should co-operate in the production of 'Ardil'. Claims, technical and economic, made by I.C.I. for the qualities of 'Ardil' were instantly challenged by Glover who compared them disadvantageously with Courtaulds' (as yet unnamed) casein fibre. He spelled it out in detail in a letter to Samuel Courtauld in August 1940. Although embodying some characteristic Coventry complacency, it pinpointed one of the main defects of 'Ardil', i.e. its low wet strength. It concluded, moreover, with a sentence which was to typify Courtaulds' attitude to the proposition: 'I.C.I. have certain patents covering the production of Ardil, but we are of the opinion that we can produce a fibre equal to Ardil without infringing any valid patent of the I.C.I.' A year later after I.C.I. had unavailingly sent further reports and samples to Coventry, they not surprisingly complained of delay, and suggested a visit to Ardeer. Glover then maintained to Samuel Courtauld that neither he nor anyone else from Courtaulds should visit Ardeer to see 'Ardil' production. He contended that such a visit would imply that I.C.I. possessed patents which would prevent Courtaulds from manufacturing their equivalent of 'Ardil' in their own way—and this he did not believe to be true.

Although this uncompromisingly hostile attitude was not communicated to I.C.I., Courtaulds (in the person of Samuel Courtauld) conveyed to I.C.I. (in the person of one of the deputy chairmen, J. G., later Sir John, Nicholson) Coventry's technical and economic findings. Courtaulds turned down the suggestion of joint production; maintained the view that the 'Ardil' process did not block their own development of protein fibres; politely indicated a vague willingness to co-operate; and wondered what I.C.I. had to propose. Despite further argument and counter-arguments about the merits of 'Ardil', this was effectively the end of the matter. A later suggestion by Courtaulds that they should take over 'Ardil', paying a contribution of £25,000 towards the cost of I.C.I.'s research expenditure, was, not surprisingly, turned down by I.C.I. in 1942. In the course of that year, I.C.I. sent further samples for testing; and again complained of delays before ultimately receiving unfavourable reports. In 1943 Courtaulds obtained a lengthy report on further samples tested by various users in the woollen and worsted trades; again the results were unfavourable.

After the end of the war, I.C.I. went ahead on their own. Large sums were invested in a plant capable of turning out 22 million lb. of 'Ardil' per year; it started production in 1951 and was closed in 1957, its yearly rate of sales having never exceeded 2·6 million lb.[1] Courtaulds, meanwhile, produced casein fibre in small quantities during and immediately after the war. Then in the later 1950s enthusiasm for it revived and Courtaulds began to market it as 'Fibrolane' as a part of the company's new interest in tufted carpets. Even so, production was never much more than on a pilot plant scale, the maximum yearly output of 2·6 million lb. being reached in 1961/2. Production closed down in 1964. Courtaulds had undoubtedly been right in turning down I.C.I.'s optimistic proposals for the production of 'Ardil'. But the episode hardly provided an auspicious start for their co-operative ventures.

III

While the 'Ardil' scheme was being bandied to and fro, sundry versions of a set of proposals for general co-operation were being drafted and discussed by the heads of Courtaulds and I.C.I. These had their ultimate origin in the 'Gentleman's Agreement' of 1928 because after the setting-up of B.N.S. it inevitably became a matter of suspicion in each company that the other might now be tempted to do precisely what that agreement had agreed should not be done, i.e. move into each other's primary fields of operation.

In the summer of 1940 Samuel Courtauld and Nicholson discussed the desirability of an exchange of letters defining more clearly 'their respective spheres of influence'. In January 1941 Nicholson sent a rought draft expressing an intent to refrain from competition and to render 'mutual assistance in their respective spheres'; these spheres the document then tried to define. A variety of objections were thought up by Courtaulds' directors. What was 'simple chemical treatment'? What was 'the chemical field' or 'the textile field'? This clause was too sweeping; that was too binding. And so on. At a meeting in June 1941, Nicholson proposed a substantial share exchange between the two companies—an idea which had been mooted in 1928. Hanbury-Williams saw some advantages in

[1] Reader, II, p. 380.

this, though worried about Courtaulds' relative weakness because of the loss of A.V.C.; he saw Courtaulds being weaker after the war whilst I.C.I. might be stronger. But nothing could be done because, at that time, no settlement had been reached with the government about the compensation for A.V.C. Both Courtaulds and I.C.I. also expressed some apprehension about government reactions to such a move and especially about the possible reactions of a Labour government should one be in office. Lord McGowan and Samuel Courtauld consulted; the former went to see Sir Horace Wilson, Lord Catto, and the President of the Board of Trade, Sir Andrew Duncan. Later Hanbury-Williams and Addison spoke with Horace Wilson, at which meeting they discovered, to their surprise, that McGowan had mentioned the possibilities of a merger between the two companies—a suggestion which has particular historical significance in view of its reappearance in the take-over bid twenty years later.

Although McGowan had indeed mentioned the idea to Samuel Courtauld, the latter had replied that he doubted whether Courtaulds' Board would be willing even to consider the possibility. At a meeting in August 1941 between Samuel Courtauld and the Chancellor of the Exchequer,[1] Courtauld emphasized that an amalgamation was out of the question. From these and other meetings with Ministers, it became clear that the government was not entirely happy about the political repercussions of financial linkages between the two companies, and counselled delay until after the war. But no objections were raised to continuing negotiations for a binding agreement.

It is evident that the senior members of Courtaulds' Board who had taken part in the discussions—Samuel Courtauld, Hanbury-Williams, and Addison—were already less than enthusiastic. Nevertheless, after further talks, Nicholson dispatched in October a draft of what he now called an 'Atlantic Charter' (on the analogy of the Anglo-American 'Atlantic Charter' just recently signed by Churchill and Roosevelt); in December he followed it with a second version, revised to meet further Courtaulds' objections. Both contained the suggestion of a £5 million investment in each other's equity. On being shown them Henry Johnson sent a letter to his chairman which contained some very pertinent observations. 'Why', he asked, 'is all this negotiation necessary now?' If it arose because Courtaulds was 'afraid of I.C.I. competition', then there was plenty of evidence both from within Courtaulds and from outside sources that I.C.I. combined excessive size with technical inefficiency:

[1] Sir Kingsley Wood.

We base our judgement on selling prices of their products, we see the scale of expenses of their Works and Head Office organisations. They have a vast number of staff, some of whom are very good and some not so good. We frequently have members of their staff come to us because they see the way to promotion blocked above them. They may seem to be efficient but may not this impression be created by mere numbers? . . . They depend for their place on a big number of sweeping commercial agreements . . . many of their products are not profitable to them . . .

It may appear in retrospect a little like the proverbial pot calling the kettle black, but it contained an element of truth. Naturally enough, converse statements were made within I.C.I., questioning Courtaulds' efficiency and doubting the advisability of any linkage.

In February 1942 Samuel Courtauld wrote to Nicholson telling him that the Courtaulds Board had concluded that 'the time is not yet opportune for a declaration of principles in such a definite form as indicated by you'. He was, however, willing that they should make a brief statement of intent, and in March sent his version of an 'Atlantic Charter'. This, predictably, aroused objections from I.C.I. More discussions, notably a high level one in May involving Samuel Courtauld, Hanbury-Williams, McGowan, and Nicholson, brought out again the basic disagreements about the 'fields' of interest. But the search for an agreement went on, and there was a little flurry of memoranda and meetings between May and October 1943. By this time, however, it was becoming increasingly obvious that influential voices on both sides were now opposed to the whole notion. Within I.C.I., Courtaulds were gaining enemies by their attitude on 'Ardil', as well as over various B.N.S. incidents; within Courtaulds, Gratwick, Johnson, and Glover were hostile and Hanbury-Williams had also come to think that the search for agreement had best be called off. So in November 1943 each Board exchanged agreed Board Minutes of a general character, recording the history of the negotiations, their failure to agree not to enter each other's fields, and expressing suitably vague intentions of future friendliness and willingness to collaborate.

Mutual mistrust had re-enforced the chemical and economic logic of current developments in man-made fibres to ensure that such an agreement could not be reached. That this particular episode did not perhaps give rise to as much acrimony as certain others in I.C.I./Courtaulds relations was largely because the transactions were conducted at the highest of Board levels and the currency used was the pious platitude and the broad generalization. Even so, it was characteristic that when preparing the final résumé, each side alleged that the other had been responsible for instigating the discussion.

IV

The quarrel about 'Terylene' was rather more disagreeable. 'Terylene' (polyethylene terephthalate) is the brand name of a polyester fibre discovered by J. R. Whinfield and S. T. Dickson working in the laboratories of the Calico Printers Association Ltd. Work on it started in 1939 but development was held up by the war. A strong patent position had been built up but, because of wartime secrecy restrictions, the applications had not been published. The Calico Printers Association brought it to the notice of the Ministry of Supply who in turn asked I.C.I. to look into it. I.C.I. did so, came to favourable conclusions, and in the summer of 1944 had brought their negotiations with C.P.A. to the point where a licence agreement was imminent.[1] Then the trouble started.

Although 'Terylene' is chemically different from nylon, it is spun into yarn in the same way, and that way is different from the spinning process used in rayon. Whereas viscose rayon is extruded from a spinneret and made into filaments by precipitation in a coagulating bath,[2] 'Terylene' and nylon are both 'melt-spun', i.e. a hot molten mass is squirted through the spinneret and the filaments, formed by cooling and solidification, are then twisted together to form yarns. So I.C.I. soon found themselves wanting the same sort of machinery to spin 'Terylene' as B.N.S. was already using to spin nylon. The official request came in a letter of June 1944 from I.C.I. to the secretary of B.N.S. and beginning with the ominous words: 'You may know that I.C.I. is starting to undertake investigations into fibre-forming polymers other than nylon, with the possibility eventually of full-scale manufacture.' The design of the machinery which B.N.S. used for nylon spinning originated from Du Pont, and B.N.S. had access to it as sub-licensees under the original I.C.I.–Du Pont nylon agreement of 1939. B.N.S. had negotiated a contract for the manufacture of the melt-spinning machinery with the firm of Peter Brotherhood Ltd. who, having to build it from Du Pont designs, had undertaken not to supply such plant to any other firm. I.C.I. now asked that B.N.S. should agree to that same machinery being supplied to them for their development of the new fibre.

However, one of the clauses of the 1939 I.C.I.–Du Pont nylon agreement forbade the application of nylon-making techniques to other types

[1] Reader, II, pp. 381–2. [2] See Vol. II, pp. 14–17, 42–8.

of fibre.[1] Was it legally possible, therefore, for B.N.S. to permit Peter Brotherhood to supply machinery to I.C.I. to spin, not nylon, but 'Terylene'? Nor was this all. One of the clauses of the 1940 co-operation agreement between Courtaulds and I.C.I., setting up B.N.S., stated that the two firms undertook to 'confer' with each other prior to developing any new products which might compete with nylon.[2] Courtaulds were formally informed of I.C.I.'s interest in 'Terylene' in July 1944, but there had been no 'conference'. So what were Courtaulds' views on this development? To Courtaulds' directors on the B.N.S. Board—then Samuel Courtauld, Hanbury-Williams, Glover, Rendall, and Henry Johnson—and also to the managing director of B.N.S.—F. C. Bagnall, an ex-I.C.I. man who now found himself in a very difficult position—it seemed as though I.C.I. were putting pressure on B.N.S. to do something which they had no right to do, and, moreover, in respect of a fibre likely to be competitive with nylon and concerning which there had been no prior consultation with Courtaulds as required in the 1940 agreement.

I.C.I. based their own legal stance in this matter, not on the I.C.I.–Du Pont nylon agreement, which was signed on 30 March 1939, but on a Du Pont–I.C.I. patents and processes agreement which provided for exchange of technical information in a broad field of chemical and allied products (including nylon and other fibres), and which was signed, three months later, on 30 June. A thicket of legal arguments quickly sprang up. I.C.I. consulted counsel and got an opinion in their favour, which they communicated to Courtaulds. Courtaulds consulted different counsel and got an opinion which, though favourable to Courtaulds in the sense that it held I.C.I.'s chosen legal base, i.e. the patents and process agreement, to be untenable, was unfavourable in that it showed B.N.S. to have a weak case; it was not communicated to I.C.I. Tempers rose on either side. I.C.I. had mistrusted Courtaulds' intentions in the plastics field; and had undoubtedly determined to keep 'Terylene' to themselves.[3] In the light of the previous

[1] Any information, knowledge, and data within the 'Licence Field' shall not be disclosed (except to sub-licensees) nor used except in each party's respective licensed territory and in connection with the exploitation of the inventions within the 'Licence Field' (Clause IX).

[2] I.C.I. and Courtaulds undertake to confer with each other prior to becoming interested or concerned in the production of any new products which might be likely to compete with or displace multifilament yarns and staple fibres produced from nylon polymers or otherwise prejudice or detrimentally affect the profit-earning capacity of the Company or any such separate Company as aforesaid (Article XVI, Clause 2).

[3] Reader, II, pp. 382–3.

breakdown of the 'Ardil' and 'Atlantic Charter' negotiations with Courtaulds this was understandable enough. I.C.I. had already turned down C.P.A.'s suggestion of a joint company, so they were not likely to accede to a proposal by Courtaulds that 'Terylene' should be handed over to B.N.S. For their part, Courtaulds, with some justification, were incensed by the fact that the full and relevant terms of the patents and processes agreements had not been communicated to them. Whatever the legal position, I.C.I.'s behaviour was held to be 'morally indefensible'—a sentiment of righteous indignation which inevitably makes such quarrels all the more satisfyingly virtuous and prolonged. Some of the I.C.I. directors themselves were not wholly comfortable about the position in which they found themselves; others had their anti-Courtaulds sentiments sharpened. In the summer of 1945 I.C.I. secured a statement from Du Pont to the effect that I.C.I. were entitled to use nylon machinery for their work on fibres other than nylon; and at the same time got permission from Du Pont to grant a sub-licence to Courtaulds to use such machinery for melt-spinning for fibres other than nylon, excluding rayon. This licence to Courtaulds was, however, for 'experimental purposes' only; if they were to pass to commercial production, then Du Pont would be prepared to authorize I.C.I. to grant a licence on 'reasonable royalty terms'. Courtaulds, who were certainly trying to make the most of the situation by getting some sort of a stake in the new fibre, did not like this suggestion as it would obviously put them in a dependent position *vis-à-vis* two competitors or potential competitors. So early in 1946 Courtaulds put forward the proposition that they would agree to B.N.S. waiving the restrictions on Peter Brotherhood supplying the machinery to I.C.I. if both Courtaulds and B.N.S. were granted sub-licences on terms no less favourable than those granted to I.C.I.

This produced an explosion from I.C.I., though the explosion was carefully controlled. With a letter to Hanbury-Williams of 1 May 1946, John Rogers, a deputy chairman of I.C.I., enclosed the draft of a tough letter which had been drawn up by the I.C.I. legal department, with some amendments by Rogers. Hanbury-Williams and Rogers then agreed to meet on 8 May to discuss the letter. In it Courtaulds were told bluntly that Du Pont had been reluctant to grant any licence to Courtaulds and that it was only by I.C.I.'s intervention that they had granted what they had; I.C.I.–Du Pont relations were 'on a very special basis'; there were no grounds for B.N.S. being involved in fibres other than nylon. As there seemed no prospect of agreement, the licensing proposal was withdrawn;

consequently, I.C.I. could not now expect B.N.S. to waive their embargo on Brotherhood's supplying the melt-spinning machinery; and I.C.I. would accordingly go elsewhere. At their meeting, Rogers inquired whether the receipt of such a letter would 'interfere with the success of British Nylon Spinners', and asked whether there was 'any body of people in Courtaulds who were particularly antagonistic towards the I.C.I.'. Hanbury-Williams stressed the bad effects of the non-disclosure of the relevant parts of the patents and processes agreement, pointing out that if there had been a public issue at the time when B.N.S. was formed, this would 'to say the least, have placed the I.C.I. in an extremely delicate position'. It was, according to Hanbury-Williams's diary notes, all conducted in a friendly manner; and it was agreed that the I.C.I. letter should be formally signed and sent. So it was. Some of Hanbury-Williams's comments were put into a formal reply in September of the same year, but in practice this particular round of the contest was ended and I.C.I. had won it. But more was to come.

The matter came up again in the early 1950s, and was to be heard yet again, in the whole context of the discussion of 'melt-spun fibres' during the take-over bid ten years later. Meanwhile, however, the immediate position had been changed by amendments to the basic nylon agreements affecting I.C.I., Courtaulds, and B.N.S. These changes, in turn, were partly dependent on the U.S. anti-Trust suit against Du Pont and I.C.I. which had been going on since 1944. It is time to examine the main axis of Courtaulds–I.C.I. relations: nylon and B.N.S.

V

The manufacture of nylon, the first of the truly synthetic fibres, uses raw materials and processes wholly different from those used in rayon manufacture. The basic raw materials are air, water, and coal or petroleum. From them, by a sequence of chemical steps, are brought into being two substances called hexamethylene diamine and adipic acid. Their molecules are then combined in a particular way so as to form another substance with long-chain molecules, capable of forming fibres. To this substance, first discovered in the U.S.A. by W. H. Carothers as a consequence of research instigated by Du Pont, was given the name 'nylon'. In the language of chemistry, it is known as a 'polyamide', being a condensation polymer of hexamethylene diamine and adipic acid. Because each of the two substances contains six carbon atoms per molecule, it was first called '66 polyamide' and later 'nylon 66'. This distinction is important because 'nylon' is effectively a generic term for several sorts of fibre-forming polyamides of this type, capable of being brought into being from the same bases but by slightly different routes and possessing slightly different qualities. To one of these, which will appear later in this book,[1] the name of 'nylon 6' has been given because it is made from one substance called caprolactam, which contains six carbon atoms and is capable of forming the requisite long-chain molecules by a process of self-condensation. By whichever route it is made, the nylon polymer emerges as a treacly liquid which is cooled, solidified, and broken up into 'chips'. These can then be stored, transported, and used for spinning. For spinning they are melted and the hot mass of molten nylon forced through spinnerets; the resulting filaments, cooled and solidified, are twisted into yarn—the same melt-spinning process which, as described above,[2] was later to be used for 'Terylene'.

The substance which was the subject of the March 1939 licence from Du Pont to I.C.I. and of the I.C.I.–Courtaulds agreements of January 1940 setting up and licensing B.N.S. was nylon 66. The commodities to be made from the polymer were primarily multi-filament yarns and staple fibres. Two clearly distinct processes were envisaged: the manufacture of the polymer, to be carried out at a plant to be erected under I.C.I. auspices at Huddersfield; and the spinning of the nylon polymer into yarn, to be carried out under Courtaulds' direction at Coventry. The production of monofils, e.g. as bristles for toothbrushes, was also covered, the I.C.I. Plastics Division at Welwyn being the chosen venue. British Nylon Spinners Ltd. was incorporated as a private company with an initial capital of £300,000 subscribed in equal shares by I.C.I. and Courtaulds. By the terms of the agreement the two founding companies were to take the major proportion of any profits in the form of dividends and not from the supply of raw materials or services to B.N.S. Courtaulds were to supply factory services for the spinning plant; I.C.I. were to supply the polymer. These two supplies were each to be paid for by B.N.S. on the basis of total cost plus a return of 6 per cent. on the capital employed—an important provision which was soon to give rise to trouble.

The commitment of B.N.S. to production entirely for the needs of warfare had resulted in a planned programme agreed with the relevant departments in the course of 1942. Special arrangements were made for reduced royalties to be paid to Du Pont under the licence agreement. In

[1] See below, pp. 176–8. [2] See p. 73.

1943 with the small plants at Coventry (repaired after air-raid damage) and at Stowmarket reaching full production, plans for post-war expansion came to the fore. Output of yarn in 1942 was approximately 300,000 lb. Plans for a factory to produce some 7 million lb. were in mind when, in the course of that year, land had been bought at Banbury. The same considerations that affected Courtaulds' own choice of proposed post-war development sites were soon brought to bear upon this choice. Continued restrictions on the availability of raw materials and government licensing thereof meant that priority was given to construction in 'development areas'. Banbury was not in such an area. In October 1943, the Board of Trade suggested Lancashire, but in the following year, after much searching, the decision was taken to build the new factory at Pontypool, to help in the creation of employment in South Wales.

It was to have a capacity of 10 million lb. per annum; and expected to cost about £6–7 million. Work started on the new factory early in 1945. Hampered by shortages of raw materials and labour, as well as by bad weather, building was delayed and production did not start until 1948. Full production was reached in 1950. The ending of the wartime concentration on yarn for making parachute fabrics brought a reorientation of output. From 1946 onwards a switch towards the production of yarns for the hosiery and knitting trades was matched by a major effort in publicity and marketing. To finance these activities, the B.N.S. capital base was widened, reaching £8 million in 1949 and £12 million in 1955, the increase having been provided in equal shares by Courtaulds and I.C.I. The expansion process continued: in 1950 an output of 30 million lb. per annum was being planned; in 1952 the target was up to 55 million lb.; and in 1953 a new site at Doncaster was bought to provide for these increases. Production, as Table 14 shows, grew apace. The rate of increase was characteristically high, an order of magnitude similar to that of viscose rayon in its early years.[1]

An essential ingredient of this expansion in B.N.S. yarn and fibre output was the corresponding expansion in the capacity of the I.C.I. polymer-producing plant. The Huddersfield unit was small and unsatisfactory and a large new plant was set up at Billingham, coming into operation in 1949. It, in turn, soon began to prove inadequate, and was increased in size in the early 1950s; and a further plant was subsequently installed at Wilton.

However much bickering went on between Courtaulds and I.C.I.,

[1] Average compound percentage growth-rate: viscose yarn 1906–8 to 1911–13: 60·1; nylon yarn and staple, 1947–9 to 1952–4: 53·2.

B.N.S. growth, in output and profits, continued; and it is important not to allow the historical record of the quarrelling to obscure the reality of the growth. As was shown earlier[1] the contribution of the dividends from B.N.S. accounted for 37 per cent. of Courtaulds' 'other income' in 1953–4. The dividends reached £1 million in 1954–5. Meanwhile, the very fact of growth in the output of nylon yarn and therefore in the demand for nylon

TABLE 14

B.N.S.: nylon-yarn and staple-fibre output, 1947–54

'000 lb.

	Yarn	*Staple*	*Total*
1947	935		935
1948	1,310		1,310
1949	3,554		3,554
1950	7,859	1,460	9,319
1951	10,052	1,648	11,700
1952	11,164	1,550	12,714
1953	12,499	1,928	14,427
1954	19,152	2,762	21,914

polymer brought to a head a crucial source of discord between Courtaulds and I.C.I. The timing of its appearance was in turn strongly influenced by the U.S. anti-Trust suit against Du Pont and I.C.I. referred to above.[2]

The progress of the U.S. anti-Trust action need not concern us here.[3] It dragged on, as is the way of such suits, for over eight years, the final judgement being given in 1952. Suffice to say that by 1946 Du Pont thought it prudent to cancel the 1939 nylon-licence agreement with I.C.I. and replace it by an arrangement more likely to commend itself to current American judicial opinion on the interpretation of the Sherman Act. By the new agreement, which came into operation at the end of 1946, Du Pont cut off the flow of technical information to I.C.I. and ceased to co-operate with what was now to be a competitor—in accordance with the appropriate economic orthodoxy. Du Pont's nylon patents for the U.K. and sundry other countries were assigned to I.C.I.; and the latter could now use them outside nylon, as for example in 'Terylene' and other melt-spun fibres. An immediate consequence was the need for a new

[1] Table 11, p. 62, above. [2] p. 76.

[3] For a detailed account as it affected I.C.I., see Reader, II, Chapter 24.

agreement with B.N.S. and Courtaulds reflecting these changes. It was duly negotiated though only in part. I.C.I. reduced the licence fee to B.N.S. for the nylon patents, and granted to Courtaulds the licence for melt-spinning of fibres other than nylon. This, of course, was precisely what Courtaulds had been asking for in the dispute about 'Terylene'.[1] The objection to I.C.I.'s using the machinery ordered from Peter Brotherhood Ltd. could no longer be sustained. Courtaulds could hardly do anything but accept the new terms; but the melt-spinning rights were of little practical use to them at the time, not least because I.C.I. continued firmly to refuse all attempts by Courtaulds and B.N.S. to persuade them to transfer the development of 'Terylene' to B.N.S.

Instead, I.C.I. used the occasion of this necessary new agreement to raise, not for the first time, the question of revising the clause of the 1940 agreement which provided for their 6 per cent. return on polymer production. This vexed problem flowed from what was undoubtedly a miscalculation by I.C.I. in accepting this clause. Courtaulds and I.C.I. both had an interest in maintaining the profits of B.N.S. as these determined the dividends to be drawn therefrom. The main determinants of profits were the cost to B.N.S. of the polymer—as this was by far the largest item (about 80 per cent.) in production costs—and the price which B.N.S.—holding a monopoly at the time—could persuade consumers to pay for nylon yarn. But polymer production was significantly more capital-intensive than spinning; and as output increased so did I.C.I.'s capital investment in polymer production increase more than proportionally to the total investment, equally shared by the two owners, in B.N.S. For what they supplied to B.N.S., both, according to the terms of the original agreement, were to draw 6 per cent.; but as output increased, the amount of capital invested in yielding that 6 per cent. would be far greater for I.C.I. than for Courtaulds. Consequently, the more did B.N.S. profits on the sale of yarn exceed 6 per cent., the greater the disparity between the return to the two owners, with Courtaulds gaining on I.C.I. all the time.

As early as September 1940 one of the I.C.I. directors on the B.N.S. Board, W. F. Lutyens, pointed out the potentialities inherent in this arrangement in a letter to Samuel Courtauld. He seems to have become aware of the situation as a result of calculations made in response to government suggestions for a much higher output. The suggestions were only partially turned into reality; and in any event there were special

[1] See above, p. 75.

contractual arrangements with the government during the war. So the problem receded though it certainly did not go away. It reappeared with the ending of wartime conditions, with building under way at Pontypool and Billingham, and with the new 1946 agreement with Du Pont. The result was that Courtaulds and I.C.I. embarked on yet another long wrangle, with lawyers and accountants in full attendance. Courtaulds had been well aware of the situation for some time and used it as a bargaining lever in their general efforts to get a better foothold on the emergent synthetic fibres, nylon and 'Terylene'. In 1943, for example, Hanbury-Williams was asking Kinnes's views on the possibility of either having B.N.S. make the polymer, in which case, 'Courtaulds would be 50/50 with I.C.I. all the way' or of Courtaulds financing half of an I.C.I.–B.N.S. polymer plant at 6 per cent. The presence of Courtaulds' large holdings of government stock, at about 3 per cent., would have made such an investment doubly attractive. Such a move by Courtaulds into chemicals, in the shape of polymer manufacture, would, however, have been wholly unwelcome to I.C.I.;[1] they no more wanted Courtaulds in polymer-making than they wanted them in 'Terylene'.

Between 1946 and 1951 the arguments continued, helped along initially by complaints from B.N.S. about the qualities, amounts, and prices of polymer coming from I.C.I., and by delays and difficulties at the Billingham plant. Meanwhile, nylon sales expanded and profits boomed. In 1948 Wilson supplied Hanbury-Williams, at his request, with some calculations setting out the increasing disparity in the returns to Courtaulds and I.C.I., on various assumptions about B.N.S. profit margins. Courtaulds knew that new terms for I.C.I.'s return on polymer supplies had to be agreed. They were, at a meeting in August 1950 when, in less than half-an-hour's discussion, it was agreed to raise the 6 per cent. to 11 per cent. This was subsequently embodied in a new formal agreement between the two companies signed in June 1951. Courtaulds re-opened the 'Terylene' issue, on which, as an internal memorandum of August 1950 shows clearly, they knew that their bargaining position was weak. As already shown,[2] it was at this time that they were having to make vital decisions on the future of viscose textile yarn and the low return on their capital invested therein. Hanbury-Williams was worried about possible competition from 'Terylene'. Wilson advised him of his views:

It would simplify relations between B.N.S., Courtaulds and I.C.I., if I.C.I.

[1] Reader, II, pp. 377, 386. [2] See above, pp. 59–61.

would agree to put all melt spinning developments into B.N.S., provided that Courtaulds agreed to do likewise. If you would induce I.C.I. to accept this point of view, I think we ought to agree to it, but I should not be unduly perturbed if we failed to reach agreement on this point. . . .

If I.C.I. insist upon developing 'Terylene' on their own, I feel that the expanded Pontypool plant is quite capable of meeting the competition which might arise.

In the event I.C.I. reaffirmed their determination to go ahead on their own with 'Terylene', confirming this to B.N.S. in October 1951; and Courtaulds pushed ahead with their own interest in acrylic fibres which was to lead to 'Courtelle'.[1] The whole issue still refused to vanish, however, because by 1954, with further expansion planned, I.C.I. became dissatisfied with 11 per cent., and there was still talk of B.N.S. taking over polymer production. What subsequently happened, even before the 1961 bid, is best dealt with in later chapters. Suffice to quote one prophetic comment, made by Wilson in a memorandum of April 1952: 'We should be on safer ground if . . . we went straight to the root of the matter, which is that the dual function of I.C.I. as sole supplier and chief competitor of B.N.S. is bound to result in future difficulties arising between I.C.I. and Courtaulds.'

VI

It is possible, though very improbable, that total harmony would have prevailed in Courtaulds–I.C.I. relations had the characters and attitudes of the directors concerned been quite different. Improbable, because they would need to have been remarkably accommodating and flexible to have settled without rancour all the problems inherent in the relationship. Given that the two companies and B.N.S. were all operating in the market economy, that relationship contained fundamental and inherent ambiguities, even contradictions, some actual, some potential. The tenor of the relations, however, especially in the early years, was worsened by the cast of mind of those who found themselves supposedly trying to reach mutually acceptable decisions.

The most active of the I.C.I. directors on the B.N.S. Board from 1940 to 1944 was Lutyens. His experience of that activity seems to have stimulated within him a thoroughgoing dislike and mistrust of Courtaulds. As chairman of I.C.I.'s Alkali Group, he was apparently accustomed to the exercise of power and the expression, in a 'masterful tone', of a confident

[1] See below, pp. 180–9.

3. Courtaulds, Inc.: Mobile, Alabama, 1955

4. Saiccor (*circa* 1959)

superiority which went with that position.[1] According to Dr. Reader, he rapidly fell out with Rendall, 'disliked almost everything about Coventry . . . , considered Courtaulds' representatives there insufferably provincial, and . . . thought Courtaulds' main Board controlled their nominees too closely'.[2] Certainly the tone is only too evident in some of his letters; and complaints of delay were soon to be heard. The indecisiveness of Henry Johnson, the self-satisfaction of Glover and his chemists, and the persistent tendency of the Courtaulds Board to discuss minutiae: these qualities, already discussed in another context,[3] are only too recognizable in this characterization of Lutyens's sentiments.

For their part Courtaulds' directors of the day were neither accustomed nor willing to make decisions without protracted Board discussions; and they were wholly unused to being harried by others with habits born of operating in a holding company. Having gained a dominant position in their own field, and in a company organized and run entirely differently from I.C.I., they did not take kindly to the intrusion of outsiders. Having also just suffered the traumatic experience of the loss of A.V.C., they were all the more likely to want to ponder lengthily about their commitments to I.C.I. and B.N.S. So if Lutyens's disapproval could be met with counter-disapproval it was. Early in 1942, when Lutyens grumbled to Hanbury-Williams about Johnson's procrastination, Johnson grumbled about the attitude of the B.N.S. secretary; Addison wrote in March 1942 to express his disappointment at Lutyens's failure to do something; in June Lutyens wrote to Samuel Courtauld complaining of delays in a B.N.S. joint-patent committee and its failure to reach agreement on virtually anything. In 1943–4, between the demise of the 'Atlantic Charter' negotiations and the 'Terylene' quarrel, a ridiculous little volcano erupted about whether 'nylon' should be classified as 'rayon'. Institutions in the U.K. such as the British Rayon Federation and the Textile Institute, their views not uninfluenced by Courtaulds, said that 'rayon' covered all man-made fibres; in the U.S. the Federal Trade Commission defined 'rayon' as a generic term for cellulosic fibres. An awareness of the very fact that I.C.I., Courtaulds, and B.N.S. were all busily engaged because of an American invention licensed by an American firm might have led their directors to a ready acceptance of the American definition. Instead, I.C.I. launched a tactless campaign, without reference to Courtaulds, to the effect that nylon was not rayon; and Courtaulds were moved to make elaborate historical enquiries and write ponderous letters about their 'many years of textile

[1] Reader, II, pp. 354–5. [2] Ibid., p. 375. [3] See above, pp. 19–21, 28–30.

experience', all in order to prove that nylon, as Samuel Courtauld put it, 'should be permitted to flow along the rayon stream' (whatever that meant). That Courtaulds had ultimately to accept the American definition doubtless rankled in the minds of such men as Hanbury-Williams and Samuel Courtauld; but the whole trivial episode was only too symptomatic of relations at this time.

Later, the climate improved. Much of this had to do with the accession in 1944, as one of I.C.I.'s nominees on the B.N.S. Board, of A. J. Quig. Although Lutyens remained on the Board, Quig came to play the dominant role. He was also instrumental in bringing in Bagnall as managing director in place of the original I.C.I. choice who had proved uncongenial to Courtaulds. Quig seems to have been far more dexterous and successful in his dealings with Rendall and other Courtaulds directors, so much so indeed that when he retired, in 1956, Hanbury-Williams asked the then chairman of I.C.I. (Alexander Fleck) whether he could remain on the B.N.S. Board. Bagnall, too, not only proved a successful and independent-minded managing director but showed himself, in Courtaulds' eyes, to be far from just another I.C.I. man. But he quickly made it clear that he would not brook continual interference from the Courtaulds and I.C.I. bosses. In a firm and courageous letter he wrote to Samuel Courtauld in February 1945 he complained of three matters in connection with the Pontypool factory which had been delayed because of Courtaulds' insistence upon referring them to higher authority:

> If this practice is allowed to continue there will be two results. In the first place, it will be quite impossible for me to carry out the instructions given to me at the time of my appointment by Sir John Nicholson and Mr. Hanbury-Williams, which was to manage B.N.S. as an independent company, subject only to the administrative control of the Board of Directors. . . .
>
> In the second place, there will be delay upon delay. It is already apparent that even if everything goes according to plan, the 3·3 million lb. unit will not be in operation till about the beginning of 1948. Indecision and changes of mind such as we are now experiencing may very well postpone this date for a year or two.

On the Courtaulds side, the diminishing role of Henry Johnson, the supersession in 1946 of Glover, and the arrival on the B.N.S. Board of Wilson[1] were major gains. Wilson's arrival brought not just a high-class intellect to the Board but a mind free from the hampering emotional remembrance of Courtaulds' past. The speedy conclusion of the new

[1] Gratwick was appointed to replace Glover with Wilson as his alternate, but Wilson became increasingly involved in B.N.S. affairs from about 1948 onwards.

agreement on polymer pricing and I.C.I.'s rate of return in 1950–1 had much to do with Wilson's approach. The whole tenor of his memoranda to Hanbury-Williams on various B.N.S. and I.C.I. matters was utterly different from the niggling obstructiveness and self-satisfaction only too often found in those of Glover.

In a variety of ways, therefore, the personalities of the leading directors exacerbated or modified the temper of the relationship between Courtaulds and I.C.I. They determined, in part at least, the timing and form of the sundry battles, even though the basic conflict was inherent in the relationship itself; and in a few years time, when some of the actors had changed, another such explosive mixture was to set off a new and much bigger outburst of corporate warfare.

CHAPTER V

The Return to North America

I

AFTER the sale of American Viscose Corporation in 1941, Courtaulds retained certain direct interests in the company. They still held 5 per cent. of the common stock of A.V.C.[1] They had one seat, occupied by Hanbury-Williams, on the newly constituted Board; and the agreement for the exchange of technical information, which had been signed in 1937, continued in force. Power on the new A.V.C. Board rested in the hands of the banking and other interests which now controlled the company. Some of the former Courtaulds' appointees still kept titular leadership: William C. Appleton, former sales director, continued as president, and the lawyer John G. Jackson as chairman; and Sir Samuel Salvage, former chairman, remained on the Board. But there was not much satisfaction with Appleton's performance as president; and Jackson was only a part-time chairman. In 1943 Salvage and Jackson proposed to Hanbury-Williams that he should become a candidate for the full-time chairmanship of A.V.C. The phraseology of their letters on this matter reveal the suggestion as an interesting testimony both to the impressive nature of the image of Hanbury-Williams as a leader in British business and to the cloud-cuckoo land in which these two elderly remnants of an earlier era were apparently living. Not surprisingly Hanbury-Williams declined, commenting *en passant* that he wondered whether 'the bankers and especially the authorities in Washington' would welcome an Englishman as chairman of the A.V.C. Board. Indeed after a short visit to the U.S.A. in 1943, he resigned his directorship because of the obvious impossibility of attending meetings; S. G. Dixon, president of Courtaulds (Canada), took his place. Arrangements were made for the opening of an office for Lustre Fibres in New York, to act partly as a channel for the expected flow of information in accordance with the technical agreement, and partly as a general listening post for the developments in the rayon world in America.

[1] See Vol. II, p. 472, n. 1. They also held some A.V.C. preferred stock but this was sold in 1943.

The post-war years soon brought change and realism to A.V.C. and its relations with its former owner. In the course of 1946 Jackson made known his wish to retire from the chairmanship as soon as possible; and the decision was taken to replace him by F. H. Reichel, one of the new A.V.C. directors who was also president of the Sylvania Industrial Corporation. A.V.C. took over Sylvania and Reichel became chairman of A.V.C. Later in the year the troubled relations with Appleton came to a head. He was sacked; and Reichel took over the presidency of A.V.C. Meanwhile, in July Salvage died, not far short of his seventieth birthday, thus removing the last of the major personal links with Courtaulds. The technical agreement was the next casualty. In June 1945 both sides had announced their intention of keeping it in being, an intention which Courtaulds went so far as to record in their Board minutes; in November 1947, however, the A.V.C. Board voted to terminate it, and this was done as from December. Apart from all the high-flown sentiment attached to its perpetuation Courtaulds had a particular reason for wishing to keep it alive: their discovery that, in certain important fields, A.V.C. production methods were now well in advance of their own, particularly affecting their own re-equipment of the Greenfield plant;[1] and the flow of information and machinery for the new staple fibre plant which Courtaulds (Canada) were setting up. A.V.C. had more than one reason for seeking to end it. There was no particular indication that they were likely to gain from its existence and some of the new directors felt that they owed nothing to Courtaulds; the recent decision of Du Pont to end their agreement with I.C.I. in consequence of the continuing anti-Trust action[2] provided a precedent for the termination of arrangements which were not likely to be looked upon with favour by the Federal Trade Commission; and, most obviously pertinent, Courtaulds themselves were busy with plans to re-enter the American scene as a producer.

II

The compensation for the enforced sale of A.V.C. had barely been awarded before Courtaulds let it be known that they would seek to re-establish themselves in the U.S.A. In July 1942 Dixon, on behalf of Courtaulds, broached to a meeting of some of A.V.C. directors the possibility of A.V.C. acquiring an interest in Courtaulds (Canada) in return for Courtaulds acquiring A.V.C. stock. The A.V.C. directors made

[1] See above, pp. 49–50. [2] See above, p. 79.

it clear that they did not approve of the idea of Courtaulds regaining effective control of A.V.C.; Courtaulds, for their part, were not prepared to sell more than one-third of their holdings in the Canadian company. Nothing came of the proposal. The continuation into the post-war years of British currency and exchange controls, requiring special permission for the remittance of funds overseas, frustrated further efforts of this sort for some time. About 5 per cent. of the A.V.C. common stock was held by the Salvage family. On Salvage's death, correspondence between Hanbury-Williams and H. A. Siepmann of the Bank of England was unavailing in securing permission for Courtaulds to obtain dollars to buy the stock from the family. The following year Courtaulds set in motion enquiries about the possibility of bidding for the German assets of two U.S. rayon companies, North American Rayon and American Bemberg, which had been taken over by the U.S. Custodian of Alien Property. Again, Siepmann reported discouragingly on the likelihood of permission for this dollar investment. In the event, it did not matter because the U.S. Attorney-General's office announced that bids would be accepted only from U.S. nationals.

Gradually, however, the dollar situation improved, and between 1948 and 1951 Courtaulds put much effort, finally successful, into the task of reinvesting in a production unit in the U.S.A. As already mentioned,[1] the director mainly responsible along with Hanbury-Williams for the re-establishment of what was seen as Courtaulds' prestige overseas and specifically in the U.S.A. was F. T. Davies. 'Colonel' Davies, as he was always referred to in Courtaulds' proceedings, was a vigorous and assertive man who liked issuing orders and getting things done. As one of his foreign business acquaintances put it, he was 'très bousculant'.[2] Capable of generating a good deal of enthusiasm for schemes which appealed to him, and generally regarded as something of a 'plunger' or 'hustler', some of his ideas were good and shrewd and some far from both; he was by no means universally popular with those who had to work with him. Some of the expansionist projects with which he was associated proved profitable to Courtaulds; some were to prove thoroughly unprofitable. But there was little opposition to his and the chairman's urge to return to the U.S.A. One director, however, expressed characteristically different views on the subject. In May 1948, when the draft of Hanbury-Williams's speech to the A.G.M. was circulated around the Board members, Freeman alone pointed out that every year there had been some statement deploring the sale of

[1] See above, p. 26. [2] For Freeman's views of Davies, see below, p. 135.

Courtaulds' A.V.C. interests. The time had come, he said, to 'make up our minds that this is the last occasion on which we should refer to the A.V.C. deal'. Later in the same year he underlined his lack of enthusiasm for the whole American adventure by telling Davies that Courtaulds were quite wrong in contemplating re-entry into the U.S.A. because, as he shrewdly commented, they were doing it 'out of pique'.

In the summer of 1948 Davies departed to the U.S.A. to make sundry investigations into the possibility of Courtaulds returning there. He talked to bankers and lawyers and looked at the premises of a company which was thought to be in the market. He reported his findings in letters to Hanbury-Williams. Amongst the conclusions he came to was that Courtaulds needed a 'finder', an 'homme de confiance', a 'fixer', who would 'launch us again in U.S.A.' In time he came at least reasonably close to filling that role himself, in the intervals of bouts of ill-health which put him periodically into hospital.

In October 1948 he recommended that Courtaulds should set up a company to operate a rayon-staple plant in the U.S.A. Investigations continued, but in the following spring he was writing gloomily about the advance of nylon and about a lack of enthusiasm in some American quarters for further investment in rayon. However, after some fruitless efforts to interest Reichel in the idea of selling one of the A.V.C. plants to Courtaulds, there was a revival of confidence and Davies departed again to the U.S.A. in February 1951. He had more than one item on his agenda of possibilities: collaboration with an American company in the development of an acrylic fibre; the starting of 'Cellophane' production in both the U.S.A. and Canada; and, the main item, the setting up of a company to operate a staple fibre plant in the U.S.A. In a sense all were subordinate to one overriding intention: the re-establishment, as Hanbury-Williams described it, of Courtaulds' 'position on the American continent which had been lost by the requisitioning of the American Viscose Corporation'. The staple-fibre project, however, had commended itself as the chosen route of return. Once again, and this time with the periodic assistance of various technical experts, Davies launched himself on a furious round of talking, lunching, negotiating, exploring, dining, visiting, discussing, cabling, and writing long letters to Hanbury-Williams. Soon he was apologizing for 'pasting you with projects'; schemes and notions abounded, involving sundry American companies—Bigelow-Sandford, Kelloggs, Koppers, Textron; various bankers were talked to and reported on as possible issuing houses—with much ambivalence about Morgan Stanley and J. P. Morgan in view of their connection with A.V.C. and the sale. ('I should like to make Morgans do our issue purely to make them swallow their own medicine'.) But one theme was often reiterated. Courtaulds must hurry; speed was essential; the time was ripe; conditions had 'never been more favourable for the return of Courtaulds to the American market'.

From all this there emerged a report and in April he returned to England for its discussion. The staple-fibre project had now been given the significant code name, 'Phoenix'. The U.S. market for staple fibre was put at about 400 million lb. for 1953–5;[1] and there was believed to be a gap between this and known present capacity and future plans by existing firms. So if Courtaulds could act rapidly and erect a plant with a 50 million lb. capacity there were profits to be made. He estimated the total capital cost at $35 million and the pre-tax rate of return at 16·7 per cent. He warned that by American standards it was a marginal project: 'I therefore deem it of the very highest importance that the rate of return on this, our first venture back into the American market, should be made as high as our ingenuity and resources can achieve.' On 26 April the Board discussed the report and resolved that 'it was of paramount importance that the Company should at the earliest favourable opportunity return to the U.S.A. as producers of rayon and more particularly of rayon staple fibre'. To this portentous resolution was added the proviso that Courtaulds should have at least a 51 per cent. interest in any relevant undertaking. It was agreed that application should be made to the Exchange Control authorities for up to $35 million, on the understanding that any balance of funds required would be borrowed in the U.S.A. At a special meeting on 7 May, at which Davies elaborated on his proposals, approval was given for the preparation of more detailed plans, involving capital expenditure of some £7 million.

Hanbury-Williams set in motion the necessary machinery and Exchange Control permission was on this occasion rapidly forthcoming. By the summer of 1951 a considerable planning effort was hard at work, involving lawyers and engineers, London and Coventry, and a small team operating through the New York office of what had now become Lustre Fibres Inc., working with Davies in the U.S.A. The over-all guidance was in the hands of Freeman whose relations with Davies were not totally harmonious though he seems to have abandoned his earlier objections to the whole

[1] This proved to be an underestimate. In 1955 U.S. staple fibre *production* totalled 396 million lb.; with exports at 7 million lb., and imports at 172 million lb., the amount available for consumption was 561 million lb. (*Textile Organon*).

venture. It was a complex and demanding operation. Three main tasks had rapidly to be tackled: designing and planning the factory and making arrangements with the chosen contractor; forming the requisite company; and, most important, obtaining the necessary permission from the U.S. authorities in Washington to go ahead with the whole project.

A company had formally to be registered and general details of the plant and site prepared and submitted before application to Washington could be made. The Korean War had brought a massive surge in American military spending and complex controls over investment projects involving the use of various raw materials; particularly relevant to the Courtaulds project were steel and sulphur. It was thought that it might be necessary to import constructional steel and sundry items of steel equipment. But it was deemed vitally important to get into the queue of applicants to Washington as quickly as possible, and Davies made arrangements to file Courtaulds' case to the National Production Authority (part of the Department of Commerce) in Washington towards the end of May. A site was found at Huntsville, Alabama, and options taken on it; a company, Courtaulds Inc., was registered on 25 May; and preliminary plans were drawn up and agreed with the contractors for the factory. The exercise with the bureaucracy gave rise to a fascinating crop of suspicions, rumours, sentiments, and suggestions. The British were thought to be especially unpopular and anti-British sentiment was said to prevail in the N.P.A. offices; interested parties, notably A.V.C., were believed to be lobbying against Courtaulds on the grounds that another staple plant was unnecessary; the British ambassador was consulted; sulphur proved especially troublesome. After hours of talking with first one set of officials and then another, Davies, in understandable frustration, observed that 'Washington is like Whitehall only a hundred times worse.' Doubts arose about the site and an alternative was found. A wild, last-minute suggestion that the plan to make staple fibre should be abandoned in favour of one to make tyre yarn—on the ground that Washington might look more kindly upon the latter as representing, if marginally, a defence requirement—moved even Hanbury-Williams to send a mild rebuke to Davies, pointing out the need to 'keep our eye' on the relevant ball. Early in June, after more talking with different officials concerned with different commodities—chemicals, constructional materials, textiles, and so forth—a small light of progress seemed to be visible. On 19 June the N.P.A. granted the necessary authority.

The congratulatory letters and cables inspired by the vaulting of this crucial hurdle contained some interesting phrases, revealing of the sentiments behind the whole exercise. Davies wrote to Hanbury-Williams to tell him:

> It was with the greatest possible pleasure that I was able to call you yesterday that Washington had granted the permit. I know how much you felt the loss of Viscose—which was unavoidable but very galling. You can take great pride in knowing that far the hardest part was getting the necessary foreign exchange and that in the whole of England I am sure that nobody but you could have done that.

And H. A. Siepmann of the Bank of England, on being told the good news, wrote to Hanbury-Williams a brief note containing this reference to the old bone of contention: 'Wrongs cannot be righted: but this is a turning point and a great occasion, on which I rejoice with you.' Some of the Board, perhaps following Freeman's earlier doubts, had had reservations about the scale of the project and Davies's plans. Davies, in turn, had expressed to Hanbury-Williams his disappointment at the Board's seeming lack of confidence in him, as well as resentment at some 'little quips' from Butler. Nevertheless, there can be little doubt that the majority of the directors readily followed Hanbury-Williams's lead in seeing the act of re-investment in the U.S.A. as symbolizing both some restoration of the company's prestige and some alleviation of a sense of injustice. Certainly it was intended to be profitable; but mere profitability was not the prime mover. As a business act, it does not fit readily into the textbook world of profit-maximization; it was nearer to prestige-maximization.

In choosing the specific site within the U.S.A., many of the relevant considerations were much the same as those which had early influenced the location of rayon plants.[1] Water supply, effluent disposal, electricity, transport, and labour supply all loomed large. But certain particular influences bore upon this decision. In the course of May and June some 50 possible sites were considered, all in the south-eastern states. According to Davies, reporting in July, there were three reasons for this limitation. Transport costs precluded going west of the Mississippi river; their customers were in the south east; and 'extensive industrialisation and highly organized labour' ruled out 'New England, the middle Atlantic states and the mid-western states'. By this time two possible sites were in contention: the one at Huntsville, in the north of Alabama, on the Tennessee river; and the other near Mobile in southern Alabama, on the Mobile river. This latter

[1] See Vol. II, pp. 196–8, 290.

site, the last to be examined, had, despite its distance from the textile customers, substantial advantages in terms of construction costs, water supply, communications, and effluent disposal. There were also chemical plants not far distant which could supply such needed raw materials as caustic soda and sulphuric acid. At the end of July the decision to choose the Mobile site was taken; permission for the change was shortly obtained from the Washington authorities; and in early August a press release told the interested world that the new factory of Courtaulds Inc., at Mobile, Alabama, would be planned to produce an annual output of 50 million lb. of viscose rayon staple.

Whatever the rationale of returning to the U.S.A., Davies had shown considerable skill and determination in the rapid and successful organization of the project. He had lived up to an intention expressed in one of his letters: 'by hook or by crook we must try to pull it off'. H. L. Johnson visited the site in September and wrote enthusiastically about it to Hanbury-Williams, adding the comment: 'I have not always been very friendly disposed to Tommy Davies in the past, but if the further progress of the job is as good as that made so far it will be a very great credit to him.'

The financial and organizational arrangements made for the new venture did not in the end include the raising of capital in the U.S.A. The whole of $35 million was in due time transferred and Courtaulds Inc. remained a wholly owned subsidiary. Complex questions of financial control and taxation arose in both America and Britain. In part they derived from the British 1951 Finance Act, but they also included that old issue of effective management and control being exercised by a U.K. company of an overseas subsidiary thereby rendering the U.K. company liable to British taxation on the unremitted profits.[1] An operating company, Courtaulds (Alabama) Inc., was registered. Its initial share capital of $4 million was subscribed entirely by Courtaulds Inc. (which had been incorporated in Delaware); this in turn thus became a holding company, with its share capital of $35 million entirely held (save for directors' qualifying shares) by Courtaulds Ltd.; Courtaulds Inc. was also to acquire the capital of Lustre Fibres Inc. Davies remained effectively in control of Courtaulds Inc., but the executive vice-presidency of Courtaulds (Alabama) was exercised by Charles Paine who under Davies had been in charge of the American end of the team organizing 'Phoenix'.

[1] The internal company memory recalled that this issue had arisen in 1916 in relation to Courtaulds and A.V.C., and subsequent changes in the degree of 'control' or 'advice' had to be made with an eye upon this tax situation. See Vol. II, pp. 147–52.

Construction of the factory went ahead. The controls, consequent upon the Korean War, brought some minor delays—without imports of some steel from Luxembourg and the U.K. they could have been worse—as did also some late deliveries of equipment. In general, however, progress was rapid, and on 18 November 1952 Davies was able to send a cable announcing the production of the first bale of staple fibre by Courtaulds (Alabama) Inc. Quality, however, soon proved to be below that of the standard either of Courtaulds' U.K. plant at Greenfield or of other American producers such as A.V.C. It improved, but large stocks of inferior quality remained; competition stiffened and prices sagged below what they had been in the optimistic days of planning for the return to the U.S. A year after that first bale came off the production line, Paine was stressing that if the Alabama plant was to do more than break even at a production rate, already 1 million lb. per week, they would have to aim at a 75 million lb. annual output and the production of more 'spun dyed' fibre. The latter was already being made and marketed under the trade name of 'Coloray'. Paine's report on operations in 1953 contained some ominous phrases: 'The current financial results compare very unfavourably with estimates made at the time when the decision was taken to proceed with the Phoenix project. But for the fact that the capital cost of the plant is substantially lower than was estimated the position would be even worse.' Plans for increasing output were put in hand, but it was not until the financial year 1954/5 that the operation of Courtaulds (Alabama) realized any significant profit. The contribution to the pre-tax profits of Courtaulds Group in this period were:

	£000
1951/2	−44
1952/3	−299
1953/4	−481
1954/5	+564

In achieving profitability, 'Phoenix' was to prove a bird with limited powers of take-off and very variable in flight.

The development of the Alabama enterprise brought a new strain on the relations with A.V.C. and, ultimately, the final severance of the remaining financial links. Some apprehension was expressed by Davies and his team in the early days of 'Phoenix' about the likely reaction of A.V.C. to the intended use of some A.V.C.-type machines in the proposed factory. Specifications of them had been made available to Courtaulds under the former technical agreement and, with various modifications, some were in use both at Greenfield and in the newly developed staple-fibre plant of Courtaulds (Canada). To what extent were they covered by U.S. patents? Were there legal rights which might prevent Courtaulds use of them or of the 'know-how' involved in their use in the U.S.A.? Would it be necessary to approach Reichel on this topic? Relations between Davies and Dixon were affected by this issue; they cooled, and those between Reichel and Dixon warmed. After sundry investigations by patent experts and lawyers, as well as some minor technical changes, Courtaulds satisfied themselves that no patents were being infringed and that they had neither legal nor moral obligation to consult A.V.C.

Although this particular matter proved an issue of no consequence, the ambiguity of Courtaulds continuing to have a seat on the A.V.C. Board after Alabama began to produce in competition with A.V.C. could not remain indefinitely unresolved. In April 1953 Davies, at Hanbury-Williams's request, sought the advice of both Sir Edward Peacock at Barings and the Governor of the Bank of England on possible procedures for realizing their remaining investment in A.V.C. He advanced three reasons for their proposal to sell the A.V.C. holding: the incompatibility between the holding and their competitive activity in the same market; the currently favourable position at U.S. law (which might be altered at some future date) whereby a foreign corporation would not pay capital gains tax on such a sale; and, least important, some expressed unhappiness about the present administration of A.V.C. On 22 April 1953 Courtaulds Ltd. sold their remaining direct holding of A.V.C. common stock for $11,165,000 (£3,942,309).[1] The price per share in this 1953 sale represented an increase of 167 per cent. on the price per share embodied in the £27 million compensation for the 1941 forced sale. A calculation to this effect was made at the time by the chief accountant, at the request of Pedder, and circulated to the Board.[2] How far they testified to changes in the value of money and to an enhancement of A.V.C.'s prospects in the view of the American stock market need not concern us here. But they no doubt fed, once again, the sense of grievance at unjust loss nourished by the older directors of Courtaulds. This view of the loss probably received further

[1] A small amount still held by Courtaulds (Canada) Ltd. was sold in November 1955, thus severing the very last link between Courtaulds and A.V.C.

[2] Pedder also suggested that a history of A.V.C. might be compiled. Freeman poured cold water on the proposal, believing that nothing of historical value had survived and expressing doubts about the worth of the immense labour and expense likely to be involved.

support from some of the accountants' other calculations. They revealed that in the 40 years 1913–53, Courtaulds Ltd., after taking over from the predecessor company, Samuel Courtauld & Co., shares in A.V.C. valued at £735,254, had received from A.V.C. profits which, after tax, totalled more than £72 million.[1] The cessation of a net return averaging some £1·8 million annually for 40 years could hardly have failed to evoke a sense of loss—just or unjust.

III

The performance and prospects of Courtaulds (Canada) had been far from rosy in the years immediately before the outbreak of war.[2] Low profitability, complaints of poor quality yarn, bad management: such familiar troubles had all been detected by an anxious parent. The post-war period was not much happier. As the figures of Table 15 show, despite

TABLE 15

Courtaulds (Canada): capital and profits, 1940–54

	$(Can.) mn.	
	Loan and share capital	*Net profits (after tax)*
1940	10	0·6
1941	10	1·1
1942	10	0·7
1943	10	0·2
1944	14	0·5
1945	14	1·6
1946	14	0·5
1946–7*	14	1·1
1947–8	14	1·6
1948–9	14·6	0·8
1949–50	14·6	−1·0
1950–1	20	2·1
1951–2	22·125	1·4
1952–3	22	1·1
1953–4	22	0·7

* 15 months adjusted to 12. Accounting year change, as in Table 6.

[1] £32,435,777 in dividends plus £39,898,751 in capital profits (after allowing for the cost of the A.V.C. tax claim—see Vol. II, pp. 409–11).

[2] Vol. II, pp. 425–8.

injections of capital, the net profits refused to climb significantly or consistently during the fifteen-year period 1940–54. Taking three-year averages at the beginning and end of this period, the weaknesses of the subsidiary's performance are very evident:

	Gross profits	*Gross sales*	*Gross margins*	*Net profits*	*Loan and share capital*	*Return on capital*
	$(Can.) mn.	$(Can.) mn.	%	$(Can.) mn.	$(Can.) mn.	%
1940–2	1·8	7·7	23·4	0·8	10	8·0
1952–4	2·3	22·7	10·1	1·1	22	5·0

Neither a doubling of capital nor a trebling of sales values could prevent lower margins and a lower rate of return. In the period 1946–54 inclusive Courtaulds (Canada) paid no dividend to its parent company. This dispiriting experience did not come from lack of interest by Courtaulds Ltd. The poor results of 1942–4 caused alarm, brought a good deal of trans-Atlantic correspondence and some visits, as well as various attempts to remedy what were thought to be the Canadian shortcomings. A new executive vice-president (later to be managing director and then president), Drummond Giles, was appointed in 1943; other appointments were made from time to time in an effort to improve unsatisfactory managerial and directorial teams; sundry reports lectured the Canadians on excessive waste, low productivity, and labour troubles. In 1944 Courtaulds obtained permission from the Bank of England to remit $(Can.) 5 million to the Canadian company to provide funds for the establishment of a staple fibre plant. The decision to start making viscose staple fibre represented a considered preference in both Montreal and London for staple rather than for acetate yarn; the latter, produced by Canadian Celanese, had since the mid-1930s been steadily gaining ground on viscose textile yarn in Canadian markets. By 1949 the staple plant was starting to produce but costs remained high. Meanwhile, the sales position of textile filament yarn had grown worse; acetate had overtaken viscose in the Canadian market for textile yarn; and the company's tyre-yarn output suffered from some defects of quality. In the autumn of 1949 the bank overdraft had reached $(Can.) 2 million, and for the financial year ending in March 1950 Courtaulds (Canada) Ltd. recorded its biggest loss of (gross) $(Can.) 1·4 million.

Although the immediate, precipitating cause of the loss can be ascribed to the general recession which was then sweeping across the North American economies and later affected Britain, Courtaulds were aware of underlying troubles which continued to dog their Canadian subsidiary. A renewed spurt of activity, visits, reports, and appointments was capped by an injection of a further $(Can.) 3 million from the parent company. The transformation of the biggest loss into a record profit (gross $(Can.) 3·7 million) in 1951 did not mark a real turning-point, for the downward slide soon recommenced, as Table 15 showed only too clearly. Nevertheless, by the time that that 1951 profit was earned a substantial post-war programme of re-equipment had been completed. Not only had the staple fibre plant been built, with A.V.C.-type spinning machinery,[1] but modernization and expansion of the yarn plant had included installation of continuous-spinning tyre-yarn machinery, also of A.V.C. origin. Between 1943 and 1950 some $(Can.) 19 million had been spent, of which $(Can.) 6 million had been remitted from the U.K. Installed capacity was equipped to produce annually 13·5 million lb. of textile yarn, 10 million lb. of tyre yarn, and 12 million lb. of staple fibre. In 1950/1 sales of textile yarn were 13·5 million lb.; by 1953/4 they had dropped to 7 million. The difficulties facing the sales of ordinary viscose textile yarn in Britain and elsewhere were still more severe in Canada partly because of the success of acetate yarn, boosted by the vertically integrated enterprise of Canadian Celanese; and partly because of the substantial penetration of the Canadian market, for yarn and fabrics, by American producers. Although the quality of the Canadian company's textile yarn had much improved, it had lost further ground to acetate. Tyre yarn continued to do well but faced increasing competition from nylon though more particularly from higher quality rayon tyre cord from Du Pont and other American producers. Courtaulds (Canada) tyre yarn, as an internal report of 1953 put it, was regarded 'together with that of A.V.C., as the least satisfactory of all the North American tyre yarns'. Improvements in quality led, in the short-run at least, to both lower margins and a lower output. Staple fibre also continued to generate some hope and confidence despite some stickiness in sales; further plant was put in, bringing installed capacity in 1954 to 23 million lb.

So by the end of the period of post-war recovery the general position of the Canadian company, for all the money and time spent on it, was not wholly encouraging. The following extract from a letter which the chairman sent to Drummond Giles in September 1953 will serve to illus-

[1] See above, p. 50.

trate Hanbury-Williams's cast of mind, the matters which worried that mind when it contemplated Canada, and the ponderous turn of phrase in which concern was expressed:

we are deeply grateful to you personally and to your team for the loyal and devoted service which you continue to give to the Company. We must, however, face facts and according to the information we have here the facts are that we are not holding our own in Canada; indeed, the textile figures show that we are getting a smaller percentage of an expanding market. Our aim must be to arrest this and make every endeavour not only to get back the business which we have lost, but to obtain a greater percentage of the market. How this can be achieved is a problem, but you and others must continue to direct your minds to the question, and we on this side will also give the most careful thought to the whole position.

Such sentences do not bring to mind the dynamic leader, the vigorous entrepreneur ablaze with the fiery pursuit of gain. The pivot of the letter, significantly enough, is the share of the market; it mentions profit not at all.

IV

One further episode in Courtaulds' renewal of activity in North America needs to be briefly examined. As mentioned above,[1] when Davies departed across the Atlantic in 1951, amongst the items in his shopping bag of possible enterprises was the establishment of 'Cellophane' production in both America and Canada. The Canadian venture proved only too irresistible, but the enthusiasm which he lavished upon it had some unexpected and indirect consequences.

As early as February 1951, he was writing to Hanbury-Williams telling him of propositions soon to be submitted to the Board. With much emphasis on the need for quick decisions, a set of recommendations duly arrived from Davies in March. Hanbury-Williams had meanwhile been obliged to pour, albeit in a gentle fashion, some cold water on Davies's pursuit of the American 'Cellophane' project: 'I hope', he cabled, 'that this valuable work which is now occupying your thoughts so much will not interfere with the major object of your visit to the American continent, namely starting up staple fibre manufacture . . .' The U.S. 'Cellophane' proposal came to nothing, being turned down by the Board of British Cellophane in June. The optimistic recommendation for a Canadian plant, however, were sympathetically considered by Courtaulds' Board in April.

[1] See p. 89.

The plan involved the setting up of film-making machinery by the side of the existing factory at Cornwall (Ontario), so that the viscose supply could be derived therefrom. Agreement in principle to the project which Davies presented was given at a special Board meeting in May. The Board approved an investment by Courtaulds of approximately £900,000. Various problems of finance arose because of the joint ownership of British Cellophane and negotiations with the continental European shareholders proved more protracted than the impatient Davies had hoped. Eventually, a new company, T.C.F.[1] of Canada Ltd., was formed. It soon began to run into trouble; in the summer of 1953 it was reported to be making substantial losses and as being unable to supply 'either the quality or the type of film required'. Not until November 1955 did it register a small monthly profit.

Meanwhile, however, the evident difficulties of this enterprise had aroused in the Courtaulds Board not simply concern but retrospective disapproval of Davies's original recommendations. So strong were feelings on this matter that in December 1953, on the discovery that the likely cost was much greater and the market less favourable than had originally been supposed, the Board set up a special committee[2] to investigate the position of T.C.F. of Canada. In particular it was asked to examine the data originally submitted to the Board, on which it had been decided to proceed with the project; to compare the present position with that data; and to consider future prospects and policy. An interim report in January 1954 was followed by a full report in February. The latter contained the damning conclusion that the proposals put to the Board in April 1951

> were misleading as to the financial prospects of the T.C.F. venture because they forecast a profit of $708,710 giving a yield of 11·9 per cent. without the essential qualifications that (a) this estimate of profit was a maximum (b) a profit was unlikely to be realised from the first and very probably also the second year's full running of the plant, and (c) a second producer might have to meet substantial competition involving losses.[3]

It was decided to let T.C.F. operate for a further six months, with a further review to follow; that an interest-free loan of $(Can.) 2¼ million should be made to T.C.F.; and that the T.C.F. Board should be strengthened as soon as possible by the appointment of 'someone with substantial

[1] T.C.F. = Transparent Cellulose Film.

[2] The committee consisted of P. S. Rendall (chairman), W. P. Courtauld, C. F. Kearton, R. A. Kinnes, and C. W. Sheldon.

[3] The existing producer was Canadian Industries Ltd.

practical experience of the cellophane business'. The need to remedy so bizarre an omission was bad enough. Worse than that, the report as a whole undoubtedly reflected adversely upon Davies's judgement, observing, indeed, that the document submitted to the Board in April 1951 did not 'in many instances, reflect exactly the data prepared by the team who visited Canada'. Eventually, in February 1955, it was decided to reprieve T.C.F. It still survives and has proved not unprofitable. But early in 1954, Davies, who had been seriously ill and absent from the Board for six months, left Courtaulds.[1]

[1] See below, pp. 134–5.

CHAPTER VI

Europe, Africa, and Australia

I

ALTHOUGH the ambition to re-establish the company in the U.S.A. was one of the sentiments uppermost in Hanbury-Williams's mind, it was far from being the sole item of overseas concern. During this post-war period, matters arising from those of the company's foreign rayon investments which were unconnected with North America fell into three main categories: the rehabilitation of the existing European subsidiaries at Calais and Cologne; collaborative ventures with Snia Viscosa, one of which, designed to deal with difficulties in the supply of wood-pulp, led to investment in South Africa; and a new investment in rayon production, this time in Australia. This chapter will consider each in turn.

Meanwhile, however, it is worth noting that these major projects did not exhaust the company's foreign interests, real or potential. Sometimes approaches from outside were a portent of possible investment. Between 1944 and 1947, for instance, proposals were made to Courtaulds that they should invest in rayon production, or in a plant for spinning and weaving staple fibre, in Egypt. A mission, headed by Sir Edward Crowe,[1] was sent out in 1946; despite the customary threat that if Courtaulds did not plunge other interests would (on this occasion the American Kohorn company was produced as the bogey), the mission's conclusions were not encouraging. The proposals were rejected; neither politically not economically did Egypt prove attractive. A similar decision was reached, for similar reasons, about the possibility of investment in India. Only a few years after the yarn-processing and weaving enterprise, Courtaulds (India), had its loss-making life ended by sale in 1940,[2] the Board were listening to proposals emanating from Indian government sources, for participation in the development of rayon production in India. Despite expressions of regret for lost opportunities, voiced by Davies, they were turned down in November 1946. Although Courtaulds (India) Ltd. was resuscitated in 1950 simply as a sales outlet for Lustre Fibres, further proposals for invest-

[1] A director of Lustre Fibres. [2] See Vol. II, pp. 279, 379–80.

ment in rayon production there were rejected in 1954 and again in 1956. In another area of the company's unfruitful pre-war investment, Spain (Courtaulds Hispania was finally sold in 1943[1]), the answer to a proposal was more favourable. But the suggested embrace was of a different kind: investment in the provision of machinery and 'know-how' for acetate yarn production by an existing Spanish enterprise, the Barcelona-based firm of Industrias del Acetato de Cellulosa S.A. (I.N.A.C.S.A.). The deal was concluded in 1948; it cost Courtaulds little, it yielded some small returns, and Courtaulds continued to hold some 11 per cent. of the Spanish company's capital. To the shareholders, it was presented by Hanbury-Williams at the A.G.M. of July 1950 as a product of 'pursuing the policy of extending our foreign interests where suitable opportunity presents itself'.

II

As was explained in Volume II, neither the French nor the German company was the product of a straightforward investment decision with a prime aim of making profits. The original move into America had been of that nature, had certainly achieved its purpose, and had come to acquire an aura of retrospective prestige. The 50/50 creation, with V.G.F. in 1925, of Glanzstoff-Courtaulds, however, had arisen out of a dispute over certain patent rights and was associated with a complex structure of technical and marketing agreements. The wholly owned French subsidiary, Les Filés de Calais, had been set up in the same year in part, at least, as a bargaining weapon, a strategic device, in Courtaulds' relations with the French rayon producers.[2] Furthermore, by the time that war broke out neither investment had produced any monetary returns to Courtaulds in the shape of dividends;[3] nor had there been any very evident successes in marketing or business strategy. When hostilities ended, the original reasons for the establishment of the companies, if they had not been forgotten, had become virtually irrelevant. They had no associations of former glory. So the immediate response to the re-opening of access to them was to see them primarily as damaged capital items needing rehabilitation, potential absorbers of cash for a profitable return.

The Calais plant presented the more formidable and immediate problem for, as already mentioned,[4] it had been seriously damaged by bombing. Until the summer of 1942 it had continued to operate under arrangements

[1] See Vol. II, pp. 279, 379. [2] See Vol. II, pp. 277–9, 284.
[3] See Vol. II, pp. 375–7. [4] See above, pp. 3–4.

laid down by the Vichy regime; its predominantly British shareholding was concealed from the German authorities, only the British directors' qualifying shares being declared as 'enemy owned'. Its output, between December 1940 and June 1942, of some 4·3 million lb. of textile filament yarn and 4 million lb. of staple fibre showed a much higher proportion of staple than before the war.[1] The air-raid of May 1942 put the factory out of action and destroyed about a third of the machinery. To forestall the possible commandeering by the Germans of the remaining machinery, some of it was sold to another French company. Only the yarn-processing and carbon-bisulphide plants continued to operate. To bring the factory back into full production, as well as to modernize it, obviously needed much expenditure. Between January 1946 and March 1949 some £430,000 was spent to this end by its parent company as were also substantial war damages eventually received from the French government. To textile-yarn and staple-fibre production, tyre yarn was added. But Calais remained a relatively high-cost plant. In 1955 factory production costs for Snia Viscosa, Courtaulds' British plants, and Calais were as shown in Table 16.[2]

TABLE 16

Rayon production: comparative factory costs, 1955: France, Italy and U.K.

	Frs./kg.		
	Textile yarn	*Tyre yarn*	*Staple fibre*
Courtaulds' U.K. plants	300	225	140
Snia Viscosa	283	260	172
Calais	376	276	201

In 1953–5 Calais' average annual output was:

	mn. lb.
textile yarn	9,316
tyre yarn	2,873
staple fibre	7,723

Although modest trading profits had begun to appear earlier, they were consistently earmarked for ploughing back into modernization and expansion. These demands together with the difficult trading conditions of the

[1] See Vol. II, p. 375.

[2] These comparisons take no account of financial and administrative costs.

early 1950s[1] ensured that in this entire period of post-war recovery Courtaulds Ltd. could take no dividends from its French subsidiary, and only a modest one in 1955.

At its peak of production during the war, in 1942–3, the Cologne factory was turning out annually some 13 million lb. of textile yarn and 20 million lb. of staple fibre. The former output was about the same as in 1938; but the latter, spurred on by the demands of the German war economy, represented an increase of about 12-fold on the 1938 output. At the end of 1944 raw-material shortages had brought total production down to an annual rate of some 3 million lb. of fibre only. In March 1945 American troops occupied the factory and production ceased. In July of the same year, however, there arrived at St. Martin's-le-Grand[2] a letter from Glanzstoff–Courtaulds G.m.b.H., starting with the words, 'We are very glad to send you the first official message for six years', and ending with a hope for 'a soon visit of a representative of our English partner'. A detailed survey of the current position, full accounts, and a résumé of productive activity over the fifteen-year period 1928–42 were also sent. The factory had experienced but trifling damage; permission to start production had been granted by the British Military Government; all that was wanted was labour and raw materials.

Eventually these arrived and production, first of textile yarn and then of staple fibre, was resumed. But the problems posed to Courtaulds by their half-owned German subsidiary were complex. What was the value of the investment to Courtaulds? Was it worth while putting in further capital for modernizing this plant, sitting as it was in a ruined economy? To contemporary eyes, moreover, that economy seemed to have little immediate chance of early recovery. Nobody on the Courtaulds Board is likely to have foreseen the so-called 'German economic miracle'; and few can have felt kindly towards Cologne. For six years it had vigorously contributed to the support of the Nazi war machine in fighting which so many lives had been lost. Furthermore, it was only during the war that the trading losses of the 1930s and the capital investment of 1937–9 were followed by profits—of which Courtaulds had had no share. During the years 1939–45 inclusive, net profits totalling some 5·5 million Reichsmarks had been made, and dividends of 2·2 million Reichsmarks paid in 1942 and 1943. Courtaulds had not, of course, received these dividends, nor had they

[1] In 1952 the factory was completely closed for several weeks.

[2] 16 St. Martin's-le-Grand remained the head office of Courtaulds until July 1964 when it moved to the present premises in Hanover Square.

received since 1937 payments of interest and repayments of principle of a loan earlier provided to Glanzstoff–Courtaulds.[1] The net result of this combined indebtedness was that by the end of the war Courtaulds were due some 5·1 million Reichsmarks, or, at the rate of exchange then prevailing, about £255,000. If the debt were to be paid out, operations would collapse; and in any event, there was virtually no chance of getting it from blocked accounts.

If these considerations tended to engender doubts about the desirability of providing the further money which would undoubtedly be necessary to sustain the plant as a profit-maker, others pulled in the opposite direction. Cologne had provided a flow of technical advantages. Its staff had shown themselves resourceful, efficient, and technically advanced, and under the terms of the agreements negotiated in 1926, Courtaulds had benefited from processes and experiments worked out at Cologne. Reality had proved quite different from expectations. The marketing arrangements for which the original agreements had provided had not worked out as expected; the technical advantages had flowed not from Courtaulds' partner, V.G.F., as had been supposed, but from Cologne itself. Both in textile yarn and in staple fibre, various technical practices worked out at Cologne had been subsequently adopted by Courtaulds in Britain. The basic system of staple-fibre production was different from that used by Courtaulds; and, as mentioned earlier,[2] visits to Cologne just after the war were instrumental in helping to change decisions and save money in the further development of the staple-fibre plant at Greenfield.[3]

To make the situation still more complicated, Courtaulds' partner in Cologne, V.G.F., had in 1929 been acquired by the Dutch concern, A.K.U. As indicated earlier,[4] Courtaulds' relations with A.K.U., particularly in relation to selling policies and to problems arising over the use of the Liechtenstein companies, had been less than happy. The war, however, had further complicated the relations between the Dutch and German concerns, A.K.U. having been divested by the Nazi government of its ownership of V.G.F.; it was not until 1953 that A.K.U. formally re-acquired a 76 per cent. ownership of V.G.F.[5]

[1] See Vol. II, pp. 280, 377. [2] See above, p. 49.

[3] Courtaulds made no secret of the benefits derived. In a letter to the President of the Board of Trade in March 1940, Hanbury-Williams wrote of 'the substantial advantages which we have derived from technical visits to German factories'.

[4] See Vol. II, pp. 376–7.

[5] Courtaulds retained during this period their own small investment in A.K.U. Gross dividends from 1945 to 1955 averaged £7,600 per annum.

In the light of these considerations, it is hardly surprising that the Board called for a detailed internal report on past, present, and possible future of the Cologne factory. Drawn up in 1947,[1] its general conclusions, despite having rehearsed in some detail both its thwarted hopes and the frustrations then inherent in the German economic situation, were broadly optimistic. 'If', it concluded, 'the value of the German investment can be maintained or even increased, there is little doubt that it will represent a valuable asset to Courtaulds Ltd. in years to come.' In practice, however, this agreeable vision proved more than occasionally elusive.

Of especial concern to Courtaulds was the situation created by the old technical agreement of 1926; if it was still valid, the Cologne plant would have access to the I.R.C. continuous spinning patents which Courtaulds had bought in 1945.[2] Courtaulds successfully maintained that the 1926 agreement was no longer valid. A new and much more limited agreement with V.G.F. was devised early in 1948 but, influenced by A.K.U., the V.G.F. Board refused to ratify it. Consequently, all proposals for providing technical help to Cologne had to be separately assessed and considerable pains were taken to ensure that no valuable information was conveyed to Cologne which might find its way to V.G.F. or A.K.U. as business competitors. By 1950 nothing had been received in the form of loan interest or dividends. Although some sterling was received in 1952, in respect of the outstanding sum due, it was not until 1954 that it became possible to get payment, in sterling, of current earnings; these were, moreover, no longer subject to taxation in both Germany and Britain. An agreement dealing with the outstanding indebtedness to Courtaulds was signed. In 1953–5, average annual output was:

	mn. lb.
textile yarn	11,402
tyre yarn	2,025
staple	18,493

But in 1952, 1954, and again in 1955 the Courtaulds Board considered whether they should sell their share in the Cologne enterprise or, alternatively, acquire V.G.F.'s half. Although Cologne had been rehabilitated and tyre yarn added to its output, and although it was making a reasonably good return on capital and had paid some dividends, the factory's situation *vis-à-vis* its joint owners remained unsatisfactory. As a Board paper put it

[1] By J. P. Koppel, subsequently a director of Courtaulds. See below, p. 139.

[2] See above, p. 48, and Vol. II, pp. 278–9.

in April 1955: 'Neither partner has been prepared to give Glanzstoff-Courtaulds the benefit of their best technical knowledge for fear that the information might become available to the other partner or its associated companies.' Yet circumstances did not seem propitious for the sale or purchase of the other half. So no change was made; the problem, like others, was shelved.

III

Of all Courtaulds' continental European investments that in Snia Viscosa was the largest and, in some ways at least, the most cherished by Hanbury-Williams. That this should have been so was not due simply to the latter's evident enjoyment of his Italian visits and of the luxurious flattery which he received at the hands of Snia's president, Franco Marinotti. It also represented an awareness that Marinotti was still one of the most astute and enterprising businessmen in the international rayon industry; that Snia was a big, profitable, low-cost producer with a small home-market and therefore a powerful competitor in export markets; and that Courtaulds had derived, and might continue to derive, benefit from technical exchanges with Snia. So it seemed that an investment worth around £2·5 million at the outbreak of war, even if it no longer commanded the control originally intended in 1927,[1] was still worth preserving and possibly extending.

In 1945 the position of Snia, and Courtaulds' interest therein, had been affected by sundry happenings during or consequent upon the course of Italy's involvement in World War II. These can be broadly summarized under four headings. First, war damage had impaired productive capacity. Worst hit were the plants in the south belonging to the C.I.S.A.[2] part of the Snia combine, that at Naples being totally destroyed; the Snia yarn and staple-fibre factories in the north, however, were virtually undamaged. Second, Italy's effective bankruptcy at the end of the war put Snia as a rayon enterprise in a particularly difficult position as it was heavily dependent on imports both for raw materials and coal fuel. Thirdly, in 1941

[1] See Vol. II, pp. 281–5, and 377–9. The £2·5 million was the valuation then put on 378,168 shares in Snia plus 40,205 shares in S.A.G.E.P.I. and S.A.F.R.A. (Società Anonima Gestioni e Partecipazioni Industriali and Società Anonima Finanziara Rayon) two investment companies holding and controlling Courtaulds' plural voting shares in Snia and owing their existence to Italian government regulations affecting foreign holdings of such shares.

[2] Snia had merged with the French-controlled Commercia Seta Artificiale in 1939. See Vol. II, p. 378.

Snia had made a substantial increase in its registered capital. Courtaulds, unable to participate in this issue because of the state of war, thereby lost some of their voting power. From 1939 to 1944 considerable profits were made and dividends had accumulated. So by 1945 large sums of lire, much depreciated in value, were due to Courtaulds; and there was also considerable scope for argument about the ownership of shares. Fourthly, the personal position and attitudes of Marinotti gave rise to some nicely balanced ambiguities of loyalty. That this leading Italian industrialist should have been involved with the Fascist party at a high level is in itself hardly surprising. More remarkable is that, by his personal intervention with Mussolini, Courtaulds' shares in Snia were never sequestrated; only the directors' qualifying share met that fate.[1] After the fall of the Fascist government in 1943, Marinotti busied himself trying to preserve the factories and work-force of Snia from German requisitioning. Although this involved him in deals with the German authorities, he was arrested in March 1944. After a short time in prison, however, he was released. But in September he deemed it expedient to escape to Switzerland. And there he was, in Zürich, when the war in Italy ended in April 1945, uncertain how long the Swiss would allow him to stay. Back in Italy the left-wing provisional authority, the Comitato della Liberazione Nazionale (C.L.N.) which seized power in northern Italy as the war finished, had promptly issued a warrant for his arrest in May 1945, along with others of his kind, on the grounds of being notable Fascists who had collaborated with the Germans.

The resolution of the difficulties arising under these four categories depended much, of course, upon economic recovery and political settlement wholly outside the control of Courtaulds. The holding of a general election in Italy in June 1946 and the effective victory of De Gasperi and the Christian Democrats brought a measure of political stability. It opened the way to American aid and economic recovery; and, more specifically, signified the removal of the threat to existing capitalist enterprise represented by the C.L.N. But what happened within Snia depended to a quite remarkable extent on what happened to Marinotti. The complex relationships and delicate manœuvring between him and Courtaulds merit a brief examination.

A variety of intermediaries and emissaries spoke with Marinotti during

[1] The directors in question being Hanbury-Williams, Bourne, and Arthur Johnson, an English lawyer practising in Paris who had looked after some of Courtaulds' continental legal manœuvres, and who also sat on the board of S.A.F.R.A.

and immediately after the war. In 1943 a Courtaulds representative had talked with him in Barcelona; reports on him and on Snia generally came to Hanbury-Williams via the British High Commission in Rome in 1944; and early in 1945 letters between Hanbury-Williams and Marinotti began to flow through an intermediary. Later in that year Arthur Johnson,[1] now in Zürich, had some lengthy conversations with the self-exiled industrialist; and Courtaulds sent out a representative to Italy who reported in full on the current views of Snia in general and Marinotti in particular. The disfavour attaching to Marinotti at this time was far from being confined to left-wing quarters in northern Italy. His dealings with the German authorities in Milan had been well-known; and even in Switzerland his actions were not wholly tactful. He sought signs of approval from Courtaulds; yet at the same time his actions aroused suspicions of double-dealing and familiar allegations of unscrupulousness. On the other hand, Snia without Marinotti looked like a rudderless ship. Courtaulds might well have an interest in the restoration of amicable relations with him; in his continued stay in Switzerland until political passions had cooled in Italy; and in his eventual return to power in Snia. Such, indeed, was the policy they followed and the outcome that ensued. Marinotti stayed in Switzerland, visited London, and conversed with Hanbury-Williams in April 1946. Courtaulds put in good words for Snia and Marinotti in various appropriate places. In May, for example, Hanbury-Williams was telling an official of the Board of Trade that Marinotti was 'the best person we knew of to head up the Snia organisation';[2] and Davies saw the Italian Premier, De Gasperi, and the British ambassador in Rome to press for Marinotti's return. Talking to him in Switzerland in July, Davies found him very 'prima donna-ish' and suspicious, but eventually concluded that 'our friend has a very soft spot for Courtaulds and I think it is essential that we back him up'. The new Italian government came to look more kindly upon Marinotti. Despite some minor setbacks, by May 1947 he had once again become President of Snia Viscosa.

Meanwhile, the process of renewing amicable relations with Snia and its dictatorial and mercurial boss was proceeding apace. The primary objectives of Courtaulds' policy, as set out by Davies in a memorandum

[1] See above, p. 109, n. 1.

[2] He also explained that 'Marinotti had been responsible for safeguarding the English shareholders in Snia during the war and had thus saved this country several millions sterling; if Marinotti had not done this the shares would have been put on the market and probably passed into German hands.'

of February 1947, were to ensure continuing technical collaboration, to receive profits on their shareholding, and, in general, to 'exercise as great an influence as possible on the formulation of policies within Snia Viscosa'. Though voicing some protestations about other commitments Hanbury-Williams was readily persuaded to resume his seat on the Snia Board. Arrangements had already been made for the grant of licences to Snia for yarn manufacture under the I.R.C. patents,[1] and part of the consideration for this was an increase in Courtaulds' shareholding. After some participation in a new share issue in 1948, they came to hold approximately 14 per cent. of the equity and, through the operation of the plural voting shares,[2] some 24 per cent. of the voting rights. Dividends received from Snia were the largest of all overseas receipts during this period, averaging 51 per cent. of all (gross) interest and dividends from overseas sources. As the following figures show, however, they were heavily concentrated in the years 1949–53:

	£000
1945	—
1946–7 (15 months)	—
1947–8 (year ended 31 March)	—
1948–9	192
1949–50	75
1950–1	162
1951–2	242 (+370 arrears)
1952–3	318
1953–4	—

In 1949 despite some increasing market difficulties and a refusal to join Marinotti in some of his wilder proposals, Courtaulds committed themselves to a joint 50/50 project with Snia for the production of acetate yarn in Italy.

This venture (then known as Filaceta, and later as Novaceta—which name it still retains) initially resembled that with I.N.A.C.S.A.[3] in Spain, i.e. the provision of machinery and 'know-how'. However, as the textile recession deepened and Snia found itself in heavy economic weather, rescue soon came to mean the provision of cash—thereby stimulating some suspicious comments by Freeman who was certainly no friend to all of the directorate's fits of expansionist fervour. The first provision of money was made by Courtaulds handing over their share of war damage claims

[1] See above, p. 43, n. 3. [2] See above, p. 108, n. 1. [3] See above, p. 103.

in Italy, the money not being transferable in sterling. In January 1953, on news of more cash demands, Freeman, who had already criticized the commitment on the grounds that it had been entered into without proper estimates of profitability or market surveys, observed tartly that 'credit is given to the President of Snia for obtaining, by aid of bribes supplied by us, settlement of our claim; when in fact settlement of our claim entails possible heavy commitments and a drain on our technical staff for which we will receive no payment.' Not everybody on the Board necessarily shared the sentiments implicit in Hanbury-Williams's glowing tributes to 'the untiring efforts of the President' and the 'able management of this great Italian undertaking' of which he told Courtaulds' shareholders at the A.G.M.s of 1950 and 1951. On 8 January 1953 the Board minuted the fact that Snia had been informed in writing that Courtaulds considered themselves as having no legal or moral commitment to provide any funds for the project beyond the lire received in Italy on account of war damage. But by July 1954, with threats of the Novaceta factory having to close down for want of working capital, Courtaulds were having to face the dilemma of either pulling out or helping out. The latter was the chosen course. Circumstances were hardly propitious for the sale of their share in the venture; and longer term expectations still seemed promising. So by 1955 Courtaulds' investment in Novaceta amounted to some £600,000.

IV

The Novaceta venture was to prove of small consequence by comparison with the other co-operative enterprise which Courtaulds started with Snia during the post-war years: SAICCOR (South African Industrial Cellulose Corporation Ltd.).

As already observed,[1] Courtaulds never seriously considered investing in wood-pulp manufacture until after World War II. Difficulties of supply arising during the war itself were dealt with by government policy.[2] But the Board's conventional view of the long-term situation was clearly enunciated by H. L. Johnson in February 1940 in commenting upon a proposition to invest in pulp production in Canada:

> we are not inclined to put money into pulp manufacture unless there is any particular feature about the proposition. The manufacture of pulp is an industry of its own and, taken over a period of years, the profits realised are not large so

[1] Vol. II, p. 342, n. 1. [2] See above, pp. 4–5.

that we could not anticipate any very satisfactory return on our capital and trouble were we to engage in the business . . . I am not in favour of our embarking on pulp manufacture unless it were in this country to make a pulp from home-grown plants or timber. That is another story and the time for it is not yet ripe.

As the price of wood-pulp began to rise after 1945 the time began to look riper, not so much for experiments with home-grown production as for further examination of overseas sources. A report by Wilson in November 1947 emphasized the need to investigate the possibility of using pulp from hard wood or from such new sources as the tropical or subtropical forests of eucalyptus trees. The paper trade was putting heavier and heavier demands on soft-wood pulps, mainly from North American and Scandinavian spruce, which were also used in the production of textile yarn and tyre yarn, but the increasingly important staple fibre could use these other pulps. 'The primary requirement', Wilson observed, 'is to produce a pulp whose characteristics are sufficiently good for staple fibre manufacture.' Various investigations already put in hand by the research laboratories had included a visit to Italy to discuss with Snia Viscosa their own experimental work on the manufacture of pulp from cane, beech, poplar, and eucalyptus.[1] Early in 1948 Davies and Rendall were urging rapid action to ensure alternative sources of pulp and trying to speed up Wilson's research activities. Further reports eliminated schemes based on home-grown timber and recommended detailed investigation of the possibilities of building a pulp mill in East Africa or South Africa to produce pulp from eucalyptus or wattle (mimosa). By the end of 1949 wood-pulp prices, at £48 per ton, had risen 220 per cent. above their 1937 level while staple-fibre and textile-yarn prices had risen by only 80 and 74 per cent. respectively. To this disturbing situation was now added the short-term circumstances engendered by the Korean War and economic recession. At a high point in 1951 pulp prices had more than doubled since 1949.

Meanwhile, in July 1950, Davies had brought before the Board a paper in which he spelled out the desirability of examining a joint venture with Snia to establish a rayon-pulp plant in south east Africa, using *eucalyptus saligna*. Pulp prices were likely to go on rising as less economic sources of soft-woods were tapped; the only available large reserves were in the dollar area; as for those in Scandinavia, 'in the event of war, part or all of Scandinavia may be occupied'. But South Africa was in the sterling area, a

[1] As a consequence of wartime studies Snia had acquired much experience herein and had extensively planted cane (*arundo donax*) in an area between Venice and Trieste.

British Dominion, and less likely to be affected by war than other sources of supply. Large plantation forests of these trees already existed; coal, transport, and cheap labour were available. Apart from providing supplies for home rayon production, the venture was seen as likely to benefit Courtaulds' Australian investment[1] and to put them in an advantageous position if and when rayon production was started in South Africa. The case for collaborating with Snia rested on two main grounds. First, they had experience and technical knowledge of manufacturing pulp by the processes which would be necessary if eucalyptus were used; and they had been associated with pulp-mill development in Spain and South America. Second, as already noted in relation to the Novaceta project, Courtaulds' outstanding war-damage claim in Italy was to be payable only in non-transferable lire. Snia, on the other hand, had access to sterling loans via the Italian government which could be used only in the sterling area. There were, as Davies put it, 'indications that Snia might be prepared to advance sterling to us to enable us to participate in a South African pulp project, against eventual repayment in lire'. Provided that the amounts receivable from the Italian government were large enough and that the transaction was approved by the exchange-control authorities, here was an attractive way of using non-transferable lire to secure, eventually, a sterling income. Also proposed was possible participation in the scheme of Canadian pulp and paper interests and, for political reasons, some South African involvement.

The Board gave its approval for further investigations without commitment. A joint Courtaulds–Snia Viscosa mission visited South Africa. In January 1951 the Board considered a report by this mission, the major recommendation of which advised proceeding with a scheme involving Snia, Courtaulds, and the South African Industrial Development Corporation (I.D.C.), a concern owned by the South African government.[2] An investment for Courtaulds, up to a maximum of £2 million was envisaged as a contribution to a total cost of £4·85 million. The opinion was also expressed that despite likely delays in the settlement of the Italian war-damage claims, the project should go ahead because of the world shortage of wood-pulp supplies: pulp was then costing £72–8 per ton. At the same time as examining this report, the Board also heard of 'certain tentative proposals' which Davies had discussed with Marinotti. By 8 May, Sheldon was reporting to the Board the signing of an agreement with Snia and the

[1] See below, pp. 116–21.

[2] The Canadian pulp and paper interests dropped out of the scheme.

5. (a) Sir Wilfrid Freeman

5. (b) F. T. Davies

6. (a) H. R. (later Sir Reginald) Mathys (in 1967)

6. (b) A. W. (later Sir Arthur) Knight (in 1961)

I.D.C. for the establishment of a development company to proceed with negotiations preliminary to the setting up of the main concern. The capital needs of the latter had been advanced to £6·35 million, exclusive of working capital.

So Saiccor came to be set up. But its formal birth was long drawn-out, and proceeded to the accompaniment of many directorial pangs and much argument with Snia Viscosa. Indeed, the company was not formally registered until May 1952; bickering about the appointments to top management continued into the autumn of that year; details of necessary loan finance remained unresolved by early 1953; and by December 1955, when Courtaulds finally bought the whole of Snia's interest in Saiccor, the plant was still not in commercial production.

To understand this disturbed process of industrial procreation, it is important to recall the economic context, specific and general. A variety of cautions, conditions, and qualifications imposed on the project by Courtaulds' Board during 1951–2 have to be seen against the background of existing commitment in Australia as well as those in the U.S.A. and Canada presented with such enthusiasm by Davies and accepted by the Board.[1] And some more evident reluctance undoubtedly owed something to mistrust of Marinotti. Outside the Boardroom lay the general context of economic recession and the Korean War; rising raw material prices; and unmistakable signals of decline in the appeal of rayon textile yarn in face of competition from nylon. So in October 1951, when the Board discussed a further report by Sheldon, who had taken over control of the project, it determined upon a re-examination of capital costs. In November these were reported as being likely to reach £7·7 to £9·1 million; and sundry doubts were expressed about the high level of costs for the plant—which Snia were to erect on the selected site near Umkomaas, south of Durban. In December the Board demanded that Courtaulds should not invest more than £1·4 million in the project; that independent consultants should provide a report on the design and costs of the proposed factory; and that top management with requisite experience and standing should be obtained from North America or Scandinavia. Wilson, indeed, proposed that Courtaulds should withdraw unless the latter two conditions were met. When these resolutions were conveyed to Marinotti early in 1952, he countered with an expressed dislike of showing the plans of the pulp plant to any outside party, and with a demand that the plant should

[1] See above, pp. 88–101.

be managed by Snia's nominees. The I.D.C. also proved unenthusiastic about imported experts from North America or Scandinavia, as well as being unhappy about raising the necessary loan finance if the partners' subscription to the equity capital were limited to £1·4 million each.

Throughout 1952 the meetings and arguments went on. In July the estimated cost was £8,859,000; each partner had by then agreed to invest up to £2 million in equity capital and to assume responsibility for one-third of £2 million loan capital. Courtaulds toned down their more extreme demands and Marinotti accepted Courtaulds' nominees both for plant manager and general manager. By March 1953 Snia had at last provided detailed costings of the factory, and the project cost was now put at £9 million, i.e. nearly double that given by the 1951 mission. Arrangements were made for a debenture issue at 6 per cent. During the next two years, however, whilst work continued in South Africa, Snia Viscosa's internal position worsened; and a serious cash shortage developed. Early in 1955 Hanbury-Williams pointed out to Marinotti the need to liquidate some of the Snia assets in order to reduce bank indebtedness at high rates of interest. Marinotti, having unavailingly approached Courtaulds for a loan, proposed the liquidation of part of Snia's participation in Saiccor. Courtaulds pressed home their advantage. If, the Board argued in December 1955, the whole of the Snia interest could be bought, then Courtaulds would possess both a source of pulp supply outside the dollar area and a means of restraining prices charged by pulp suppliers elsewhere. Snia were offered £2·1 million for the whole of their interest. They accepted.

Ultimately Saiccor proved to be one of the more profitable ventures with which Davies was associated. But it took time for its value to become evident. For the moment, suffice to note that, in this period of post-war rayon recovery but rising pulp costs, Courtaulds' involvement with Snia had resulted in an investment which represented a move towards vertical integration entirely foreign to pre-war policy. And, moreover, that their stronger financial position, together with some growing disenchantment with Marinotti, had led them to buy out their partner.[1]

V

Courtaulds' post-war investment in Australia sprang directly from the pre-war importance of that country amongst the company's overseas

[1] I.D.C. retained its one-third interest.

markets for yarn. During the years 1935–9, Australia took an average of 38 per cent. of Courtaulds' exports of textile yarn, and in 1939 alone took 57 per cent.[1] In 1940 rumours reached London of the Australian government considering an application from a local company for permission to manufacture rayon in Australia. So perhaps it is not wholly surprising that even in the dark days of 1942–3 the Board was seriously examining the possibility of production in Australia. F. Williams, Courtaulds' yarn sales manager in Australia, prepared an enthusiastic report; options on possible sites were taken out; and in November 1944 authority was given for the purchase of land. Estimates of costs and profits proved disappointing, however, and the blame for this was largely attributed to the absence of a double-taxation agreement; with both Australian and British taxes to pay, the net yield of the investment looked very low. However, in March 1946, after a second report by Williams, the Board recommended that steps should be taken to set up a rayon-spinning plant at Tomago, near Newcastle, N.S.W., provided that satisfactory water supply could be ensured and the double-taxation difficulty resolved. In October, Davies was nominated as the director responsible for the Australian project. A special Board meeting of May 1947 was addressed by Williams, who reported that the water-supply questions had been solved; and that a Bill for a double-taxation agreement was expected to be ratified shortly by the Australian Parliament. He also expressed his confidence that were foreign competition to become embarrassing the Australian government would grant tariff protection.[2] Estimates before the Board showed a return on capital ranging, on various assumptions, from 9·7 per cent. to 17·3 per cent.; and a possible capital outlay by Courtaulds of between £3·8 million and £4·5 million, these amounts representing about 51 per cent. of total capital. It was made clear that profits would depend on the maintenance of prices at the current levels which in turn would 'depend to some extent upon the degree of tariff protection'. Though reserving decision about the date when work on the project should be started, the Board gave its approval in principle, providing that the double-taxation agreement was ratified, to the erection of an Australian plant for producing acetate yarn, textile yarn, and tyre yarn.

In October Davies and Freeman went together to Australia to see for themselves. What they saw and heard and reported on was clearly rather

[1] See Vol. II, p. 380.

[2] Currently, imports from sources other than the U.K. paid 20 per cent. *ad valorem*; U.K. imports paid no duty.

different from the paradise on which Williams had reported. They were alarmed at a serious labour shortage. Indeed, although the proposed factory site had many advantages, they discovered that there was 'no labour within reasonable distance' of it. Considerable provision of housing and social amenities would be necessary to attract labour thereto. Moreover, despite what they had been led to believe by both Williams and the Australian Federal authorities, the Premier of New South Wales 'far from welcoming the establishment of a factory and promising assistance in our housing problems . . . gave the coldest possible reception to the whole project'. More generally, they were alarmed at the political posture of the Australian Labour government. They concluded that on this count the dangers were much as in Britain but 'with this difference—that Chifley is a more fanatical Socialist with dictatorial ambitions more marked than in our own mild-mannered Mr. Attlee'. However, the Australian Labour government was as much, if not more, disposed to support the establishment of secondary industry as its Liberal rival;[1] and the country as a whole was seen as holding out opportunities for expansion and development. Provided that Courtaulds were prepared to take a risk on finding both adequate labour and competent executives, the project, they recommended, should go ahead. But they were critical of the company's local representative and concluded that somebody of 'more driving power and greater intelligence' than Williams had to be found if negotiations were to continue.

As well as sending in their joint report, Davies and Freeman both wrote a number of separate letters to Hanbury-Williams. Passages from them are quoted in another context,[2] containing as they do some of those comments about each other or about other directors, so often occurring in letters to the chairman. One of Davies's first letters about Australia, however, is worth quoting at some length here, for it conveys a brief but characteristic impression of the reaction to that country by an English businessman of his age, class, and social origins. From Sydney, he wrote thus in November 1947:

Hotel life here is rather primitive and it all takes getting used to. However, by now we are almost Australian except, I hope, for the accent!

[1] In 1944, Chifley, not yet Prime Minister, had written to Williams saying 'that it is the established policy of Australia, whatever the government, to encourage secondary industry in Australia which can be justified from the economic standpoint and that the Customs Tariff is a means of promoting that policy'.

[2] See below, pp. 135–6.

Life here is very provincial. It is just like living in Manchester. They are most hospitable people and it is often that one is embarrassed by invitations to every sort of function. They live pretty hard—they drink like fishes—are very 'sportif'—You are very much out of it if you don't play a game. They are very refreshing, though, in being very uninhibited people. They are very what's called to-day 'democratic', in that there aren't very many 'Sirs' flying about!!

So far Wilfred [*sic*] and I have been impressed by the wealth and enthusiasm of the people. They all seem to look forward to a rosy future which is more than one can say of Europe . . . As a European though one does feel the lack of the antique. There is practically no building more than 100 years old. This lack of a cultural background goes right through Australian life.

Back in London, the Board of Courtaulds, whatever its members may have thought of culture and democracy in Australia, blew hot and cold about the project during the course of the next two years. After a meeting with Barings early in 1948, Hanbury-Williams corresponded with J. B. Chifley, the Australian Prime Minister, on the tricky subject of housing and tariff protection. By the latter part of that year, other possible sites were still being investigated; the intended venture had narrowed down to an acetate unit only; and, although Chifley had been assured of the company's intention to proceed with 'the development of a rayon spinning industry in Australia', illness had caused Davies to postpone a further visit there. In February 1949, the Board finally agreed that a sum not exceeding £1 million should be made available provided that various Australian interests which had been consulted were ready to put up a similar amount. But at this meeting and at others in March and April, considerable misgivings were aired: Freeman and Kinnes emphasized sundry hazards and the latter contended that the whole scheme should be shelved for five years; instructions were given to the company's negotiators to try to obtain written assurances, from both the Australian government and the chief opposition parties, on adequate tariff protection and the granting of priorities for labour and materials. Although at the April meeting the February resolution was agreed, five directors out of the fifteen present voted against it.[1] In May, however, Gratwick, an enthusiast for the scheme, persuaded the Board that Davies should be given flexible powers of negotiation, despite the constraints imposed by the April vote. Davies departed. Then the negotiations took a slightly different turn, consequent upon the Australian authorities having shown themselves eager—with an

[1] S. A. Courtauld, Stanier, Verrall, Whittaker, and Kinnes: Freeman abstained.

eye on defence purposes—to have a tyre-yarn plant; some directors still remained unconvinced.[1] But with Chifley showing signs of impatience with Courtaulds after five years of indecision, with news of a rival firm in the offing (Kohorn[2]), and an awareness of an obligation to the Australian government to honour, the enthusiasts got their way. In the summer of 1949, Davies, assisted by a financial expert,[3] was busy, as he put it, 'tapping the financial market' with two objects in mind: '1) to stop Kohorns, 2) to put Courtaulds in the "right" with the Government and the public'. By late July, though admitting the need for 'patience and tenacity', he was coming to believe that if the negotiations succeeded 'it will be a good deal for Courtaulds'. In October, the Board, not without reluctance, raised their expenditure limit to £1,500,000. In November, Courtaulds (Australia) Ltd. was incorporated in the state of New South Wales.

The company had an issued capital of £A6,750,000. Of this £A675,000 was in deferred shares taken up entirely by Courtaulds as part consideration for the provision of technical 'know-how';[4] of the ordinary capital of £A6,075,000, Courtaulds subscribed in cash £A1,500,000 and the same amount went to various Australian interests; £A2,350,000 was underwritten by Australian financial firms and institutions and a small balance offered to the public. The issue was successful. Courtaulds thus had a minority interest; this was reflected in the composition of the Board the chairman of which was R. J. Vicars, a leading figure in the Australian wool-spinning industry. Factories, for acetate and tyre yarn, were to be erected on the Tomago site; the local authority was to assist in the provision of housing, though the company was to provide finance for house construction. The prospectus also contained some important statements about protection. It observed that 'suitable and adequate protection' was 'fundamental to the project', and noted that the necessity for this had been brought to the attention of the Australian government. The latter had stated that it 'would be prepared to give favourable consideration to ensuring that an efficient industry received a reasonable degree of protection particularly in its initial stages'. This fairly vague promise was further qualified:

[1] Notably, S. A. Courtauld, Kinnes, and Nankivell.

[2] Kohorn International of New York was an American firm specializing in the construction of rayon plants. (See above, p. 102.)

[3] A. Burney from Binder Hamlyn & Co. (later Sir Anthony Burney and chairman of Debenhams)

[4] The balance of consideration was £A75,000 cash.

The Directors appreciate that a decision as to the nature and extent of the protection to be granted is subject to a Tariff Board Enquiry and may have to be deferred until the factories are nearer the production stage and conditions then prevailing can be taken into account. However, in the light of past experience and of what has been said above, the Directors feel confident that in due course a degree of protection will be afforded which should enable the Company to make satisfactory profits.

The gamble was spelled out for all to see. Still, hopes were high. Although it was not expected that the plant—intended to produce some 6 million lb. annually of tyre yarn and 3 million lb. of acetate yarn—would be ready for four years, this comparatively slow-yielding investment was seen to hold out great promise for a Courtaulds' future in the expanding Australian economy.

In 1953 acetate-yarn spinning began, early in 1954 tyre-yarn spinning. But costs were rising; original estimates of construction expenses were substantially exceeded; and acetate-yarn sales soon began to suffer from competing imports. Tariff protection looked more vital than ever. In October of that year Courtaulds made a formal application for protection. Rather over a year later the Tariff Board gave its recommendations. On acetate yarn, Courtaulds failed to get the tariff protection for which they had asked but a small production bounty was awarded instead; on tyre yarn they were granted tariff protection but at rates considerably lower than those submitted as desirable. In 1955—by which time Prime Minister Chifley was dead and the Liberal Party under Menzies in power—an appeal against the acetate-yarn recommendation had some success. A measure of protection—though again not as much as requested—was granted in addition to the bounty. So a little of the much-requested tariff wall had been built. But already in 1956 the bank overdraft of Courtaulds (Australia) was so large as to move Hanbury-Williams to dispatch to Vicars in Sydney, one of those suave and long-winded letters, so characteristic of his literary style. Its closing sentence, after a recital of rising costs, rising debts, and too optimistic forecasts, admirably conveyed the flavour of a hesitant iron fist in a padded velvet glove: 'I would be most interested to have your views as not only do I value them but I have little doubt that you will agree with me the whole situation requires a careful study.' Not until 1957 did any dividend flow back to Courtaulds as a return on an investment begun—in the purchase of land—in 1944. And even that was not to be the herald of a future gold mine.[1]

[1] See below, pp. 265–6, on the fate of Courtaulds (Australia) Ltd.

TABLE 17

Income from overseas investments, 1945–54

£000

	Calais	Canada ord. div.	Canada loan int.	Cologne ord. div.	Cologne loan int.	A.K.U.	A.V.C.	Snia	Total	Percentage total gross income*
1945	—	101	—	—	—	—	41	—	142	3·8
1946–7†	—	—	—	—	—	18	71	—	89	1·7
1947–8	—	—	—	—	—	—	74	—	74	1·4
1948–9	—	—	—	—	—	5	93	192	290	4·3
1949–50	—	—	—	—	—	5	126	75	206	2·3
1950–1	—	—	7	—	1	6	187	162	363	2·3
1951–2	—	—	39	29	48	11	178	242‡	547‡	3·4‡
1952–3	—	—	30	—	—	8	178	318	534	4·8
1953–4	—	—	—	26	—	12	35	—	73	0·4

* For definition, see above, pp. 41 and 61–2, Tables 6 and 11.
† 15 months, January 1946 to 31 March 1947.
‡ Exclusive of £370,000 arrears.

VI

As already indicated in Chapter III[1] income from overseas investments during the post-war decade was of trifling consequence. Table 17 breaks down the sources of contributions, by dividend and loan interest, to gross income. Investments in what had all become rival concerns—A.K.U., A.V.C., and Snia—produced the largest share of the overseas income. Calais, Canada, and Cologne took a long time to revive.

These contributions all sprang from what survived of the pre-war investments. The main new outlays produced no returns during this period. That this should have been so is perhaps not surprising, though it presents a very striking contrast from the instant success of A.V.C. between its incorporation in 1910 and its first inflow of profits in 1911.[2] The following sequence is not uninstructive:

	First active interest	*Incorporation of company*	*Start of production*	*First dividends or profits*
Australia (Tomago)	1944	1949	1953	1957
U.S.A. (Alabama)	1948	1951	1952	1955
Saiccor	1950	1952	1956	1957
T.C.F. of Canada	1951	1951	1952	1955

As this summary of progress reveals, although in the North American enterprises production began rapidly, profits did not. Various internal difficulties delayed factory construction and start-up in Australia and South Africa. Common to all the new ventures, however, was their concentration in or about the recession years 1950–1. By the time they had come into operation—and this was especially true of the new plants in Australia and the U.S.A.—their output was not flowing into a textile world avid for a new product as in 1911 but into one in which there was over-capacity in rayon, especially in textile yarn, and an intensifying threat from nylon.

At home and overseas alike, the ensuing decade was to bring radical change to Courtaulds in response to an increasingly difficult situation.

[1] Table 6, p. 41, and Table 11, p. 62. [2] Vol. II, pp. 111–13.

PART II

IN SEARCH OF A POLICY, 1954–1962

CHAPTER VII

The New Context and the Changing Board

To some commentators, the famous I.C.I. take-over bid for Courtaulds in 1961–2, together with its immediate consequences, have seemed, naturally enough, to mark the crucial turning-point in Courtaulds' development in recent years. Only to a limited extent is this true. The bid and the opposition thereto precipitated certain important changes; in this sense they were the proximate causes of those changes. But neither the nature of the reaction to the bid nor even the bid itself is comprehensible without examination of what had been happening within Courtaulds (and in Courtaulds' relations with I.C.I.) over the previous seven or eight years. Indeed, it might be said, by those disposed to risk counterfactual propositions of this sort, that had it not been for certain developments within Courtaulds during those years, the bid and therefore the consequential reactions might not have taken place when and how they did.

The seven or eight years preceding the bid and its resolution have as good a claim as any period in the company's history, to that exceedingly over-worked phrase which historians deploy in their efforts to chop up time into manageable slices: 'a transition period'. As so often, when nothing very striking appears to be happening on the surface of events or according to familiar criteria, much is happening below the surface. Such changes are not always easy to pick up; they do not readily attract the attention of contemporaries; their significance remains concealed until, in time, these hidden roots burst into sudden and spectacular flower. Not everyone may instantly admire those blooms. But that matters less than that we should examine the growth from which they sprang.

This chapter will, first, sketch the general outlines of performance, the nature and context of achievement and failure, during these years. Second, it will examine in some detail certain changes in the Board, changes which crucially affected the direction and development of policy. Subsequent chapters in Part II will then pursue specific productive activities in some detail, looking, as earlier in Part I, at the roles played therein by particular directors or groups of directors.

I

As shown in Chapter III, the period of post-war recovery and expansion brought a real increase both in profits and in the yield on assets. These gains were overwhelmingly derived from the production and sale of viscose rayon, with staple fibre and tyre yarn coming to be responsible for the largest share, as textile yarn declined. In the economy as a whole, as in Courtaulds, the recession of 1951–3 was followed by the reappearance of comparative prosperity.[1] Courtaulds' profits for the financial years 1953–4 and 1954–5 showed a marked recovery from their low point in 1952–3. In December 1953 a 1-for-1 bonus issue was made, bringing the issued ordinary capital to £48 million. This represented a capitalization of reserves arising from the A.V.C. compensation, from capital gains made by dealings in government securities, as well as from ploughed-back profits on operations and reductions in taxation. Spending on the various new investments had absorbed some of these reserves and the issue was largely a recognition thereof. The level of dividends (pre-tax) had stood at $7\frac{1}{2}$ per cent. annually for some years until 1951 when it was raised to $11\frac{1}{4}$ per cent. at which it stood when the issue was made. In June 1955 the creation of a further £2 million of ordinary shares was authorized to provide for issues under a newly introduced employees-co-partnership scheme. The formal capital of the company thus stood at £58 million (£48 million + £2 million ordinary + £8 million preference).

This happy state of affairs did not last for, as Table 18 shows, the accounts for the next period, to March 1962, spelled out a very different message. Courtaulds were now diverging unfavourably from the performance of the economy in general. Save in the good year of 1959–60, such results elicited a flow of disappointed comment from the financial press, ranging from 'Poor outlook for Courtaulds' in the *Guardian* in July 1958 to 'More gloom from Courtaulds' in *The Times* in June 1961. The assets had more than doubled in value but the downswing and recovery in pre-tax profits left the level virtually the same at the end of the period as at the beginning. Despite the high profits of 1959–60, which the chairman applauded in the annual report for that year as being 'the highest, in absolute terms, ever recorded by the Group', the pre-tax yield (column (f)) on the group's growing assets was falling, and had fallen in 1961–2 to less than half what it had been in 1953–4. Whatever the longer term merits of the process of acquisition which was increasing the value of the assets—a

[1] Worswick & Ady (eds.), pp. 259–61.

TABLE 18

Financial results, 1954–62, Courtaulds Group

Year ending 31 March	(*a*) Profit and interest before tax*	(*b*) Tax	(*c*) Dividends less tax	(*d*) Retained profits†	(*e*) Total net assets	(*f*) Return on capital employed (*a*) as percentage of (*e*)
	£ mn.	£ mn.	£ mn.	£ mn.	£ mn.	%
1953–4	18·2	11·4	2·3	4·5	111·7	16·3
1954–5	19·4	8·8	2·9	7·4	125·8	14·6
1955–6	17·7	7·8	3·0	6·5	130·7	13·5
1956–7	15·2	6·7	3·0	5·1	139·7	10·9
1957–8	13·9	7·0	3·0	3·3	169·2	8·2
1958–9	13·5	6·2	3·7	3·0	174·5	7·7
1959–60	21·0	9·2	4·7	6·5	202·0	10·4
1960–1	18·7	8·2	5·4	4·4	207·8	9·0
1961–2	17·7	7·4	6·7	2·9	234·6	7·5

* But *after* deduction of debenture and/or loan interest.

† Excluded from the figures are small amounts representing deduction in respect of minority interests; these account for the disparity between columns (*a*) and (*b*)+(*c*)+(*d*).

process to be examined in Chapter VIII—there was certainly no short-term increase in their yield. Comparison with Table 5, moreover, shows that the average yield of 8·5 per cent. in the 5 years 1957–8 to 1961–2 was only slightly above that for the worst of the war years, 7·0 per cent. in 1941–5, and barely above half that for the last five years of the recovery upswing, 1950–1 to 1954–5, when it averaged 16·9 per cent.[1] Furthermore, whereas in the post-war period the increase in pre-tax (and indeed post-tax) income well exceeded the rise in prices,[2] in these years it just kept pace with them, both the pre-tax income and the retail price index rising by 26 per cent. between 1952–4 and 1960–2.

The shifting sources of the profits which Courtaulds were making during this period can again be illustrated by examination of the profit and loss account. The figures in Table 19 are those of Courtaulds Group (*not*

[1] For further data and comments on the relationship between assets and the yield thereon, see Chapter XIV, pp. 314–16.

[2] See above, p. 39.

Courtaulds Ltd.)[1] and show the contribution of subsidiaries to Group pre-tax profits in the years immediately before the I.C.I. bid.

TABLE 19

Contributions to pre-tax profits, Courtaulds Group, 1959–61

Percentages

	1958–9	*1959–60*	*1960–1*
Courtaulds Ltd.	45·3	49·5	43·8
Celanese (Group) (acetate)	14·5	17·8	20·3
Cellophane (Group) (packaging)	21·9	15·7	18·9
Saiccor (Group) (wood pulp)	7·1	5·0	7·3
Pinchin Johnson (Group) (paint)			5·7
Other subsidiaries and minor items	11·2	12·0	4·0
	100·0	100·0	100·0

The various subsidiaries testify (aside for what they say about changes in accounting procedures) partly to improved yields from past investments and partly to the process of acquisition and diversification to be discussed in ensuing chapters. The contributions concealed under the heading of Courtaulds Ltd. still mainly comprised the gains from the manufacture and processing of viscose rayon in its various forms. But even here there were new sources coming in to replace, in part at least, the failing allure of rayon. And if the contributions, by dividend, of British Nylon Spinners are taken into account, then, as Table 20 reveals, the range of the sources from which at the end of this period Courtaulds were deriving their profits can be seen to be much wider and more diverse than hitherto. Although rayon in its generic sense—viscose and acetate, yarn and staple fibre—was still the largest single source of Courtaulds' income, a growing share was coming from their stake in nylon, via B.N.S. and their own development of an acrylic fibre ('Courtelle'); from the sale of chemicals and of engineering services (largely in the form of exported rayon plants); from the ownership of forests and the manufacture of wood-pulp; from viscose film and other investments in the production of packaging materials; and from a new entry into the paint business.

[1] C.f. p. 62, Table 11, above.

TABLE 20

Contributions to the pre-tax profits of Courtaulds Ltd., 1959–61

	1958–9	*1959–60*	*1960–1*
Total mill profits* (£000)	9,470	14,061	12,545
Percentage contributed by:			
Viscose textile yarn	8·1	8·1	4·5
Viscose tyre yarn	19·7	19·0	16·3
Viscose staple fibre	64·8†	54·0	52·8
Chemicals	9·0	9·2	8·1
Synthetic fibres (mainly 'Courtelle')	—	1·0	10·8
Engineering (mainly sale of plants)	0·1	6·0	5·2
	101·7‡	97·3	97·7
Income from dividends and interest (£000)	2,484	2,686	3,253
Percentage thereto contributed by British Nylon Spinners Ltd..	65·2	67·0	73·8

* For definition of mill profits, see above, Table 6 and pp. 39–41.

† This was an exceptionally high figure; the preceding 3-year average was 45·1 per cent.

‡ Losses, mainly on textiles and plastics, offset the gains represented by these items.

The process of widening and diversifying the Group's business interests was directed by a Board whose membership was also undergoing radical changes during this period. Some of the moves which had been initiated under an earlier regime, for example, those in North America, South Africa, and Australia, came to fruition and presented problems for resolution by the new men. Others, for example, the absorption of British Celanese, the new interest in paints and packaging, and the contracts for the erection of factories in Russia and China, themselves owed much to the doings of the new rulers. It was these men, too, who had to deal with the internal problems of organization presented by the merger with British Celanese as well as questions of policy created by such external changes as the proposed British involvement in E.E.C. (European Economic Community). Who were these men?

II

Hanbury-Williams's 'Gentlemen's Club' memorandum of 1952[1] typified the idea of continuity with the past; the existence of 'Gentlemen' and 'Players' in joint leadership of business belonged likewise to a longer continuity, to Victorian and Edwardian England. The educational patterns, class structure, and paths of promotion to the Boardroom—reflected in Courtaulds' Board as in many others in British industry—had long historical roots. In a dozen or so years after 1952, something approaching a transformation was wrought in the membership of that Board, a transformation which again mirrored changes in British society. In very general social and educational categories the longer term dimensions of change are suggested in the comparative figures of Table 21.

TABLE 21

Education of Courtaulds' Directors

		Percentages of total at:			*Percentages of those at university who read:*		
	Total number	*Public Schools*	*Oxford or Cambridge*	*Other universities*	*Arts*	*Science and/or engineering*	*Economics*
1938	17	82	43	6	not available		
1952	16	69	31	6	50	50	
1970	17	47	29	35	18	64	18

Even by 1970 this was not a total transformation, nor is it necessarily irreversible. Such data are social indicators as much as educational facts. They are not offered as necessarily revealing anything about the attitudes and behaviour of individuals. But in pointing to certain characteristics of a group, they signify the drawing to an end of that English duality of 'Gentlemen' and 'Players', so typical of the pre-war Board. The advent of a preponderance of men whose social and educational background comprised attendance at a maintained or grammar school followed by science or economics at university—and increasingly at universities other than Oxford or Cambridge—contributed much to destroying that duality.

These changes were, in their general direction, far from peculiar to the

[1] See above, p. 24.

Courtaulds Board. Various sample surveys of the educational background of directors and managers in Britain, published between 1955 and 1978, although sometimes exhibiting conflicting results based on differing samples, suggest a similar pattern of change: more directors with university education, especially of a scientific character, more from universities other than Oxford and Cambridge, fewer from Public Schools.[1] The trend seems to have been rather less pronounced among the top direction of the largest companies and in the financial institutions of the City; and rather more pronounced in manufacturing industry and in management as a whole. For reasons to be considered later,[2] Courtaulds may have moved rather further in this general direction than some other companies of comparable size and status.

The force of such changes within the Courtaulds directorate cannot therefore be assessed, however roughly, without seeing them as a part of the larger shifts in social attitudes in Britain generally. They cannot be isolated from such seemingly dissimilar realities as an increased accessibility of university education and a decreased regard for the older symbols of status and prestige. To the characteristics of the group must be added, too, the force of individual personalities on the Board. Heed must be taken of the departure of the extended Courtauld family and its nominees from the ruling body of the company which bore its name: instead of the six out of seventeen in 1946,[3] by 1970 not one remained. Within the period considered in this chapter, i.e. to December 1961, the transformation was far from complete. Certain crucially important changes took place; though not all fitting neatly into the period, their net effect was to point unmistakably towards the newly emerging Board composition. Had these changes not happened those which were to follow would have been less likely to have occurred when and how they did though they would almost certainly have happened at some time and in some other way.

After the appointment to the Board in 1952 of C. F. Kearton and J. G. Smith,[4] the next changes came in 1953–5. There were three departures: Freeman died in May 1953; Davies resigned with effect from the Annual General Meeting of 28 July 1954; and two days after the A.G.M., Gratwick died suddenly. The three appointments—which were not, however,

[1] For a useful survey of the surveys, providing historical background to its own 1976 sample, see the British Institute of Management's publication *Profile of the British Manager* (London, 1978).

[2] Chapter XIII, especially pp. 295–300.

[3] See above, p. 25.

[4] See above, p. 37.

direct replacements—were H. R. Mathys as from March 1954; Sir Dallas Bernard in June 1954; and D. R. B. Mynors in December 1955. The ages of the leavers were, respectively, 64, 47, and 69 making an average of 60; and the arrivals 46, 66, and 40 thus averaging just under 51. So the Board got a slight access of relative youth. The death of Gratwick removed an elder deputy chairman who represented one of the surviving links with the 1930s; that of Freeman removed another deputy chairman but one whose outstanding qualities had perhaps never realized their full potential in Courtaulds. It was characteristic of current attitudes that *The Times*'s obituary which paid tribute to his achievements during the war did not even so much as mention the fact that he was a deputy chairman of one of the country's biggest companies.

The departure of so important and energetic a member of the Board as F. T. Davies calls for some examination; it provides an interesting example of the attitudes of a Board to one of its own number. Davies's bouts of ill-health became more frequent as his intercontinental journeyings in aid of Courtaulds' expansionist policies became more hectic. The autumn and early winter of 1948 found him ill, first in New York and then in London; in November 1949 he had an operation in New York; early in 1952 he was ill again and expressed himself as 'quite humiliated at being so sick so long'. Disgust at his own condition expressed itself in his remark, in the course of a letter to Hanbury-Williams: 'If this kind of thing goes on much longer, I had much better retire and grow pigs or mushrooms or whatever broken down people grow.' In June the Board welcomed him back after several months' absence. But in the summer of 1953 there were more operations and further enforced absences. By September though hoping to return soon, he was preparing to resign from various subsidiary Boards on which he sat and indeed offering Hanbury-Williams 'any resignations you so wish'. But his hopes for return were not fulfilled; he remained away during the ensuing months, referring to himself gloomily as 'a broken down colleague'. Meanwhile, in December the Board's growing worries about Davies's recommendations which had led to the investment in T.C.F. of Canada were made manifest in the setting up of the special investigatory committee.[1] Its reports, already quoted, reflected damningly on Davies's judgement. In January his resignation from the Board was accepted. In a subsequent letter to Hanbury-Williams he wrote in glowing terms of how much he had owed the latter in their twenty-five years of association,

[1] See above, p. 100.

and observed of himself: 'a sick man, however, in an important job like mine can under certain circumstances prove to be a liability; the only gentlemany [*sic*] thing for me to do was to relieve you and the company of that responsibility'. Thus did a combination of circumstances bring about Davies's departure. It seems unlikely that Hanbury-Williams would have allowed ill-health alone to have stood in the way of retaining one so intimately associated with him and so useful as a 'henchman', to use Davies's own description of his role. But Davies's judgement was under attack; he had made enemies; and some, who had little affection for him, including Kearton, were on the committee whose report was for him so unfortunately timed. So he went. A generous settlement was provided; he accepted the familiar formula of 'acting on medical advice' not offering himself for re-election at the A.G.M.; and the Board Minutes and the Chairman's Speech were dressed out with the customary eulogies.[1]

As a final comment upon two of the men who left the Board at this time it is perhaps worth quoting their remarks about each other. After their joint visit to Australia in 1947 Davies and Freeman each wrote letters to Hanbury-Williams. Freeman, having seen off his colleague by air to South Africa and America, lamented the strain of air travel and observed of Davies:

Tommy is not the type that can sit back and relax with a book: instead he spends a restless time putting right the world and Courtaulds.

I shall miss him very much, and not least because he doesn't allow anybody to rest. Indeed, that is my only criticism of him—inability to sit back and think a problem out: he will plunge in and strike out on all sides with all his limbs.

We have, I believe, worked well together, but not of course without heated disagreements at times. Possibly we have each found the other a bit uncompromising, but since we have reached agreement in the end on all fundamental points it has meant that the problems have been examined in some detail.

When Davies had arrived in Canada he provided his version:

I should say on the whole our mission was a moderate success. It is a little difficult two people working on the same ground. Though I am the best of friends with Wilfred [*sic*], each one has his own way of doing things. Wilfred is by far the most [*sic*] prominent of us both and also the older man so I had

[1] In due time Davies's health recovered. He joined the Gulf Oil Co., and had a second successful business career which ended by his becoming chairman of one of Courtaulds' competitors in man-made fibres, British Enkalon Limited.

really to tow [*sic*] the line with him. Don't think for one moment we had any serious disagreement on matters of principle but I don't think I would do in quite that way again.[1]

So much for two Courtaulds' directors reporting on each other to their chairman.

The first of the three who joined the Board at this time, H. R. Mathys, came with a very specialized experience. Mathys was a chartered patent agent who had been in general practice as such from 1929 to 1936. After the war he joined Courtaulds in 1946 as head of their patents department. No previous occupant of that position had ever reached the Boardroom, and Mathys's elevation owed something to the increasingly important role played by patents—already of considerable consequence in rayon—as Courtaulds sought to diversify their productive activities. An aggressive and resourceful man with an almost unlimited capacity for talking, his appointment was seen, in part at least, as providing a counterweight to the emerging power of Kearton within the Board. Although in reality he proved not to possess the requisite authority for such a role, he was to figure quite prominently in some aspects of the company's future development, and especially in the episode of the I.C.I. bid. The second arrival at the Board, Sir Dallas Bernard, came in initially as a part-time director. The channel of communication along which he moved into Courtaulds was provided by Hanbury-Williams and the Bank of England. Bernard's career showed some similarities to that of Hanbury-Williams. After spending many years in the Far East, mainly with Jardine Matheson & Co., he became a director of the Bank of England in 1936 and was deputy-governor from 1949 to 1954. He was made a baronet in January 1954. A man of wide experience in commerce and banking, Bernard had a notably well-balanced judgement. Earlier in life he had been impressed by the curious doctrines of Mrs. Eddy and became an enthusiastic Christian Scientist. Whether for this reason or some other, he proved in the event to be one of the more useful of those wise and distinguished outsiders so much sought after by some members of Courtaulds' Board.[2]

Before the last of the 1953–5 batch of appointments was made, a reshuffle of Board duties had to be carried out as a consequence of the 1954 changes. In December of that year, Dallas Bernard joined Rendall as a deputy chairman and both Wilson and Pedder became managing directors.

[1] Davies consistently misspelt Sir Wilfrid Freeman's name.

[2] See above, p. 22.

Two vacancies remained in the Board's authorized strength of eighteen. One of them was filled by means of an internal appointment from the very small band of middle-class and university-educated young men which the company had recruited before the war. Like Davies and Verrall, a product of Eton, D. R. B. Mynors went up to Oxford and then joined Courtaulds in 1937. Returning after six years' military service during the war, he went into the Textile division, became manager of Halstead mill and was then sent out to gain administrative experience in Canada and Australia, in Saiccor and in British Cellophane. He had in the course of time earned the commendation of both Davies and George Courtauld, who was the director responsible for staff matters. The death of Gratwick—who thought less of his abilities—cleared the way for Mynors's promotion, although this did not take formal effect until December 1955.

With these changes made, and the phase of economic recovery having brought a peak of profits in 1954–5, some euphoric comment was virtually inevitable. George Courtauld (also gratified by a recent increase in his salary) provided it. In December 1955 he told the chairman:

> Courtaulds I think is fundamentally in better heart than I have ever known it. We have some very stiff fences indeed in front of us (such as the decline in profitability of textile viscose), but with Alan Wilson and now Frank Kearton and David Mynors on the Board and us old steadies to keep them on the rails I believe we can face the future with confidence, so long as we do not face it with complacency. We have too at last a first-class 'younger generation' coming on and beginning to bear some of the brunt—those people whom we recruited 10 years and more ago with such care for their character and brains and who by now have gained experience as well. So I am pretty hopeful.

This happy vision was soon to be blighted.

The 'younger generation' on whom the senior directors had had their eyes over the past few years largely comprised four men. Mynors had been one. The others were R. J. Kerr-Muir, A. W. Knight, and J. P. Koppel, all of whom joined the Board between 1958 and 1961. Each had a university education, Kerr-Muir and Koppel at Oxford, Knight at the London School of Economics. Each had carried out various executive duties connected with the company's overseas expansion, thereby coming within Davies's ambit and being reported on by him to the chairman. Kerr-Muir was the oldest; a scientist by training, after a spell as a schoolmaster before the war, he had joined Courtaulds in 1946 on leaving the Army. Having served on the British Army staff in Washington, he was quickly drafted into liaison work for Courtaulds' American interests and ambitions. He became President of Lustre Fibres Inc., and earned Davies's approval as a contact man and a 'nice fellow' though not possessing 'the instincts of a "finder" or "fixer"'. Davies indeed thought him 'better suited to technical supervision than commercial and administrative affairs' and in 1950–1 he was made manager of the chemicals works at Trafford Park and a director of the newly created Chemicals Division. After Davies's departure, however, Kerr-Muir became executive vice-president of the Canadian company in 1954. He remained a likely candidate for the Board. One vacancy still remained and others were being created by the already announced intention of Kinnes to retire in September 1957 (when he would be 65) and of the aged Sir William Stanier not to seek re-election in 1958 (when he would be 82). George Courtauld—who had a good ear for the prevalent views of his colleagues—was probably voicing a generally agreed sentiment when he told the chairman in September 1957: 'For years now we have talked about putting Ronnie on our board: don't you agree that it is now high time that we did it? Not only would he be useful in running a Division, but I think he is needed generally as another young policy making director—to join the younger set of Mynors, Kearton and Mathys.' So Kerr-Muir joined the Board with effect from January 1958.

A. W. Knight had joined Courtaulds in 1939 after having left school at 16 and graduating from L.S.E. as an evening student. His service during the war had included a spell at sundry staff activities in S.O.E.; and on his return to the company he soon found himself working with Davies, becoming the senior executive in what was then known as the Overseas Investments Department. He was closely involved in the administrative and financial arrangements attending both the Alabama and Australian ventures, and carried out investigations into the functioning of other plants, including the Canadian company. Davies thought very highly of him; and suggestions that he should be dispatched for a longer period, to rejuvenate the ailing and unprofitable business of Courtaulds (Canada), evoked the response that he should be 'earmarked for London'. Comparing the merits of various of the young hopefuls in 1953 Davies observed to Hanbury-Williams that Knight had 'a more balanced mind' than two other contenders[1] and was 'the most promising of the three'. He added, characteristically, 'but of course he is not so polished socially if that means anything these days'. George Courtauld again brought his support to bear, expressing the view that Knight should be charged with the company's activities

[1] Mynors and Koppel.

in 'the New World'. His appointment, like that of Kerr-Muir, took effect from January 1958. Although he did continue for a time to look after the North American interests he also became involved with new diversification schemes, a move which brought him into much closer contact with Kearton.

The last of the four to reach the Board also waited the longest, a circumstance not unproductive of some later resentment. J. P. Koppel, after leaving Rugby and having a brief attendance at the University of Freiburg, read P.P.E. at Oxford and then joined Courtaulds in 1935. So he thus waited 26 years, including the usual gap whilst serving in the Army during the war, before being made a director in September 1961. His earlier commendation from Davies had been earned whilst being concerned with the rehabilitation of Cologne[1] and, more especially, with the Australian company of which he became general manager in 1952. In 1953 he returned to Britain and joined the Board of British Cellophane, of which he was deputy chairman and managing director from 1956 to 1961.

Meanwhile, there had been departures from the Board and one other arrival; a major reshuffle of positions and responsibilities had been started; and a big decision taken about the future. To the already mentioned retirements of Kinnes and Stanier was added that of Rendall who, after more than 41 years with Courtaulds, retired (aged 66) in September 1961. In August 1959 after a brief illness Pedder had died, thus ending one of the few surviving links with the older regime at Coventry. The arrival was another of those outside directors of whom Hanbury-Williams was always entertaining such high hopes. This time it was the Rt. Hon. Aubrey Jones, M.P., who, at the chairman's instigation, was rather suddenly invited to join Courtaulds' Board.[2] He accepted, and took his place as from March 1960. It proved to be the shortest and probably the least successful of all such appointments. Two crucial moves in the reshuffling of offices within the Board, particularly affecting the men who were now emerging as the foci of power, took place at the end of 1957 and four years later, at the end of 1961. In December 1957 Kearton was made a managing director and Wilson became a deputy chairman in addition to retaining his managing directorship; in December 1961, Kearton and Mathys were both made deputy chairmen. The latter moves, however, must be seen in the context

[1] See above, p. 107.

[2] Like Knight, a product of the L.S.E., Jones became Minister of Fuel and Power in the Conservative government in 1955, and of Supply in 1957. The latter office was wound up in October 1959.

of the major decision, which was taken on an issue which had long been engaging the minds of the Board: the future of the chairmanship.

III

In the course of 1959 Hanbury-Williams let it be known that he was proposing to retire, probably in 1962 when he would be 70 years of age. He then made use of that invaluable sounding board of directorial opinion, George Courtauld, to test reaction to the idea of getting in an outsider as chairman of the company. A counting of heads in November 1959 revealed opinion to be in favour of an outsider, though not unequivocally so: nine approved (Hanbury-Williams himself, George and Peter Courtauld, Verrall, Nankivell, Mynors, Kerr-Muir, Bernard, and Sheldon); four did not; and three were reported, for varying reasons, as 'queries'. But the process of consultation had also elicited the obvious sort of qualifications amongst those who approved: an outside appointment should not create a precedent and become a 'City plum'; the chosen man should be of exceptional ability, and so on. More interestingly, it also sketches for the historian an impression of the evolving lines of a power struggle, an impression which can be built up from what George Courtauld reported as his colleagues' views of their fellow directors, views for which other sources offer a fair degree of independent support. Wilson was reported as believing that an outsider would not understand what was going on and would be at the mercy of the managing director (he almost certainly had Kearton in mind); George Courtauld believed Wilson wanted the job himself. Though Kerr-Muir thought an outsider was probably desirable, he was alleged to feel that Wilson was 'so clever and receptive' that he should be groomed for the appointment. As for Kearton, 'I cannot see him stomaching any of our present colleagues who would be prepared to undertake it'; and Knight was reported as backing-up his anti-outsider opinion by the intriguing proposition that 'the only way of forcing C.F.K.[earton] to delegate anything to anybody would be to make him Chairman'. Mathys talked for 'half-an-hour non-stop' without committing himself though George Courtauld confessed with some surprise that he believed Mathys's vote against an outsider stemmed from 'his own strong ambition'. Rendall, kind and well-liked, was patently upset because it had to be made clear to him that his own ambition could not be gratified if only because he was a mere three years younger than Hanbury-Williams himself. Almost certainly, a number of those who were willing to have an outside man took the attitude because of dislike or apprehension about the internal alternatives; though probably not all expressed themselves as unequivocally as Verrall who is alleged to have replied that 'almost anybody from outside the company would be better than anybody from within it'.

Behind these suggestive impressions of a power struggle lay a reality only too tangible to those intimately affected. The 'present rift between Alan and Frank' to which Rendall referred in a letter to the chairman (then in South Africa) in February 1959 could readily be attributed to disagreements over matters with which Kearton was closely involved, for example, the Russian contracts[1] or the 'Courtelle' project[2] or diversification,[3] but these were merely the proximate causes, the precipitating factors. Beyond or below them were the antipathetic personalities of the only two men then on Courtaulds' Board who combined outstanding intellectual qualities with powerful business ambition. Both had achieved scientific distinction via the route of grammar school and Oxford (Kearton) or Cambridge (Wilson); both became Fellows of the Royal Society.[4] Both wanted to be at the top; but they went about the climb in utterly contrasting ways. As a pair of prima donnas they sang not only in different keys but sometimes as though they were in different operas. Alan Wilson, possessed of an extremely lucid penetrating and quick mind, thought through problems with consistent rationality; but in action remained largely devoid of those qualities which are summed up by that useful but tiresome word 'charisma'. Frank Kearton, five years younger combined his high intelligence with a thrusting impulsiveness and a fluctuating temper which showed the familiar signs of the mildly manic-depressive—hurtling from euphoria and great personal charm to gloom-laden paranoia or violent abuse. The two men did not complement each other. They lurched from mutual admiration to mutual antagonism, pausing only for occasional periods of mutual comprehension.

The high voltage thus generated might have been much lower or, at least, might have been appropriately insulated if the chairman had been capable of controlling it. But it was precisely during these years that Hanbury-Williams's reign became almost disastrous. His own powers were failing yet he clung to office. The investments or re-investments in Courtaulds' overseas prestige which he so cherished were not producing worthwhile returns. The unmistakable downward slide of the company's profits from 1955 to 1959 left him dispirited, and especially about the

[1] See below, pp. 191–200.
[2] See below, pp. 181–9.
[3] See below, pp. 153–6.
[4] Wilson in 1942, Kearton in 1961.

prospects for rayon. The absorption of British Celanese, and of the other companies, created problems of organization which he did not understand, any more than he understood the technical issues raised by acrylic or triacetate fibres. He did not much care for either of the rising stars, but Kearton he actively disliked. Such people certainly failed to fit into his concept of the Gentlemen's Club. Kearton, in turn, had little but a barely concealed contempt for Hanbury-Williams. The chairman's divide-and-rule technique was conducive to setting director against director. But if such positive action was hardly needed to ensure friction between Kearton and Wilson, the very absence of any consistent efforts to bring about mutual comprehension, the very failure to act, or to give clear leads in policy, in brief the very inertia at the top, exacerbated the conflict between the two men. During his periodic progresses round Courtaulds' overseas empire the chairman was fed with information about the doings of the demon king. He was told that 'Frank' was in 'a peculiarly difficult mood'; or about an 'unpleasant' Board meeting in which 'the principal actors were A.H.W. and C.F.K.'. Already in 1959 Kearton occupied a remarkable number of important posts within Courtaulds, carried great responsibilities, and worked extremely hard at a wide range of tasks.[1] Not surprisingly, he overworked and got into a paranoid state. In May 1959 Wilson sent to Hanbury-Williams a summary of a lengthy Wilson–Kearton conversation during which Kearton was said to have complained bitterly to Wilson about the way in which he (Wilson) was behaving. Amongst other crimes, Wilson was alleged to be doing everything he could to ruin the 'Courtelle' project; to have undermined the morale of chemists working on this and other research; to have written to the chairman about the Russian contracts behind Kearton's back, an act 'absolutely indefensible in any circumstances'; to have become, over the previous eighteen months, 'extremely dictatorial, secretive and vindictive'; to have exhibited a 'pathological dislike of free discussion'; and in general to have behaved in such a way as to bring 'nothing but harm to the company as a whole and to him [Kearton] in particular'. Conversely, Kearton presented himself as having been 'treated like dirt'; to have been loaded, by Wilson, with various inadequately remunerated jobs; to have been forced to have 'an old decrepit car'; to

[1] For details see below, Chapter VIII, p. 172. In addition he had various outside commitments, e.g. part-time membership of the U.K. Atomic Energy Authority, the chairmanship of the Electricity Supply Research Council, membership of the Railway Planning Board and, in 1960, of the Advisory Group to inquire into the British Transport Commission.

have had to put up with incompetent typists; and to have been, along with his wife, 'socially snubbed at various functions'.

This near-classical portrait of mild paranoia is reminiscent, almost to a phrase, of the language, behaviour, and sentiments of Kearton's nineteenth-century predecessor, Samuel Courtauld III.[1] To this topic, and to what it may suggest about entrepreneurs, we may return later. For the moment, suffice to note that it was only a few months after he had thus been regaled by one of his deputy chairmen with this account of the views of one of his managing directors, that Hanbury-Williams got George Courtauld to sound out opinions on the succession. The results, as we have seen, were not wholly conclusive; nor were subsequent attempts discreetly to interest various distinguished persons in the chairmanship of Courtaulds notably successful. Towards the end of 1960, and coincident with a temporary improvement in profits, Wilson–Kearton relations seemed to have entered a more peaceful phase. Wilson reported to Hanbury-Williams, 'a very long conversation with Frank today which encouraged me greatly'. Kearton took a holiday; Wilson got a knighthood.[2] But the tension remained; and so did the issue of the chairmanship. In the course of 1961 the former worsened as efforts to solve the latter were resumed. In May 1961 George Courtauld, after more soundings, was once again reporting to his chairman. He made clear his own views—and as, in this matter, they coincided with what was in fact done, we may assume that they represented general opinion. He proposed four moves: Wilson should be designated as the future chairman; Kearton and Mathys should be appointed simultaneously as additional deputy chairmen; Knight should be finance director, with definite terms of reference so that he would be 'in no doubt of what were his duties and powers'; and Koppel should be made a director.

Some of these proposals were more readily acceptable than others. Koppel's appointment to the Board was thought, by some of the older members at least, to be overdue. The need for a finance director was recognized—Kinnes had never performed such a function, being simply an accountant on the Board—and the opportunity was welcomed to harness Knight's abilities to a specific task and thereby disengage them from his association (sometimes involuntary) with Kearton's wilder diversification schemes. The notion of Wilson as chairman-designate was accepted, though not with unalloyed enthusiasm; his assumption of the chairmanship was

[1] See Vol. I, pp. 120–8. [2] 31 December 1960.

to take effect as from the A.G.M. in July 1962. The 'simultaneous' appointment of Mathys and Kearton as deputy chairmen evidently envisaged the former as counterbalance to the latter, who would perhaps have preferred to be the sole deputy, alongside the ageing and part-time Bernard. In June the Board had another 'dreadful meeting'. That favoured nostrum, the distinguished outsider, was again invoked. And so, in July 1961, at the same time as formally resolving Wilson's appointment as chairman-designate, the Board also agreed that Hanbury-Williams should 'invite a gentleman now named to join the Board'. The gentleman in question was distinguished indeed, no less than Lord Cobbold, Governor of the Bank of England but due to retire shortly. The plan was that he should succeed Dallas Bernard when the latter retired, as a deputy chairman, thus providing a weightier countervailing or restraining force to Kearton. The title of managing director currently held by Kearton and Wilson, would be abolished for main Board directors. A formal Board agreement to the invitation to Cobbold—though not mentioning him as a possible deputy chairman—and to the various appointments of Wilson, Mathys, Kearton, and Koppel was passed in September. But it was not until November that the Board finally resolved on the appointment of Mathys and Kearton as additional deputy chairmen with effect from 1 December and only 'for the period ending 31 March 1962'. Cobbold accepted the invitation to him and a draft press release (for 15 December) announcing his appointment as a director as from January 1962 was prepared.

It was not to be. The I.C.I. bid burst upon Courtaulds in December. Rather than be involved in such a controversial matter, Cobbold withdrew and never joined Courtaulds' Board; and, for reasons to be examined in detail later[1] Wilson never became chairman of Courtaulds Ltd.

IV

The results of the changes of the preceding years are shown in summarized form in Table 22 which sets out the Board of Courtaulds Ltd. as it was in December 1961. This was the Board which had emerged from this period of trouble, transition, and tension. And this was the Board which had to deal with the I.C.I. bid.

It was also, or nearly, the Board which in about 1959 prompted George Courtauld to start writing, for his private amusement, a skit on its proceedings. What survives is incomplete. It is sometimes rather heavy-handed,

[1] See below, pp. 241–4.

TABLE 22

The Board, December 1961

		Age	
Chairman	Sir John Hanbury-Williams, C.V.O.	69	Retirement (July 1962) announced
Deputy chairmen (full-time)	Sir Alan Wilson, F.R.S.	55	Chairman-designate (July 1962)
	H. R. Mathys	53	
	C. F. Kearton, O.B.E., F.R.S.	50	
Full-time directors (in age order)	W. H. Nankivell, O.B.E.	64	
	G. T. Verrall	63	
	J. G. Smith	61	
	G. Courtauld	58	
	C. W. Sheldon	56	
	R. J. Kerr-Muir, O.B.E.	51	
	J. P. Koppel	48	
	D. R. B. Mynors	46	
	A. W. Knight	44	
Part-time directors (in age order)			
Deputy chairman	Sir Dallas Bernard, Bart.	73	
Directors	H. L. Johnson	57	
	W. P. Courtauld*	51	
	Rt. Hon. Aubrey Jones, M.P.	50	

* Had ceased to be a full-time director after 1959.

Median age: 55

but by its invented names and by some of its imaginary verbatim minutes. it provides a thoroughly unflattering picture of the attitudes and behaviour of this important business body. George Courtauld's vision of the Board of the company which bore his name fell a long way short of admiration. The skit was called simply 'Draft Minutes of the 1,951st meeting of the Board of the Gadarene Manufacturing Co. Ltd. Great Slope Works, near Dedbete.' The *dramatis personae* (and their equivalents) included Sir Galahad Allenbury-Jones, Cav. Rust. (Hanbury-Williams), Sir Bernard Banker, Bart. F.R.G.S. (Dallas Bernard) Mr. Tom Plodder, J.P. (Pedder), Mr. Fred Kittler, D.V. (Kearton), Sir W. Simon Gadarene, Bart. (Peter Courtauld), and Mr. Rufus Bullswind, Q.C. (Mathys). The introductory stage directions read:

The Directors of the Gadarene Manufacturing Company Limited are discovered seated around an oval table. In appearance they are a distinguished body of men, well-fed, well-groomed, some even smoking cigars. Having assembled, they complain bitterly to each other in low voices about everything. Enter the Chairman. The Board staggers to its feet and for 10 minutes stands in profound silence with bowed heads to mark its deep sense of appreciation of the fact that The Monarch has graciously bestowed the Order of the B.E. on the Chairman Himself. Sir Galahad is a strikingly handsome man, representative of all that was best in an England of Yesteryear.

After a passage of dialogue tilting in various ways at Hanbury-Williams, Bernard, and Pedder, the following speech by 'Fred Kittler' gives an only too likely parody of how Kearton and his doings then appeared not only to George Courtauld but probably to other members of the Board:

You will remember, Mr. Chairman, that Board Minute 979,999 laid down that 'From now on Mr. Kittler can do what he likes, when he likes, where he likes and how he likes'. With these somewhat restricted terms of reference (and suffering as I do from this perpetual and malignant persecution by my colleagues and so forth) I am a trifle handicapped; but ... I am delighted to inform you that ... we bought the B.P.F.C. [British Prodigal Finance Corporation] for 35 million pounds and so forth: we now find that on a highly conservative valuation ... it is today worth ... £11. 17s. 9d. ... Under my own close personal supervision and so forth the losses for the coming year may well amount to less than £2,900,000 ...

In reality, of course, the Courtaulds Board was by no means a comic body. It was a group of men who exercised considerable power by being in charge of a very large company. If it was periodically riven by internal dissensions this was true of many other such bodies. Although, as we shall see later, the outside business world, and specifically I.C.I., had correctly suspected the existence of divided opinions within the Courtaulds Board on certain matters, little was known of the power struggle and the conflict of personalities. However imperfectly, the Board maintained a continuum of decisions on a variety of important issues; it examined major matters of policy; and was responsible, directly and indirectly, for some crucial advances and improvements which, even in these difficult years, were made by the company. To these we must now turn.

7. The Board, in the Board Room at St. Martins-le-Grand March 1960,
From l. to r. H. R. Mathys, R. J. Kerr-Muir, W. H. Nankivell, W. P. Courtauld, C. F. Kearton, G. Courtauld, G. T. Verrall, P. S. Rendall, Sir John Hanbury-Williams, H. L. Light (secretary), H. L. Johnson, J. G. Smith, A. H. Wilson, Aubrey Jones, A. W. Knight, Sir Dallas Bernard. (absent: C. W. Sheldon and D. R. B. Mynors)

8. Spondon, 1961

CHAPTER VIII

Acquiring and Diversifying

I

On the last day of December 1956 Wilson sent to his chairman a letter which began with these words: 'In view of the many difficulties which face the Company, I feel that we are spreading our energies too widely and that we are in danger of failing to tackle the really important long-term problems because of our pre-occupation with day-to-day matters.' In so far as this observation commented on the habits of the Courtaulds Board it was no more than the latest of many reflections on its tendency to deal with minutiae at the expense of policy.[1] But the 'many difficulties' were real and specific. Wilson's list was formidable: the inroads that nylon was making into sales of tyre yarn; the possible insolvency of the Canadian and Australian companies; the need to raise or maintain prices as well as increase sales of both yarns and staple fibre; the desirability of getting more money from B.N.S.; the need for a successful launching of their new acrylic fibre; and the possibility of diversification. Other Board members, Wilson conceded, might have different priorities; some might not understand what the problems were. Running through this letter—and indeed other comments by other directors, then and later—is the growing awareness of one main underlying and continuing difficulty. How were Courtaulds to replace the profits which once came from rayon but were now everywhere slipping away? The question had been posed earlier, specifically in relation to viscose textile yarn, but the recovery of 1953–5 had left the long-term problem no nearer to solution. The later 1950s indeed saw the external situation worsen. Rayon was coming to be regarded, in Europe and America, as a dying industry; Du Pont and A.K.U. closed down or curtailed production. The great expansion internationally of the rayon industry in the post-war years had created over-capacity evident by the mid-1950s. Prices, as is clear from Fig. 5, fell either absolutely or in real terms as inflation in the general price level proceeded. Courtaulds, with so much investment in rayon, made some determined efforts to find answers to these difficulties. They covered a wide range,

[1] See above, pp. 28–31, 83.

from attempts to find new sources of profits at home to rejoining, in 1957, certain European rayon-exporting associations which they had abandoned as useless in 1953.[1] This miscellany of actions should not be represented as adding up to a single conscious and coherent policy; there was plenty of improvisation and chance. But the varied results were to prove of great consequence to the future of the company; they owed little to Hanbury-Williams but much to the tension-ridden leadership of Wilson and Kearton, with the latter playing an increasingly energetic role.

The deliberate attempts simply to diversify the company's activities represented only *one* part—and not in itself the most important—of that search for answers. Taken together, however, the various acquisitions,

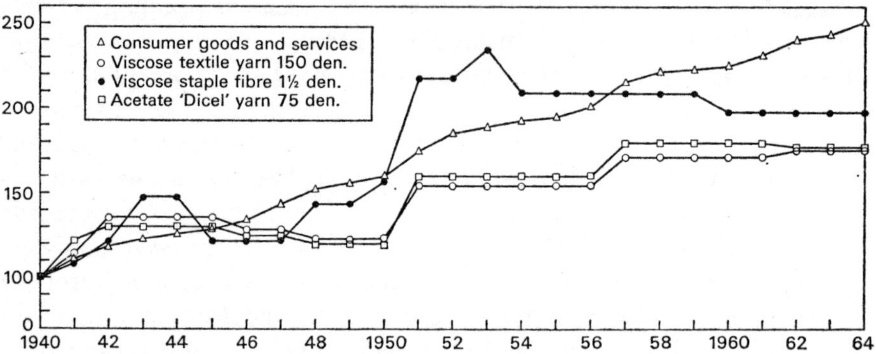

FIG. 5. *Index of U.K. prices: rayon and consumer goods and services, 1940–64 (1940 = 100)*

The index of prices is based upon prices prevailing in January of each year.

Sources: consumer goods and services: Feinstein, Table 61, re-plotted on base 1940 = 100. rayon prices: M.C. *Man-made cellulosic fibres*, Appendix 3, Table 3, supplemented by internal sources for war years.

mergers, and new projects brought to fruition meant that the Courtaulds which faced the I.C.I. bid in December 1961 was in many ways a very different entity from the Courtaulds of six years earlier. It was different not only in the rather more varied sources of profits, as shown earlier,[2] but in its structure and its potential for further change and advance. The first steps formally to inaugurate the diversification policy were taken in January 1957, before the acquisition of British Celanese. A memorandum called 'Some Considerations relating to Expansion and Diversification' was sent to Hanbury-Williams over the joint signatures of Wilson and Kearton. Concluding that the man-made fibre industry had reached a

[1] M.C. *Man-made cellulosic fibres*, pp. 18–19.

[2] Tables 19 and 20, above, pp. 130 and 131.

stage at which further expansion was likely to be slow, it advocated that Courtaulds should expand within the industry by amalgamations which could lead to greater efficiency and higher margins and/or by the entry into new fields through buying up moderate-sized companies which showed promise of expansion. After a tedious exchange of letters occasioned by Hanbury-Williams's failure to understand certain points and some patient explaining by Wilson, the Board agreed to Kearton being charged with the task of 'instituting enquiries into the possibility and desirability of the Company diversifying its activities into cognate industries'. A year later a diversification team, operating as a subsidiary company, Group Developments Ltd., started work in earnest. But meanwhile British Celanese had been acquired.

II

The possibility of renewing the negotiations which in 1937–40 had nearly led to a merger between Courtaulds and British Celanese[1] floated to the surface again after the death of Henry Dreyfus in 1944. Some time in 1946, George Whigham, who had assumed the chairmanship of British Celanese, had mentioned the desirability of reopening the negotiations. Conveyed via Lord Bicester[2] to Hanbury-Williams and thence to the Courtaulds Board, the idea had not been greeted with approval because of fears that the Labour government then in office would seek to nationalize the rayon industry; the near-total monopoly possessed by a merged Courtaulds–Celanese would provide a ready pretext. At a further meeting arranged by Bicester in July 1947, Whigham pressed the advantages of amalgamation as a defence against American export competition but Hanbury-Williams repeated his objection to 'handing the Government a ripe plum for nationalization'. A decade later, however, changed circumstances had combined to put the whole idea in a different light. The return of Conservative governments in 1951 and again in 1957 had fended off the threat of nationalization; the onset in 1956 of the European Free Trade Area proposals and the creation of the European Economic Community in 1957 had signalled the desirability of larger groupings to exploit the possibilities of competition in larger markets; and falling profits in rayon had given an extra urgency to moves towards lower costs and higher

[1] Vol. II, pp. 357–9.

[2] Partner in Morgan Grenfell who, with Lord Catto, had been active in the 1937–40 negotiations.

efficiency. There had already been ominous signs amongst the lesser rayon companies, those that had survived the crash of the 1930s.[1] In 1953 both Breda Visada and British Bemberg closed down, the latter going into liquidation; of those that still tottered along, Kirklees ceased to pay dividends after 1951,[2] North British Rayon after 1952, Harbens after 1954, and British Enka after 1955. North British approached Courtaulds in 1955 with a view to being taken over; Courtaulds declined and North British went into liquidation in 1956.

If Courtaulds' directors got little cheer from their slipping profits after 1954–5 their opposite numbers at British Celanese must have got very much less, as Table 23 suggests.

TABLE 23

Courtaulds and British Celanese: profits and interest, before tax, 1949–57

£ mn.

Year	*Courtaulds*	*British Celanese*
1948–9	6·6	3·1*
1949–50	8·0	4·1
1950–1	16·8	7·3
1951–2	18·5	2·5
1952–3	9·8	1·8 (9 months only)
1953–4	18·2	4·1†
1954–5	19·4	3·3
1955–6	17·7	2·4
1956–7	15·2	1·6

* 1948–9 to 1951–2, year ending 30 June.
† 1953–4 onwards, year ending 31 March.

Although sales of the main product of British Celanese, acetate textile yarn, had not fallen as much as those of Courtaulds' viscose equivalent, the Celanese subsidiary products—acetate staple fibre, chemicals, knitted and woven fabrics and garments—had not provided as much counterbalancing expansion as did Courtaulds' other viscose products, staple fibre and tyre yarn. Nor had the promising new Celanese ventures, triacetate yarns (marketed as 'Tricel') and nylon 6 ('Celon'), been developed in time to contribute as much to profits as had Courtaulds' participation in B.N.S.

[1] See Vol. II, pp. 333–4.
[2] They recommenced in 1959, but see below, p. 163.

The unsatisfactory financial record of British Celanese in the inter-war years had led to a high proportion of preference capital, debentures, and mortgage loans. Having been in arrears on its preference dividends and failed to pay an ordinary dividend until 1944 the unwonted access of profits in the 1950s apparently induced the company to go to the other extreme, distributing an average of nearly 28 per cent. of its profits as dividends over the years 1952–7. Even so, the balance sheet at March 1957 revealed the existence of £5·5 million in cash and government securities, representing about a quarter of the net tangible assets. Despite his sometimes bizarre behaviour Dreyfus had imparted a remarkable momentum to British Celanese;[1] since his death nothing had quite replaced it. By the beginning of 1957 when negotiations with Courtaulds recommenced, British Celanese had rising costs, poor profits, and underutilized assets but some real potential for future development.

In February 1957 Whigham lunched with Hanbury-Williams and other Courtaulds directors, and was sounded on the likely Celanese reactions to the creation of some form of mutual association designed to strengthen their joint position in an expected European Common Market. Discussions were then entrusted to their financial advisers, Barings for Courtaulds, and Morgan Grenfell for Celanese. There was some toying with the idea of a holding company but by April agreement had been reached on a merger to be effected by Courtaulds making an offer for the whole of Celanese capital. The disparity between the current strength and past performance of the two companies was very evident. Courtaulds' net tangible assets were put at £118·3 million, those of British Celanese at £21·9 million; stock-market prices for £1 ordinary shares on 11 April were 35*s*. 3*d*. and 15*s*. 3*d*. respectively. The offer was 2 Courtaulds ordinary for 3 Celanese. To deal with the Celanese 7 and 7½ per cent. first and second preference stocks, a new Courtaulds second preference stock at 6 per cent. was created. The offers for this were 6 for 5 of the 7 per cent. and 5 for 4 of the 7½ per cent. Celanese recommended acceptance of this take-over bid. By 3 June over 90 per cent. acceptances had been received.[2]

The acquisition of British Celanese marked a turning-point in Courtaulds' history in a number of ways. It was the first increase in capital other than by bonus issues. It brought the company much nearer

[1] See Vol. II, pp. 354–9; also my 'War Demand and industrial supply: the "Dope Scandal", 1915–19', in J. M. Winter (ed.), *War and Economic Development* 'Cambridge, 1975), which looks at the origins of British Celanese during World War I.

[2] For consequent changes in Courtaulds' capital structure, see below, p. 165.

to a complete monopoly of all British rayon production by making it the dominant producer of both viscose and acetate. In particular, it enabled Courtaulds greatly to expand two promising new outlets for acetate: triacetate yarns and acetate tow for cigarette filter tips. Courtaulds had been working on the former for some time and in 1955 had moved, somewhat tentatively, to commercial production at the Little Heath plant in Coventry, using the trade name 'Courpleta'. Disappointing sales ensued, however, and the Celanese product, together with the livelier and less cumbersome trade name 'Tricel', was taken over with encouraging results in sales for dress fabrics.[1] So too with cigarette tow. Courtaulds had been trying to push their 'Fibroceta' in this direction before the merger but thereafter—and coincident with a big shift towards the use of filter tips in cigarettes (2 per cent. in U.K. sales in 1954–5, 16 per cent. in 1955–60, and 65 per cent. in 1967)—a greatly increased output was concentrated in the Celanese plant at Spondon.[2]

If by this act of horizontal integration Courtaulds thus secured a wider base in fibre production, of much greater significance was the substantial increase in vertical integration effected by the merger. Despite its origins in textiles, the Courtaulds enterprise had consistently refrained from going further in textile manufacturing than the maintenance of Samuel Courtauld & Co., and of a small warp-knitting unit, with garment manufacture confined to Luvisca Ltd., surviving, like the knitting unit, from an experiment of the 1930s[3] In complete contrast British Celanese had a substantial investment in weaving, knitting, dyeing, finishing, fabric printing, and garment-manufacture; and, as already shown,[4] had been built up in the inter-war years by the skilful advertising of Celanese as a brand name for women's underwear. Much of the investment had been at the main Celanese plant at Spondon, but there were also several yarn spinning or processing plants as well as weaving and knitting mills in various parts of Britain. In addition, one series of subsidiaries made up garments and another marketed, sometimes using their brand names. There were also knitting subsidiaries in South Africa and New Zealand. But the creation of a vertically integrated, chemical-textile enterprise—which had indeed been Henry Dreyfus's main contribution to the rayon industry—also demanded substantial investment in basic production facilities. And in acetate these were of a different and more chemically

[1] For data on output, see below, pp. 190 and 272.

[2] M.C. *Man-made cellulosic fibres*, p. 126.

[3] See Vol. II, pp. 367–70. [4] See Vol. II, p. 271.

complex kind than in viscose. Celanese had directed much research effort before World War II into seeking methods of lowering the production costs of its basic raw materials, acetic acid and acetic anhydride. Substantial investments to this end had been made at Spondon.[1] So with Courtaulds' own step towards vertical integration in the form of the wood-pulp producing venture, Saiccor,[2] the newly merged Courtaulds–Celanese group had a very wide vertical range from owning forests to selling underwear, and including on the way the production of sundry organic chemicals relevant to the paint and plastics industries.

III

Having thus absorbed Celanese, Courtaulds got busy with the diversification policy. Group Developments Ltd., the vehicle for carrying out the policy, was controlled by Frank Kearton and Arthur Knight, with the former as chairman. It was run from an office in Hanover Square, London headquarters of British Celanese, of which company Kearton had already become a managing director. In a statement of March 1958, Kearton and Knight made it clear that their concern was neither to find new uses for surplus physical assets within the group nor to seek means of extending existing sections of the business. They were looking for medium-sized businesses, with prospects of rapid growth, preferably in some way cognate to skills existing within Courtaulds and requiring a capital investment of perhaps £250,000–1,000,000 which could rapidly secure effective control. By the autumn of 1959, their staff had made some 54 detailed reports on companies in such diverse fields as paint, packaging, tyres and rubber products, hotels, jewellery, electronics, plastics, scientific instruments, engineering, building materials, mechanical handling, refrigeration, paper and board, aluminium foil, and travel agencies. Their scrutiny was clearly nothing if not wide; and cognateness had evidently assumed a prodigious extensibility. But already in the summer of 1958 Group Developments' thoughts had come to be concentrated especially upon paint and packaging.

In June of that year the Board received a memorandum from Kearton and Knight recommending paint as a desirable field of investment on the grounds that return on assets was good (15 per cent. and upwards); that it used raw materials which could be provided by the Courtaulds Group (meaning in practice the Celanese chemical plant at Spondon); and that

[1] See above, pp. 51–2 and Vol. II, p. 354, n. 1. [2] See above, pp. 112–16.

there were various technical and financial advantages to be gained by such a venture. Group Developments Ltd. consequently sought borrowing facilities from Courtaulds Ltd. of up to £500,000 with a view to buying into an existing company. The Board granted them. Certain proposals had already been made to Cellon Ltd., a firm manufacturing various industrial coatings, largely based on nitro-cellulose;[1] and a further paper, 'Plans for entering the Paint Industry', was presented to the Board in July. This envisaged the acquisition of Cellon as a spring-board for a 'major entry' into the paint industry the profit potential of which was sketched in optimistic terms. A bid was made for all the ordinary capital of £160,000 (nominal) of 5*s.* shares at £1 per share, i.e. £640,000. The Cellon Board recommended acceptance and by September control had been gained. Group Developments quickly came back for more, securing approval from the Board for further investment of up to £2 million in diversification over the next six months.

Investigations into the packaging industry were pursued with speed and vigour. In November the Board pondered upon a set of proposals from the Group Developments team which bore the title 'Policy for investment in packaging'. The advantages of the packaging business were paraded. American experience and research in Britain suggested that expenditure on packaging was likely to grow twice as fast as the national income; despite the development of some large companies, notably Metal Box Ltd., medium-sized enterprises were available; the technologies employed were diverse and many fitted in with 'know-how' already extant in the group, such as cellulose film and plastics. A loosely organized 'Packaging Group' was envisaged. A very brief sketch of the structure and organization of the group began with the disarmingly bland remark that 'the form of the Group and its organisation would evolve'. Noting the existent tendency toward either vertical integration, for example in the paper and packaging firm of E. S. & A. Robinson, or of the horizontal integration typified by Metal Box, it was agreed that the proposed group should attempt to cover a variety of types of packaging. To this end the Board was asked to consider the acquisition of three companies: the Pearlite Box Co., making waxed boxes and cartons; Betts & Co., manufacturers of collapsible tubes[2] and capsules for bottles; and Reads Ltd., Liverpool-based producers of steel drums and tinplate cans. The first was a small private company with

[1] For the origins of the firm see 'War demand and industrial supply: the "Dope Scandal", 1915–19', loc. cit.

[2] i.e. the sort used for toothpaste and the like.

most of the 1,869,000 issued ordinary 1*s.* shares in the hands of one controlling family. A bid of 2*s.* 2*d.* per share was thought to be acceptable, thus involving an investment of approximately £202,000. The second was a slightly larger public company for obtaining control of which an investment of some £380,000 was thought to be necessary. The third company was by far the biggest. Starting as a partnership in 1869, Reads had become a private company in 1909 and public only in 1953. With the assistance of the American Can Co., it had recently entered the 'open-top' can market.[1] It was believed that an offer of 21*s.* per share for the whole of the ordinary capital would be recommended by the Board to the shareholders. This would mean an investment of some £1,430,000. All three companies had respectable profit records. And all three were bought, control having passed to Group Developments Ltd. by December 1958.

The acquisition of these four companies in paint and packaging—Cellon, Pearlite, Betts, and Reads—together made up the spearhead of Courtaulds' diversification offensive. But they were only a fraction of the investment programme taking imaginative shape in Kearton's mind. In October 1958 he had already told the Board about negotiations with companies involving possible commitments of £4½–5 million, and had indicated a rate of investment in diversification of the order of £20 million in the next five years reaching £50 million over ten years. Not surprisingly, the Board began to show signs of wariness, pressing periodically for more consultation before commitments and demanding pauses in what its more conservative members must have apprehended as a headlong rush into the unknown. The reality behind 'Fred Kittler's' speech in George Courtauld's skit is evident enough.[2] Group Developments assured the main Board that diversification was 'well worth while and must be vigorously pursued'. More companies were gobbled up. A firm of painting contractors, T. H. Kenyon & Sons, was bought in May 1959, at a cost of a mere £71,250. The use of steel in tyres had earlier been investigated by a special panel set up by the Board and in November 1958 Kearton and Knight submitted a scheme for the establishment of a company jointly with British Ropes Ltd. The Board agreed and a new company, Steel Cords Ltd., was formed in January 1959. Group Developments subscribed £40,000 of the capital, British Ropes £10,000. Looking for an opening

[1] 'Open-top' is the technical name for the standard type of can which is filled, closed on special machinery, and then requires to be opened by the ultimate consumer with the aid of a tin-opener.

[2] See above, p. 146.

in the plastics field Kearton came up with National Plastics Ltd., a company with potential, but so poor a recent record that it offered the merits of a tax loss. By November 1959 it had been bought for £552,833. In the course of 1959 and 1960, the Board agreed to a further £1,500,000 to be invested in expansion of Reads and some £362,000 in Steel Cords.

Then, in January 1960, came a very much bigger acquisition, so big that although Group Developments carried out the initial negotiations, the purchase was done directly by Courtaulds Ltd. rather than through the medium of the diversification subsidiary. The chosen target was Pinchin Johnson & Associates Ltd., the second largest manufacturer of paints in U.K., and possessed of a string of subsidiaries and associates in France, Belgium, Italy, Germany, Switzerland, South Africa, Hong Kong, India, Pakistan, Argentina, U.S.A., and Canada, with a world turnover of nearly £30 million annually. The firm's main concentration was in industrial paints and lacquers, with a small interest, which it was proposing to increase, in decorative paints for the retail market. Talks in 1959 had indicated that Pinchin Johnson were open to an offer, as advantages were seen in an association which would offer a supply of the requisite organic chemicals which were increasingly forming the raw materials of paint manufacture, and which would thereby put them in a better position to compete with I.C.I. To Group Developments the merits of acquisition lay precisely in an extension—after the satisfactory experience with Cellon—of the profitable outlet for the raw materials available within the group from the petrochemical plant at Spondon. After Kearton and Knight had commended the purchase, the Board agreed that an offer should be made on a share-exchange basis for the ordinary capital, accompanied by a cash offer for the preference shares. The basis of the ordinary-share exchange was 2 Courtaulds £1 shares for 3 Pinchin Johnson 10*s*. shares. At current prices the bid as a whole was worth about £17,000,000. The operation was successful and by February sufficient acceptances had been received. So Courtaulds had taken another major step on the path of integration and diversification.[1]

IV

This was the last of the acquisitions carried out as a direct result of the doings of Group Developments Ltd. At the end of 1961 the companies which it had acquired and run as subsidiaries were in various ways absorbed

[1] For the consequent increase in capital, see below, p. 165.

into Courtaulds as a group[1] and Group Developments itself ceased to operate. But there were yet more acquisitions and new projects which, though not conducted under the aegis of Group Developments, gave further momentum to the progress of Courtaulds' diversification. There was the setting-up in 1959 of British Lego Ltd. on the basis of a licence from A/s Lego of Denmark to make toy building-bricks from cellulose acetate. There were sundry new projects overseas or under the aegis of British Cellophane. But of the major acquisitions to be considered here two ostensibly lay at the extreme ends of the vertically integrated structure which was taking shape: the buying up of Gossard (Holdings) Ltd., which brought, *inter alia*, a chain of retail lingerie shops and a department store; and the foundation of the Usutu Pulp Co., which added to their investment in African forests. In reality, this latter venture was an act of horizontal rather than vertical expansion. So too was Courtaulds' entry into the field of glass fibre production, which included the purchase of Marglass Ltd. More obvious examples of horizontal integration were the taking-over of Harbens, British Enka, and, eventually, Kirklees, thereby almost completing Courtaulds' absorption of all the remaining native rayon producers.

Early in 1959 the then chairman of Gossard (Holdings) Ltd. wrote to one of the directors of British Celanese, whom he happened to know, telling him that he believed a bid for Gossards would be forthcoming from an American source. He wished to forestall this bid and inquired whether Group Developments might be interested in acquiring his company. The matter was referred to Arthur Knight who, after some investigations, decided that Gossards would not be an appropriate acquisition for Group Developments but might be of interest to Courtaulds' group of garment companies gathered under the Celanese wing, and specifically to Kearton, this time in the latter's capacity as managing director of Celanese. The upshot was a proposal by Kearton, put forward to the Board in June 1959, that Courtaulds should make an offer worth £2,342,500 for the ordinary shares of Gossard (Holdings) Ltd. The bid represented a price of 13*s*. 6*d*. for the 5*s*. Gossard ordinary shares and a 40 per cent. advance on the book value of the equity. However, the assets were thought to be undervalued, and the Board accepted Kearton's evident enthusiasm for buying Gossards. The bid was made and succeeded. In August 1959 Courtaulds had thereby completed another diverse purchase and moved into the world of making and selling corsets and brassières (so oddly known as 'foundation garments')

[1] Except Pearlite Box which was sold in July 1961, see below, p. 168.

not to speak of laundering, dry cleaning, tailoring, and retail shopkeeping. An admittedly somewhat ramshackle empire with outliers in Germany, Switzerland, and South Africa, it also included a firm of knitting-machine manufacturers and an exceedingly run-down retail department store in Swindon. The logic of the acquisition appealed to Kearton: it would link up with the burgeoning garment division as well as providing outlets and experience in marketing. And so it was bought. When Courtaulds had merged with British Celanese, Rab Butler had remarked, in a letter to Hanbury-Williams, 'I only wish Sam were here, for I feel sure he would have been very pleased.' The pleasure of Samuel Courtauld IV at the acquisition of a string of bra shops and a laundry in Poplar would perhaps have been less readily predictable.

The origins of the Usutu Pulp Co. could hardly have provided a greater contrast. In 1948 the U.K. High Commissioner for the British Protectorate of Basutoland, Bechuanaland, and Swaziland was Sir Evelyn Baring—later Lord Howick and, of course, a member of the same family whose banking business advised Courtaulds from time to time. He apparently originated the idea of a massive afforestation scheme by which some 100,000 acres of land by the Great Usutu river in Swaziland should be planted with conifers suitable for both timber and wood-pulp. The Colonial Development Corporation (C.D.C.) bought the land and started planting in 1950. In 1955–7 the paper and pulp firm of Bowater investigated the possibility of building a pulp mill, with an output of 50,000 tons, in the area but decided against it on the grounds that the costs would be such as to make the product uncompetitive in world markets. In 1957–8 Courtaulds had discussions with C.D.C. and in February 1958 Kearton and Sheldon visited Usutu. In November, as a consequence of reports to the Board by Kearton a development panel was set up jointly with C.D.C. to carry out detailed investigations in Swaziland. The panel's report arrived in May 1959. In his covering letter to the chairman, Kearton, sending a copy of the report, commented: 'The project involves a degree of risk but to my mind it looks attractive.' The report was optimistic in tone. It accepted the contentions of Courtaulds members of the panel that they could build a mill of 100,000 tons capacity embodying new techniques derived from their experience with Saiccor more cheaply than the Bowater mission had estimated; and it advocated the setting up a company jointly-financed by Courtaulds and C.D.C., with an initial capital of £5 million, further money to be raised by debentures to cover an investment expected to total about £11 million. In June—at about the same time as he was proposing the acquisition of

Gossards—Kearton put these proposals to the Board. They were accepted and in July 1959 the Usutu Pulp Co. was registered in Swaziland. Courtaulds' initial investment was £2,500,000 representing its equal share of the ordinary capital. It should be emphasized that the output of the Usutu mill—unbleached sulphate pulp—was intended for sale to the paper and board industry and *not* for providing the raw material of viscose-rayon manufacture. The latter was the rationale of Saiccor and thus fitted in to the pattern of vertical integration. The Usutu venture, on the other hand, represented a horizontal expansion of the new involvement in making wood-pulp. To market the Usutu product a selling company, known as the Springwood Cellulose Co. Ltd., was formed in March 1961.

The move into glass fibres and fabrics started with some informal discussions between some Courtaulds directors and their opposite numbers in the big American textile company, United Merchants and Manufacturers (U.M.M.). Originally concerned with the possibility of a joint venture in North America, the discussions turned to the British market. Rendall, and later Knight and Mynors, took an active part in forwarding these discussions during 1960. A market survey was completed and in November the Board, approving a paper submitted by Knight, agreed to further investigations. The net result was that in July 1961, after another report submitted jointly by Knight and Mynors, the Board approved proposals to set up a joint company with U.M.M. This envisaged the development over a five-year period of a vertically integrated enterprise, stretching from furnaces producing the glass from which the yarn was to be spun through to weaving, finishing, and the marketing of fabrics; it would involve a joint capital expenditure of £4·2 million. The joint company, Spun Glass Ltd. was incorporated and a site for the enterprise was sought. The notion of converting and equipping the disused yarn mill at Wolverhampton[1] seemed attractive but the Engineering department's estimate of nearly £2 million to do so was so far from attractive as to be horrifying. Mynors, now responsible for the project, proposed in November a less ambitious scheme and the immediate acquisition of one of the very small number of companies engaged in glass fabric weaving and finishing, though not in the yarn-extrusion process. The firm in question was Marglass, whose mill was located at Sherborne in Dorset; it was owned by Frederick Marsden (Holdings) Ltd. who also ran a small rayon-weaving business in Coventry; Mynors had known the chairman, Frederick Marsden, for some years. Discussion involving Mynors, Knight,

[1] See above, p. 48.

and Marsden finally produced an agreement to sell. The Board approved and in January 1962 Spun Glass Ltd. bought the whole of the share capital of Marglass Ltd. for £365,000. The press notice announced the intention of developing and enlarging Marglass and to 'produce glass yarn in a fully integrated business'.

Ever since the rayon boom of the 1920s, those of the smaller British rayon producers that survived had perforce to live in the shadow of Courtaulds. Sometimes they objected, in vain, to Courtaulds' low prices; in the 1950s as in the 1930s, as members of the British Viscose Association before the war or of the Man-made Fibres Producers Committee after it; sometimes they undercut Courtaulds in particular lines.[1] But their lack of resources and a narrow range of products made it increasingly difficult for them to stay alive in rayon as it came under market pressure. As already shown, some had gone under by the mid-1950s. Just as Courtaulds had decided against initiating any take over of the small competitors in the 1930s, so they did in the 1950s.[2] But later, after more approaches by the competitor companies, they took over Harbens in 1959, British Enka in 1961, Kirklees in 1962, as well as Lustrafil and Nelsons Silk in 1963. The immediate context of this apparent switch in policy is provided by the slump in rayon sales between 1956 and 1960. Fig. 6 plots the values of Courtaulds' sales of textile yarn, tyre yarn, and staple fibre. Although the last of these showed only a 6 per cent. drop between 1956–7 and 1957–8, those of viscose textile yarn suffered a fall of 34 per cent., and tyre yarn of 27 per cent. between their respective peaks in 1956–7 and 1955–6 to the trough of 1958–9. In his letter of December 1956 Wilson had written of the need to increase or maintain both prices and sales of both yarn and staple fibre. Prices of tyre yarn were reduced in January 1956 and again in March 1957; sales fell nevertheless. Prices of staple were maintained and a small drop in sales ensued; those of yarn, after the good year 1956–7, were raised in January 1957 and a massive drop ensued. In the circumstances, the existence of excess capacity in rayon yarn seemed a logical economic corollary. The old yarn mill at Aber was closed down; and the merits and demerits of taking over and closing down some of the smaller companies began to be reconsidered.

In 1955 the prosperity which Harbens Ltd. had been enjoying for some years began to collapse and worsened in the following years. A new spun-dyed yarn marketed by Courtaulds began to undermine hope of recovery,

[1] See Vol. II, pp. 237–40, 332–45; M.C. *Man-made cellulosic fibres*, p. 62.
[2] See above, p. 150.

and early in 1959 Kearton was approached by one of Harbens' directors. In March he set out a paper on the advantages and disadvantages of taking over Harbens. Calculations suggested that if production were continued then the marginal profit on both textile yarn and tyre cord (which Harbens also produced) was such that a take-over would be worth while at the low price for which the company could be acquired; alternatively

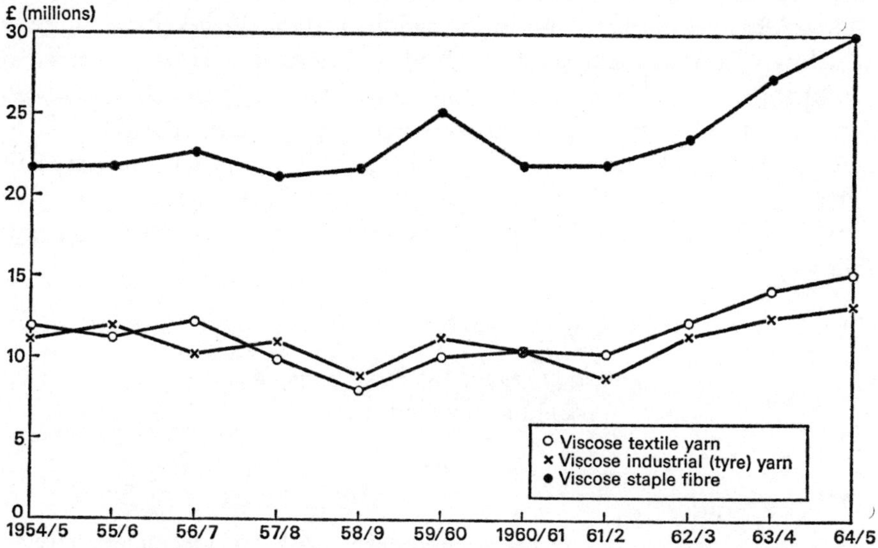

FIG. 6. *Courtaulds, U.K.: rayon sales, 1954/5–1964/5*

if the plant was closed down the break-up value of the company was 'not negligible'. He recommended the continuance of negotiations. In May a formal offer was made on a basis of 1 Courtaulds £1 ordinary for 9 Harbens 5*s.* ordinary; it was accepted.[1] Harbens' works were partly closed down, their customers' yarn orders being met from Courtaulds' currently surplus capacity; tyre-yarn production was continued there for some time, as demand and sales recovered sharply from 1960–1 onwards.

British Enka, a subsidiary of A.K.U., found its textile and tyre-yarn profitability falling sharply in the 1950s. The former suffered from the general fall in demand, the latter was burdened by higher costs which made it hard to compete with Courtaulds, especially when Courtaulds cut tyre-yarn prices again in 1960 in order to meet competition from nylon tyre yarns. An expensive investment was made in a viscose-film plant,

[1] See p. 165 below for the resulting changes in Courtaulds' capital.

installed in their works at Aintree. But although a large net loss in 1956 was followed by only smaller losses in the next two years and a profit in 1959, a loss reappeared in 1960. In the summer of 1961 Wilson was approached by a representative of A.K.U. with the idea of providing aid in one form or another. After the inevitable talk of surplus capacity, the Board, having accepted proposals put forward by Wilson for Courtaulds to make an offer for the whole of the subscribed capital of British Enka, resolved to do so as a 'desirable further step in the rationalization of the rayon industry which would be in the interests of all concerned (and not least the staff and workpeople)'. By November the bid, worth some £1,875,000, had been accepted. The cellulose film unit was closed down immediately, having run for five weeks at a loss of £60,000; the tyre-yarn plant ceased in February 1962, and the output concentrated in Courtaulds' existing factories. The Aintree works was subsequently turned over to 'Celon' and knitting.

TABLE 24

Production capacity of Rayon companies taken over by Courtaulds

mn. lb.

Company	*Viscose textile yarn*	*Viscose industrial yarn*	*Viscose staple fibre*	*Acetate yarn and fibres*	*Total rayon*
1955 Courtaulds	70	62	223	19	374
British Celanese	—	—	—	57	57
Lustrafil	1·5	—	—	—	1·5
Nelsons Silk	—	—	—	2	2
British Enka	11	15	—	—	26
Harbens	4	—	—	—	4
Kirklees	5	—	—	—	5
	91·5	77	223	78	469·5
1962 Courtaulds Group	60	65	290	79	494

Source: adapted from M.C. *Man-made cellulosic fibres*, p. 103.

The purchases of Harbens and British Enka together constituted the most important, after British Celanese, of the acquisitions of other rayon companies by Courtaulds, as Table 24 shows. It will be convenient to consider in this context the fate of the remaining companies even though they were not absorbed by Courtaulds in these years before the I.C.I. bid.

Kirklees Ltd. made its first approach to Courtaulds, suggesting a take-over, in 1959. A producer solely of viscose textile yarn, it ran into difficulties in the depression of 1951–2 and came to rely largely on chemical production for its profits. Even this proved inadequate and late in 1961 a further approach was made, resulting in Courtaulds making a successful offer for Kirklees in June 1962, at the cheap price of one Courtaulds £1 ordinary for every 12 Kirklees 5*s.* shares. Lustrafil and Nelsons Silk were both subsidiaries of James Nelson Ltd. The former ceased production after a serious fire in 1961; Courtaulds took over its yarn business but did not acquire the company until 1963 when the parent company, which was both a knitting concern as well as a small acetate producer, was bought for rather different reasons.[1] Only one survivor was not acquired: in 1962, after some abortive discussions with Courtaulds, Lansil Ltd., which started life as the Cellulose Acetate Silk Co.,[2] was eventually bought by the American firm of Chemstrand Ltd. (part of the Monsanto group).

The rayon acquisitions of this period were subsequently explained by Courtaulds—in evidence to the Monopolies Commission inquiry initiated in 1965—as part of a deliberate policy of 'the rationalization of the U.K. viscose industry'; and, as we have seen, the phrase occurs in the Board minutes of the day. If all was not quite so carefully planned as the wording would imply, there is no doubt, as Table 24 indicates, that by securing maximum control Courtaulds were able by these moves and without a price-cutting conflict to change the types of rayon produced within an increased total output by closing down inefficient plants producing the decreasingly wanted viscose textile yarn, and concentrating on the efficient production of more of what was in demand. Courtaulds were probably right, despite the doubts subsequently expressed by the Monopolies Commission,[3] in their diagnosis that sooner or later the smaller companies would have collapsed anyway or, as happened to Lansil, sold out to one of the American giants—thus providing bridgeheads which Courtaulds had no reason to encourage.

V

Some possible costs or benefits of this policy of acquisition and diversification will be considered later.[4] For the moment, suffice to look at three

[1] See below, pp. 278–9.
[2] See Vol. II, pp. 272, 351, 355.
[3] M.C. *Man-made cellulosic fibres*, p. 62.
[4] See below, pp. 311–18.

sorts of short-run consequences, mainly evident in the years before the I.C.I. bid: the changes in capital structure; certain short-term, unforeseen disadvantages of the policy which helped to produce the falling return on assets within the period, as already shown in Table 18 in Chapter VII; and the changes in organization made in an attempt to fit the new parts into the old structure.

In Table 25 are shown simply the major acquisitions made by Courtaulds during the five years between the January 1957 memorandum by Wilson

TABLE 25

Main acquisions by Courtaulds, 1957–61

Company	*Date of bid*	*Value put on bid at the time*	*Direct cost to Courtaulds*		
			Cash	*Ordinary shares*	*2nd preference shares*
		£	£	(£ units)	(£ units)
British Celanese	Apr. 1957	19,471,930	1,062,500	5,012,356	9,512,500
Cellon	Aug. 1958	640,000	640,000	—	—
	May 1961	150,000	—	—	171,000
Reads	Dec. 1958	1,430,000	1,430,000	—	—
Harbens	Apr. 1959	675,000	253,125	266,900	—
Gossards	July 1959	2,362,000	2,362,000	—	—
National Plastics	Oct. 1959	552,833	552,833	—	—
Pinchin Johnson	Jan. 1960	16,500,000	865,000	5,259,600	—
British Enka	Oct. 1961	1,875,000	1,875,000	—	—
Total		43,656,763	9,040,458	10,538,856	9,683,500

and Kearton[1] and the I.C.I. bid in December 1961. It takes no account of new investments, such as the Usutu venture; of smaller acquisitions, such as T. H. Kenyon Ltd.; of companies re-sold during the period; or of take-overs by British Cellophane or other subsidiaries at home or overseas. Even so, it shows that successful bids with a total contemporary valuation of nearly £44 million had been made during these years; and purchases effected, in cash or by share exchange, to the approximate value of, respectively, £9 million and £20 million. The consequential changes in the cash-flow position was beginning to cause the Board some apprehension in the summer of 1961—a matter which is, however, best considered as a part of the circumstances preceding the I.C.I. bid. The changes in the

[1] See above, p. 148.

capital structure were there for all to see. Those set out in Table 26 cover all the acquisitions involving share issues up to and including the purchase of the Cellon preference shares in May 1961.

TABLE 26

Changes in Courtaulds' capital structure, 1954–61

Date	*Ordinary £1 shares*		*5% cumulative preference £1 shares authorized and issued*	*6% cumulative preference £1 shares*	
	Authorized	*Issued*		*Authorized*	*Issued*
	£	£	£	£	£
1954 (Mar.)	48,000,000	48,000,000	8,000,000	—	—
1956 (Mar.)	50,000,000	48,079,453*	8,000,000	—	—
1958 (Mar.)	65,000,000	53,337,730*	8,000,000	9,512,500	9,512,500
1961 (Mar.)	100,000,000	78,985,413*	8,000,000	15,000,000	9,512,500
1961 (Dec.)	100,000,000	79,177,156*	8,000,000	15,000,000	9,683,500

* These figures include amounts issued under the co-partnership scheme, see above, p. 128.

The main increases in ordinary and preference shares were made, as is evident from Table 26, to cover the Celanese and Pinchin Johnson mergers; a 1 for 3 bonus issue during the financial year 1960–1 capitalized, for the benefit of shareholders, some of the company's still substantial reserves.

Not surprisingly this tremendous rush of company gobbling produced some indigestion. Failures in expectation of return on capital invested became only too evident in some schemes; managements of acquired companies proved to be weaker than had been supposed; mistakes in strategy quickly showed up in others. To cover all gains and losses would be impossible; some illustrations must suffice.

The ventures in southern Africa provide a range of indications. The Usutu Pulp Co. rapidly presented problems and incurred costs which suggest that Courtaulds had been more than a little over-optimistic. Work began in 1959 but the proposed starting date of July 1961 had to be put back because of sundry delays and difficulties. By early 1962, however, it was reported that although the mill had started it had been working with virtually no output but with maximum expenses—trial runs, training of staff, start-up expenditure, etc. The total of such expenses was approaching £1 million. The overdraft was large, the cash drain serious. The project was admitted to 'bristle with difficulties'. Not for some years and after some written-off investment did the Usutu Co. begin to make profits. Saiccor itself, the investment from which Usutu was a sort of horizontal 'spin-off', continued to encounter difficulties during this period. There were two interrelated problems: the maintenance of quality in its pulp output; and the reduction of costs in face of the fall in world wood-pulp prices which set in after the rise that had stimulated the original enterprise in 1951. Throughout the period covered by this chapter and on into the 1960s, Kearton maintained a barrage of letters to the manager of Saiccor on the subject of quality, productivity, cost reduction, and pulp prices. These had fallen from £72–8 per ton in 1951 to £55–60 in November 1961. As fast as this lowered the cost of viscose production, so it also put pressure on Saiccor costs. And if Courtaulds' rayon mills, not only in England but also in North America, as well as British Cellophane's factories, were to use Saiccor pulp—and heavy pressure was put upon them to do so—then the quality of the pulp had to be improved and maintained. Some real success was achieved; by the end of 1961, the Saiccor output had risen from some 44,000 short tons per year to well over 100,000 tons; all of it was being absorbed within the Courtaulds group; the Greenfield staple-fibre plant was using 60 per cent. Saiccor pulp in its pulp requirements; and Saiccor was making profits. But not very large ones—and its liquidity position was soon to worsen. In contrast to these difficulties, the South African off-shoot of Gossards rapidly proved to be the best profit-earner in the whole of that particular acquisition; in 1961, for example, it was responsible for some 46 per cent. of the profits of Gossard (Holdings) Ltd. Similarly South African Fabrics, one of the British Celanese knitting subsidiaries, also proved a profitable concern, increasing their sales and profits from 1960 onwards.

To move nearer home, a clear example of over-optimistic forecasting was provided by the glass venture. Plunging into a field in which they had no experience, Courtaulds found that this piece of enterprise rapidly proved to be more costly and less profitable than the survey of 1960 had predicted. Market demand was less buoyant, over-capacity became evident, and various difficulties developed at the production end. By 1964 rates of return on it had not come up to the levels forecast and only in 1965 did an up-turn become evident.

Certain developments in the paint and packaging area of the diversification programme suggest mistakes in strategy or, at least, an excessive optimism about the likely reactions of competitors into whose preserves Courtaulds had charged with no little gusto. Before examining this topic, however, it is necessary briefly to look at certain aspects of the development of Courtaulds' subsidiary British Cellophane Ltd. Formed in 1937, with the French proprietors of the 'Cellophane' trade mark,[1] this venture represented the earliest significant move by Courtaulds outside the field of rayon and textiles. After experiencing falling output and profits during World War II, it emerged, with Courtaulds owning 75 per cent. of the equity, to participate in the post-war recovery boom as demand for cellulose-film wrappings in such trades as confectionery reasserted itself. Along with recovery and hopes of further expansion there also re-emerged a question which had long exercised the minds of those Courtaulds' directors who were concerned with British Cellophane's affairs. Much of the output of film was bought by converters who received rebates varying with the size of their purchases; by far the biggest was the British paper and packaging firm of E. S. & A. Robinson Ltd. Should British Cellophane integrate forward by moving into the converting business itself, thereby acquiring more control over the disposal of its final products and participating more directly in the profits of the packaging industry? And, if this were done, would the most appropriate move be the setting up a company jointly with Robinsons? Discussions went on sporadically for many years, before, during, and after the war. By 1943 it was agreed that an unwritten understanding existed by which Robinsons would not go in for the manufacture of film and British Cellophane would not go into the printing and bag-making trade without prior consultation. Neither company found these restrictions satisfactory, however, and negotiations continued. Eventually in 1947 after Ennemond Bizot of C.T.A.[2] had taken a hand, a joint company, Colodense Ltd., was set up to operate and develop film printing and converting using British Cellophane's film output.

This co-operative move in pursuit of vertical integration was the first example of such integration by Courtaulds, or by one of the companies in which it had a controlling interest, in the post-war years. It antedates Saiccor, and, of course, all those acquisitions which form the main subject of this chapter. The co-operation proved to be disastrous. No sooner had Colodense started than disagreements arose: about prices and rebates, about the factory in Bristol, and about a subsidiary company in Australia,

[1] See Vol. II, pp. 371–4. The French interest was then controlled by C.T.A.

[2] See Vol. II, pp. 373, 378.

In March 1953 Robinsons gave 12 months' notice of their wish to terminate the Colodense agreement. After an attempt by Robinsons to retreat from this notice and a hardening insistence by Courtaulds on securing control, relations worsened still further resulting in an acrimonious wrangle over the value of the shares which had to be settled by arbitration. British Cellophane duly acquired control and thus took a further step towards forward integration. In the later 1950s both British Cellophane and Colodense were expanding their turnover and in 1955, Mathys, by then chairman of the former company, announced the intention to go ahead with a new plant at Barrow-in-Furness. It started production in 1959 and in 1960 reinforced their earlier step towards integration by the purchase of an independent converter, Donaldson & Filer Ltd.

So when Kearton and Knight, in the guise of Group Developments Ltd., started Courtaulds' buying into the packaging industry, there was within the group both an existing stake in that industry and a certain fund of experience, not all of it happy, of difficulties of co-operation therein. The purchase of Reads, Betts, and Pearlite in 1958 seemed an appropriate set of building blocks with which to develop the packaging side of the group. As Kearton put it: 'Packaging as an investment theme was originally adopted by G.D.L. [Group Developments Ltd.] because of growth prospects. The thought was to acquire a number of packaging companies and to build up by degrees a balanced group. It was also felt that we could finally have a captive market for board and, in turn, pulp.' But by the end of June 1961 Pearlite, the only one of the companies which used board (and thus, indirectly, pulp), had been sold off. Its profits slumped in 1960 to a third of their pre-acquisition level and a loss was registered in the first quarter of 1961.

Pearlite was sold, with a capital profit, to Metal Box Ltd.—a firm which had by this time demonstrated a capacity to react very vigorously to Courtaulds' challenge to their dominance in the 'open-top' can market as represented by Courtaulds' purchase of Reads. No sooner was Courtaulds' financial strength seen to be behind Reads in their intention to extend their 'open-top' can business, than Metal Box rapidly fired off a battery of diverse competitive weapons. Metal Box, according to its historian, 'had no great opinion of Courtaulds' abilities in the packaging industry'[1] and, having foreseen the expansion in packaging, were unwilling to surrender the position which they had gained therein. In due time their doings were referred to the Monopolies Commission and were not recorded with

[1] W. J. Reader, *Metal Box. A History* (London, 1976), p. 170.

favour by that body.[1] But Courtaulds and Reads, meanwhile, both underestimated the cost of their expansion programme and wholly failed to foresee Metal Box's reaction. Kearton, in a memorandum to the Board asking for money for Reads in January 1960, admitted as much:

No one at Reads foresaw the energetic way in which the Metal Box Company would oppose their entry into the field . . . Every method Metal Box could use has been brought into operation: price cutting; special terms for long-term contracts; threatened withholding of supplies to complete a range; personal 'persuasion' visits by their Chairman, Sir Robert Barlow,[2] to their main customers; and the prohibition of the use of Metal Box closing machines for Read's cans.

At precisely the same time as these complaints—with a flavour, albeit faint, of righteous indignation—were being put forward to explain the need for more money for Reads, the Board was agreeing, also under the enthusiastic prodding of Kearton, to the purchase of Pinchin Johnson. By so doing Courtaulds promptly put themselves in a disadvantageous position in relation to Metal Box for not only had Pinchin Johnson and Metal Box long collaborated in the development of lacquers and varnishes for cans, but Pinchin Johnson's sales to Metal Box at home and overseas, amounted to some £800,000 annually.

Neither Group Developments nor Courtaulds' Board—with very little experience of the metal-container business—seem to have foreseen the trap into which they had walked. Metal Box promptly threatened to close the trap. In February one of the Pinchin Johnson directors was talking of 'definite signs of a "go-slow" movement' by Metal Box in relation to technical liaison with Pinchin Johnson and admitting that Metal Box could move 50 per cent. of their business elsewhere within six months and that all of it could be lost within twelve months. By May Metal Box had made it quite clear that instructions had been given to 'clamp down' on development work with Pinchin Johnson; and to use sources of supply other than Pinchin Johnson's; and that any reversion to previous arrangements depended upon Courtaulds' plans for the development of Reads. Courtaulds consulted their lawyers who advised them that there was a clear case for bringing the matter to the attention of the Board of Trade for action by the Monopolies Commission. Reads' management, on the other hand, asked how this would benefit them in their competitive struggle and

[1] M.C. *Report on the Supply of Metal Containers* (1970).

[2] Who, incidentally, was at that time also a director of the Steel Company of Wales, the major suppliers of tin plate.

looked to treating with Metal Box in the hope of coming to some mutual arrangement. Barlow of Metal Box suggested to Kearton that Metal Box should take over Reads against shares in Metal Box. Neither this proposal nor an alternative one that Metal Box should acquire a minority shareholding in Reads proved acceptable.

By November 1960 a rough mutual understanding had been reached. It was agreed (though *not* in writing) that Metal Box would resume collaboration with Pinchin Johnson; would not reduce its purchases from Pinchin Johnson providing that they met Metal Box's requirements as to quality, service, and price; and would 'grant dispensations' to customers who wished to use Metal Box machines for closing Reads' cans. The quid pro quo was the formidable one that Reads would confine its production of 'open-top' cans to the Liverpool area.[1] Metal Box had the balance of advantage in the result of this contest, and they strengthened their position in the course of it by taking a 25 per cent. interest in another firm of lacquer suppliers. Courtaulds, it was being said in some quarters, had been unwise in taking over Pinchin Johnson. At the beginning of 1961 Knight was disposed to believe that the willingness of Metal Box to adopt a 'live-and-let-live' attitude was 'a victory which justifies the persistence which has been shown in the face of their discouragements'. But the course of Pinchin Johnson's trade with Metal Box over the next few years hardly reflected a victory for Courtaulds in this episode as Pinchin Johnson's *share* of the expanding Metal Box business declined; and as Reads incurred big development losses and suffered in their expansion as a result of management difficulties and of the handicap of having to confine their operations to the unsatisfactory site in Liverpool.[2] In 1967 Courtaulds sold 60 per cent. of the Reads equity to the American Can Co. Mistakes were bound to be made in so headlong a pace of acquiring and diversifying but the combined prescience of the directors of British Cellophane and Courtaulds seems to have been less than impressive in their efforts to form a packaging group.

VI

The merger with Celanese obviously posed problems of organization and structure, thus instantly regenerating that interminable debate which, as shown earlier,[3] so much pre-occupied the Courtaulds Board. The

[1] There are, not surprisingly, some variant versions of the understanding, cf. Reader, *Metal Box*, pp. 170–1, and M.C. *Metal Containers*, p. 30, and notes.

[2] M.C. *Metal Containers*, p. 31, and notes. [3] See above, Chapter II.

subsequent rush of further acquisitions ensured that every corner of the group was brought into new plans for rationalization and reorganization—not all of which worked or endured.

In February 1957 Wilson sent some rough notes to Hanbury-Williams for a holding company scheme in which to accommodate the expected acquisition of British Celanese. He himself regarded it as unsatisfactory and nothing came of it. In the course of 1957 and 1958 a committee was set up to look into company organization; and the Textile Division appointed a committee to examine textile policy and the division's relations to other parts of the group. Meanwhile, sundry new divisions and groupings came into being to cope with the arrival of British Celanese and the first of the paint and packaging companies. The lines between product divisions and operating functions were, inevitably, imprecisely drawn and sometimes changed. For example, the knitting activities of Celanese were first transferred to the care of the Textile Division and then sent back to Celanese. In December 1958 it was decided to segregate the knitting companies and bring them together under the control of one of the Celanese subsidiaries, which was renamed the Furzebrook Knitting Co. Ltd. The garment-making companies were also put into a separate group. Rationalization of the weaving facilities within the group led to removals and closures in Celanese and transfers to Samuel Courtauld & Co. In addition to the existing Chemicals Division, a Plastics Division of British Celanese was created to look after the petrochemical products of Spondon; a new entity called the Synthetic Fibres Division was created to look after 'Courtelle' and 'Fibrolane'; Celanese's acetate activities were transferred to a new Acetate Division of Courtaulds. As more companies were acquired, and in order to co-ordinate the selling and promotion of the growing range of activities, a Marketing Division was brought into being. Engineering Headquarters was turned into the Engineering Division; and yarn processing spawned a Processing Division. Early in 1961 a Packaging Panel was set up to advise on the future of the packaging companies which were still then under the control of Group Developments; the upshot was the creation early in the following year of a new Packaging Division to combine the interests of British Cellophane, Reads, and Betts. Meanwhile other acquisitions or diversifications as Pinchin Johnson and Saiccor continued to operate as separate companies.

Whilst all these practical things were happening under the force of practical circumstances—sometimes rather hectically and with scant planning—a debate on the nature, significance, and degree of change continued in the Board. In particular, it was periodically asked, as it had been in the past, whether there should be more drastic hiving-off into separate companies. Wilson put the problem, as he saw it, in a memorandum of September 1959:

The arguments in favour of 'hiving-off' centre around the impossibility of a Board of 18 people being sufficiently homogenous in outlook and knowledge to control the component parts of the Company, while the arguments against 'hiving-off' largely arise from the fact that about 80% of the Company's activities (and about 95% of the Board's time) are concerned with fibre manufacture. If the fibre operations are hived-off properly, there will be practically nothing left for the Board to do except to look at the financial results, and if the other operations are hived off the lightening of the burden on the Board would be insignificant.

Rehearsing various possible courses of action, he admitted that he did not see clearly what was 'the best line to adopt which would meet both the short-term and long-term requirements of the Company *and be acceptable to the various personalities involved*' (my italics). Amongst those 'various personalities' one man must have loomed large. By the end of 1959 Kearton was a director of 16 companies within the group; was chairman of several of them as well as of the Processing and Synthetic Fibres Divisions; had become the senior managing director of British Celanese and was particularly responsible for the knitting and garment companies; and was especially concerned with a variety of overseas interests such as Saiccor and Usutu as well as the plant-selling operations of Prinex. Wilson's recommendation was effectively to abandon plans for hiving off divisions into separate companies and to build up along the lines already being laid down, viz. the integration of recent acquisitions; and the strengthening both of existing operating and functional divisions and of the central organization. Characteristically, he supported his views by reference to an academic work[1] which included a chapter dealing with the similar difficulties experienced in Associated Electrical Industries (A.E.I.). Wilson concluded:

There are remarkable similarities between A.E.I. and ourselves and the history of A.E.I. shows that the solution of these problems cannot be divorced from the past history of the Companies or from the personalities of the people involved and it also shows how bad an effect these problems can have on a Company unless some reasonable and acceptable solution to them is found.

[1] To which he had also contributed: R. S. Edwards and H. Townsend, *Business Enterprise. Its Growth and Organisation* (London, 1958), pp. 311–16.

The author of the chapter on A.E.I. referred to that company as having 'at the head of affairs a man with a profound understanding of organisation'.[1] Alas for such admiration! Within a decade of these words, A.E.I. had suffered falling profits and severe difficulties, not a little due to defects of an internal organization based on divisions, and had been the object of a successful take-over bid by the General Electric Company.[2] In the light of subsequent events, Wilson's words and references were more than a little ironic.

Fortunately for Courtaulds, the *ad hoc* path of a mixture of product and process divisions and of separate operating units apparently proved less disastrous. Or was that the reason? Was it rather that here, as elsewhere, 'the personalities of the people involved' turned out to be more important than patterns of organization? What at least is clear is that certain sweeping changes which came after the I.C.I. bid merely built upon vital underlying changes which had happened before then; and that Kearton, not without blunders, had done much to provoke them.

[1] Ibid., p. 311. The man in question was the chairman of A.E.I. at that time: Oliver Lyttleton, Viscount Chandos. The author of the chapter was its then secretary. It originated as a paper given to the seminar on problems of industrial administration run at the London School of Economics by Prof. R. S. (later Sir Ronald) Edwards.

[2] See Robert Jones and Oliver Marriott, *Anatomy of a Merger. A History of G.E.C., A.E.I. and English Electric* (London, 1970), esp. pp. 241–55, and D. F. Channon, *Strategy and Structure of British Enterprise*, pp. 134–5.

CHAPTER IX

Fibres and Factories

WHILE all these companies were being absorbed and new ventures undertaken, Courtaulds' research and development organization, earlier revitalized by Wilson, had not been idle. That other line of search for a replacement source of profits, so characteristic both of the old textile industry and of its modern chemical-textile counterpart—new finishes, new fabrics, or even new fibres—was being actively explored. And, seemingly fortuitously, yet another possible source of profit was opened up as a consequence of a piece of enterprise which put together two otherwise quite unrelated instances of resources and wants: the prior existence in Courtaulds of an engineering department, substantial in size and with underemployed capacity; and the policy decisions of the U.S.S.R. and other Communist countries to buy certain advanced technical skills which the western non-Communist world could alone supply.

I

The search for new fibres or the creation of new qualities in old fibres was rewarded with one oustanding success, the acrylic fibre 'Courtelle', the development of which forms one of the main subjects of this chapter. But it was not the only reward of the work at Courtaulds' research laboratories. Apart from the staple fibre from casein, 'Fibrolane',[1] which yielded some profits in this period, various sorts of true synthetics were the subject of experiment, and in some instances of commercial production. Some important improvements were made in the quality and characteristics of rayon yarns and fibres. Furthermore, the acquisition of British Celanese put into Courtaulds' hands the pilot plant at Spondon for making and spinning nylon 6, the type of nylon made from caprolactam[2] which Celanese had been exploring quite independently from the nylon 66 made by B.N.S. and which had certain advantages in industrial uses.

Amongst the synthetic fibres which were developed was the polyethylene (or polythene) yarn marketed as 'Courlene', and which found

[1] See above, pp. 68–70. [2] See above, p. 77.

such end-uses as fishing nets and deck-chair fabrics. Research on it started in 1948 and production on a small scale began in 1952. Output, from a plant at Little Heath, was running at about 1 million lb. per annum by 1960. Research into the technically related polypropylene fibres was also pursued from about 1956 onwards, though Courtaulds' work was less advanced than that already under way in North America and in Italy by the Montecatini organization which held the basic U.K. patents for making the requisite polymer. Small-scale commercial production began in 1959. Efforts to improve the characteristics of existing rayon fibres had considerable success in the development of a polynosic viscose staple fibre which came to be marketed under the name of 'Vincel' during this period. It had a markedly higher wet strength and was thereby made more competitive with the better grades of cotton. The increasing manufacture of tufted carpets provided both an outlet for staple fibres of various sorts (viscose, casein, and acrylic) and a stimulus to the improvement of standard viscose staple. This particular stimulus helped into being a better-wearing, crimped viscose staple fibre for carpets, marketed as 'Evlan' in growing quantities during the early 1960s. The achievement of higher tenacity in yarns and fibres was an important element in maintaining rayon sales in face of competition from other fibres. This was particularly true of the increasing strengths obtained in various industrial yarns and especially tyre yarn which in the late 1950s and early 1960s accounted for some 95 per cent. of end-uses of all the company's industrial yarn sales. Successive improvements produced the T.105 or 'Tyrex' yarn which began to be marketed in 1958, followed by the still stronger T.140 yarn in 1962. Experiments in yarn processing included the successful establishment of spun-dyed yarns and fibres in which colour is introduced in the manufacturing process; and the development of various sorts of crimped and twisted yarns to give different effects. One of the latter which loomed large in this period was a false-twist process developed during the 1950s and used particularly with nylon 66 yarn; it was used mainly in the knitting trade, and achieved some success as 'Courtolon'.

All these advances belonged in part to the continued tradition of empirical research which in the 1930s had improved the technical qualities of Courtaulds' rayon output;[1] and in part to the new capacity for research introduced by Wilson and which facilitated the enquiries into the new synthetics. Certain developments in regard to nylon 6, however, raised

[1] See Vol. II, Chapter XII.

rather more complex issues which demand some attention now although some of their consequences did not become evident until the 1960s.

The acquisition by Courtaulds of British Celanese and thereby of the small nylon 6 ('Celon') plant at Spondon instantly posed a problem. Under the terms of the original I.C.I.–Courtaulds agreement[1] the signatories were obliged to produce nylon only through the medium of B.N.S. Commercial problems were bound to arise if one or the other of the parents of B.N.S. were to compete with it in nylon manufacture. What therefore was to be done with the 'Celon' plant? At the time of the take-over Celanese had in mind the erection, in collaboration with British Enka, of a 10-million-lb.-per-year plant at their Wrexham factory. This notion was abandoned as potentially disastrous to the future collaboration in developing B.N.S. But after a series of talks involving Rendall, Wilson, Kearton, and the B.N.S. directors, a *modus vivendi* was arrived at whereby the 'Celon' plant continued in operation, at its existing output; all yarn was to be converted into fabric within the Courtaulds group; and all technical information on operating procedures was to be available to B.N.S. without any reciprocal obligation on B.N.S. to provide technical information to Celanese. One of the reasons adduced in support of the continuance of the plant was that the existence of a caprolactam pilot plant in the group could be useful to B.N.S., as B.N.S. had from time to time considered the possibility of expanding via nylon 6 rather than nylon 66.

But what was to be the source of the caprolactam? Although made and used fairly extensively in Germany, Italy, and U.S.A. for the production of nylon 6 yarns, there was no major U.K. source as its use in Britain was only on a very modest scale. The normal process by which caprolactam was made started with phenol and then involved the production of a substance called cyclohexane, from which by further chemical steps the requisite caprolactam was derived.[2] In 1960 Snia Viscosa patented a new process for making caprolactam starting not with benzene but with toluene, which they claimed to be cheaper than the cyclohexane process. Both Hanbury-Williams and Wilson showed an eagerness to acquire the rights which Marinotti was offering for sale. Its attractions were evident. I.C.I., as we shall see, consistently maintained its grip on polymer manufacture for nylon 66. If Courtaulds could get a comparable grip on caprolactam

[1] Terminated by mutual consent in February 1957. See below, p. 179.

[2] At the time phenol was normally derived from benzene obtained from coal. Today both phenol and cyclohexane are mainly derived from benzene obtained from oil-cracking.

manufacture for nylon 6, there might be both economic advantages and some shift in the balance of power in relation to B.N.S. I.C.I.'s determined stand in keeping Courtaulds out of 'Terylene' had not been forgotten and the move seemed almost to offer scope for the redress of grievances. And Hanbury-Williams's liking for Marinotti predisposed him in favour of buying the Snia process. In February 1960 he cabled Wilson: 'most anxious we should take some initiative regarding possible manufacture caprolactam in U.K.'. In May the Board, presented with a report from Wilson and Sheldon, approved a recommendation that 'action be taken with all speed' to secure for Courtaulds the exclusive rights to the Snia process in U.K., Australia, and Germany and to proceed with the design and ordering of a plant to produce 10,000 tons per year. It is clear that Hanbury-Williams himself was a prime mover in pushing through the deal—which involved a down-payment to Snia of £1 million, plus a royalty—and it is equally clear that Kearton violently opposed it, insisting upon his reservations being recorded in the Board minutes. Thereby was created yet another source of friction between him and Wilson.

The decision to buy the Snia process led instantly to difficulties in negotiations with Marinotti; and in the longer run to a minor furore when, in 1963, Courtaulds threatened not to pay some £250,000 due out of the £1 million on the grounds that the original estimates on which the contract was based had in effect misrepresented the cost-savings inherent in the process and hence its value.[1] Meanwhile, despite mounting evidence from Snia's development work that the cost of the process would be higher than had been supposed, in June 1961, after an optimistic recommendation from Wilson, the Board agreed to go ahead with plans to build a caprolactam producing unit. A public announcement was made of Courtaulds' intention to build a plant with an annual capacity of 10,000 tons, using the process acquired from Snia. I.C.I., meanwhile, had gone ahead with a caprolactam plant based on the cyclohexane process. In correspondence with Wilson at the time, one of the I.C.I. directors made it plain that I.C.I. (like Kearton) did not believe the Snia process to have any cost advantages over existing processes. So the two partners in B.N.S. were about to compete in making caprolactam for nylon 6—a curiosity which did not pass unnoticed in the press.[2]

The plant was never built. The 'Celon' unit continued to operate on a small scale at Spondon. But new intentions were being formulated as well

[1] For further details see below, pp. 268–9. [2] *The Economist*, 6 June 1961.

as valuable experience being gained with nylon 6, the results of which were to become evident in the new climate which emerged after the I.C.I. bid.

II

While Courtaulds and I.C.I. were thus seen publicly to disagree over the ways of producing the raw materials for nylon 6, they continued privately to argue over a matter which was already a favourite topic of contention:[1] polymer production for nylon 66.

After sundry talks in 1953–4, the Courtaulds Board finally determined, in March 1954, upon a twin resolution: first, that it was not prepared to negotiate with I.C.I. with the intent to acquire an interest in 'Terylene' at the price of becoming only minority shareholders in B.N.S., which had been suggested; second, that it should be proposed to I.C.I. that as I.C.I. had again expressed dissatisfaction with the return on polymer production, B.N.S. should take it over. A letter on these lines was sent by Rendall to the I.C.I. chairman, Alexander Fleck, in April. A new polymer plant was already planned, so discussions were set in motion about the possibility of Courtaulds financing it, thus moving towards an equalization of the capital contributions of the two firms to the whole process of nylon manufacture, i.e. from polymer production to spun yarn. Courtaulds envisaged capital expenditure of about £15 million on a polymer plant near the new B.N.S. factory at Doncaster; I.C.I. thought that if it were erected at their Wilton site the cost would be about £13·5 million. Under the pressure of demand, construction began at Wilton but during 1955 discussions continued on the possibility of transferring all the polymer production to B.N.S.[2] A valuation of £16·4 million had been put on the plants and, in the spring of 1956, Hanbury-Williams asked Sir Alexander Fleck (as he had by now become) what I.C.I. would want for goodwill or 'intangibles'. In May Fleck sent his reply: 'in order to ensure that I.C.I. suffers no loss of income', the answer was £33 million. And that was that. As Hanbury-Williams observed, such a figure 'put the matter out of court as a practical proposition'. Which, perhaps, is precisely what it was intended to do.

[1] See Chapter IV, pp. 76–82.

[2] At the end of 1955, the position was that the plants at Billingham, brought into production in 1950 and 1955 had a total annual capacity of 35 million lb.; and work had commenced on the Wilton plant, with a projected capacity of 20 million lb., to come into operation in 1958.

9. Grimsby, 1959. The 'Courtelle' Plant, in its early stages, is on the right of the picture

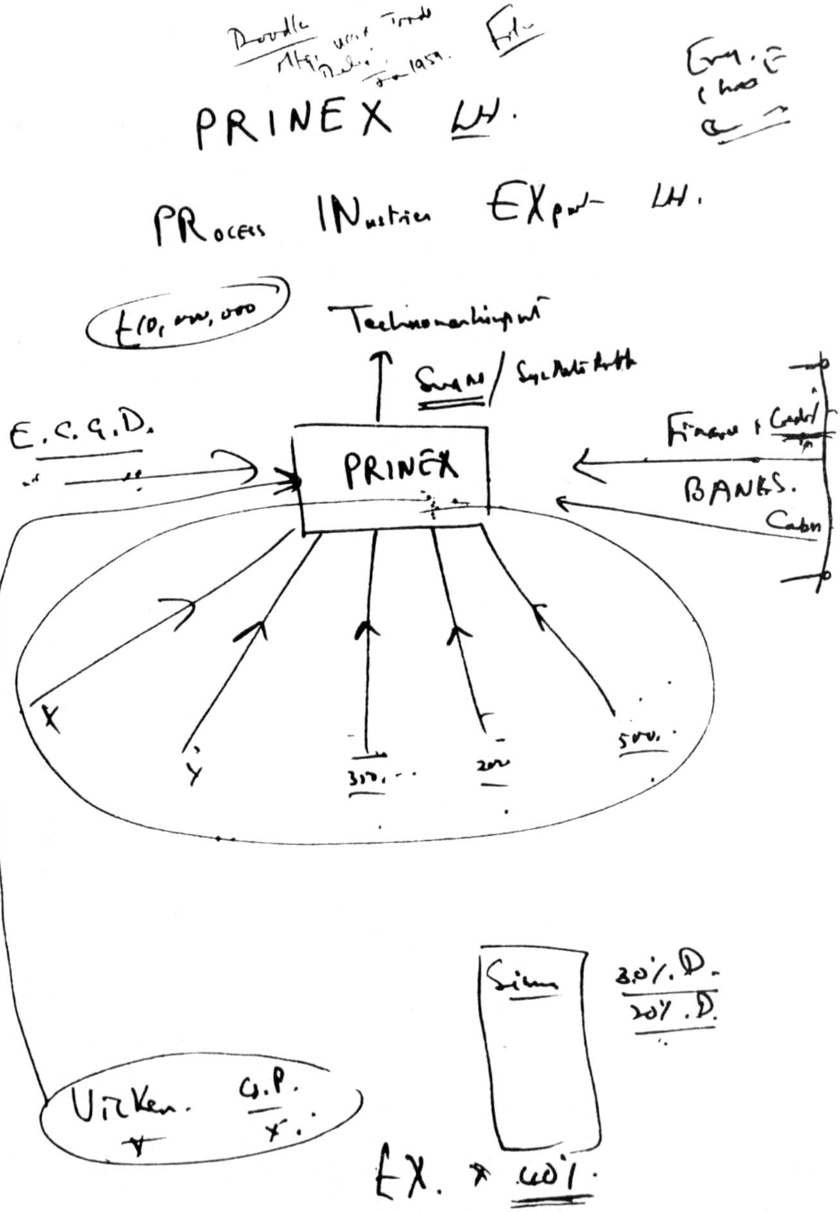

10. The origins of Prinex: a Kearton doodle

So negotiations on the terms of the polymer-supply agreement recommenced on more familiar lines. In the course of 1956 they were given a jolt by the passage of the Restrictive Trade Practices Act which forced Courtaulds, I.C.I., and B.N.S. to look at the whole of the co-operation agreement of 1940 because it contained various restrictive clauses.[1] Discussions soon reached approval of the termination of the 1940 agreement, the passage of various resolutions by B.N.S., and the adoption of new articles of association. But the crucial article of the 1940 agreement which set out the conditions relating to polymer supply was, temporarily, re-enacted until a new agreement could be reached on this thorny matter. In September, Courtaulds agreed that negotiations should continue on the basis that I.C.I. would supply B.N.S. with all the polymer required now and in future at a price representing cost plus 15 per cent. Finally, a new polymer-supply agreement was signed in May 1959, applying retrospectively to dispatches from January 1958, and then amended by supplementary letters in November 1960. The net effect was indeed to raise the rate of return to 15 per cent., instead of the 6 per cent. of the 1940 agreement and the 11 per cent. of the 1951 agreement.[2] Once again, I.C.I. had won.

Meanwhile, B.N.S. itself went from strength to strength. Table 27 continues for 1954–61 the production figures given, in Table 14, for 1947–54.[3]

TABLE 27

B.N.S.: nylon-yarn and staple-fibre output, 1954–61

mn. lb.

	Yarn	*Staple*	*Total*
1954	19·2	2·8	22·0
1955	27·6	4·5	32·1
1956	27·8	6·9	34·7
1957	37·7	6·7	44·4
1958	38·9	6·6	45·5
1959	45·1	9·1	54·2
1960	60·7	10·5	71·2
1961	66·9	13·8	80·7

[1] The 1940 agreement would have had to be registered under the terms of the Act unless terminated beforehand. Typical restrictive clauses were those which, for example, prevented B.N.S. from making yarn other than nylon, or limited the territory of their operations.

[2] See above, pp. 80–1. [3] See above, p. 79.

In 1959–61 B.N.S. net profits averaged £5·17 million annually, an increase of 177 per cent. over the corresponding average of £1·87 million in 1951–3. The £8 million issued capital of 1949 was increased to £12 million in 1955, to £18 million in 1956 and, by a bonus issue, to £24 million in 1960. Fig. 7 compares the rate of growth of total B.N.S. nylon output with the comparable data for the various sorts of Courtaulds' rayon. Even after including the additional output from the acquired rayon companies,[1] as this graph does, the contrast is still obvious, both in the longer-term growth rate and in the ability to weather the recessions of 1951–3 and 1957–9. Courtaulds certainly needed a new fibre.

III

As a part of the expansion of the synthetic-rubber industry in the U.S.A. during World War II, there was developed a substantial capacity for the production of certain chemicals. Amongst them was the substance known as acrylonitrile the molecules of which will join together to form polymers capable of forming fibres. This fibre-forming capacity had been known before the war but despite research, particularly in Germany (by I. G. Farben) and the U.S.A. (by Du Pont), no commercial production of polyacrylonitrile fibres had been reached. By 1945, however, Du Pont had a pilot plant at work for the production of what in 1948 became known as 'Orlon', large-scale production of which began in 1950.

Courtaulds were well behind such developments. In October 1950, at a meeting in Coventry, Wilson and Kearton told Davies, anxious that Courtaulds should get into pure synthetics, that the company's research staff was as yet quite inadequate, and that the best way was to buy 'know-how'. Early in January 1951 it became known that the American Cyanamid Company had developed and patented a new acrylic fibre which they called 'X 51'. Davies on one of his many American trips visited Cyanamid in March and April and reported enthusiastically on the prospects of some sort of collaboration agreement between Cyanamid and Courtaulds. Kearton, not yet on the Board, accompanied Davies as a technical adviser. In a letter to Wilson he commented on the urge to get Courtaulds back into the U.S.A., so characteristic of Davies and Hanbury-Williams, and which seemed to lie behind the former's enthusiasm: 'the Colonel seems very keen on coming to an agreement with Cyanamid, as much as a means of getting back in the U.S. market as anything else'. In

[1] See above, pp. 160–3.

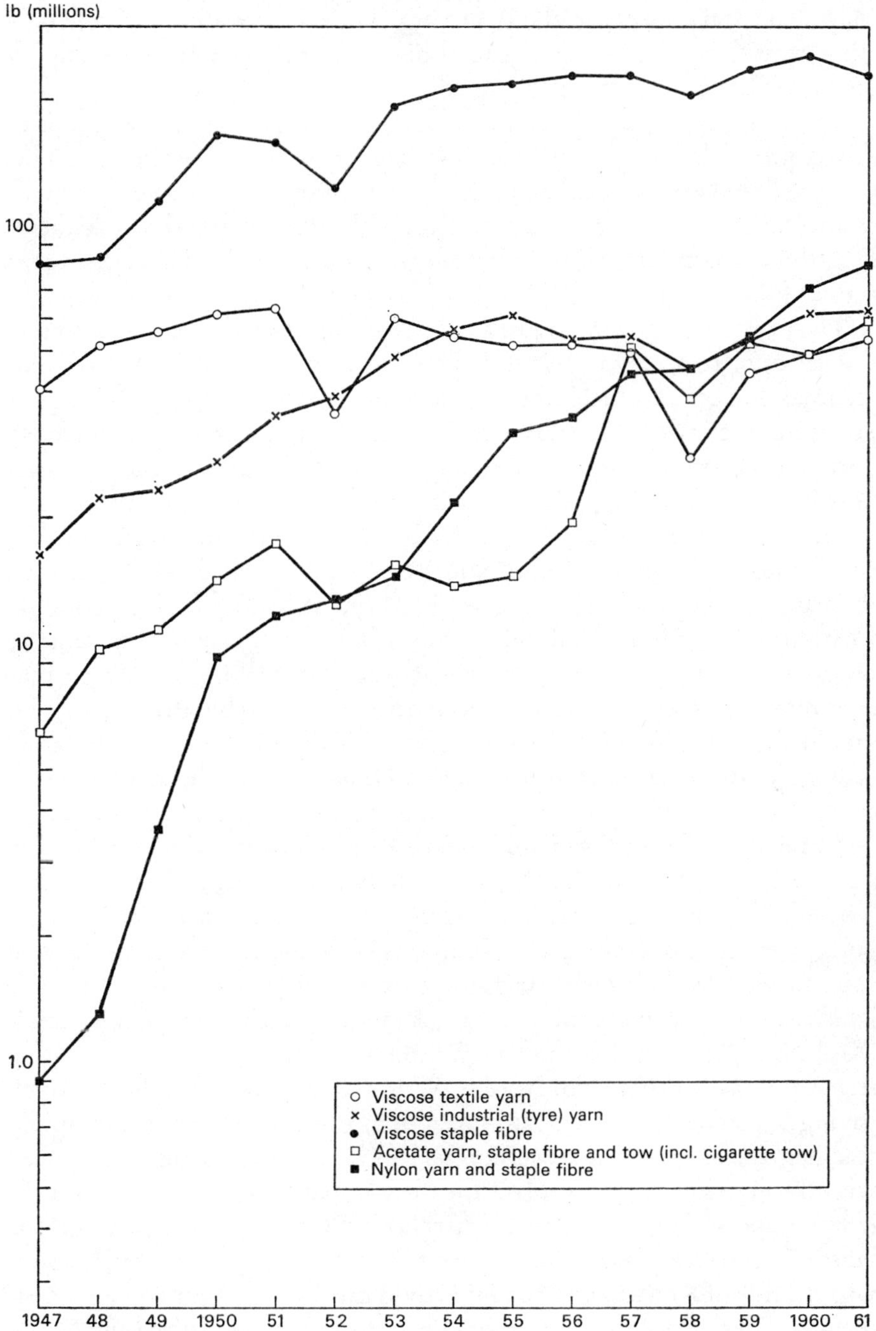

FIG. 7. *Courtaulds, U.K., and B.N.S.: rayon and nylon output, 1947–61*

May, at a special meeting, the Board agreed to the possibility of collaborating with Cyanamid on the general lines of a 50/50 company to exploit the new fibre in America and Canada.

From that time and for the next four years, to July 1955, two trains of events proceeded apace with varying degrees of leisureliness or urgency. On one line there rambled along a train of negotiations between the two companies; on the other, there travelled, with growing speed and deliberation, the work in Courtaulds' research laboratories in pursuit of their own acrylic fibre.

The negotiations were so protracted as clearly to indicate that each side had its own reasons for delay. A draft agreement in July 1951 did not command assent; by September Cyanamid had begun to think the proposals impracticable; in December the project was regarded as completely dormant. Discussions in the following year revealed that Cyanamid were now interested in an appraisal of their fibre by Courtaulds, a disclosure of technical information for a fee, and a licence agreement. Courtaulds had already tested samples of 'X 51' and were pushing ahead with their own research on various synthetics. In January, at a technical meeting in Coventry chaired by Wilson, the decision was made to concentrate research on the production of an acrylic staple fibre. At a research-committee discussion in May it was recorded as desirable that Courtaulds should delay the decision on taking out a licence under the Cyanamid patents 'until the last possible moment'. Desultory talks between the two companies continued but the matter was effectively left in abeyance.

At the end of 1953 Cyanamid announced that they had now produced a much improved fibre, 'X 54', which they considered to be better than 'Orlon'. During 1954, however, Courtaulds own research advanced to the point when the company was having to balance the chances of a successful commitment to their own fibre as against the merits of paying $250,000 which Cyanamid were asking for the disclosure of information about 'X 54'. Early in 1955 Kearton and Wilson had come to the conclusion that it was not worth that sum. In May Wilson suggested it might be worth paying $50,000 and told a Board meeting in June that research was rapidly reaching the stage when a decision had to be made whether to go ahead with the erection of a pilot plant for the company's own acrylic fibre. As it was impossible to tell how far advanced Cyanamid were, it might be worth while paying to see their process. The Board agreed to negotiations with a limit of $150,000. Cyanamid stood out for that sum and an agreement was signed in July. A Courtaulds team thereupon visited the Cyanamid plant, and concluded that the process contained neither revolutionary features nor indications that it had yet reached the stage of being commercially viable. In the words of a report, prepared by Mathys, in November 1955:

Having examined the information put at their disposal by American Cyanamid, Courtaulds Ltd. find that the process developed by American Cyanamid is similar in general, but different in detail, to that developed by Courtaulds Ltd.; that the problems involved in scaling up either process are of the same order of magnitude; that on the research and development side, Courtaulds Ltd. are as far advanced as American Cyanamid; and that in progress towards designs for a full-scale plant Courtaulds Ltd. seem to be somewhat ahead.

Moreover, there was a possibility that the Cyanamid process could involve a patent dispute. So Courtaulds decided not to take up the offer of a patent licence from Cyanamid; and in January 1956 the agreement was formally terminated.

Meanwhile, the American firm, Chemstrand, had announced its intention to build in Northern Ireland a plant to produce its acrylic fibre ('Acrilan') with an annual capacity of 10 million lb. Already in September 1955 the Courtaulds Board had approved expenditure on a large pilot plant to produce 1 million lb. per annum. In October Wilson pressed for the speeding up of the project and for a larger initial output. By stages this was approved; the capacity was to be increased to 2 million lb.; plans were drawn up for the installation of the project at Little Heath; a market survey of likely U.K. and overseas demand was set in train; the trade name of 'Courtelle' was adopted after the abandonment of the previously favoured but curiously unattractive alternative 'Crylton'; and by April 1956 Wilson was telling a Research Department meeting of the importance of 'directing all development efforts towards the attainment of the 10,000,000 lb./year output of "Courtelle" staple fibre'. In October 1957 this Little Heath plant started production.

Before going on to consider the emerging plans for the construction of larger units and the market reception of 'Courtelle', it is worth briefly digressing in order to examine the nature of this technical breakthrough. When Wilson and Kearton told Davies in October 1950 that the company's research staff was inadequate, they were doing no more than confirm the gloomy reports on the laboratories and on staff recruitment which Wilson had made earlier. In a comprehensively damning report in 1947 Wilson had observed of the No. 1 laboratory at Coventry (just put under control of the newly appointed Kearton) that its general condition was bad and that the buildings were unsuitable for experimental work by modern standards. The legacy of past neglect, the habit of limited empirical work, and the difficulties of war conditions were now being rendered more difficult to combat by the drift of scientists to government contracts. In April 1948 Wilson wrote gloomily to the chairman telling him categorically that he was satisfied neither with the small laboratory, which had been set up at Maidenhead to conduct 'pure' research, nor with any of the other laboratories of the company. He saw little prospect of things getting better; young science graduates 'lack drive and adopt an escapist attitude'; most of the university staffs had abandoned serious research and 'sit on Government Committees instead'. He had said in 1945 that it would take ten years to 'put the Company's research on its feet . . . and my estimate is still ten years, which means that I just don't know when there will be any improvement'. So to be producing and selling an acrylic fibre, albeit in small quantities, within ten years of making those remarks represents a considerable achievement in research and development. Much of the work itself was inevitably channelled into certain directions by the combination of Courtaulds' late start and the prior existence of other firms' patents. The task boiled down to discovering paths to a type of fibre, new to Courtaulds but already developed elsewhere, through the rocks represented by the patents; and then finding out whether its qualities and its costs of production were such as to make it, by this route, a marketable entity. Despite a large number of patents no one company held a broad monopoly for the production of an acrylic fibre in the U.K. Du Pont held a key patent for 'Orlon' covering the use of a particular solvent for polyacrylonitrile and certain of its co-polymers. Research at Courtaulds, with a gradually improving team and under vigorous direction, was steered towards producing a new co-polymer and finding a new solvent. Success in doing this at the Acetate and Synthetic Fibres Laboratory at Coventry resulted in the development of a fibre with good dyeing and bulking qualities (acrylic fibres, having a warm and soft feel, compete with wool); and this was paralleled by testing the textile qualities of the fibre, in the early days by the Textile Research Laboratory at Bocking and later at the company's Arrow, Westcroft, and Bull Royd mills.

Plans for the development of a much larger 'Courtelle' unit than that at Little Heath began to be formulated well before the latter came into production. In the summer of 1956 investigations into suitable sites were carried out. The three most important influences taken into account were labour supply, ease of effluent discharge, and accessibility to raw materials. Possible locations considered were Flint, Grimsby, Wolverhampton, or Carrickfergus, all sites of existing company plants. After a discussion with experts on water pollution it seemed likely that Grimsby would be the only suitable place. Various estimates of production cost and profitability were prepared. That finally submitted to the Board in March 1957 recommended Grimsby as the best choice, 'offering ready access to both Lancashire and Yorkshire customers as well as room for eventual expansion and acceptable effluent disposal'. Despite a higher capital cost, and the loss of a 25 per cent. capital grant from the Northern Ireland government, available if the plant were built at Carrickfergus, Grimsby was calculated to offer a slightly better return. 'Courtelle' production costs were markedly different from those of viscose textile yarn, raw materials being of much greater consequence in the production costs of the acrylic fibre.

TABLE 28

Proportionate costs: 'Courtelle' and viscose textile yarn

Percentages

	Labour	*Raw materials*	*Other*	*Total*
'Courtelle' estimates (Grimsby 1957)				
at 100% capacity . . .	3·7	81·5	14·8	100·0
at 50% capacity . . .	6·5	73·8	19·7	100·0
Viscose textile yarn (actual all plants, average)				
1954 (peak, output 54·3 mn. lb.).	17·3	39·2	43·5	100·0
1958 (trough, output 27·8 mn. lb.)	15·6	33·7	50·7	100·0

Although for various reasons the two sets of figures in Table 28 are not strictly comparable, they give an adequate indication of the very different role of raw materials in the two cost structures. The project, for a plant with an annual capacity of 10 million lbs., was estimated to cost £2·4 million (new capital £1·6 million + £0·8 million working capital) and envisaged a profit which would represent a 50 per cent. return on the cost at 100 per cent. capacity working. On 14 March 1957 the Board approved the capital expenditure on a 'Courtelle' plant at Grimsby.

Meanwhile, a general assessment of the current position of the whole project[1] had been done and discussed at a meeting in January of a group which became known as the 'Courtelle Steering Committee'. The two main Board members were Kearton and Wilson, with the former as chairman; later they were joined by Verrall. The assessment, although presenting the 'major portion of the Courtelle process' as satisfactory, had indicated a number of problems as yet quite far from solution. Some were of a highly technical nature; one involved devising a way round a patent; the deficiency within the company of knitting machinery and personnel to carry out development work and trials had somehow to be circumvented; more machines (called 'turbo-staplers') used in preparing the yarn were needed; the textile mills at Bocking were regarded as unhelpful; the research laboratory at Maidenhead had been 'of no practical help'. Kearton told the meeting of the need to proceed 'on the basis of limited objectives, clearly defined responsibilities and a vigorous attack on a narrow front'; and, as already recorded, plans were put to, and approved by, the Board in March. Wilson, as in other matters, was markedly less eager to push ahead whilst such problems remained unsolved. In June of the previous year, he had already become alarmed and seemed hesitant about pushing ahead quickly towards the 10-million-lb. unit, despite his earlier remarks in April.[2] Now, in February 1957, he wrote one of his apprehensive letters, this time to the head of the Maidenhead laboratory. He set out certain problems and asked that work should be put in hand urgently to try to solve them, but he prefaced these instructions with some general comments.

A detailed examination of the 'Courtelle' project has revealed a most alarming situation. While we have 95% of the information required for the design and operation of the plant under erection and the proposed extension, there is still a residuum of unsolved problems which are likely to be of vital importance. As you know, the difference between success and failure in launching a new fibre is a very narrow one, and I feel that unless we have answers to these problems in say six months the whole 'Courtelle' project may well founder. If such an unhappy event were to materialize you can imagine its effect upon the Company's future.

This was hardly the phraseology of a man *seen* to be determined upon success; resolution and willingness to take risks scarcely leap to the eye.

[1] Made by Dr. G. A. R. Hartley, the head of the Acetate and Synthetic Fibres Laboratory at Coventry and later (1973–7) a director of Courtaulds Ltd.

[2] See above, p. 183.

Perhaps such sentiments would have been inappropriate anyway in writing to a chemist in charge of a pure research laboratory. But it is not too difficult to see why here was another field of conflict for Wilson and Kearton and why the latter came in time to feel, however wrongly, that Wilson was hampering his efforts to drive forward.[1]

The problems were real enough and not only of the sort likely to be solved by the sort of research which the Maidenhead laboratories might carry out. A firm seeking to manufacture and market an acrylic fibre in the U.K. had to face one price-relationship which was significantly different from what prevailed in the U.S.A. The natural fibre with which it was to compete, wool, was notably cheaper in the U.K., as is shown by the following prices for acrylic staple and wool, derived from the company's market survey in 1956:

	U.S.A.	*U.K.*
	d./lb.	
Orlon (3 denier)	107	127
Acrilan (3 denier)	96	108
Wool (64's clean)	127	99

So despite the immensely rapid increase of output in the U.S.A. (acrylic-fibre output had risen from negligible quantities in 1950 to 58 million lb. in 1955), the U.K. market was obviously likely to present a stiffer task in that both price and quality would have to match the cheaper and more familiar wool. The survey calculated that in 1960 the total home market for acrylic fibres, mainly in knitwear such as sweaters and cardigans, would extend to 35 million lb., assuming a price of 70*d.* per lb. A small export market of 5 million lb. was also thought likely. But all this was built on the presumption that 'Courtelle' could compete in quality with 'Orlon' and 'Acrilan' between which there already existed some differences in textile characteristics. All did not go smoothly at first. Reports from trials in 1956 and 1957 showed that the current output of 'Courtelle' was as yet unable to compete satisfactorily, particularly in regard to its bulking properties. In the course of 1957 and 1958 important improvements were made; the output of the Little Heath plant began to appear on the market; an advertising campaign was launched. The steering committee was periodically praised for its achievements or berated for its shortcomings by Kearton who dominated it but did not always endear himself to the

[1] See above, p. 142.

chemists.[1] Wilson had dropped off it, Verrall attended only occasionally.

In June 1958 Wilson revealed more worries in a letter to Kearton:

> I have been seriously disturbed at the failure of the Little Heath plant to reach its designed output, even after it has been in operation so long, and I fear that the Grimsby plant may similarly fail to reach its design figures. The financial consequences of working at a low capacity would of course be very serious, quite apart from its effect upon the competitive position vis-à-vis Chemstrand.

After specifying what he considered to be the trouble, he ended on this chilly note: 'During the past month or so I have emphasized these points to those in charge of the "Courtelle" project but I would be glad if you would raise the matter again at the "Courtelle" Steering Committee.' Kearton, it should be remembered, was at this time also heavily involved in the diversification programme, in acting as managing director of the newly acquired British Celanese, and in trying to run several other companies or projects. Nevertheless in February 1959, at precisely the same time as Rendall was writing to the chairman about the rift between Wilson and Kearton,[2] the latter was able to report to the Board that the Grimsby 'Courtelle' plant had produced its first bale of fibre.

The launch of 'Courtelle'—the need for success in which had been stressed by Wilson in his letter to the chairman in December 1956[3]—was in fact highly successful. Production and sales soared as Table 29 shows.

TABLE 29

'Courtelle': output and sales, 1958–61

	'000 lb. *Production*	*Sales*
1958–9	1,039	884
1959–60	5,050	4,273
1960–1	10,699	10,428
1961–2	14,016	12,982

[1] An oblique but interesting comment on how Wilson and Kearton appeared to different groups within the company is provided by the following contrast. A chatty article (passed for publication by Wilson, Kearton, Verrall, and others) for the house-journal *The Rayoneer* early in 1958 did not so much as mention Wilson. An internal technical history of the 'Courtelle' project, prepared in 1962 by one of the company's chemists, barely mentioned Kearton but named Wilson on a number of occasions and with laudatory inflections; it also had him, incorrectly, as chairman of the steering committee.

[2] See above, p. 141. [3] See above, p. 147.

The home market took over 90 per cent. of the output and demand soon overtook available supplies. It became popular in the tufted carpet trade and for a time Courtaulds gave exceptional terms to Cyril Lord Ltd. who pushed it vigorously. Despite costs of production being rather higher than the earlier estimates had suggested, a high price was secured initially (1st grade, 3 denier was 96*d*. in 1960) and profits were substantial. As indicated earlier,[1] by 1961 they were beginning to make a small but significant contribution to total group profits. These successes rapidly induced in Kearton grandiose schemes for starting production in the U.S.A. (where total acrylic output had soared from 55 million lb. in 1955 to 142 million lb. in 1960): in October 1960 he was envisaging a 30 million lb. or perhaps even a 50 million lb. unit there. For various reasons—the danger of a patent dispute and weaknesses in the current management of Courtaulds North America amongst them—the idea was dropped and a promotion campaign substituted for it.[2] But for the U.K. he quickly promoted the expansion of Grimsby plant to double its capacity to 20 million lb. The requisite £1·7 million for this was approved in November 1959. France also recommended itself as a site for 'Courtelle'. In June of the same year the Board approved the establishment of a plant at Calais to produce initially 5 million lb. to be expanded to 10 million lb., which expansion was agreed in February 1961.

In January 1961 Kearton, replying to an enquiry from Hanbury-Williams, was telling him his views about building 'Courtelle' factories in various parts of the world. There were commitments to France, Russia, and Yugoslavia; a hope for a contract in Poland; the possible venture in America; he remained 'lukewarm' about 'Courtelle' projects in Germany, Australia, and Scandinavia, though at some future date a plant to serve Australia and New Zealand 'might be likely'; in due course 'we might sell plants to countries such as China'. Before we move on to consider some of these sales of factories, it is worth drawing together, in Table 30, the major commercial output of fibres from the Courtaulds group in the years just before the I.C.I. bid. As is evident from the Table, the oldest products showed the least growth, the newest the most rapid. Nylon yarn and staple depended on continued co-operation with I.C.I. Hopes for independently based vigour rested on 'Tricel', cigarette tow, and, above all, 'Courtelle'.

[1] See above, p. 131. [2] For the result of this, see below, p. 284.

TABLE 30

Output of fibres, 1959–61

mn. lb.

	Viscose textile yarn and staple	*Viscose industrial yarn*	*'Dicel' yarn and staple**	*'Tricel' yarn and staple**	*Acetate cigarette tow**	*'Fibrolane' (casein staple)**	*'Courtelle' (acrylic staple)**	B.N.S. *nylon yarn*	B.N.S. *nylon staple*
1959	282·0	53·2	42·6	11·4	4·8	1·6	5·0	45·1	9·1
1960	305·7	61·9	32·9	12·2	5·9	2·2	10·7	60·7	10·5
1961	283·0	62·3	40·3	16·8	7·8	2·6	14·0	66·9	13·8

* Years are March–March, 1959–60, 1960–1, and 1961–2; the remainder are calendar years.

IV

In the course of the three years immediately preceding the I.C.I. bid, 1958–61, Courtaulds signed six contracts for the supply of machinery, 'know-how', and/or complete plants for fibre manufacture. The sequence started not with the new achievement in acrylics, but with acetate ('Dicel') and the false-twist process. Four of the contracts were with the U.S.S.R., two for acetate, one for viscose tyre cord, and one for acrylic fibre. A fifth contract with the U.S.S.R.—for triacetate—was negotiated during the period but not signed until early in 1962. The remaining contracts signed before the bid were with Yugoslavia and Poland, both for acrylic fibre. The total value of the seven contracts was nearly £30 million. Without any doubt, Kearton was the driving force behind this whole piece of enterprise.

In 1955 and 1956 some Russian delegations interested in textiles and man-made fibres visited Courtaulds. As a follow-up, Kearton went to Moscow in August–September 1956, in company with the chairman of Lustre Fibres. Courtaulds had an almost negligible export trade to Russia and after reports on a fashion show in Moscow in June of that year, Kearton had expressed himself on the desirability of getting into the Russian market. But during his visit, conversations with Soviet officials revealed an interest in buying complete plants for the production of acetate yarn for warp knitting as well as for viscose staple fibre; in machinery for the false-twist process; in additional acetate spinning machinery; and in chemicals used in the spinning of acrylic fibres (which Kearton pointed out was unrealistic as this really meant asking for 'know-how' in 'Courtelle'). Hints were also dropped about spinning machinery and 'know-how' for the strongest type of tyre cord. All this was conveyed by letter to the chairman and subsequently reported to the Board. With a warning to get the official view on such matters from the Board of Trade, the Board agreed that Kearton should continue his discussions with the U.S.S.R. representatives. After some further correspondence and consultation, in October 1956 Kearton sent to Technopromimport (the U.S.S.R. department then concerned with these matters) a set of preliminary tenders, hedged about with sundry qualifications, and all excluding packing, shipment, and, where appropriate, erection costs. The figures, given below, were not those on which in fact any of the contracts were entered into, but their very presentation, in this letter, gives an idea of what was involved and what Kearton, in conjunction with the Engineering department, was disposed to offer:

	£
1 acetate filament yarn plant, capacity 15 tons per day	1,850,000
10 acetate yarn spinning machines	430,000
5 viscose staple fibre plants, capacity each 30 tons per day	5,925,000
machinery for production of 'stretch' nylon yarn by the false-twist process, capacity 1 ton per day	88,000
information on and chemicals for acrylic fibre process	500,000

For a firm which, as he had explained in a previous letter, made no claims to being machinery manufacturers and which was 'presented with a new situation' by requests for man-made fibre plants, this preliminary tender marked a very remarkable departure for the company.

It was also the first shot in a long bargaining battle during which Courtaulds, like other British firms engaged in similar negotiations at that time, discovered that the most relevant weapons in dealing with Soviet officialdom were great patience and considerable tenacity. As sellers they found themselves dealing with buyers who were very well-informed, who shopped around (to Snia, for example), sometimes changed their minds but at other times could be very rigid and inflexible, and were very tough bargainers. A large number of inquiring balloons were sent aloft, only a small number of which were intended to be taken seriously. By February 1958 over a dozen schemes had been put forward. By the summer of 1960, by which time the first four U.S.S.R. contracts had been signed, 22 separate projects had been specified and tendered for, covering a wide range of processes and chemicals, viz. acetate spinning and acetate moulding powders, acetic anhydride, caprolactam, viscose staple fibre and tyre cord, petrochemicals, acrylics, and more besides. Many came to nothing. Between 1957 and 1960, eight visits were paid to the U.S.S.R., involving some 50 Courtaulds technicians; five different departments or organizations within the U.S.S.R. administrative machine were dealt with. On the first contract negotiations seemingly broke down completely in the course of 1957 only to be resumed with changed specifications. Ignorance by Courtaulds of Soviet regulations and contract techniques undoubtedly contributed to the delay; much of the time spent on the first contract was in reality given over to the two sides gaining some confidence in each other's intentions. Not until the early summer of 1958 were the negotiations for the first contract—covering a cellulose acetate ('Dicel') spinning plant together with twisting and false-twisting machinery—approaching the stage when the possibility of signing seemed at last to be in view. At the time, moreover, the Russians also made it clear that they were seriously interested in tenders for plants to produce high-tenacity tyre cord and acrylic fibre. And it was just at this time, too, that Wilson took an important step in furthering his objections to the Russian contracts as a whole.

In June 1958 Wilson, hearing that Kearton was about to sign the acetate contract, wrote to Hanbury-Williams, setting out his views at some length. Once that contract had been signed, then, he wrote, 'I feel very strongly that we ought to withdraw diplomatically from our conversations regarding a tyre cord and acrylic plant'. He had always, he said, been dubious about the advantages to Courtaulds of these contracts, regarding them as highly advantageous to the Russians. The arguments in favour of them were four-fold: large payments for 'know-how'; favourable terms for export of Courtaulds' yarns and fibres; other firms would undertake the projects if Courtaulds did not; and 'a much-needed base load for E.H.Q. [Engineering Headquarters].'[1] He saw these arguments as having doubtful validity though conceding that the fourth argument provided a justification for going through with the acetate contract. 'Apart from the temporary important relief it gives to E.H.Q. while E.H.Q. is being reorganized to deal with our smaller future capital expenditure, I think that the financial advantages are negligible in the short run, and may be negative in the long run.' The tyre-cord and acrylic projects he saw as diplomatic bait for the acetate contract; they should be killed off. There was 'no future in building large fibre plants abroad in which we have no financial interest'. Whilst the company suffered no harm as a consequence of giving temporary assistance to E.H.Q. by the sale of a standard acetate plant, it would be giving away its life-blood and building up even greater competitive forces by handing over new and advanced designs and chemical processes, embodied in the new tyre-cord and acrylic plants, which were, moreover, still in the course of development. Wilson, who wrote from Brussels, asked Hanbury-Williams to put forward his views at the next Board meeting, when the subject might come up.

Whatever the force of Wilson's arguments, there is no doubt that he was correct in presenting the whole Russian venture as having originated, in part at least, as an operation to provide work for unused capacity in the company's engineering section.

A brief digression must be made into the provenance of Courtaulds'

[1] The engineering department at Coventry was often known as Engineering Headquarters even after it became the Engineering Division.

engineers. The existence of a significant engineering department within the company had its roots in the earliest days of the Courtaulds family enterprise, in 'Steam Factory' at Bocking in the 1820s making silk-throwing machinery and power looms, growing into Frederick Johnson's little empire at Coventry, making rayon-spinning machinery and designing the company's yarn mills in the 1920s and 1930s.[1] In 1945, in anticipation of post-war re-equipment and expansion, the Engineering department was itself expanded, a lease being taken of a government-owned factory at Accrington in order to increase machinery-making capacity.[2] After Frederick Johnson's retirement in 1947 the post of chief engineer was briefly occupied by a non-directorial appointment, but with Verrall's arrival in 1949 and the part-time appointment of Sir William Stanier, engineering was doubly represented on the Board. No sooner had the Accrington factory been leased than delays and indecision were experienced in the re-equipment programme, thus inevitably raising the policy question: should the Engineering department undertake outside work in order to keep its capacity profitably employed? This question was to recur and be debated over the ensuing decades, even after the Accrington factory was given up in 1950. The converse proposition was of course that more use should be made of specialist engineering firms by putting the company's needs out to tender, and reducing the size of the Engineering department. Both Gratwick and Freeman had adhered to this school of thought, and in 1952 Freeman tried hard to cut down the Engineering department which he scathingly referred to as 'one of the biggest overheads which the company has to support'. Whilst Courtaulds were continuing to expand their activities during the 1950s a respectable case could of course be made for the maintenance of the engineers' traditional role. But relations between the Engineering Division and the Research Division, and particularly its Chemical Engineering section, became somewhat strained. The substantial build-up and modernization of the Research Division by Wilson and the work of the Chemical Engineering section, of which Kearton had been put in charge when he first joined Courtaulds, had led them to develop their own engineering facilities outside the Engineering department. The latter had been left with its traditional concern with plant layout and the repairs and manufacture of machinery but excluded from the design and development of the new processes. Representations

[1] See Vol. I, pp. 71–2, 76, and *passim*; II, pp. 222, 231, 248, 271, 277, etc.

[2] It was intended to use it for making the continuous-spinning machines which the company was to make as a consequence of obtaining the I.R.C. patents (see above, p. 48).

by Verrall and Stanier led to the commissioning of a report on the Engineering Division from an outside expert and the net result of its recommendation, made in 1956, was in effect to sustain the size and power of the Division, with certain organizational changes designed to improve its relations with those responsible for the new developments. The Board accepted the report despite the opposition of those (including Hanbury-Williams and Wilson) who wanted to see the Engineering Division cut down and who, as can be seen from Wilson's letter, expected future capital expenditure to fall. But at that particular time work was not forthcoming. The Russian contracts provided the opportunity for one sort of work and in 1957 a subsidiary called Courtaulds Technical Services Ltd. was created to do other sorts of outside work.

So here was a further source of friction and disagreement between Wilson and Kearton. The former was anxious to curtail E.H.Q., thereby economizing at a time of falling profits and in the light of expected retraction in capital commitments of the sort which provided work for the engineers; the latter was keen to press E.H.Q. into the service of his expansionary and diversifying zeal. Wilson's letter of June 1958 caused trouble or, to be more exact, what Hanbury-Williams did with it caused trouble. For he promptly showed it not only to Kearton but also to Pedder[1] whose relations with Kearton were known to be less than cordial. Kearton took offence; it was to this letter which he referred when, according to Wilson's memorandum of May 1959, he complained of Wilson having written to the chairman about the Russian contracts behind his back.[2] But having showed the letter to others, Hanbury-Williams, to Wilson's chagrin, then did nothing further about it. The negotiations continued, and in July 1958—at the same time as the signing of the first acetate contract, worth approximately £4 million, was announced—preliminary estimates were given for the tyre-cord and acrylic plants. When the Board was told, Wilson was joined by Mathys and Peter Courtauld in voicing reservations. Nevertheless, a majority was in favour and Kearton was authorized to continue. The formal tender for the tyre-cord factory was submitted in November 1958. By this time Russian habits were becoming familiar: 'I would be very surprised if anything much now happens for another two or three months,' Kearton observed to Verrall, 'I don't put the chances of it coming off much higher than

[1] The letter is endorsed in Hanbury-Williams's handwriting: 'seen by C.F.K. and J.E.P. 24/6/58'.

[2] See above, p. 142.

about 25% at this stage.' Negotiations on the acrylic-fibre project were also pushed ahead but not without more reservations from the Board. Early in 1959, on a further visit to Moscow, Kearton and George Courtauld, who had accompanied him, had been obliged to break off the negotiations because of cabled instructions from Rendall stipulating conditions which they regarded as unacceptable. It was not until clarification had been secured at a Board meeting in February that they were resumed. They then took the form of talk about a package deal for three plants: tyre cord, acrylic fibre, and a second acetate unit.[1] The matter was again discussed by the Board in April and Kearton was given permission to go ahead on a basis that the contract would yield about 10 per cent. profit and that he would have to come back to the Board if it appeared necessary to go significantly below that margin to secure agreement. By the end of the month the contracts had been signed; and with some muted trumpet-blowing Courtaulds publicly announced the conclusion of contracts to supply to the U.S.S.R. complete plants and technical processes for the manufacture of viscose tyre cord, acrylic staple fibre, and cellulose acetate yarn, the total sum involved being approximately £15 million.

These contracts were formally concluded between Techmashimport,[2] and Prinex Ltd. The latter was a subsidiary of Courtaulds, specifically set up in January 1959 for the export of factories and processes. Its name was derived, as Kearton's doodle shows (see Plate 10), from the words *Pr*ocess *In*dustries *Ex*port. The immediate pretext was a Russian enquiry about matters outside Courtaulds' purview, viz. a sugar factory, but Prinex became in practice a legal device for handling the plant contracts after the first acetate contract. An important *raison d'être* for Prinex, and certain other similar subsidiaries created for specific contracts of this sort, was to buy from Courtaulds Ltd. for a lump sum the 'know-how' attributable to the particular plant being sold. Until a final judgement delivered by the House of Lords in May 1962 lump-sum payments for 'know-how' or 'secret processes' were treated as capital receipts and therefore not liable to tax.[3] This method was used both for the £15 million batch of Russian contracts and for those with Yugoslavia and Poland.

The Yugoslav contract arose from conversations between a Yugoslav delegation and one of the British Celanese directors, W. A. Dickie, in June

[1] They were to be built at, respectively, Balakova, Saratov, and Kirovakan.

[2] Instead of Technopromimport as in the first contract.

[3] The sums received from these sales made their contribution during the battle against the I.C.I. take-over bid. See below, p. 228, n.1.

1958. The potential buyers showed interest in an acetate plant and, later, an acrylic unit. Dickie referred it to Kearton. The latter's response, in a letter written shortly after Hanbury-Williams had shown him Wilson's letter deprecating the Russian contracts, recommended playing for time, as the controversial nature of the business hardly made it opportune to submit formal proposals for the Yugoslav suggestion:

There are very mixed opinions inside Courtaulds Ltd., about doing business with the U.S.S.R., and although I have agreement to submit quotations, etc. for the tyrecord and acrylic fibre units, there is no certainty as yet that the Company would in fact accept a contract. This doesn't worry me over much at this stage, since the Russians have tenders from many other sources and I think that our own quotes are in any case a little more expensive than competitive quotations.

The negotiations continued. Delegations visited Skopje first from British Celanese and then in March 1959, as it became apparent that the acrylic plant was foremost in the Yugoslavs' minds, from Courtaulds. Kearton submitted a £2·2 million tender for an acrylic plant in June. Eventually a contract was signed in May 1960 and for the purposes of the lump-sum sale of 'know-how' a subsidiary called Luna Ltd. was created, buying the 'know-how' for £500,000.

The Polish contract followed a not dissimilar course. A request from the Polish authorities for a tender for an acetate plant in the summer of 1958 was followed by a switch to an acrylic-fibre plant, a first tender for which was submitted in December 1960. After a good deal of bargaining—in the course of which the Poles claimed to have ten separate tenders for an acrylic-fibre plant—a contract worth approximately £2 million was finally signed in July 1961 for the supply of a plant with a capacity of 10 million lb. per annum to be built near Lodz. Courtaulds had meanwhile sold to another Prinex-type subsidiary, Procindus Ltd. its acrylic-fibre 'know-how' for the sum of £800,000.

It was one thing to win all these contracts but quite another to carry them out on time. Delays were inevitable and some of them became so serious as to give rise to protracted battles of words. The first U.S.S.R. acetate contract, after its long period of gestation, seems to have gone fairly smoothly and was completed on time. With the second acetate contract, however, the delays began. Some small complaints were heard in the summer of 1960, but by the autumn of that year it became evident that problems were arriving, and were likely to continue arriving, on two fronts: delays by sub-contractors supplying various machines or constructional materials; and difficulties in E.H.Q. because of the enormous pressure of commercial work put on an organization initially designed to fulfil service functions within Courtaulds. Not a great deal could be done about the former except exert appropriate pressure; the latter represented the logical outcome of embarking on a venture which ultimately went so much further than finding employment for some under-utilized engineering capacity as to bring about some expansion of that capacity. Early in 1961 Russian complaints of delays in deliveries on the acrylic and second acetate plants were answered by suitable apologies and promises from Verrall; but they were met, in part at least, by the completion of deliveries under the second acetate contract in April, one month beyond the grace period which was allowed after the formal completion date of 31 January. Further delays and complaints on the acrylic contracts worsened during 1961; it, too, was finally completed, but not until May by which time it had run four months beyond the period of grace, the contract's completion date having been 30 November 1960.

The tyre-cord venture experienced these difficulties in a more acute form. To secure this contract, the most valuable of all, Kearton had agreed to a reduction on the originally quoted price, a shortened delivery time, and penalty clauses on late deliveries. Furthermore, the project as a whole was full of technical risk for the simple reason that the plant which was the subject of the contract had no equivalent already at work in Britain, nor had the very high-strength tyre cord which the Russians demanded yet been produced commercially. Although the T.105 cord, which was already in production by Courtaulds, formed the basis of the original contract, capacity to produce the higher strength (T.140) was also needed; and it was this cord which Courtaulds had not yet produced in factory conditions. Even when the contract was signed in April 1959, many of the technical details were still under discussion. Thus fundamental design work was required and considerable problems arose in producing the technical documentation specified under the terms of the contract. To try to meet the contract dates large orders were put out to engineering firms. But by the summer of 1960 the situation in the engineering industry had changed substantially as the slow economic advance of the later 1950s gave way to something of a boom in 1959–60 and order books filled up. By February 1961 the backlog of plant due for delivery but which had fallen behind the original schedule amounted to nearly £1·4 million. Outside suppliers were berated; apologies offered to the Russians; counter-arguments put forward, attacking the shortcomings of the Russian shipping agent; the Board of Trade was consulted. Moreover, even by April, Kearton was still wondering whether the work at the research laboratories had reached the stage which would ensure the achievement of the requisite 'super-super cord' which the Russian plant was destined to produce. 'I did not see many signs that we have yet reached specification for 140 level tyre cord,' he wrote to the head of the Viscose Research Laboratory at Coventry;[1] 'Are you still quite confident that we shall be able to meet the Russian specification?' The reply reassured him, though the margin left was obviously thin: 'I have no doubts that, given reasonable raw materials, we shall be able to meet the Russian strength specification.' But it was still only at the pilot-plant stage, and the completion date was supposed to be 31 August, a mere four months away. The shipments of plant were finally completed in October 1961. Thereafter, there were long and complicated delays and disputes about the erection and operation of the plant itself, many of which were in no way the fault of Courtaulds, but which resulted in the final instalment of the 'retention money' under the contract not being received until 1966.

This tyre-cord contract provided yet another, and particular, cause of disagreement between Kearton and Wilson. The latter disapproved strongly of entering into a contract to supply something, i.e. the T.140 cord, which was still based on expectation rather than achievement. But his objections came to nothing in face of Kearton's drive and Board majorities in favour of proceeding with the various contracts. By the autumn of 1961 Wilson had had to accept such engineering ventures as one of the company's sources of profits even though he still regarded the Engineering Division as excessively large. The delays in the contracts had, after all, not prevented the Russians from continuing negotiations in the course of 1961 for the triacetate plant.[2] The hazards of dealing with the first major Communist power in the world and some of its satellites had not prevented Kearton from departing on a trip to China in 1959 in the hope of interesting the second major Communist country in the idea of buying Courtaulds' machinery and 'know-how'. Although the Yugoslav and Polish contracts were not completed for some time, negotiations began with Romania for an acrylic-fibre plant.

Because of the long and varying periods involved in these contracts, and the complex pattern of costs and benefits—ranging from the price of

[1] Donald Entwistle, subsequently (1967–79) a Courtaulds director.
[2] To be erected in Kaunas, Lithuania.

financing those in which credit terms were negotiated with the assistance of E.C.G.D.[1] to the gains from consequential exports of home-produced fibres or machinery spares—consideration of their general profitability to Courtaulds must be deferred to a later chapter.[2] Suffice, meanwhile, to draw together some of the results of the U.S.S.R. contracts as they had appeared by 1961. The four contracts can be summarized as follows:

TABLE 31

U.S.S.R. contracts, 1958–9

Date of contract	*Name and purpose*	*Approx. value £ mn.*	*Terms*
15 July 1958	First acetate	4·0	Cash
30 Apr. 1959	Second acetate	3·8	Credit
30 Apr. 1959	Acrylic	2·2	Cash
30 Apr. 1959	Viscose tyre cord	9·0	Credit

To the financial year ending in March 1961, the total value of sales made in connection with these contracts was £12,232,079.[3] Out of this the sum of £1,500,728 was attributed to sales of 'know-how', treated as a capital transaction and hence was not taxable. Against the balance, £10,731,351, were set costs of £9,509,374 which left a net revenue profit of £1,221,977, i.e. a margin of 11 per cent. on sales over two years. Whatever value one cares to put upon the tax-free gain of selling 'know-how', this residual gain was clearly not high. However, not only was it incomplete at this date but it was also in some senses merely a bait to catch other and more profitable fish in the future.

[1] Export Credit Guarantee Department, a branch of the Board of Trade. Courtaulds found it sometimes a rather slow, expensive, and bureaucratic machine.

[2] See below, pp. 282–4.

[3] Of this sum £8,235,144 went through Prinex, the balance of £3,996,935 representing the first pre-Prinex acetate contract.

CHAPTER X

The I.C.I. Bid

ON Monday 18 December 1961 British newspaper readers learned, under such headlines as 'Stock Exchange Sensation: The Biggest Take-over Bid in Britain's History',[1] that the largest industrial company in the country, Imperial Chemical Industries, had made an offer for that most respected, if rather doleful, giant Courtaulds Ltd. Rather over a fortnight later, on 5 January 1962, Courtaulds issued a press statement recommending the rejection of the bid. For more than two months there followed, to the accompaniment of much debate in press and Parliament, a public business quarrel which was not merely the largest take-over battle which had ever been seen in Britain but behaviour of an unprecedented kind in the eyes of the City. Its termination with the announcement on 12 March that I.C.I. had then gained some 38 per cent. of Courtaulds' equity represented a defeat for I.C.I. and only a partial victory for Courtaulds. It left a legacy of resentment as well as much mystery about how it all came to happen; it carried very important consequences for Courtaulds' future; and some for I.C.I. (which are *not* the concern of this book).

I

The hinge of Courtaulds' relationship with I.C.I. was B.N.S. The inherently unstable position pointed out by Wilson in his prophetic comment of 1952[2] continued in being. For not only was B.N.S. dependent on I.C.I. for the basic raw material but its product competed both with Courtaulds' rayon and with I.C.I.'s 'Terylene'. Despite the success with 'Courtelle' it was perhaps hardly surprising that some Courtaulds' directors —despairing about the future of rayon and worried about the stuttering performance of profits in the later 1950s—should have come to believe that salvation might lie with some sort of amalgamation with I.C.I. Conversely, it is equally unsurprising that some I.C.I. directors—as they read their experts' rosy predictions for the future of synthetics,[3] as they observed the take-off of 'Courtelle' and pondered their own earlier decision not to

[1] *Evening Standard.* [2] See above, p. 82. [3] See below, p. 206.

develop acrylics,[1] as they experienced some difficulties in the launch of 'Terylene' and bore in mind the expiry of its patents in 1963—should have wondered whether there was not something to be said for acquiring 'Courtelle' and the other half of B.N.S. at the price of taking over Courtaulds.

The first significant moves in this direction were taken in 1960. In January of that year the chairmanship of I.C.I. passed from the hands of Sir Alexander Fleck[2] into those of S. P. Chambers. Totally different both from Fleck and from his opposite numbers in Courtaulds, Paul Chambers, then aged 56, had had an exceptionally brilliant career as a civil servant in the Inland Revenue and had gone straight on to the main Board of I.C.I. in 1947.[3] He differed from Hanbury-Williams in age, background, education, and manner. Although virtually the same age as Wilson, he differed from him in the possession of a notable capacity for voluble and, in the judgement of many who met him, highly persuasive talk.

In July 1960, chatting to Hanbury-Williams at a social function, Chambers suggested that they should meet to talk about 'matters of mutual interest to Courtaulds and I.C.I.'. They did so and talked of a share exchange or holding company. Further meetings in August and September resulted in the production by Chambers of a document in which he argued the merits of 'a complete merger of the two groups'. Competition between them was growing in fibres, chemicals, raw-material supply; there was overlapping in research and development; the opportunities for friction and discord were likely to grow rather than decline. A holding company had serious disadvantages, so a complete merger would be the simplest solution. An expanded I.C.I. Board would contain 'the leading members of the Courtaulds Board'; Courtaulds would continue to be run as a separate company. In the light of later events his observations on possible terms have a piquant flavour:

An offer of one I.C.I. share for one Courtaulds share might mean that I.C.I. stockholders were paying a premium of some millions of pounds for the advantage of being merged with Courtaulds. A large sum may be involved but I believe the long-term advantages would make it worthwhile for I.C.I. stockholders.

[1] I.C.I. had in 1950 secured an exclusive licence to the 'Orlon' patents in the U.K. from Du Pont but had decided against exploiting them commercially.

[2] Later (1961) Lord Fleck.

[3] Reader, II, p. 310. Chambers is generally credited with the invention of P.A.Y.E. He became Sir (Stanley) Paul Chambers, K.B.E. in 1965.

In sending these secret proposals, Chambers observed that 'the matter has not been discussed by my Board'; it was 'in no sense an agreed document'.

There followed, a week or so later, a meeting in which Hanbury-Williams, Dallas Bernard, and Wilson, representing Courtaulds, discussed the matter with Chambers and two of his deputy chairmen from I.C.I.[1] The I.C.I. representatives pressed the desirability of a merger, advancing the arguments of increased strength and savings in costs. Hanbury-Williams, Bernard, and Wilson each expressed doubts of various sorts. It was agreed that the matter should be discussed by both Boards. The Courtaulds representatives were offered the important reassurance that 'no bid over the heads of the Board of Courtaulds was in contemplation'.

Over the next couple of months the Courtaulds' directors pondered upon this notion of a voluntary merger with I.C.I. And the more they pondered the less some of them liked it. The chairman himself, however, approved of the idea. In October Hanbury-Williams circulated a paper to his Board. Though evidently troubled by the possible political implications and by the likely adverse effect upon staff morale, he found the profit forecasts for the next five and ten years so depressing as to imprint upon his mind the advantages of a merger. Their combined strengths would make them 'more efficient and more competitive with other large companies' in the U.S.A. and continental Europe. So, though leaving a slender loophole, he committed himself: 'I believe that unless a satisfactory alternative solution can be found we should decide to negotiate on the basis of a complete merger'. Four directors, Mynors, Knight, Mathys, and Peter Courtauld, put their observations on paper and sent them to Hanbury-Williams. All, in effect, said: No. By far the most interesting remarks were made by Knight. Noting that as the youngest member of the Board, he could expect, in the normal course of events, to have to live longer with the consequences of the decision to be made on this matter, he set out some explicit and forthright comments. He emphasized that the Board had had no considered assessment of possible profits or losses in particular areas of the two company's activities, e.g. paint, 'Courtelle' and 'Terylene' as rival fibres, or nylon and rayon in the tyre-cord market; and that careful study of such issues was needed before an informed decision could be made. Meanwhile, 'the case for our agreeing to a merger on these grounds is by no means obvious'. He noted the rate of growth of I.C.I. profits and

[1] R. H. (later Sir Ronald) Holroyd, F.R.S., and E. A. (later Sir Eric) Bingen.

asked whether the prospects of further growth therein were so much more attractive that Courtaulds should encourage shareholders to exchange their holdings for an equity interest in I.C.I.'s prospects. As for the estimates to which the chairman referred they were of little help, being merely 'accounting and statistical exercises reflecting no coherent plan'. He specified examples of the company's inadequate investment planning, damning it comprehensively with the remark that 'we are not at present organising ourselves to prepare a sensible coherent plan for the next ten years'. He pointed to a currently sensitive spot on the company's direction: the continuing argument over the succession to the chairmanship and the factions arising therefrom: 'leadership and therefore management are impaired by personal frictions which have become worse since you declared your intentions and in the absence of any decision about your successor'.[1] A merger would not solve the problem; it would merely transfer it to I.C.I. He concluded that Courtaulds should take action to set its own house in order and should tell I.C.I. meanwhile that 'we do not at present see the justification for a merger'.

On 24 November 1960 the Board discussed the whole issue. It was unanimously agreed that the chairman should tell his opposite number at I.C.I. that the Board was opposed to a merger. There had been a few waverers: Henry Johnson, probably beset, like Hanbury-Williams, by memories of past rayon glory now slipping away, confessed that though his heart was against it his head was in favour. But the many and various objections, not least that of monopoly, triumphed. So in December Hanbury-Williams told Chambers that the Courtaulds Board was against a merger; and it was agreed that although the two of them might meet from time to time 'to see if there were matters of mutual interest which could form the basis of a more detailed discussion', it would be wiser meanwhile to leave things as they were.

And so they were. Before moving on to the way in which their slumbers were disturbed a year later, it is perhaps worth emphasizing two points about this 1960 episode. First, despite the gloomy forecasts for the future, the decision to oppose the merger scheme was made against the background of improved profits for the financial year ending March 1960 when, indeed, pre-tax profits at £21 million had been a record.[2] One may reasonably wonder whether the stand would have been so bold had the 1959–60 results been as poor as those of the two preceding years. Second,

[1] For this enduring source of conflict within the Board, see Chapter VII above.

[2] See Table 18, p. 129, above.

the chairman's doubts, pessimism, and general lack of faith in the future of Courtaulds were made clear to all who had eyes to see.

II

In April 1961 Chambers entertained Hanbury-Williams to lunch at I.C.I.'s massive head office on Millbank. Conversation turned to the matters discussed the previous summer and Chambers showed a clear disposition to reopen the issue. On a similar occasion later, in September, he did precisely that. The amalgamation between Rhodiaceta and Rhône-Poulenc had created a large new man-made fibre group in France, like Du Pont in America. Perhaps I.C.I. and Courtaulds might contemplate a sort of amalgamation different from the merger mooted and rejected in 1960? What about the creation of a new company with some such title as 'Chemicals and Courtaulds Ltd.', thus disposing of the anachronistic 'Imperial' in the name of I.C.I.? No details were discussed but it was agreed that a closer link between I.C.I. and Courtaulds seemed desirable 'in the coming years'. On 3 October Chambers called on Hanbury-Williams at the latter's invitation and aired some more notions on the topic. These included a revival of the idea of a holding company, this time to rule over two subsidiaries, one of which would control all fibres and the chemicals used therein, the other everything else.[1] Hanbury-Williams, however, was just about to leave in a few days' time to visit the Usutu and Saiccor plants. So it was agreed that Wilson should continue the discussions with Chambers in London. As, moreover, Chambers himself was likewise going briefly to South Africa, a further meeting there between the two chairmen was also planned.

All these various meetings took place. Alan Wilson met and talked with Paul Chambers on seven occasions between 17 October and 16 December inclusive, either at Millbank or at Chambers's house. In addition he had two meetings with another I.C.I. director particularly interested in these matters, Leslie Williams, on 19 October and 8 November. Meanwhile, Chambers and Hanbury-Williams met in Johannesburg. The whole sequence of twelve duologues is set out in Table 32. One vital point about these meetings must be stressed. *At none of them was anyone else present.* This is a matter of crucial importance to the history of this whole episode

[1] A rough diagram of this arrangement is sketched, in Hanbury-Williams's hand, in his notes on the meeting, made at the time.

TABLE 32

Merger duologues, Sept.–Dec. 1961

Date	*Participants*		
18 Sept.	Hanbury-Williams	and	Chambers
3 Oct.	,,	,,	,,
17 Oct.	Wilson	,,	,,
19 Oct.	,,	,,	Williams
3 Nov. (Johannesburg)	Hanbury-Williams	,,	Chambers
8 Nov.	Wilson	,,	Williams
23 Nov.	,,	,,	Chambers
29 Nov.	,,	,,	,,
7 Dec.	,,	,,	,,
12 Dec.	,,	,,	,,
15 Dec.	,,	,,	,,
16 Dec.	,,	,,	,,

because much of the subsequent bitterness arose from conflicting views about what had been agreed on these occasions.

According to Wilson,[1] when he saw Chambers on 17 October, the latter told him that he and some of his senior colleagues were convinced that a merger would bring both short-term economies in fibres and paints and long-term expansion in profits. Wilson said that his Board had yet to be convinced that joint rather than separate action would produce such major benefits. It was eventually agreed that Chambers would get one of his deputy chairmen to provide general substantiation for the claims made. Two days later Wilson talked with the deputy chairman in question, L. H. Williams, and came to understand that at the base of I.C.I.'s case lay a belief, gained from a study of world markets, that demand for synthetic fibres would rise so steeply as to render it impossible for any but large groups to have the requisite financial and technical resources to match output to demand. Shortly afterwards Williams sent to Wilson some copies of the I.C.I. study on which these views were based. When they met again on 8 November, Wilson told Williams that they considered the study revealed that the main problem was the efficient expansion of melt-spun fibres. So, if there was to be amalgamation, why not let it be simply the

[1] All the statements made in this chapter about what was said at the meetings, after that of 3 Oct., set out in Table 32 are based upon (a) the correspondence between Wilson and Hanbury-Williams while the latter was in South Africa; (b) a set of notes prepared by Wilson in January 1962 and which are in Courtaulds' archives; and (c) later interviews with Sir Alan Wilson.

integration of nylon and 'Terylene', as had so often been proposed in the past but to which I.C.I. never saw fit to agree?

Just before this 8 November meeting Courtaulds did something which *may* have had some marginal effect in persuading I.C.I. to press ahead with their growing disposition to bring about a merger. Much more certainly it influenced financial opinion in its view of Courtaulds' prospects, thus in turn bearing upon the company's subsequent defence against the bid. On 2 November Courtaulds announced a cut in the interim dividend.

The decision to do this—thrashed out at a routine Board meeting on 26 October and a specially convened one on 2 November—arose from the confluence of a number of facts and notions. First, and foremost, was the enduring belief, long held within the Courtaulds Board and currently embodied in the person of Hanbury-Williams himself, that large reserves and financial strength constituted a sort of holy armour preserving Courtaulds from the buffets of a hostile outer world. Few questioned it and if they did the chairman would exert his authority in a field in which he was supposed to have some expertise. Upon this attitude of mind there came the impact of the second influence: the fact that the accounting estimates showed a likely fall in profits in the current financial year to March 1962 (which did indeed happen, as Table 18 showed[1]), this being a second fall after the high point of 1959–60. Third was a 12-page survey of Courtaulds' future prospects called 'The general problems of the next five years' written by Wilson and circulated to all directors on 23 October. Its theme was over-capacity and its tone was one of modified despondency interspersed with occasional expressions of muted hopefulness. Finally, the fourth relevant notion was Kearton's vociferously expressed idea that Courtaulds were short of money, not for the reasons that Hanbury-Williams adduced but because the company should be committed to a very large capital programme in further acquiring, diversifying, and expanding in the manner which he prescribed. The net result of all this was that although Courtaulds sat on government securities to a value which in 1960 was almost as great as in 1949 and was still over £12 million in 1961 (see Fig. 8), there was worry about a cash shortage in the summer and autumn of 1961; and, when it came to deciding upon the interim dividend, Hanbury-Williams's wish to cut it from 10*d*. to 8*d*. per £1 attracted the support of, *inter alia*, Kearton. Others thought this was too drastic. After much discussion, and agreement by cable from Hanbury-Williams, a compromise cut to 9*d*. was finally agreed.

[1] See above, p. 129.

There is no indication that in reaching this decision any significant heed was paid to the current talks with I.C.I. or that any director ever seriously supposed that it might induce a take-over bid. It is improbable that the idea would have been entertained if only because such a bid would have been unprecedented. Courtaulds was not the sort of company to which such things happened; in any event they were too big for a bid. So if anybody did mention I.C.I. in passing, the implication was ignored. The nearest approach to such an objection came from Mathys who had been

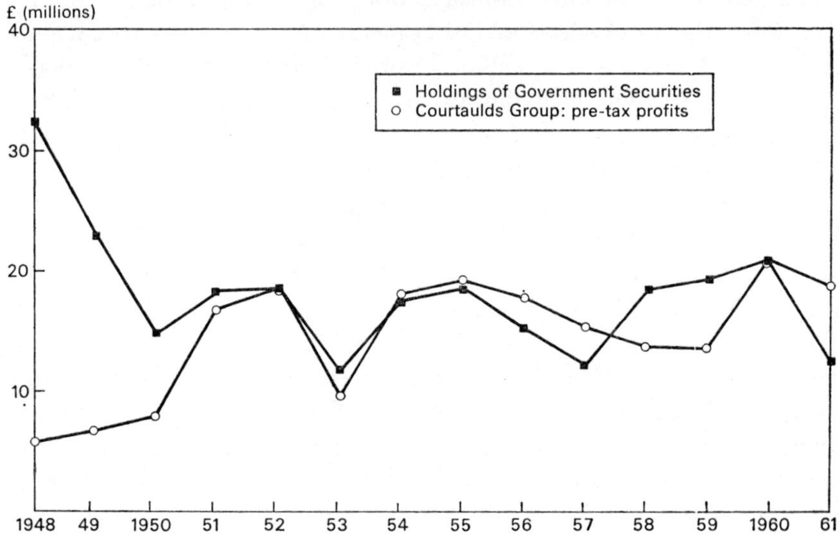

FIG. 8. *Courtaulds Group: profits and holdings of government securities, 1948–61*

The government securities were those held by Courtaulds Ltd. and subsidiaries, i.e. Courtauld Group. Profits are after deduction of debenture and/or loan interest for years ending 31 March.

much impressed by the warnings made by the company's public relations officer[1] that the announcement of a reduction in the interim dividend would be bound to cause adverse comment in the press—already prone to making unflattering comments on Courtaulds' performance.[2] Mathys indeed was the one director to vote against the cut at the meeting on 2 November. All the remainder, including Knight, the new finance director, voted in favour of the cut to 9*d*.—later to admit in retrospect that it had been a mistake.

At about the same time as this decision was being made in London,

[1] M. W. Pitts-Tucker. [2] See above, p. 128.

Hanbury-Williams and Chambers met in Johannesburg. In a letter dated 4 November the former told Wilson of the meeting and announced that in future he would refer to the matter in question as 'Operation Atlas'. He undoubtedly shared Chambers's wish for a rapid outcome and hoped that what emerged would prove more acceptable to the Courtaulds Board than it had in 1960.

He told me of his conversations with you and I understand some progress has been made. He says that his Board are now aware of the general idea and are in agreement that it would be advantageous for something to be done. I explained that by the end of this year my Board would reach a decision as to whether they wished to go ahead or drop the whole matter. I told him that if we decided to go ahead some public announcement should be made in January because a leak must be avoided at all costs, he is in full agreement with this.

On 13 November, asking for news of Operation Atlas, he added, 'the more I think of it the more I feel something should be done'. The members of the Courtaulds Board would probably have been more than a little interested to know that they had thus been committed to making a decision within a couple of months on a matter which had not been fully and formally discussed for almost a year.

Shortly after the meeting in Johannesburg Chambers returned to London and on 15 November took a further step towards his intended goal. He entertained to dinner, at his house in London, four I.C.I. directors and four Courtaulds directors. The I.C.I. contingent comprised Williams and Bingen, P. T. (later Sir Peter) Menzies, finance director, and G. F. Whitby, chairman of the Fibres Division though not an I.C.I. main-board director. Courtaulds were represented by Wilson, Knight, Kearton, and Mathys. Reports of the meeting are confused and divergent. A few features at least are clear. Courtaulds' team did not accept the implications of the I.C.I. study on the market for synthetic fibres but were disposed to consider the advantages of integrating the melt-spun fibres; the I.C.I. team contended that there were bigger economies and advantages to be gained by the integration of all fibres. At some late stage in the argument Chambers said in so many words that there was not much point in discussing the integration of melt-spun fibres; that he wanted a complete merger; and that I.C.I. were prepared to make an offer for Courtaulds' entire share capital. Rubbing salt in the wound thereby opened, Williams observed that if I.C.I. made a big enough offer Courtaulds would not be able to resist it. After the ensuing verbal mêlée it was agreed that Chambers should produce what was called a 'pro forma' of the arguments for a merger and some indication of the terms and the proposed organization. The extreme undesirability of a leak was stressed; and the meeting broke up with the four Courtaulds directors going home, feeling not a little apprehensive.

When Chambers and Wilson met on 23 November, the former sketched some organizational changes as part of his proposed merger. They seemed hardly consistent with what had been discussed, both earlier and more recently, between Chambers and Hanbury-Williams. In the new company I.C.I.'s name would be retained but Courtaulds' would be amended or added to; only two or three Courtaulds directors would be welcomed on the new I.C.I. Board; the terms would be based on equating the dividends paid by the two companies, in 1961 and 1962; there was talk of a price of 2 I.C.I. shares for 3 Courtaulds'. According to Wilson, Chambers said 'Let's assume we are going to have a merger.' All this was a long way from the notion of a 1 for 1 offer and a premium payable by I.C.I. stockholders, as set out by Chambers in 1960.[1] If it was in other respects a return to the rejected merger proposals of 1960, it was also a long way from what Hanbury-Williams, even after his meeting with Chambers in South Africa, was still regarding as Chambers's plan, i.e. the holding company with two subsidiaries, as adumbrated at the meeting of 3 October. Having heard from Wilson on the progress of the talks and the possibility of a take-over, he naturally wondered why 'we are departing from what I understood P.C. had in mind'.

On 29 November Wilson again met Chambers. Armed with a paper by Knight, he pointed out that when allowance was made for the cyclical nature of the textile trade the performances of the two companies were very similar until 1959–60 and that it was only in the past two years that they had markedly diverged. Chambers, putting more weight on current than on past results, now said that his Board thought that a price of 5 I.C.I. shares for 8 Courtaulds' was reasonable; and he was not sure whether it would agree to 2 for 3. This question of price now became the centre-piece of talk at the next three meetings between Wilson and Chambers, on 7, 12, and 15 December.

Before looking at what went on then, it is worth digressing briefly to note that it was just at this time that awareness of the changing path of these talks led to the abandonment of the plan, already mentioned,[2] for Lord Cobbold to join the Courtaulds Board. On 23 November Wilson had explained the emerging situation to him, particularly the desire to have

[1] See above, p. 202. [2] See above, p. 144.

11. Press Conference, 24 January 1962

From l. to r. J. P. Koppel, A. W. Knight, C. F. Kearton, Sir John Hanbury-Williams, Sir Alan Wilson, H. R. Mathys, R. J. Kerr-Muir

COURTAULDS, LIMITED

Advice to Stockholders

Out of the mass of paper which you have received during these past few weeks, one fact emerges quite clearly—the I.C.I. offers are not good enough.

I.C.I. have such a high opinion of your Company that they have progressively increased their offers in order to obtain a shareholding in it as large as you will permit them.

Your shares are worth more than I.C.I. are offering.

All you have to do to reject the I.C.I. offer is to destroy all the paper which you have received.

JOHN HANBURY-WILLIAMS, *Chairman*.
ALAN H. WILSON, *Chairman Designate*.

12. Courtaulds' final advice to stockholders, *The Times*, 2 March 1962

13. The Press and the Bid: a selection of cartoons

14. Sir Dallas Bernard (*circa* 1961)

a decision by January. Cobbold felt he had no option but to withdraw. Bernard cabled the news of his withdrawal 'in view possible Atlas development' to Hanbury-Williams. The latter's cable in reply reveals how much he had expected that the merger, as he imagined it, would come about. 'When West Atlas [i.e. Chambers] recently here I found it desirable to tell him in confidence about our proposed changes[1] and *he would welcome* noble lord [i.e. Cobbold] as colleague' (my italics). Whether Cobbold would have welcomed Chambers is another matter; at least it is clear that he foresaw controversy of a kind in which, as an eminent figure but as an outside director completely new to Courtaulds, he had no wish to become involved.

To return to the main line of discussion. At the meetings of 7 and 12 December, the two men swapped and argued about various papers prepared by their respective financial directors. At the second meeting Wilson said that a price of 2 I.C.I. shares for 3 Courtaulds' was too low, to which, according to Wilson, Chambers answered that he would have difficulty in getting his Board to agree to 3 for 4 and that if he did so, it would be his last word. He had a Board meeting on 14 December and might, or might not, thereafter send an official letter with an offer of 2 for 3 or 3 for 4. If he did send such a letter, he would like a reply in time to make an announcement on 1 January 1962. Wilson pointed out that such a timetable was virtually impossible and suggested that 15 January was the earliest possible time for a considered decision. Then, at their crucial meeting on 15 December, Chambers told Wilson that his Board agreed to a 3 for 4 offer; that a formal letter would be sent on 18 December; and, moreover, that he still wanted an answer by 29 December. Wilson retorted that the Board of Courtaulds could not possibly agree to produce an answer to so momentous a question in so short a time. In any event, he considered that the absorption of Courtaulds by I.C.I. was seen as unattractive by the Courtaulds Board; that it would have bad effects on the morale of the Courtaulds staff; and in general would be almost entirely to the advantage of I.C.I. He put such observations on paper and showed them to Chambers who rejected them. Impasse had been reached.

These Chambers–Wilson meetings had all taken place in considerable secrecy. All Wilson's letters to Hanbury-Williams had been handwritten. According to Wilson, he had tried, but failed to make the loquacious Chambers understand that the Courtaulds Board was in principle opposed

[1] i.e. making Kearton, Mathys, and, eventually, Cobbold deputy chairmen.

to a merger. He had also adopted the tactics of trying to force Chambers to a price position where he could no longer get the support of his Board. Wilson had explained something of this in a letter to Hanbury-Williams on 30 November:

> he [Chambers] has given up any ideas of a merger, first because his Board would not agree to it, and secondly because it would require the positive assent of 90% of each set of shareholders, which everyone thinks impracticable. He must therefore make a bid and offer sufficiently attractive terms to the Courtaulds shareholders to get 90% acceptance, but not so high that his own shareholders will refuse to vote the required increase in capital in an E.G.M. [Extraordinary General Meeting]. We know from our own experience how high a premium you have to pay to get a 90% acceptance of any offer, and the I.C.I. Board are not yet conditioned to pay any premium at all . . . P.C. agrees that any bid which proved inadequate would be disastrous, and he must avoid at all costs any public move which would merely give him a fraction of our shares.

As this last eventuality was precisely what did happen, Wilson's tactics might in one sense seem to have been successful, however indirectly. But Chambers evidently did have the support of his Board; and the bid was made. So in another sense they failed. If the initial level of the bid had been rather more generous Courtaulds could probably never have successfully opposed it. But once made, the very vigour with which it was opposed owed not a little to the emotions generated when Chambers's intentions and price eventually became known to the Board.

In his letters to Hanbury-Williams of 24 and 30 November Wilson wrote of the views of the Courtaulds Board. 'They realize', he wrote on the earlier date, 'that everything in the end depends on price'; by the later date they were said to be 'reconciled . . . to receive a bid from I.C.I.'; he had done what he said he would do 'namely to get our Board to consider the matter as dispassionately as possible'. The precise nature of the Board's consideration of this matter is unfortunately unclear. There were six Board meetings between 12 October and 6 December inclusive; all were chaired by Wilson. For none of them do the formal Board minutes record discussions of the talks with I.C.I. Discussions of them did proceed, however, at several informal meetings of directors between 12 October and 16 December. Not all directors were present at all these meetings; and only informal minutes or 'notes on the proceedings' relating to some of them seem to have survived. Despite these discussions, despite plenty of gossip, and despite the 15 November dinner party, it was not until Friday 15 December that a special Board meeting took formal, minuted cognizance of this whole issue. Even this meeting started as an informal discussion but was changed into a formal Board meeting, largely at the instigation of George Courtauld and Kearton. It was in the course of it that Wilson departed to Millbank and received the effective ultimatum from Chambers. On the following morning he visited Chambers at his home in Highgate, primarily to stress the unreasonableness of the proposed timetable. He reported Chambers as having said that if the Courtaulds Board rejected the offer he would immediately call a press conference, say that he had asked for Courtaulds' co-operation, had been refused, and intended to make a bid. 'Whilst it was desirable for the Courtaulds Board to support his offer to acquire the company *it was not essential* and he therefore proposed to go ahead as proposed for which he had the full authority of his Board.' Finally, Chambers gave to Wilson the official letter containing the I.C.I. offer. He also mentioned that his Board had asked him to seek the views of the government on the political desirability of the merger and that he had accordingly arranged to see Sir Frank Lee[1] on the following Monday morning. Wilson returned to a further special meeting of the Courtaulds Board on the Saturday afternoon, to tell his fellow-directors of Chambers's intentions and to show them the terms of the I.C.I. bid, more copies of which arrived during the meeting. He had told Chambers that the proposals would be considered by the Courtaulds Board on 20 December. This meeting was indeed held, to take formal cognizance of the bid and to issue a statement to that effect. So the Board had three formal meetings, Friday 15, Saturday 16, and Wednesday 20 December to reach a conclusion and issue a public statement on something which it had rejected in principle a year earlier—merging with I.C.I.

Before the Wednesday meeting, however, the bid had been made public as a consequence of the intervention of a press leak. Somebody had somehow got to know of the talks; somebody pretending to be an I.C.I. press officer had telephoned certain newspaper and television offices on Sunday 17th announcing that there was to be a meeting of the I.C.I. Board at Chambers's house that afternoon (as indeed there was, the directors arriving to find the press there in force); a journalist from the *Daily Mail* telephoned Chambers the same evening and asked directly about the possibility of a merger with Courtaulds; and, despite Chambers's denial, there appeared in Monday morning's *Daily Mail* an article on its City page saying that rumours of a merger between I.C.I. and Courtaulds were now so strong that it must be 'near at hand'. Seeing this, Chambers decided that

[1] Joint Permanent Secretary to the Treasury.

in view of the big Stock Exchange repercussions which would follow, he had to make a statement forthwith. So he called a press conference for that afternoon. He attempted to contact Wilson early in the morning; he failed but made no attempt to consult anyone else at Courtaulds. Wilson, who had not seen the *Daily Mail*, had also arranged to call on Sir Frank Lee on Monday morning, to tell him of the situation. Arriving, he found a message waiting for him asking him to telephone Chambers urgently. The latter told him of his intentions and asked whether Wilson would like to take part. Wilson said it was extremely unlikely. So Chambers let the very large cat out of the bag on Monday afternoon, ready for the evening papers' headlines. The leak which had been feared had duly happened. Naturally, all sorts of suspicions quickly developed. As Wilson put in a letter to Hanbury-Williams on 21 December, 'you arrive home to a confused and dangerous situation. Very ugly rumours are circulating about the leak.' The two companies, at Chambers's suggestion, jointly arranged for an enquiry.[1] It was inconclusive; there was the usual story of information supplied by someone unconnected with I.C.I. or Courtaulds whose name the *Daily Mail* would not divulge; and there was no evidence that any director of either company passed on information for the purpose of publication. In view of I.C.I.'s obvious determination to go ahead with the bid, it is unlikely, in retrospect, that the leak had any more effect than to cause the gun to be fired a few days earlier than it would otherwise have been.

To chart the fluctuating course of the individual attitudes and decisions of the Courtaulds directors at these three vital meetings, or indeed at the various informal meetings which preceded them, is neither possible nor desirable—if only because of an abundance of retrospective, and sometimes conflicting, oral evidence and a dearth of reliable documentary evidence. Suffice to pick out certain dominant themes.

But what, first, were the documents with which they were confronted? The formal bid was contained in a letter from Chambers addressed to Wilson. It offered 3 I.C.I. £1 ordinary shares for 4 £1 Courtaulds ordinary; dealt with the 5 per cent. first preference stock on a 1 for 1 basis; and offered 6 I.C.I. 5 per cent. for 5 of the Courtaulds 6 per cent. second preference shares. Chambers hoped for an acceptance by 29 December and suggested a joint press conference on 1 January 1962. The letter, dated 16 December, was accompanied by two appendices called

[1] It was conducted by the well-known firm of solicitors, W. C. Crocker, and by ex-Commander Burt formerly of Scotland Yard.

Statements A and B. Statement A was a résumé of the arguments for complete amalgamation and the expected savings: it was dated 23 November. Statement B, 'The Scheme', set out certain intentions very relevant to members of the Courtaulds Board. Although it uttered some generalized noises about preserving the names and traditions of both sides, it also made it clear that the only Courtaulds' directors who would be asked to join the Board of I.C.I. were Wilson and Kearton. Although it was not proposed to make any immediate changes in the Board of Courtaulds 'a full examination of the relationship of the businesses of I.C.I. and Courtaulds' was to be undertaken and it was envisaged that 'appropriate additions' would be made to the Board of Courtaulds. This examination would be carried out by a joint committee of seven nominated persons of whom only three came from Courtaulds: Wilson, as its chairman, Kearton, and Mathys.[1] The committee would recommend to the I.C.I. such changes in the Courtaulds Board and in lower levels of management as would enable the intended savings to be secured. Finally, there was an explicit statement that no existing members of the Boards of I.C.I., Courtaulds, or B.N.S. would become redundant as a result of the proposed merger.

Despite this apparent safeguard, it is hard not to believe that the sentiment uppermost in the minds of some of the Courtaulds directors when they came to ponder on these documents was concern about their own jobs. Some, especially Mathys, may have been disappointed at finding themselves unwanted on the I.C.I. Board. Of the two who were wanted, the ambitious Kearton may have hoped for some more specific recognition of his talents; and Wilson may have looked forward without enthusiasm at the prospect of continuing his feud with Kearton amidst the I.C.I. directorate. There can be little doubt that a number of those directors who were least well-informed about what had been going on felt a sense of resentment when they saw the stark reality of the machine bearing down upon them. Suspicion came readily into several minds that Wilson, in his talks with Chambers, had in some way gone further than he should have done, and, rightly or wrongly, some felt that his commitment to opposition was less than whole-hearted. Still more rife was mistrust of Hanbury-Williams himself. The most extreme form of this sentiment was the conviction, subsequently expressed by George Courtauld, that he had 'sold the company down the river' at his meeting with Chambers in Johannesburg

[1] The other members were Williams, Whitby and C. Paine (from I.C.I. Fibres Division), and F. C. Bagnall, the current managing director of B.N.S.

—ironically enough the same phrase which Hanbury-Williams had himself used over twenty years earlier about the sale of A.V.C.[1] There were those, like George Courtauld and his cousin Peter, with an emotional attachment to the firm whose indignation at the predatory monster from Millbank ensured expressions of instant rejection without too much heed to considerations of price or tactics. There were some waverers, anxious about the future of rayon, who initially wondered whether the bid should not be accepted or who sat on the fence, the doubters along with the inscrutable. There were others, including Kearton, who had no objection in principle to going in with I.C.I. but who did not like the terms. Courtaulds shares stood at 30*s.* and I.C.I.'s at 58*s.* 9*d.* just before the announcement of the bid. The offer thus gave an imputed price of 44*s.*[2] to the Courtaulds shares. They jumped to 40*s.* as soon as the bid was made public (see Fig. 9). If Chambers had initially offered terms which would have produced an imputed price of, say, 50*s.* then Kearton, Knight, and probably others with no particular emotional attachment to Courtaulds would almost certainly have pressed for acceptance.

Opinions seem to have shifted during the course of the various meetings, formal and informal, with anti-I.C.I. sentiment hardening, and a good deal of vigorous urging to opposition by George Courtauld, Mathys, Kearton, and Knight who provided much financial data to support Wilson in his talks with Chambers and which included some revised and improved profit estimates.[3] Verbatim notes of the meeting on the Saturday morning, 16 December, before the arrival of the terms of the bid, indicate some characteristic exchanges. Asked by Kearton whether or not he recommended co-operation with I.C.I., Wilson is reported as having said: 'I believe that if he [i.e. Chambers] bid 3 for 4 he would get his offer accepted unless we could make out a very clearly reasoned case against.' After Wilson had pointed to the difficulty, in the light of current Stock Exchange prices, of persuading stockholders that 3 for 4 would be a bad bid, Kearton demanded: 'do we or don't we believe in our own estimates?' To this question came a typical Wilson response: 'I believe in them—with all the reservations attaching to any estimates of future profits.' At an informal meeting on 18 December Wilson is reported as having said that Courtaulds had an arguable but 'not a cast-iron' case. He expressed his conviction that Chambers was determined to get hold of Courtaulds, that he had his Board behind him, and that Courtaulds could only 'fight to get the best

[1] See Vol. II, p. 469. [2] $\frac{3 \times 58s.\ 9d.}{4}$ [3] See below, p. 225.

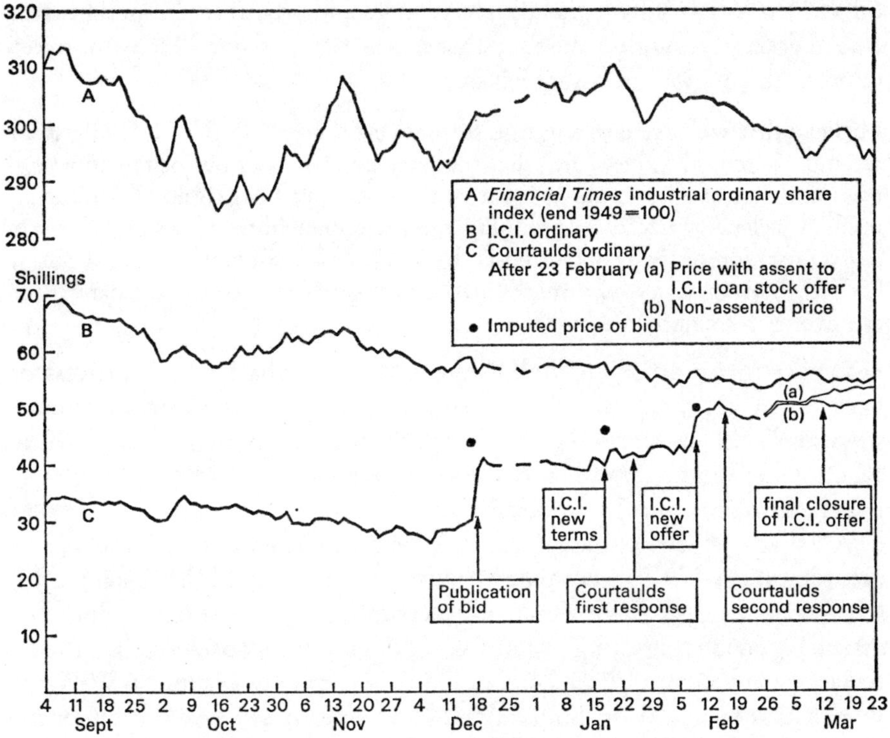

FIG. 9. *Stock Exchange prices: Courtaulds, I.C.I., and* Financial Times *index, September 1961–March 1962*

possible bargain for the stockholders'. In the course of the meeting on 15 December, what looks to have been a rather foolish attempt, sponsored by Kearton and others, to try to stave off the bid by announcing the payment of a second interim dividend, was initially carried but eventually abandoned after continued opposition led by Wilson. Only one member of the Board seems to have been in favour of accepting the bid: Aubrey Jones who, as a recently appointed outside director, had the least emotional commitment to the company. Even his stance, however, was not such as to inhibit the use of the word 'unanimous' in Courtaulds' subsequent public announcement recommending the rejection of the bid.[1] Whatever suspicions some directors may have harboured about Wilson's attitude, he himself believed that he had secured the Board's cohesion. He wrote to Hanbury-Williams

[1] Hanbury-Williams had meanwhile obtained some reassuring opinions from two Q.C.s on the question of Board unanimity.

on 21 December: 'I have had difficulty in keeping the Board together. But I have done it, though I must say that it was a close shave.' He went on to express his opinion on future action:

I believe that we have a strong case for not recommending the I.C.I. offer, but we must be constructive. I feel that the only possible way out of the appalling mess both we and I.C.I. are in is for us to renew our offer to do all we can to make Terylene a success by merging the melt-spun fibres together. This is a logical solution of the problem posed by I.C.I. Although it was rejected out of hand by P.C. on 15 Nov. it might now be acceptable to the I.C.I. Board if we can ever get it considered by them.

However many divergent trails were followed, whatever the process of decision-making, the Board finally decided by 21 December, after consultations with its advisers—the merchant bankers Baring Bros. and the accountants Binder, Hamlyn & Co.—to prepare a statement recommending shareholders to reject the I.C.I. bid.

All that was said publicly was that a statement was being prepared in consultation with the company's advisers and would be issued after Christmas. And so, with the brief interruption of Christmas, a flurry of discussing and consulting went on. Drafts were considered at Board meetings on 26 and 29 December, both chaired by Hanbury-Williams who had returned from South Africa and who could now be under no illusion about the intention of his Board to resist Chambers. Finally, after many amendments, drafts of a formal letter to Chambers and of a press announcement recommending rejection were agreed and ready for release. On 3 January, however, after further talks between Barings and I.C.I.'s advisers, Robert Fleming and Co. and Morgan Grenfell & Co., a last-minute conference between the two sides was arranged at Barings. Both sets of bankers obviously disapproved of the course of events; it would be disastrous 'if a takeover were to be "bulldozed through"'; this was clearly not the way reputable and respected British companies behaved. Moreover, it was gradually emerging that I.C.I.'s advisers had received from Chambers a report on the course of negotiations with Courtaulds which was very different from that which Barings had received from their clients. So on 3 January, a special Courtaulds Board meeting in the morning was adjourned so that Hanbury-Williams and Wilson could meet Chambers and Bingen at Barings' offices in the presence of their respective advisers.[1]

[1] Lord Ashburton and Andrew Carnwath of Barings; R. Fleming of Flemings and J. E. H. Collins of Morgan Grenfell.

This meeting, of which Wilson wrote an account a few days later, marked a turning-point, for it was then that were revealed the diametrically opposite views held by the two sides about what had been agreed by Wilson and Chambers. Hanbury-Williams read out the terms of the formal letter and the press release to the effect that the Courtaulds Board agreed unanimously that the financial terms were inadequate; that the talks had stemmed from a wish to co-ordinate the melt-spun fibres; that Courtaulds did not think that a conclusive case had been advanced for a complete merger; and that this view had been communicated to Chambers on 15 and 16 December. These announcements led Chambers to say that he had understood that a merger was in principle acceptable to Courtaulds, an interpretation challenged by Wilson. Chambers, according to Wilson, seemed surprised to be told that the Courtaulds Board was unanimous and that no conclusive arguments for a merger had been advanced. Both Chambers and Bingen were evidently incensed at the rejection of the merger as a matter of principle rather than as a matter of terms, finding the wording of the press announcement highly objectionable. Despite agreement to make some minor modifications of wording and to hold up the press release to allow for further consultation, and despite various fruitless telephone conversations between Chambers and Hanbury-Williams, on 5 January the formal letter was accepted, the press announcement was released, and the public battle began.

Before going on to consider the course of the battle it is worth pausing to look briefly at Chambers's view of the discussions. There seems to be little doubt that he had genuinely come to believe something quite different from what Wilson said. At his press conference on 18 December, asked if he anticipated opposition, he said: No. In a public statement he made on 17 January he said that the course of discussions 'had led them [I.C.I.] to believe that the Courtaulds Board were seeking a solution to the problem by a complete merger'; the 'friendly negotiations' had been 'directed towards a complete merger of interests'. An I.C.I. press release of 8 February contained the statement that 'detailed negotiations for a full merger had been proceeding from early in September last year, i.e. well before the announcement of the reduction of Courtaulds' interim dividend'. It claimed that by mid-December they had reached a stage at which the only matter for discussion was 'the terms of the offer to the Courtaulds stockholders'. On seeing this press release, Courtaulds promptly issued a counter-statement saying that it was misleading; that the discussions had never contemplated a take-over bid; and that there was no truth in the idea that at the time of the cut in the interim dividend the Courtaulds Board knew that a take-over bid by I.C.I. was 'in contemplation'. It is noteworthy, however, that the denial used the words 'take-over bid'; it did not deny that discussions might have contemplated a voluntary merger. Both sides repeated these claims and denials in subsequent documents during the battle. Such striking variance was only too evident to the interested public. On 20 February the Church Commissioners, big shareholders in both companies, sent a letter to the respective chairmen raising this very matter of irreconcilable statements and wondering how shareholders could be expected to rely on estimates, forecasts, or prophecies from boards of directors who could thus so readily contradict each other on matters of fact. After the battle was over, at a meeting between Holroyd and Kearton in March 1962, the former was reported as having said that the I.C.I. Board believed that a merger had been agreed in principle in 1960; and that at their meeting in September 1961, Chambers and Hanbury-Williams had agreed that the time was ripe to 'bring things to a conclusion'. They were surprised to learn that the Courtaulds Board was not unanimous about the merits of a full merger. In future, he said, I.C.I. would have to take care to ensure that Courtaulds' representatives were 'acting in accord with their Board opinion'. In May 1962, Bingen commenting on the 'bad blood' on both sides, told Kearton that they had been misled in the conversations at the end of 1961. Still later, in October 1962, Dallas Bernard, after a meeting with Chambers, reported the latter as having assured him that in the talks of the previous autumn he had believed that Wilson was speaking on behalf of the Courtaulds Board; they had arranged everything for the running of the two companies once I.C.I. had acquired the shares; these arrangements had included 'the interlocking of the directors' and the only point that remained unsettled was the price. He had been 'so certain that Alan had the Board behind him that he had arranged a code word to be cabled to him the moment agreement had been reached'. I.C.I. had had no intention, Chambers claimed, of making an offer unacceptable to the Courtaulds Board; and in future, in matters between the two companies, he would do nothing without prior consultation with the Courtaulds Board.

To try to explain the emergence of such an utter disparity of views by the supposition that the two men were simply lying is absurdly simplistic.[1] There is no reason whatever to suppose that Wilson deliberately deceived

[1] Though this is what a questioner at the Courtaulds press conference on 24 January 1962 (see below, p. 225) in fact suggested.

either Chambers or his own Board. But he may perhaps have unintentionally conveyed to Chambers the impression that he could persuade the Courtaulds Board to agree to a merger. Hanbury-Williams, after all, was known to be in favour of it. Certainly the Courtaulds Board became uneasy at the continued private conversations with Chambers, though there is conflicting evidence on why Wilson continued to conduct the discussions by himself. As for Chambers, there can be little doubt that—vigorously supported by Williams and with a sharp eye on the merits of 'Courtelle' as well as nylon—he was determined to push ahead with his plans in any event. It is probable that he had come to believe from information received (from what quarters is best left to guesswork) that the Courtaulds Board was at least divided or weak, even if not wholly agreeable to a merger bid; he may have supposed that he could rely on the support of some members of that Board. Perhaps that support was whittled away when the reality of the terms was spelt out; or perhaps it had never fully existed. This is still an area on which reliable evidence is lacking. It is reasonably certain that by the time of his meeting with Wilson on 15 December he had secured the authority of his own Board to make an approach to the Courtaulds shareholders over the heads of the Courtaulds Board. Wilson complained of torrents of words from Chambers; in the occasional respites from the flood, Wilson's words, cast very much in an intellectual mould, may have been more enigmatic to Chambers than he cared to admit. So each may have come to believe what he wanted to believe. If this was so then it constituted a classic case of non-communication, or at least ineffective communication, which, had it not occurred, might have prevented the battle, changed the course of British business development, and deprived the public and the press of a spectacular financial conflict—to which we must now turn.

III

The conduct of a contested take-over battle between two big firms with widespread public shareholdings demands both the provision of financial ammunition to justify (or rebut) the claims and the deployment of an effective artillery of public relations with which to fire that ammunition. Courtaulds were in the position of having relatively new men in these commands: Knight, a director for only four years, had been finance director for merely a few months; and Mathys, certainly not one of the 'old brigade' on the Board, was in general charge of public relations. The company had made various provisions for dealing with public relations, and a new public relations officer had been appointed in December 1957. Some of the older generation of Courtaulds' directors, and especially Hanbury-Williams, regarded the press rather as though it were a necessary but regrettable institution which should be told as little as possible as infrequently as possible. The task of somehow dissolving the predictable press image of the Courtaulds directorate as remote, antiquated, and prone to 'elderly indecision', not to say as simply fuddy-duddy, had by no means been completed by the time the bid broke; and, of course, it had not been aided by the dividend cut of November 1961. But, at least, just as Knight was well aware of unexploited assets, plentiful reserves, inappropriate financial policy, and inadequate financial planning, so Mathys was aware of public relations to be improved and a department anxious to improve them.

Before the ammunition could be prepared and fired however, a rather different tactic was followed. This was partly genuine and partly a delaying operation. At the meeting on 3 January Courtaulds had suggested a full-scale discussion between representatives of the two firms to report by June 1962. Chambers dismissed this notion without much difficulty. So on 8 January, after consultation with Barings and a further Board meeting, Hanbury-Williams sent a letter to Chambers suggesting consideration of two proposals: (a) a joint company to deal with melt-spun fibres, I.C.I. having a majority position; (b) a joint company to deal with all fibres, Courtaulds to have the majority position. This time the hope was expressed that matters of principle could be settled within a week or ten days. I.C.I. agreed to the talks, and a joint press statement on the discussions was issued. For the purpose of these talks negotiating teams were set up. The appointment of the Courtaulds team proved to be a most important step in the battle, for the men appointed came to figure as—and indeed be deliberately presented to the press as—'the New Team', or the 'Action Committee', conducting the defence against the aggressor, long after these particular negotiations were over. The chosen, appointed at a Board meeting on 8 January, were Kearton, Mathys, and Knight. Koppel was also selected, initially to represent Kearton whilst the latter was away in hospital (as he was from approximately 5 to 15 January inclusive) but in fact Koppel continued as a member of the team after Kearton's return. Two meetings were held at Barings on 10 and 11 January.[1] Deadlock was

[1] The two teams and their advisers were as follows. I.C.I.: Holroyd, Williams, Paine, and Menzies, with Richard Fleming from Robert Fleming & Co., and J. E. H. Collins from Morgan Grenfell; Courtaulds: Mathys, Knight, and Koppel, with Lord Ashburton

fairly soon reached. It became evident that I.C.I. wanted proposal (a) to embrace all non-cellulosic fibres including 'Courtelle', to which Courtaulds would not agree; and that proposal (b) was simply unacceptable to I.C.I. The Courtaulds team also believed the discussions revealed the two companies as holding incompatible 'philosophies': I.C.I. with a production-orientated viewpoint, seeking the best employment of their substantial capital investment; Courtaulds as market-orientated, emphasizing that in the last resort profits depended on what would sell. There was some truth in this, though it was exploited by Courtaulds more for its propaganda value than for its inherent validity. The two sides agreed to meet on the 15 January. A last minute proposition devised by Andrew Carnwath of Barings was discussed by the Courtaulds Board at meetings on both 15 and 16 January and finally put to I.C.I. via Barings. This suggested either that Courtaulds should sell their half-share of B.N.S. to I.C.I. or that the fibre interests of both Courtaulds and I.C.I. together with the latter's polymer plants should be sold to a new company. All to no avail. Formal letters between Chambers and Hanbury-Williams conceded that the discussions had failed; a further meeting[1] on 17 January had no more success.

Both sides promptly issued press releases. Courtaulds' announced failure and deprecated I.C.I.'s attitude. I.C.I.'s much longer statement emphasized Courtaulds' heavy investment in old-fashioned rayon; blew its own fibres trumpet (incidentally wholly ignoring 'Courtelle'); announced the decision to proceed with 'their proposal for a complete merger'; and, most important, raised their terms to 4 I.C.I. ordinary shares for 5 Courtaulds. This raised the imputed price of Courtaulds' shares to 46*s.*[2] Courtaulds once again rejected them. Chambers held another press conference; announced that there was to be no withdrawal nor any further alteration of terms which, when they had been 3 for 4, he had already described as 'final, final terms'; and made a variety of disparaging comments about Courtaulds.

Tempers and temperatures were beginning to rise. Courtaulds would evidently, as *The Times* put it, have to 'do something quite drastic if it is

---

and Andrew (later Sir Andrew) Carnwath from Barings. Hanbury-Williams, Wilson, Evelyn Baring, and Chambers were present at the opening of the talks, but withdrew after the two chairmen had each made encouraging noises to set the teams going.

[1] Hanbury-Williams, Wilson, Chambers, and Bingen, plus advisers.

[2] $\frac{4 \times 57s.\ 6d.}{5}$

to ward off the latest offer'.[1] Such was indeed being planned. The preparation of the commercial and financial ammunition had been going ahead for some while. The organization of this task was shared in varying ways amongst three men: Knight,[2] Andrew Carnwath, and Anthony Burney[3] of Binder Hamlyn. As early as 21 December, Burney, working on data supplied by Knight, had drawn up the first draft of a document setting out the basic arguments to show that the potential earnings of Courtaulds were much greater than the I.C.I. terms implied. It noted the earning power of the recently acquired assets as yet not fully realized, for example Pinchin Johnson, Harbens, and the most recent acquisition, British Enka. Using an analysis of the rates of return on capital in various parts of the group, it argued that by 1964 more of the capital would be in the higher-earning category and less in the lower-earning. It observed the marked undervaluation of certain assets, notably Courtaulds' share of B.N.S., carried in the books at £4 million but worth about £23 million and its holding in Snia Viscosa with a market price of some £20 million as compared with the £5 million at which it stood in the last balance sheet. Pointing to the healthy reserves and cash-flow position prepared by Courtaulds' latest estimates, it demonstrated that higher dividends could easily be paid in the immediate future. Something had, of course, to be prepared to explain the gloomy forecasts given at the 1961 A.G.M., produced to justify the interim dividend cut, as well as the slightly improved figures disclosed to Chambers in December. Of these it was said in so many words that they were prepared earlier for internal purposes and were admittedly too conservative. It is worth emphasizing, however, that they had already been subject to internal revisions before the bid broke.[4] The more optimistic forecasts had not been concocted simply to meet the I.C.I. challenge; the bid provided an opportunity, willy-nilly, to bring to light what had remained concealed, as a consequence of deference to the chairman's gloomy vision of the future. But that could hardly be said publicly. Revisions of these estimates and of the general terms of the 21 December draft were finally agreed on 4 January by Wilson, Kearton, and Knight. A further memorandum from Burney on 10 January set out a possible reorganization of Courtaulds, with trade investments separated out from manufacturing divisions.

[1] *The Times*, 19 January 1962.

[2] Who was also able to draw upon Courtaulds' Economics Department, then under the leadership of A. M. Alfred.

[3] See above, p. 120, n. 3.

[4] See below, Chapter XII, p. 256.

On 24 January Courtaulds launched their response in a widely publicized financial statement. Built up from these memoranda and estimates, variously revised and rearranged, it painted an optimistic picture of the earning power of the company's assets and offered a set of profit estimates as follows:

1960–1 (actual)	£18·7 mn.
1961–2 (final three months estimated)	£17·5 mn.
1962–3 (estimated)	£23·0 mn.
1964–5 (estimated)	£28·5 mn.

The earlier 1962–3 estimate of £18·5 million, as disclosed to I.C.I. in December 1961, was waved away as 'a routine forecast . . . in September 1961'. The optimistic tone was not enough. The statement failed in itself to make much impact in the City and certainly not on Courtaulds' share prices; it was still not easy to reconcile the £17·5 million for 1961–2 with the (approximate) £15 million which was estimated at the time of the interim dividend cut.

However, the mere publication of the statement was not the whole of this particular deployment. The public-relations side of the defence was also being planned, with much emphasis on advertisement and the need to 'get across the image of a new dynamic management, by every means including TV'. A carefully stage-managed press conference by Courtaulds on 24 January was arranged to provide a platform for Kearton. After introductory remarks by Hanbury-Williams, Wilson answered some questions in the course of which he again reiterated the absence during his earlier discussions with I.C.I. of any negotiations on terms. He also admitted that cutting the interim dividend was a mistake, but explained it as a socio-political decision, made because of a fear of alienating workers whilst closing down a factory and making other 'rationalization changes'. *The Times* claimed that this statement would 'probably command universal acceptance'.[1] Maybe it did but there is no reason to suppose that the explanation offered represented more than a small fraction of the real reasons for the decision; it was simply the best way of explaining a mistake. Wilson got into something of a muddle while dealing with questions about profit estimates and again about the date on which I.C.I. first gave signs of being interested in a take-over. After a passage by Mathys, in which he managed to extract a laugh from the assembled journalists, Kearton took over and began more and more to dominate the conference. It was an egocentric performance with plentiful use of the first person singular

[1] *The Times*, 25 January 1962.

('I acquired Cellon . . . I have sold factories . . .'), but it was also vigorous, assertive, fluent, and confident. He laid about I.C.I., damning as excessively high the prices of the raw materials which Courtaulds bought from them; contrasting the slow development of 'Terylene' with the rapid development of 'Courtelle'; and hazarding that I.C.I.'s profits for 1961–2 would be at least 25 per cent. below 1960–1. He threw facts and figures about with cheerful abandon and some inaccuracy. He raised laughs, bubbled with ideas, and was the total antithesis of the old, stuffy Courtaulds. In brief, he epitomized 'the image of a new dynamic management'.

On the public-relations side of Courtaulds' campaign, though not on the financial, this press conference was something of a watershed. The new image was being put across, with the assistance of outside consultants on advertising and public relations. From time to time Kearton provided other publicity boosts, for example by reporting in mid-February that the Russians—with whom he had been talking in yet another session in the long-enduring wrangle about the 'Tricel' contract—had expressed concern about the I.C.I. bid and had offered to help Courtaulds by speeding up the contract.[1] The continuing political debate—of which more later[2]—kept the issue in the public eye; and Courtaulds ensured that it stayed there by means of such devices as a circular to all M.P.s and a series of advertisements carrying the general message that Courtaulds *alone* could do what was needed. For whatever precise reasons, sentiment began to shift against I.C.I. The big monopolist came to be seen as the big predator; opponents of monopoly had a splendid platform in the political debate. If few yet believed that Courtaulds could win, hostility was changing to sympathy. The 'new look' was beginning to be noticed in some stockbrokers circulars, one of which expressed the hope that Chambers would 'follow the sensible and dignified course of dropping the whole matter . . . thus ensuring the usual knighthood which a thankful Government should be even more ready to accord'.

The battle flared up again on 8 February. With the now customary panoply of press conference and big advertisements, I.C.I. issued a statement to stockholders, which also contained an improvement in the terms of the bid. Courtaulds' shareholders were now given the alternative of the existing 4 for 5 offer or of taking £2 10*s*. worth of a new $6\frac{1}{2}$ per cent. convertible unsecured loan stock, 1972–7, in exchange for each of Courtaulds £1 ordinary shares. Valued at par his offer thus raised the

[1] See, e.g. *Financial Times*, 12 February 1962, and above, p. 191.

[2] See below, pp. 232–6.

imputed price of the bid to 50*s*. per share.[1] Although this was a useful I.C.I. salvo in the duel, its impact was blunted, at least in part, by the accompanying announcement that I.C.I.'s own profits for 1961–2 would be down by almost 30 per cent., to about £62 million instead of £88 million in 1960–1—even more than Kearton had predicted at the press conference a fortnight earlier. Courtaulds now got down to the task of answering the new offer. On 9 February the chief accountant[2] produced for Knight at the latter's request a set of possible offers to Courtaulds' shareholders; they included the payment of a 17½ per cent. dividend over the next three years and the creation of a loan stock. From this, and building on the previous analyses of Courtaulds' assets, Knight presented to the Board at a meeting on 13 February a paper called 'How should we counter the I.C.I. loan stock offer?' Meanwhile, Carnwath and Burney had been preparing draft answers to I.C.I.'s offer which included demonstrations that over the past eleven years Courtaulds' earnings on issued ordinary capital had generally been better than I.C.I.'s. The Board accepted Knight's proposals and the resulting riposte to I.C.I. was fired at the shareholding public on 15 February, carefully timed to explode immediately after the formal offer document from I.C.I. had been released on the previous day.

I.C.I. posted their offer to some 180,000 Courtaulds shareholders, and followed it up with a circular to the 500,000 or more of their own shareholders to give notice of the necessary extraordinary general meeting on 16 March. The offer expired on 8 March and had the customary provisional conditions of 90 per cent. acceptances to be received.[3] The formal offer document ran to 16 pages; it was accompanied by a copy of an I.C.I. pamphlet called 'The I.C.I. view' (which was also circulated to M.P.s); and sundry forms. *The Times* guessed that the exercise used up 20 tons of paper and would cram 900 mailbags. But *The Times* also had the revealing headline on its City page: 'Success of I.C.I. Bid now in Doubt'.[4] For the Courtaulds counter-attack was indeed formidable. It had four thrusts:

(1) Not less than 50 per cent. of trading profits and the whole of the investment income to be distributed in dividends. Thereby would

[1] The stock was to be first convertible in 1963 on terms equal to the current 4 for 5 offer and on slightly lower terms in 1964 and 1965. The withdrawal period for the stock was 1972–7.

[2] J. L. Fraser.

[3] Ninety per cent. was required for a company to be able to acquire compulsorily the non-assenting shareholdings within the provisions of the Companies Act.

[4] *The Times*, 15 February 1962.

be recommended dividends of 12½ per cent. for 1961–2 and 13 per cent. for 1962–3;

(2) A cash distribution of 2½ per cent. tax free out of capital profit for each of the three years 1961–2, 1962–3, and 1963–4;

(3) The capitalization of nearly £40 million of capital reserves by the issue to ordinary shareholders, credited as fully paid, of 10*s.* worth of a newly created 7 per cent. unsecured loan stock, 1982–7, for each £1 ordinary share;[1]

(4) The creation of a wholly owned investment-trust subsidiary to which would be transferred Courtaulds' main trade investments (excluding B.N.S.) and government securities, the whole of its income to be distributed as dividends.

In addition to this 'up-ending of the Courtaulds cornucopia', as the *Financial Times* put it,[2] the statement—dispatched to shareholders on 15 February and appearing as a full-page advertisement in major newspapers on the next day—also contained the demonstration, mentioned above, of Courtaulds' advantage over I.C.I. in the Company's past earnings performance. There was yet another recommendation to reject the I.C.I. terms, this time supported by figures to show that a Courtaulds shareholder would be better off to retain his Courtaulds holdings. Also enclosed was a postcard which shareholders were asked to sign and return, if they favoured 'the continued independence of your company'.

It worked. The Stock Exchange value of Courtaulds shares rose above the imputed value of the I.C.I. bid (50*s.*) to a high point of 52*s* and, as Fig. 9 shows,[3] after briefly falling back, continued to rise. There were a few more shots in the paper war: I.C.I. dispatched another statement to shareholders on 19 February; Courtaulds sent one on 27 February, urging, *inter alia*, the return of the postcards. On the following day Courtaulds

[1] The total capital profits which provided these reserves were agreed as follows:

	£000
Balance of profits as at 31 March 1953 from sale of A.V.C. shares	15,185
Profit on sale of remaining A.V.C. shares	3,460
Profit on sale of government securities 1 April 1953–31 March 1961	448
Receipts from sale of 'know-how' 1 April 1953–31 March 1961	1,805
Surplus on revaluation of B.N.S. shares	8,000
Surplus on revaluation of Snia Viscosa shares	13,000
Total capital reserve at 16 February 1962 in respect of untaxed capital profits	41,898

[2] *Financial Times*, 16 February 1962. [3] See above, p. 217.

announced that the tally of postcards received had amounted to some 44,000: there was no chance of Chambers getting a 90 per cent. acceptance rate. On 28 February and on 8 March, Chambers fired his last serious shots. On the former date he declared the offer unconditional, i.e. irrespective of percentages received by 8 March; and on the latter date he extended the deadline by a mere four days, to 12 March. In the meanwhile the issue remained undecided. Courtaulds' position, however, was strengthened partly because a majority of City opinion as reflected in press comment seemed to be supporting the 'new men';[1] and partly because a Courtaulds' shareholder need do nothing to accept the company's offer but had to sign forms to accept the increasingly doubtful I.C.I. offer. A brilliant publicity capitalization of this fact came in the form of a simple advertisement telling stockholders that all they need do was to destroy all the paper which they had received (see Plate 12).

Presumably many of them did for at noon on 12 March I.C.I. announced that the offer would not be extended. By then I.C.I. had secured, instead of the 90 per cent. for which they had hoped, some 37 per cent. of Courtaulds' ordinary share capital; the final figure worked out at about 38 per cent. The battle was over.

It had cost Courtaulds nearly £365,000 (or over £476,000 if the costs of the loan-stock issue are included) to defend themselves against a compulsory marriage with I.C.I. And to celebrate their success—or so it seemed—they promptly organized a church service to thank God for their deliverance from so satanic an embrace. Behind the St. Martin's-le-Grand head office lay the tiny City church of St. Vedast, the restoration of which, after destruction by wartime bombing, had been helped by money from Courtaulds. It had a fine eighteenth-century organ and new bells as yet un-rung since 1940; indeed no service had been held in it since the restoration had been completed. Some members of the office staff, who had worked long and late during the battle, asked the public relations officer, who was also a Churchwarden of St. Vedast's, if a special private service could be held for Courtaulds' employees and their friends. Unwisely, as it turned out, consent was given and the service fixed for Thursday 15 March. But, once again, somebody tipped off the press. So the select and well-dressed congregation, including a few directors and their wives, arrived to be greeted by press photographers and happy journalists. To the stirring sounds of 'Praise my soul the King of Heaven' and 'Now thank we all our

[1] *The Economist*, 10 March 1962.

God', as well as a splendid peal of bells, the spectre of Paul Chambers was—or so it seemed—being appropriately exorcised. Whether or not it had been intended as a thanksgiving, it could hardly fail to be seen as one. Those sections of the press given to levity on such matters had a field-day; and the earnest Canon Collins was inexorably moved to preach in St. Paul's on the theme of Christianity and the 'economic gangsterism of capitalism'.[1] After so successfully conducted a public-relations exercise as the defence against the bid, this episode was a maladroit slip which fortunately for Courtaulds seemed, in retrospect at least, rather more hilarious than disastrous.

Before moving on to examine, in Chapter XI, the profound repercussions within Courtaulds which were wrought by the bid and its aftermath, it is worth briefly considering the external impact of this remarkable event in British business history.

IV

Remarkable it was, but not just as an example of a merger. For it appeared as though borne along on a tide of merger activity which had begun to gather momentum in the mid-1950s. The figures in Table 33 are derived from two separately constructed series and give an indication of the rising extent and value of this trend towards concentration which reached a high point in the later 1960s. As was shown in some detail in Chapter VIII, Courtaulds had taken a very active part in precisely this process, accounting for a total of about £44 million of acquiring in the six years 1957–62. In relation to the triennial averages in column (d) of Table 33, this means that Courtaulds alone were responsible for about 5·6 per cent. of the total for 1957–9 and 1·7 per cent. for 1960–2. Had the I.C.I. bid gone through it would have increased the value of 'disappearing' manufacturing companies in the one year, 1962, by about two-thirds.

Public opinion, political sentiment, and government policy had each been taking cognizance of the merger movement of the 1950s well before the explosion of the I.C.I.–Courtaulds affair. The publicized doings of Charles Clore, in the building up of Sears Holdings, as well as of various property-magnates; the enthusiasm for diversification and the construction of conglomerates in the manner of the Tilling Group or Reckitt &

[1] 'Instead of casting out those that sell and buy, and over-throwing the tables of the money-changers, we now engrave their names on our communion plate and commemorate them in our stained-glass windows' (*Guardian*, 19 March 1962).

TABLE 33

U.K. merger activity, 1954–68

	(a)	(b)	(c)	(d)
	Triennial averages			
	*Company acquisitions in manufacturing, distribution, and services**		*Company disappearances in manufacturing industry†*	
	Nos.	*Values £ mn.*	*Nos.*	*Values £ mn.*
1954–6	272	108	191	93
1957–9	400	188	286	151
1960–2	668	355	493	365
1963–5	940	447	650	387
1966–8	837	1,014	576	955

* P. E. Hart, M. A. Utton, and G. Walshe, *Mergers and Concentration in British Industry* (Cambridge, 1973), p. 3.

† L. Hannah, *The Rise of the Corporate Economy* (London, 1976), p. 213.

Colman:[1] such happenings had ensured the airing of views on the old topics of monopoly and competition. That these operations should have attained the size and frequency that they did—and thereby secured attention—was a consequence of various economic circumstances. Share prices had remained low, in part because of dividends being deliberately held down in response to Labour government policies; and many companies had accumulated reserves in the form of low-yielding assets.[2] To the eye of the enterprising (and sometimes not too scrupulous) financier these presented attractive bargains. A variety of hopes for economies of scale, be they in management, distribution, or on the technical side of production, added different incentives for drives towards integration.[3] Such circumstances and hopes were present and relevant in varying degrees in Courtaulds' own take-over activities, so avidly pushed forward by Kearton, with the support of Knight; and presumably they were not absent from

[1] Channon, *Strategy and Structure of British Enterprise*, pp. 188–93.

[2] Worswick & Ady (eds.), pp. 464–73.

[3] In fact, however, the plants of large companies have not grown to anything like the same extent as the companies themselves. See S. J. Prais, *The Evolution of Giant Firms in Britain* (Cambridge, 1976), pp. 45–8.

the minds of Chambers, Williams, and other I.C.I. directors who rallied behind their chairman in seeking to acquire Courtaulds. Certainly the latter's past financial policy—which, according to Kearton in February 1962, had been regarded by Barings as 'remarkably inept and close to suicidal'—had been a standing invitation to a determined take-over bidder.

The attitudes of political parties and the doings of the State had exhibited their customary ambivalence on these topics. To the Right, monopoly was bad and competition good, but just how much intervention there should be seemed wholly indeterminate; to the Left, all capitalism was suspect, monopoly demanded the remedy of nationalization, but competition still had something to be said for it.[1] A Labour government had passed the 1948 Monopolies Act which set up the Monopolies Commission; a Conservative government passed the 1956 Restrictive Trade Practices Act which set up the Restrictive Practices Court. Much was revealed to interested experts by the operation of this legislation but little in practice was done. An occasional report made the headlines. Problems about the rights of shareholders were brought to the fore as a result of the actions of some take-over bidders. A contested bid sometimes brought the reassertion of shareholders' rights, but only too frequently the latter were left unconsidered by tycoons on the make. The legal implications of these developments resulted in the setting up of the Jenkins Committee[2] in 1959 to review Company law in the light of such trends.

So when the I.C.I.–Courtaulds bomb burst the time was richly ripe for the pursuit of further contentiousness about the flood of take-overs, the doings of big business, the spectre of monopoly—or however any politician or economic saviour cared to phrase so favourite a topic. What made the I.C.I. bid so remarkable was not merely that it was large but that it was contested. All of Courtaulds' own £44 million of taking-over had gone through unopposed by the Boards of the companies acquired. Before 1950 the contested take-over was virtually unknown.[3] Only a very small minority had been opposed during the 1950s; and of these still fewer, for example the contested bid for British Aluminium in 1958–9, reached the headlines. Consequently, when the biggest manufacturing firm in the

[1] 'We in the Labour Party take our stand on this basic principle—that where there is monopoly there ought to be public ownership and where there is private ownership there ought to be competition.' Douglas Jay, M.P., March 1957, quoted J. W. Grove, *Government and Industry in Britain* (London, 1962), p. 189.

[2] The chairman was Lord Jenkins, a Lord of Appeal in Ordinary.

[3] Hannah, op. cit., p. 149.

country, itself a monopolist in certain lines, was seen to be forging ahead with an appeal to the shareholders over the heads of the Courtaulds Board, it simply could not avoid arousing opposition right across the political spectrum. This was true well before the two companies started swapping insults. It offended the City: 'a public clash between the Boards of two such great companies might well have untold social and political consequences and do serious damage industrially'. So wrote Carnwath in the preamble to his attempt, vain as it turned out, to secure agreement in January. It was a sentiment echoed, in varying terms by many similarly placed commentators, privately and publicly. It worried the Right. And it was a gift to the Left.

The Parliamentary session ended on 21 December, but in both the House of Commons and in the House of Lords the proposed I.C.I.–Courtaulds merger was raised. The Lords got in first, Lord Shepherd raising the matter on the 20th with the ominous words: 'this is not an ordinary take-over';[1] and in the Commons both Richard Marsh and Douglas Jay asked on the following day whether the President of the Board of Trade would refer the matter to the Monopolies Commission.[2] F. J. Erroll, the incumbent of that office, said the Government had no power to do so. It soon became evident from comments by both James Callaghan for the Opposition and Peter Walker for the Conservatives that this reply brought satisfaction to the ranks of neither Labour nor Conservative. After the Christmas recess this burning issue quickly reappeared. On the first day of the new session, 23 January, Douglas Jay, who led for the Opposition on trade and industry matters,[3] formally asked the President of the Board of Trade for an inquiry.[4] The debate had begun. On 30 January Erroll refused on the grounds that it was premature; the issue was capable of being judged by results and could not be prejudged before any merger took place.[5] In any event a general review of policy since the 1956 Act was in hand. From the brief speeches made after this refusal it again became evident that the Government's decision did not much please either the Left or a number of the Right; and, moreover, that anti-I.C.I. sentiment was beginning to flow strongly. Some mildly rude remarks were made about I.C.I. by certain M.P.s who seemed to have been suitably primed

[1] *Hansard*, vol. 236, p. 810. [2] *Hansard*, vol. 651, p. 1546.

[3] Subsequently President of the Board of Trade, 1964–7. Director of Courtaulds, 1967–70.

[4] *Hansard*, vol. 652, p. 38.

[5] Ibid., pp. 895–6.

with notions not all of which could be described as totally objective.[1] But whatever the help gently provided by Courtaulds' Government Relations Department, the drift of comment was unmistakable. Hugh Gaitskell, Leader of the Opposition, gave notice that a motion would be moved.

Even more clearly did the unfavourable sentiment flow from the House of Lords when they got down to the subject two days later.[2] The Labour peer Lord Alexander of Hillsborough, pressing the case for an inquiry, observed that the merger was unpopular in the City, with the users of man-made fibres, and with some trade unionists. Other peers doubted the Government's case for refusing an inquiry and variously looked with disfavour on the whole matter. The ageing Earl of Swinton—hardly a pillar of the Left[3]—made what was in effect an attack on Chambers and the I.C.I. Board contrasting the current handling of 'this business' with the 'wise guidance and leadership' of Fleck.[4] 'Unedifying' was a word which came readily to noble tongues as a description of the battle. Lord Hailsham, defending for the Government, preached the virtues of 'silence based on discretion' but he too deplored the conflict as both 'unedifying and undignified'.[5]

Courtaulds' Government Relations Department were indeed justified in looking back on the week's Parliamentary activities as very favourable, and to note that Courtaulds had earned goodwill whilst I.C.I.'s reputation had been undermined. They recommended an end to the mass circulation of material to all M.P.s and a continuation of providing detailed briefs to particular Members; care should be taken not to dissipate the goodwill which had been generated. What weight should be attached to their activities it is impossible to say, but at least it did nothing to change these sentiments. For the full-scale Commons debate on the Opposition motion on 14 February brought out the anti-I.C.I. sentiment still more obviously. The motion was moved by Jay in these words:

That this House deplores the timid and complacent attitude of Her Majesty's Government towards the growth of private monopoly in Great Britain and

[1] For example, Mrs. Eirene White (East Flint, Labour) spoke of I.C.I.'s 'lamentable record' in man-made fibres; Brian Harrison (Maldon, Conservative) contended that I.C.I. had failed to produce one successful synthetic fibre since the war; and Sir Cyril Osborne (Louth, Conservative) talked about I.C.I.'s high raw-material prices. *Hansard*, vol. 652, p. 899.

[2] *Hansard*, vol. 236, pp. 1151–99.

[3] Minister in various Conservative/National governments, including President of the Board of Trade, 1924–9 and 1931–5.

[4] *Hansard*, vol. 236, p. 1162.

[5] Ibid., pp. 1186, 1198.

their refusal to safeguard the public interest by instituting a public inquiry into the proposed merger of Imperial Chemical Industries and Courtaulds.[1]

Both the words of the motion and the tenor of Jay's speech showed how the I.C.I.–Courtaulds affair was seen as fitting into the current concern over mergers and monopolies. He attacked the whole trend of take-over bids; cited sundry facts and figures about I.C.I. and Courtaulds which, though ostensibly neutral, were in fact more detrimental to I.C.I. than to Courtaulds; and stressed the sheer size of the combine which would result from the proposed merger. It would, he maintained, have a capital of nearly £1,000 million and a labour force of nearly 170,000 which would be 'over 50 per cent. larger than the British Navy'[2]—a comparison presumably designed to tear at the very souls of true Britons. Several other speakers adopted a similar stance, including such Labour spokesmen as James Callaghan and a number of Conservative back-benchers. Once again the unique quality of the episode was stressed: it was 'something entirely new'.[3] Rude words about I.C.I. came from the Right (e.g. Sir Cyril Osborne) and from the Left (e.g. Eirene White).[4] Although the Opposition undoubtedly put up the more spirited performance—for obvious political reasons—there was plenty of evidence, in a well-attended House, of genuine concern on all sides. The Government's negative position was sustained by Erroll[5] as well as by Henry Brooke.[6] In the vote party loyalties duly ensured the rejection of the motion by 317 votes to 230, a fairly typical Government majority of 87. A further debate on 16 February, built around a Private Member's motion on mergers and the Monopolies Commission, continued to keep the issue before the public eye—just at the time when shareholders were contemplating the final I.C.I. offer and the final Courtaulds' riposte. Once again, and despite some fiery rhetoric from Barbara Castle about Courtaulds' 'new cash bribe' to shareholders,[7] the general drift of the discussion again envinced more sympathy for Courtaulds. This was evident, for example, in the contribution made by two Conservative speakers, Peter Walker and R. Gresham Cooke.[8] Well

[1] *Hansard*, vol. 653, p. 1323. [2] Ibid., p. 1329.

[3] Ibid., p. 1411 (Sir John Barlow, Middleton and Prestwich, Conservative).

[4] Both declared their interests as having Courtaulds factories in their constituencies. Ibid., pp. 1355, 1419.

[5] Ibid., pp. 1338–55.

[6] Ibid., pp. 1437–48. Then Chief Secretary to the Treasury. Created a Life Peer as Lord Brooke, 1966.

[7] *Hansard*, vol. 653, pp. 1677–85.

[8] Ibid., pp. 1696–1702, 1711–18.

into the first half of March, Members continued to harry the Government by raising various matters or putting down questions directly or indirectly related to the bid.[1]

The general drift of this Parliamentary discussion was well reflected in a massive press coverage. That coverage was large, continuous, and nation-wide; it ranged from weighty stuff in the 'heavies' to a picture of Mrs. Chambers at home under the headline of 'Mrs. I.C.I.'.[2] There was plenty of informed and objective debate in *The Times*, *Financial Times*, *Guardian*, *The Economist*, and the like, but again the drift was anti-I.C.I. as time wore on. Between 20 January and 13 March *The Times* ran to some five leaders on the topic, including two first leaders. The changing public image may be seen in these extracts from *The Times* and *The Economist*:

> The initial impression of Courtaulds as a somnolent family textile concern, engaged in making an out-of-date product, with shaky profits and a poor chance of survival, could not last. (*The Times*, 14 February)

> Courtaulds directors are, in effect, asking the shareholders to reject completely the comparative images of I.C.I. and Courtaulds' managements in the past as any guide to the future. They are also asking shareholders to forget and forgive the cut in the interim dividend, which they now openly admit was an absurd mistake. At this late stage, can the Courtaulds' directors, able and fierce as some of them have proved themselves to be in the latest bout of in-fighting, create a brand new image. (*The Economist*, 27 January)

> by their conduct they [I.C.I.] have alienated important parts of the City and industry as well as many Courtaulds shareholders. (*The Times*, 10 March)

And when it was all over:

> The present unsatisfactory position is due entirely to their [I.C.I.'s] precipitate action in deciding to go for a complete merger of the two companies and to throw away any possibility of co-operative action. (*The Times*, 13 March)

> Many investors resented the aggressive, dogmatic manner in which Mr. Paul Chambers and I.C.I. saw the only possible answer to the problems of the man-made fibre industry in submitting Courtaulds to a total merger. (*The Economist*, 17 March)

Not every commentator wrote like this, but it is easy to see why I.C.I. came to feel resentful about the rough handling they had received in press

[1] *Hansard*, vol. 654, questions, pp. 20, 68, 168, vol. 566, pp. 1126–9, 1513–17; questions, p. 174.

[2] *Daily Express*, 19 December 1961.

and Parliament alike. It is also evident that the I.C.I. leadership—however much it may be said that a higher initial offer would have won a quick victory—was unwise to have taken the action that it did at a time when informed public opinion was alarmed about the rising trend in mergers and monopoly. Nobody knew that there were more and still bigger battles to come—notably the famous G.E.C., A.E.I., and English Electric affair in 1967–8[1]—but in 1962 many knew that they did not like the look of the I.C.I. Goliath even though the Courtaulds David was not quite what it seemed. To the press I.C.I. became personified as Chambers, already known as a thrusting business leader; Courtaulds offered a variety of new faces emerging from comparative obscurity. The fullest exploitation of these journalistic possibilities was made in a series of three articles in the 'Weekend Review' section of the *Observer*.[2] They were written by Roy Jenkins, Labour M.P., journalist and author, future Chancellor of the Exchequer and President of the Council for Europe. They were highly personalized, moderately accurate so far as they went, and very readable. Despite having been based on interviews voluntarily given, their probing sketches of personalities began to arouse strong feelings in Courtaulds and I.C.I. alike. Representations were made to those who edited and controlled the *Observer*. It seems probable that a decision was reached to conclude what had been intended as a four-article series with the third instalment, which was certainly more impersonal and general than the first two articles. There were some very bruised and tender feelings—and not all of them were on Millbank.

[1] See Jones and Marriott, *Anatomy of a Merger*.

[2] 'The Untold Story of how I.C.I. became the Thwarted Giant', 18, 25 March, and 1 April 1962.

PART III

THE NEW ORDER

CHAPTER XI

Direction and Disengagement

IN the aftermath of the I.C.I. bid the leaders of Courtaulds were clearly seen to be presented with three major tasks. In order of immediacy they were: (1) to reconstitute or rearrange their own directorate and management structure so as to reflect the 'new look' which had successfully emerged during the bid; (2) to devise some mutually tolerable method of living with their big new shareholder, whom they had spent the previous two months reviling so heartily; and (3) to turn into reality, over the next three years, the profit estimates upon which the defence against the bid had been grounded. These tasks neither existed *in vacuo* nor comprised the totality of problems to be solved. Chapter XII will examine the broad developments in policy in the three years after the end of the bid battle; in that context it will also examine the company's performance and profits, and thereby the third of those so obvious tasks. The present chapter will deal simply with (1) and (2).

I

Public comment on Courtaulds' directorate varied from the highly general to the very specific. Here, for example, is a pro-Courtaulds apologia in February: 'Courtaulds top financial management and also its public relations—until very recently—have not been all that they might have been.'[1] And here is *The Economist* after the conflict: 'Sir Alan Wilson . . . figured prominently in last year's discussions with I.C.I. but took no great part in the battle from December onwards; his somewhat aloof, intellectual personality appeared to be smothered by the fire and smoke.'[2] This *Economist* article went on to point a finger at an ostensible alternative candidate should Wilson withdraw from his role as chairman-designate, in the person of Kearton whose 'fire, courage and ability' had made a decisive mark. Nevertheless, the obviously well-briefed author of the article concluded, 'it may still be true that the task of building bridges may be better undertaken for a few years by someone from outside'. And

[1] Eirene White, 14 February 1962, *Hansard*, vol. 653, p. 1362.

[2] *The Economist*, 17 March 1962.

indeed the little rondo which went under the name of 'Hunt-the-distinguished-outsider', so familiar in the repertoire of the Courtaulds Board, was already being played.

During the battle, when it had become evident that certain financial institutions had little faith in the Courtaulds Board, Wilson told Barings that if the support of such institutions depended upon the appointment of a new chairman he would be prepared to relinquish his position as chairman-designate. It was thought unwise to let such a proposal be known during the battle; and in the event most of these institutions sold out their Courtaulds shareholdings to I.C.I.[1] But the offer to retire had been made. However sensible it seemed to Wilson at the time, he was soon to see it in a different light. For on 7 March, ten days before the appearance of *The Economist* article, Mathys had delivered to Wilson what was in effect an ultimatum. Acting as the spokesman of Kearton and his supporters he went to see Wilson to ask him to implement his promise to make way for a strong and independent outside chairman. Thereby would be demonstrated to the world and the company's staff that Courtaulds 'really meant business'. By this time Wilson was a depressed and weary man. He had borne a heavy burden in his talks with Chambers, and had listened to a public outcry about the mutual misunderstandings created therein. He had long found exhausting the very process of dealing with Hanbury-Williams, devious and difficult, failing in his powers but still capriciously autocratic. The worsening relations between Hanbury-Williams and the tempestuous and ambitious Kearton spilled over to aggravate the existing tensions between the latter and Wilson. Wilson's perception of himself as cool, rational, and realistic was readily translated by his colleagues as aloof, intellectualized, and pessimistic. As those colleagues, or some of them, began to wonder what he was up to, so he saw his colleagues as a body prone to lurch from euphoria to hysteria. Small wonder that already in February he had remarked that for years he had been disposed to quit Courtaulds to find something which he could enjoy doing. And small wonder that when confronted by the ultimatum of 7 March he unhesitatingly announced that he would not only relinquish the chairmanship but would resign from the Board.

[1] The biggest of such holdings disposed of in this way was that of the Prudential Assurance Co. which sold the whole of its £1,390,066 of Courtaulds' ordinary shares. Other insurance companies to sell all their Courtaulds' holdings included the Commercial Union (£102,000), London Assurance (£60,000), North British & Mercantile (£167,000), and Scottish Life (£68,888).

15. (a) George Courtauld

15. (b) Walter Pierre (Peter) Courtauld

16. C. F. (later Lord) Kearton, 1962

But who should succeed him? For all his achievements there was certainly no majority for Kearton—who would in all probability have cheerfully sacked several directors on the spot. So who should be the distinguished outsider? Wilson agreed to set in motion the traditional process of making discreet enquiries; and at a Board meeting on 8 March it was agreed that Hanbury-Williams should continue as chairman, with Wilson, Kearton, and Mathys as deputy chairmen, pending further consideration as soon as practicable and in any case not later than mid-June. By the end of May the front-runner in the 'Hunt-the-Chairman' stakes was the former textile industrialist and Conservative politician Derek Heathcoat Amory, created Viscount Amory in 1960 after some two-and-a-half years as Chancellor of the Exchequer in the Macmillan government. He was currently serving as High Commissioner for the U.K. in Canada, a post which, however, he was not to relinquish until some time in 1963. Hanbury-Williams saw Amory—referred to in cables and memoranda on this issue under the code name of 'Alpha'—in New York and reported him as sympathetic. There was much consultation at a high level, but there was no certainty that he would accept; and in any event he could not take up the post before 1963. So there was still an interregnum to be filled and an announcement to be made at the A.G.M. in July. Only one man on the Board could attract a clear majority of votes for such a caretaker post: Dallas Bernard.

Although already 74 years of age, Bernard commanded considerable respect as a man of balanced judgement, detached from the Board's in-fighting, and possessed of a high sense of responsibility. At a chairman's meeting on 29 May attended by Hanbury-Williams, Bernard, Wilson, Mathys, and Kearton, he agreed to take on the job; and Wilson, when asked to stay on as an executive director, refused. He had earlier been urged, though not perhaps with whole-hearted conviction, to remain to help ease Amory into office. But, bitterly resentful of what he saw as the Board's failure to support him and keenly aware of the great gulf between his and Kearton's views of business life, he could not tolerate the idea of remaining—even if Amory were to come, which he doubted. He regarded Kearton not as a believer in collective wisdom and responsibility, like himself, but as a dictator who believed in centralized control and *ad hoc* methods for the solution of every problem. Conversely, Kearton had come to see Wilson as yet another defeatist who had lost confidence in the future both of rayon in particular and of Courtaulds in general; and who in 1961–2 no more believed in the ability of the company to reach the revised profit estimates than he had earlier believed in Kearton's various profit-seeking sallies into the unknown. Above all, perhaps, Kearton saw him as an obstacle, a personified deterrent equipped with a sober armour of rationality, to his own insistent urge to take risks in pursuit of an ambition to force, batter, lure, cajole, shout, or somehow to lead Courtaulds into a new and more profitable shape. There was no real hope of the two men ever working harmoniously together, and Wilson knew it. A suggestion that he should stay on as a non-executive director he likewise rejected. At a meeting on 7 June the Board passed final resolutions for the ending of his contract by mutual consent. And so, on 25 June the resignation from Courtaulds of Sir Alan Wilson was duly made public. Some three weeks later, at his last A.G.M., Hanbury-Williams announced that Dallas Bernard was to succeed him.

Meanwhile, on 12 July, notice had been received from Amory that, because of the length of time which would elapse before he would be free from his present official duties, he did not think it likely that he would be able to accept the invitation to become chairman. Although the door was thus not completely closed the likelihood that the interim reign of Dallas Bernard would be followed by the accession of Frank Kearton was correspondingly increased.

The going of Wilson and the appointment of Bernard to replace Hanbury-Williams were not the only Board changes. On 12 April Nankivell had retired, having reached the customary retiring age of 65; and on 31 May Smith also departed, at the age of 62, 'having felt obliged to follow his doctor's advice'. To fill the gap in the upper echelon of the Board created by the resignation of Wilson, Peter Courtauld was appointed to be a deputy chairman. The four departures reduced the number of directors to thirteen as compared with the authorized eighteen. Nor was this all; the immediate future held further reductions. George Courtauld gave twelve months' notice of his wish to retire as an executive director as from 30 June 1963, though indicating his willingness to stay on in a non-executive capacity if so desired. Verrall was due to retire in December when he would be 65 years of age. And then there was the problem of Aubrey Jones. His contract would bring him up for re-election at the A.G.M. of 1963, but his one-man stand for the I.C.I. bid had lost him the favour of the Board. It was conveyed to him that he was no longer a welcome colleague. At the A.G.M. of 1963 he did not stand for re-election. To counter-balance the withdrawals four new appointments were made in November 1962 and one in December 1963. C. H. Colton and J. G. N. Drewitt both joined the main Courtaulds Board from British

Celanese where the former was a manager director and the latter personnel manager. Recognition of the continuing importance of rayon, Coventry, and the Viscose Division came with the appointment of J. H. Givens, who had been much involved with the technical development of high-tenacity yarns and tyre cord.[1] The high-level outside man who came in as a non-executive director was David Eccles, created Lord Eccles in 1962[2] on ceasing to be Minister of Education in the Macmillan government. He had City interests and had been President of the Board of Trade in 1957–9. The appointment in December 1963 of G. A. Samuel, like those of Colton and Drewitt, represented a tapping of the expertise of absorbed companies; he had come from Harbens in 1959 and had wide experience in textiles and rayon.

So by the end of 1963 the Courtaulds Board was constituted as in Table 34.

TABLE 34

The Board, December 1963

		Age
Chairman	Sir Dallas Bernard, Bart.	75
Deputy chairmen	H. R. Mathys	55
	W. P. Courtauld	53
	C. F. Kearton, O.B.E., F.R.S.	52
Full-time directors	C. H. Colton	61
(in age order)	J. H. Givens	59
	G. A. Samuel	59
	C. W. Sheldon	58
	R. J. Kerr-Muir, O.B.E.	53
	J. P. Koppel	50
	J. G. N. Drewitt	49
	D. R. B. Mynors	48
	A. W. Knight	46
Part-time directors	G. Courtauld	60
	H. L. Johnson	59
	Lord Eccles of Chute, P.C., K.C.V.O.	59

Median age: 55

Its median age of 55 was identical with that of its predecessor of December 1961 (Table 22),[3] but in composition there had been substantial change, for six out of the 17 of the immediately pre-bid Board had gone. More important than names and numbers was a radical change in the organization of the Board.

[1] See Vol. II, pp. 188, 230, 357.

[2] Created Viscount Eccles, 1964.

[3] See above, p. 145.

At a meeting on 15 March 1962, when the defeat of the bid was evident, the Board resolved, 'it being recognised as urgently necessary greatly to simplify and streamline the way in which the Company operates', to create two new committees of the Board. These were called the Policy Executive and the Operations Executive. The corollary of the formation of these two bodies was the elimination of numerous existing committees—finance, research, appointments and personnel, textile industry policy, and more besides—which had either long existed (e.g. finance) or had been created to deal with particular problems (e.g. textile industry policy). Both Executives were responsible to the Board as a whole. Broadly speaking, the role of the Operations Executive was to examine and monitor the implementation of plans and policy; that of the Policy Executive to examine high-level administration and to discuss issues of long-term strategy. In practice the Operations Executive proved to be the more powerful and important. Membership of these bodies and especially of the Operations Executive clearly conferred influence; membership of both went far to identify the true seat of power within the new command structure. As the membership at their early meetings shows, the 'new men' had come into their own.

TABLE 35

Membership of the Operations and Policy Executives, 1962

Operations Executive	*Policy Executive*
C. F. Kearton (chairman)	A. H. Wilson (chairman)*
H. R. Mathys (deputy chairman)	C. F. Kearton
A. W. Knight	H. R. Mathys
J. P. Koppel	
D. R. B. Mynors	
R. J. Kerr-Muir	
C. W. Sheldon	

* After Wilson's departure, Dallas Bernard became chairman of the Policy Executive and Peter Courtauld joined it.

Efforts to secure that elusive distinguished potential chairman from outside had, however, not yet been given up. Further correspondence and a discussion with Amory early in 1963 ended with a final confirmation of his refusal. Other names were considered for non-executive directorships and/or for the chairmanship. There were too many uncertainties, not least about relations with I.C.I. The suitable were unwilling, the willing unsuitable. The hunt was abandoned. In October 1964 the Board formally resolved that C. F. Kearton be appointed chairman as from 1 November.

Dallas Bernard retired from Courtaulds in March 1965. In his caretaker role he had proved notably successful, holding in balance contending forces within the Board, allowing Kearton and the 'new men' to have their way but maintaining restraint the while, and playing an effective part in the negotiations with I.C.I. over the issue of disengagement. His task had not been to initiate but to facilitate; to help an outside chairman if he could be found or, if not, to smooth the way for the one insider who was outstandingly able to do the job but who was not personally to everybody's taste. By the time that Kearton addressed the A.G.M. in July 1965 for the first time as chairman, others had gone too. Peter Courtauld, then aged 55, decided that he had had enough of business life and retired in May 1965. John Givens, for different reasons, came to conclude that life on the main Board with Kearton was less than appealing, and returned to Coventry, as chairman of the Viscose Division. Two newcomers joined the Board in November 1964—J. B. Whitehead and W. T. Winterbottom—both from the cotton industry and both arriving as a consequence of Courtaulds' absorption of the Lancashire Cotton Corporation and Fine Spinners & Doublers in 1964.[1] Eight of the Board which faced the bid had now gone. And of the Board of 1940 only two survived, both non-executive part-time directors—Henry Johnson and George Courtauld—both effectively passengers in a train powered by an engine very different from anything that had appeared in the recent experience of Courtaulds Ltd.

II

The directors of Courtaulds and I.C.I., after the heady delights of bombardment by insult had been replaced by the prosaic tensions of peace, approached each other again with a caution verging on the apprehensive. Both chairmen made public statements of a kind appropriate to the signing of a major armistice. A 'period of tranquil reflection' was deemed appropriate. Suggestions that certain persons in the City might act as 'peace makers' between the two firms were greeted with no enthusiasm by I.C.I., where bitterness about all that had been said about the company extended to many luminaries of the City. Nevertheless, pressing matters of business had to be attended to by the two companies, most obviously in regard to

[1] See below, pp. 270–9.

B.N.S. and to raw materials purchased by Courtaulds from I.C.I. These, principally caustic soda and acrylonitrile, were worth some £4–5 million annually. Although during the battle Courtaulds made much capital about I.C.I.'s prices thereof nothing very startling was likely to occur afterwards, partly because Courtaulds' purchases comprised only a very small portion of total I.C.I. sales of chemicals and partly because the supplier was now the biggest shareholder. Gradually, discussions got under way on sundry practical matters, such as acrylonitrile (for which Courtaulds had a rapidly growing demand, already the subject of negotiations with the Distillers Company); the combined use of 'Tricel' and 'Terylene'; or the scope for mutual co-operation in the home market to avoid being played off against each other by big buyers such as Marks & Spencer. Kearton and Mathys had meetings with Holroyd and Williams in March; with some effort to keep off the subject of the bid, co-operative noises were made and signs of mutual tolerance showed themselves. There were further meetings, formal and informal, in the ensuing months. By the summer, press comment—perhaps taking a cue from Chambers's remark in a speech in which he referred to the bid as a 'sad history of misunderstanding' and spoke of emotion having got the better of reason—was seeing signs of 'time healing the breach' between the two firms.

Although substantial progress was indeed made in the course of 1962 on a number of matters, for example those concerned with a B.N.S. investment in Australia and on nylon and rayon tyre-cord prices, there still remained for Courtaulds a big question mark hanging over I.C.I.'s intentions as a consequence of their 38 per cent. shareholding. No approach had been made for representation on the Courtaulds Board but it would have been difficult to refuse if it were made. There was reason to suppose that Courtaulds' efforts to strengthen the Board by attracting distinguished outsiders were being affected by uncertainty about Chambers's intentions. Should I.C.I. be consulted about possible major acts of policy by Courtaulds? These and like matters were aired in a paper about the possibilities of disengagement put up by Knight and discussed by the Policy Executive in October 1962. Although it seemed from their dealings with Courtaulds that I.C.I. directors were pursuing a policy of wishing to avoid the appearance of exerting pressure, there was also evidence that Chambers still believed in the merits of a full merger. If that were true the I.C.I. could not regard their shareholding merely as a passive investment. Was there something to be said for trying to resolve the situation either by pursuing the notion of a new fibre company, as suggested by Carnwath of Barings back in January, or by seeking a transfer of some Courtaulds' assets to I.C.I. in exchange for a corresponding reduction in share capital, with a view to eliminating the I.C.I. shareholding? Neither idea then commended itself to the deputy chairmen who feared the lopping off of assets such as B.N.S. or Pinchin Johnson and were worried about the competition from a B.N.S. under I.C.I. control. It was decided that proposals on these lines should not be given any publicity at this time but that other possible methods, such as seeking a shareholding in I.C.I. in exchange for the Courtaulds shareholding in B.N.S., should also be examined.

As 1962 gave way to 1963 and as Courtaulds' results began to show the promised improvements,[1] there were signs amongst some members of the Board of a resurgence of strong anti-I.C.I. sentiments, coincident, too, with a belief that Chambers still nurtured designs on a controlling interest or a merger. But in reality it had become abundantly clear by the summer of 1963 that however much Chambers might continue to entertain such ideas, he also knew full well that they were politically out of the question. The death of Hugh Gaitskell in 1963 and the advent of Harold Wilson to the leadership of the Labour Party combined with the growing probability of a Labour government at the general election due in 1964 was seen by the I.C.I. Board as making it far too dangerous to embark upon a merger at that time. These views were conveyed by Chambers and Holroyd to Bernard and Kearton at a meeting on 24 May. (Later, in a different context, Chambers let it be known that he had regarded the 38 per cent. as giving I.C.I. control of Courtaulds but that it was for political reasons that the control had not been exercised in the direction of integrating the two companies.) The corollary of this decision was the increasingly serious consideration by Courtaulds of the technique of some form of swap so as to secure disengagement. Knight prepared a detailed paper on the finance of a possible swap of I.C.I.'s holding against Courtaulds' share of B.N.S.; the head of the legal department[2] looked into the difficult legal complications involved in a reduction of capital. Holroyd had proposed, but then withdrawn, the idea of a phased transaction by which I.C.I. would dispose of *some* of their holding in exchange for Courtaulds' share of B.N.S. Kearton made it clear that the value of B.N.S. to Courtaulds was such that the transaction must include the value of I.C.I.'s 38 per cent. plus something extra to compensate for the loss of half of B.N.S.; and, moreover, that an essential condition would be Courtaulds' freedom to enter into polyamide

[1] See below, p. 256. [2] J. B. Bransbury.

and polyester production in the future. This view was conveyed in a letter from Kearton to Holroyd on 31 May, putting forward unofficial proposals for a disengagement on these lines.

From that time on, the whole issue of disengagement was a matter of negotiating, bargaining, and manœuvring to find mutually acceptable terms. Knight's calculations had suggested in April that, depending on what assumptions were made about future earnings, the value of B.N.S. could be put anywhere within a range of £137–223 million. The price of nylon was falling; but B.N.S. expansion was planned or contemplated in Australia, South Africa, even America. Consultations proceeded with Barings and with Counsel on the necessary legal procedure. Discussion on the financial arrangements and possible terms were conducted between Arthur Knight for Courtaulds and Peter Menzies for I.C.I. In the manœuvres and counter-manœuvres carried out by each side an important part was played by the future role—intended or imagined, believed or alleged—for 'Celon' and the Courtaulds/Celanese knitting capacity. The build-up under Kearton's aegis of the Furzebrook Knitting Co. as the centre-piece of Courtaulds' developing warp-knitting activities was publicized with an increasingly familiar gusto in a press release of December 1962. In April 1963 Kearton sent a memorandum to the chairman of Furzebrook telling him of plans for a major expansion in 'Celon' production at Spondon and possibly later at Aintree which would in turn demand further expansion of Furzebrook. At almost precisely the same time Kearton was busily playing down to I.C.I. the significance of 'Celon'—the output of which, as already shown in Chapter IX,[1] was limited by agreement—in order to play up the value to Courtaulds represented by the possible loss of half of B.N.S. 'The importance of British Celanese's 'Celon' has been much exaggerated,' he wrote in his letter to Holroyd in May. 'It is a tiny plant.' Admittedly, because the yarn supplies from B.N.S. to the Celanese warp-knitting plant were proving inadequate, a little 'Celon' had been used, but the idea that the 'possession of this limited spinning know-how in any way puts Courtaulds in a position to minimize the importance of their B.N.S. interest is ludicrous'.

The take-over by Courtaulds of two knit-wear manufacturers—Foister, Clay & Ward Ltd. in May and Bairns-Wear Ltd. in June[2]—could hardly have persuaded I.C.I. to ignore the possibility of an intended build-up of 'Celon' production. Nor did such actions in themselves readily appeal either to Chambers and his colleagues or to the B.N.S. directors. The

[1] See above, p. 176. [2] See below, p. 278.

balloon went up at a meeting in July between Bernard and Kearton for Courtaulds and Chambers and Holroyd for I.C.I. Chambers specifically complained that such acquisitions were 'not in the spirit of the accord previously reached that major matters of this kind would be discussed by the two sides before they were decided upon', and, moreover, that such moves appeared to provide confirmation to B.N.S. that they were designed to provide captive markets for the output of a big planned expansion of the 'Celon' plant at Spondon. Kearton explained them in terms of 'Courtelle'. Chambers now declared that the disengagement suggestions previously discussed were too complicated and therefore unacceptable. He suggested that instead I.C.I. should put the polymer plants into B.N.S.'s hands in exchange for shares, thus making Courtaulds a minority shareholder in B.N.S. without a seat on the Board; to compensate for this Courtaulds would now be free to go in for nylon manufacture in competition with B.N.S. The 38 per cent. shareholding, he had come to the conclusion, was no great problem and could be left, at any rate for the time being. Dallas Bernard made it clear that these notions were unacceptable to Courtaulds. This counter-manœuvre having been parried, it soon became increasingly evident that I.C.I. were anxious to reach a settlement; that Chambers knew that a deal over B.N.S. was inevitable; and that he was anxious to avoid any accusations of monopoly in order, as Bernard put it, to 'keep the face of the I.C.I. bright and shining before the public'. It was a matter of bargaining. On 14 August Chambers wrote to Bernard suggesting a 'straight exchange of Courtaulds' B.N.S. shares for I.C.I.'s Courtaulds share'. Bernard said that this was not equitable and that he could not put it to the Courtaulds Board; he suggested instead that Knight and Menzies should meet again to talk about the value of Courtaulds' share in B.N.S. After further correspondence and meetings in September and October this was eventually agreed by Chambers. The whole procedure of consultation by the finance directors and reference to the Boards was carefully prescribed in the minutes, with yet another deliberate reference, presumably at Chambers's request, to that much-disputed misapprehension:

Bearing in mind the events of two years ago, when he thought that the take-over of Courtaulds by I.C.I. was merely a matter of price, but found that the Courtaulds Board were opposed to it on principle, Mr. Chambers proposed that on this occasion the Board of each Company should approve discussions taking place in regard to the I.C.I. acquiring Courtaulds share in B.N.S., that the Finance Directors of each Company be asked to work out their estimate of the value of the 50 per cent. interest and if they disagree each make his comments on the figures of the other.

Various procedures were then set down in the event of disagreement.

The I.C.I. holding in Courtaulds' equity was £30,672,404 of ordinary shares which in September 1963 was worth about £106 million. By this time Knight's valuation of B.N.S. had been raised. B.N.S. pre-tax profits rose from £13·6 million in 1962 to £18·7 million in 1963; and its issued capital had gone up again from £30 million in 1962 to £45 million in 1963. Improved profits forecasts now seemed to justify a valuation of some £300–350 million, i.e. £150–175 million for Courtaulds' half thus leaving a gap between that and the market worth of the I.C.I. holding of some £44–69 million. There were outstanding obligations to B.N.S. which reduced this to £35–60 million. This was simply a possible bargaining position, and, not surprisingly, it did not commend itself to the other side. The process of negotiating was now entrusted to Barings for Courtaulds and Schroder Wagg for I.C.I. A further bout of trouble over 'Celon' revealed that the prospect of Courtaulds building up a large nylon 6 capacity was viewed with much apprehension by B.N.S. or at any rate was claimed to be so viewed for this alarm was usable as an argument for diminishing the sum which Courtaulds sought to compensate for the loss of their half. In March 1964 Barings reported that they had proposed to Schroder Wagg a swap plus £20 million. Then Chambers backed away seemingly suggesting that agreement could not be reached. Was this just another bargaining manœuvre? Or was it an excuse to get out of disengagement? The Courtaulds Board discussed the matter on 23 April. It confirmed the previous decision to negotiate an arrangement on the lines set out in the previous October, and authorized Bernard and Kearton, at a forthcoming meeting with the I.C.I. representatives, to settle somewhere between a straight exchange and an exchange plus £20 million. They did. On 27 April 1964 a press release announced the swap plus £10 million in cash, payable by I.C.I. at the rate of £2 million per annum for five years.

The procedure was fairly complicated involving as it did the preparation of a Scheme of Arrangement under section 206 of the Companies Act 1948; an application to the Chancery Division of the High Court for the reduction of Courtaulds' capital; and three special shareholders' meetings. The former I.C.I. holding of Courtaulds stock was then to be held in a Special Capital Reserve. The scheme became effective at the end of July 1964 at which time the I.C.I. holding was worth approximately £126 million thus giving an imputed value of about £136 million to Courtaulds' lost half of B.N.S. At the same time as these changes were made the opportunity was taken to change the denomination of the ordinary shares from £1 to 5*s*. The effect upon Courtaulds' issued capital structure (after further changes consequent upon some acquisitions involving share issues, see below, Table 42, p. 271) was such that in September 1964 it stood as follows:

Ordinary (5*s*. units)	*Cumulative preference* (£1 units)		*Loan stock* (10*s*. units)
	5 per cent.	6 per cent.	7 per cent.
£	£	£	£
54,534,463	8,000,000	13,190,070	39,588,578

The authorized ordinary capital was still £100 million, but the structure as a whole showed a marked difference from its conventional and 'traditional' pre-war pattern.

So after 24 years of life B.N.S. lost one of its parents by divorce on the grounds of commercial incompatibility. A few days before agreement was reached on disengagement, when it looked as though I.C.I. were retreating from the proposed swap, Dallas Bernard asked whether Courtaulds could continue as joint owners of B.N.S. The reply given by Mathys is worth quoting *in extenso* because it sums up neatly, if inelegantly, the accumulated experience of years of tension as that experience had appeared to one of the parents:

> You asked me if I believed we could go on with B.N.S. as fifty-fifty shareholders with I.C.I.
>
> My answer was only with the greatest difficulty and with the certainty of another major tussle with I.C.I.
>
> B.N.S. is the classic example of the inherent instability of a fifty-fifty company with the inevitable pulls of individual interests against joint interests.
>
> Specific problems, such as polymer prices, I.C.I.'s Terylene, Courtaulds Courtelle, tyre yarn prices, can be met and a practical solution worked out by understanding people in both Companies. But B.N.S. is now so big its future commercial policy and development are of major importance in the fibre industry and both partners must want to ensure their view prevails. When these views coincide all is well, but every conflict is inevitably blown up into a major issue . . .

He went on to add that he believed I.C.I. to want 'the dominant voice'. Whether or not he was correct does not really matter: it was a suspicion widely believed in the Courtaulds leadership. Nor does it matter very much whether fifty-fifty companies have 'an inherent instability'; and certainly B.N.S.'s relations with its joint owners were so complex as to make it exceptionally unstable. If it was a 'classic case' of anything then, to an economic historian at least, this history of B.N.S. typifies the interaction between technical or economic relationships on the one hand, and the role of personalities on the other. As already indicated in Chapter IV, this interaction was only too evident in the 1940s and early 1950s, despite pious generalizations about co-operation and an 'Atlantic Charter' mouthed at the highest of boardroom levels. And once again, in the final battle and resolution of the 1960s, the inherent difficulties so accurately diagnosed by Wilson in 1952 were first exacerbated and then ignited by failures of personal understanding. Some degree of mutual distrust between Mathys and Williams; Chambers's unwitting gift to Kearton of a new and more public platform for his vocal belligerence; the antipathies within the Courtaulds Board; above all, the mutual misunderstanding between Wilson and Chambers: such personal stimuli provoked reaction and went far to determine the timing of events. But they would in themselves have been meaningless flags fluttering in the breeze without the tensions inherent in the triangle I.C.I.–B.N.S.–Courtaulds, tensions unpredicted and perhaps unpredictable in 1940.

CHAPTER XII

Profits, Problems, and Policies

THE historical task of achieving the profits forecast in those seemingly optimistic estimates of January 1962 was closely entwined with the pursuit of policies which were radically to alter Courtaulds' relationships with the British textile industry. Numerous observers of the business scene at the end of the bid battle could have been found to lay bets on the chances of Courtaulds reaching the estimated profits. But few would have put much money on the idea that in three years Courtaulds would have carried out a series of take-over bids exceeding in total value those of 1956–61; would have come to control a significant and growing share of the country's spinning, weaving, and knitting capacity; and would not only have reached but well surpassed those profit estimates. That these things did happen was largely, though certainly not entirely, a result of the circumstances of the bid having put Kearton into such a position of power that he was able, with the support of the 'new men', to push through his policies. The latter were not newly formed by the bid; their execution was facilitated by its legacy. They were influenced by certain external circumstances, such as the course of the trade cycle and, especially, the expectation, and then defeat of that expectation, that Britain would enter the European Common Market.

All these changes were conducted on the home front. At the same time Courtaulds had to deal with those outposts of their overseas empire which had been acquired in the days of rayon's glory—real or supposedly still surviving after the war—and which were contributing little but headaches to the Board. The solutions which were found to those problems varied both in nature and in degree of success. Some, again, were crucially affected, even facilitated, by the legacy of the bid.

This chapter will first set out the quantitative fulfilment of what was promised at the time of the bid; then consider in broad terms the various policies pursued in relation to overseas investments; and finally examine the pursuit of vertical integration at home.

I

In its barest form the comparison of promise and performance is set out in Table 36.

TABLE 36

Promise and achievement in profits, 1961–5

Years ending 31 March	*Profit* estimates 24 Jan. 1962*	*Profit* achieved*
	£ mn.	£ mn.
1960–1 (actual)	18·7	18·7
1961–2	17·5	17·7
1962–3	23·0	23·6
1963–4		33·3
1964–5	28·5	36·4

* Profit and interest before tax but after deduction of debenture and/or loan interest.

Whether these absolute totals of estimated profits would have been achieved had the Courtaulds Group remained the same size as it was at the time of the publication of the estimates in January 1962 is of course open to debate. The question is considered below in the light of the rates of return on capital which were achieved. Suffice to note for the moment that estimates made *before the bid*, though supporting only £24 million as the 'reasonable' profit expectation for 1964–5 and £25 million for 1965–6 also offered £33 million as 'possible' for the latter year. These estimates envisaged capital expenditure totalling some £78·5 million over the five years 1962–6 but none of this included the acquisition of other companies. In fact, approximately £60 million was spent on taking over other firms during the years 1962–4.[1] Table 37, which is effectively a continuation of Table 18, shows in more detail the performance of the company over the seven-year period 1961–7.

These figures bring out the reality of the achievement in the improved profits and suggest strongly, though they do not prove, that it was not based merely on the acquisitions of 1963 and 1964. The increase in the return on capital employed (column (f)) in 1962–3 was obtained on virtually the same capital as in the very poor year 1961–2 and then improved again on the increased capital of 1963–4. This was very substantially a

[1] See below, Table 42, p. 271.

TABLE 37

Financial results, 1961–7, Courtaulds Group

Year ending 31 March	(a) Profit and interest before tax*	(b) Tax	(c) Dividends less tax	(d) Retained profits†	(e) Total net assets	(f) Return on capital employed (a) as percentage of (e)
	£ mn.	£ mn.	£ mn.	£ mn.	£ mn.	%
1960–1	18·7	8·2	5·4	4·4	207·8	9·0
1961–2	17·7	7·4	6·7	2·9	234·6	7·5
1962–3	23·6	9·7	8·1	4·7	238·9	9·9
1963–4	33·3	15·8	10·5	6·0	262·4	12·7
1964–5	36·4	15·9	8·8‡	10·5	293·9	12·4
1965–6	37·0	11·4	10·3	13·6	308·7	12·0
1966–7	32·2	11·5	14·5	4·7	320·2	10·0

* But *after* deduction of debenture and loan interest.

† Excluded from this column are small amounts representing deductions in respect of minority interests; these account for the disparity between columns (*a*) and (*b*)+(*c*)+(*d*).

‡ The cancellation of the I.C.I. holding of £30·7 million in 1964 reduced the cost of the ordinary dividend.

result of cost-reductions and improved productivity in existing assets, including the major acquisitions of the 1958–62 period, which at last began to show themselves in the results for the financial years ending in March 1963 and March 1964. The good results were achieved, moreover, despite the fact the companies taken over during the financial year 1963–4 included some with very low yields[1] which took some time to improve and which would thus have tended to lower the over-all yield on capital for 1963–4. That the profitability of the group's trading activities was genuinely improving is also suggested by the data in Table 38 giving the margins on total sales for the decade 1958–67.

Ignoring the peak years of 1959–60 and 1963–4, the trend in sales margins over the decade was upward, even though not strikingly, and there was a very real recovery from the depressed years of 1960–1 and 1961–2. The percentage increase over the average of the two 4-year periods 1957–8 to 1960–1 and 1963–4 to 1966–7 was 10·5.

[1] See below, pp. 277–8.

TABLE 38

Sales margins, 1958–67

Year ending 31 March	(a) Total sales	(b) Pre-tax trading profits*	(c) Margins (b) as percentage of (a)
	£ mn.	£ mn.	%
1957–8	109·5	11·23	10·3
1958–9	104·5	10·71	10·2
1959–60	139·9	17·76	12·7
1960–1	171·9	15·00	8·7
1961–2	173·3	14·16	8·2
1962–3	185·4	21·57	11·6
1963–4	227·7	29·74	13·1
1964–5	301·4	35·52	11·8
1965–6	340·5	38·88	11·4
1966–7	349·5	35·10	10·0

* i.e. excluding investment income.

Both the sales margins and the profits and profitability figures do suggest, however, that Courtaulds may at least have been helped towards their goal by the particular timing of the trade cycle. When the improved figures were announced in 1963 and 1964, some sceptical observers, in I.C.I. and elsewhere, made comments to the effect that they simply reflected the upswing in the textile trade cycle, and that they would soon be followed by a fall. Tables 37 and 38 have carried the data to 1967, beyond the terminal date of this book, in order to demonstrate that although these critics were right in predicting the downswing (which came in profits, profitability, and margins, though not in the total value of sales) they were wrong in thinking it would come soon, for it did not in fact arrive until 1967. To test the suggestion of help from the cycle implicit in Tables 37 and 38, the trend, and deviations therefrom, in Courtaulds' profits for the two decades 1948–67 have been calculated. The result is exhibited in Fig. 10. As it shows, a cycle there certainly was. The bid was made during the trough; and the upswing nicely coincided with the period when promises had to be turned into bigger profits.

This does not mean, however, that without the cyclical upswing the promises would not have been fulfilled. The upward trend would have

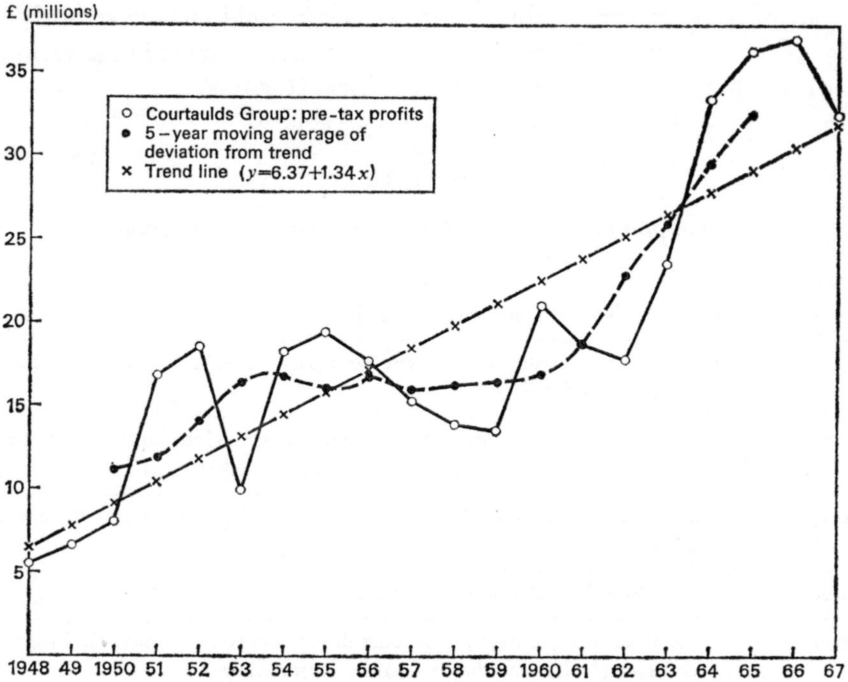

FIG. 10. *Courtaulds Group: profits, 1948–67, trend and cycle*

Profits are after deduction of debenture and/or loan interest, for years ending 31 March.

taken them there; the upward cycle gave them the impetus handsomely to exceed the promises.[1] If the low rate of return on capital achieved in 1960–1 or 1961–2 had remained as low on the higher capital of 1964–5, then the estimates would not have been reached without the aid of a cyclical boost;[2] but if the capital had remained the same in 1964–5 as it was in 1961–2 but the rate of return had been as high as that actually achieved in 1964–5, then the estimates would have been reached.[3] Contained within the trend, it must be remembered, was the long-term change in the sources of profit within the enlarging group. The change had started, as already shown in Chapters VII and VIII, well before the bid, but it continued and became increasingly marked for a decade thereafter. Calculations assembled

[1] 1964–5 trend value, £29·15 million; estimate, £28·5; actual £36·4.

[2] i.e. 9·0 per cent. on £293·9 million = £26·45 million (estimate for 1964–5, £28·5 million). See Tables 36 and 37.

[3] i.e. 12·4 per cent. on £234·6 million = £29·9 million (estimate for 1964–5, £28·5 million). See Tables 36 and 37.

as part of the preparations for defence against the bid include an analysis of profits according to the rates of return on capital invested in the various sources of profit within the group for the fiscal year 1960–1. Rearranged in 5 per cent. bands the data are exhibited in Table 39.

TABLE 39

Rates of profit on capital employed in main activities, 1960–1

per cent.	*Activities/plants*
losses	Canada (viscose); Calais ('Courtelle')
0–5	U.K. Viscose yarns; Calais (viscose yarn); U.S.A. (Courtaulds North America); miscellaneous
6–10	U.K. Viscose yarn processing; textiles (Samuel Courtauld & Co. and Gossard Ltd.); paints (Pinchin Johnson and Cellon Ltd.)
11–15	U.K. Acetate yarns, etc.; U.K. staple fibre spinning (Arrow and Westcroft mills)
16–20	U.K. Packaging (Cellophane, etc.); Saiccor
Over 20	U.K. Viscose staple fibre; U.K. chemicals; Prinex and similar engineering contracts;* U.K. synthetics (mainly 'Courtelle')

* Including capital profits on sales of 'know-how'.

Within the over-all rate of return on capital employed, i.e. 9 per cent., as shown in Table 37, there was evidently concealed a very wide range. Over the next few years a vigorous attack was mounted on the weak performers in the group, at the same time as the process of acquisition and integration was maintained. It is time to look at some of the weakest performers overseas.

II

As Table 39 makes only too evident, Courtaulds' possessions in the North American continent were, in 1960–1, among their least lucrative ventures. Table 40 shows that over the decade 1952–61 neither the older Canadian subsidiary nor the new plant in Alabama could sustain a worthwhile performance. For two companies which, by the end of that decade, had invested capital worth approximately £24 million (£13·1 in Canada and £11·0 in U.S.A.) the yield had been remarkably poor. It was not until 1964 and 1965 that the American venture showed much improved results.

TABLE 40

Contribution to pre-tax profits, Courtaulds Group, by the Canadian and American companies, 1952–65

Year ending 31 March	*Canada*	*America*
	£000	£000
1952	1,619	−44
1953	1,989	−299
1954	1,394	−481
1955	978	564
1956	1,229	727
1957	259	516
1958	158	414
1959	814	311
1960	342	994
1961	−747	139
1962	−293	−202
1963	520	815
1964	700	1,924
1965	250	2,025

The Canadian subsidiary went from bad to worse after its improved profits in the early 1950s when, as shown earlier, though sales margins were down, absolute levels of profits were better.[1] But this was followed by the collapse in 1957. Wilson's comment about the 'impending insolvency of Courtaulds (Canada)' in his memorandum of December 1956[2] to Hanbury-Williams was only too pertinent (despite the chairman's reception of it by putting a question-mark in the margin). A 'Canadian Panel' was set up in London to investigate the alarming situation.[3] It made a variety of recommendations and some action was taken. But after the little recovery in 1958–9, profits fell again, tumbling down to a loss of over $(Canadian) 1 million in 1960–1. Yet more investigations were set in train; and Wilson and Knight produced a detailed joint report in December 1960. There ensued some drastic changes in organization and management in 1961 and 1962; and, at last, some improvements in profits in 1963–4, improvements which owed something to success in reducing costs, something to the revaluation of the Canadian dollar early in 1962, and something to the general economic upswing of the early 1960s.

[1] See above, pp. 96–7. [2] See above, p. 147.

[3] Its members were Rendall, Bernard, Kearton, Mathys, and Mynors.

Throughout this period of acute difficulties Courtaulds (Canada) faced three main sorts of problems: its products, already under pressure in other parts of the world, suffered particularly severe competition both from American producers and from Japanese imports; the Canadian textile industry was a poor thing, demoralized and shrinking, thus offering a far from buoyant market for the yarn and fibre output of the Cornwall (Ontario) plant; and the local management and direction were not good. At various times consideration was given to merging with Canadian Celanese (who proved unenthusiastic) or to trying to sell the plant (but it was not clear who would buy it). Sundry efforts at diversification, including plastic boats and tufted carpets, proved of no great value. Some limited success was achieved with a campaign to boost tyre-yarn sales; technical efficiency was improved considerably; and intensive pressure upon the Canadian government brought an increase in tariff protection. In 1963 work began on introducing the manufacture of nylon 6 ('Celon'). As for the management, letters were dispatched by Hanbury-Williams to S. G. Dixon (chairman) and Drummond Giles (president), not dissimilar to that quoted in Chapter V,[1] and including a lengthy ultimatum of March 1960 which though not actually asking for Dixon's resignation did all but that. Eventually, Dixon retired, at the age of 70, in 1961; Giles was shifted into his place in a purely honorific capacity and he, too, finally went in 1964. But these and other changes were interrelated with those also affecting the Alabama plant and Courtaulds' whole organization in North America.

The problems of the American subsidiary were rather different from those of its Canadian counterpart in that as a staple-fibre producer it was, as Wilson put it in February 1960, 'a small struggling company in a country of giants, and its small size means that its overheads are relatively very high'. With its sales accounting for rather less than 20 per cent. of the total U.S. market for staple fibre, it seemed to need a broader base to achieve maximum efficiency. Sundry efforts were directed at this end via the channels of diversification or attempts to link up with other producers. The former led to the setting up in 1959 of a new company, Courtaulds North America (Inc.) with a view to acquiring substantial interests in external but cognate fields, rather in the manner of Group Developments Ltd. in the U.K. A complex series of negotiations then ensued with the American chemical firm, Koppers Company, Inc., with the intention of expanding in plastics and petrochemicals. Wilson and Knight were fairly enthusiastic; Kearton, observing that 'the history of our enterprises in

[1] See above, p. 99.

Canada and the U.S.A. since the War isn't exactly such as to fill one with confidence', was notably less so. In the course of 1961 Courtaulds bought some $4 million of shares in Koppers; and Arthur Knight joined the Koppers Board. Consideration of the possibility of linking up with another producer had usually run foul of potential anti-Trust difficulties, but in July 1962 the Board began to look seriously at the possibility of a joint enterprise with Koppers to acquire the fibre and Cellophane interests of A.V.C. which was actively seeking a purchaser. The scheme would have involved the sale of the Alabama plant—in order that the anti-Trust laws should not be infringed—and a 50/50 exercise with Koppers, without any remittance from the U.K. There were other bidders in the field. The upshot of a sequence of bids and counter-bids, acceptances and withdrawals, understandings and misunderstandings, was that the deal fell through. A.V.C. was in February 1963 bought by F.M.C. (Food Machinery Corporation); and a rift developed between Koppers and Courtaulds, where the enthusiasm of Kearton and Mathys for the scheme was less than total. The Koppers shares went into the portfolio of Courtaulds Investments Ltd.,[1] and in time were duly sold off; and Knight left Koppers Board.

So all these exercises came to nothing. In June 1962 Mynors was gloomily recommending sale as probably the best method of dealing with the American subsidiary (unless the Koppers–A.V.C. negotiations proved fruitful). But Kearton began to be more optimistic, observing to Dallas Bernard in September 1962, after reading a technical report on Alabama and Canada, that there was 'no need to be defeatist about either venture'. In practice, change came in a fashion rather similar to its arrival in Canada: reorganization in management; the new energies of the 'new men' aided by the more favourable economic climate of the mid-1960s which brought better results; and the introduction of nylon 6 ('Celon') manufacture. Rearrangement of the company structure in the U.S.A. was carried out in two separate stages: in March 1961 and in May 1962. The main result was the liquidation of the company called Courtaulds North America Inc. in the form in which it had been created in 1959, and its re-emergence as the new name for what had previously been Courtaulds (Alabama) Inc. Courtaulds North America Inc. and Courtaulds (Canada) remained two separate companies, but viscose operations came, for a time at least, under the control of a joint-management committee and some directors sat on both boards. As in the Canadian company, various directorial changes

[1] The investment trust set up during the I.C.I. bid. See above, p. 228.

were enforced, the former president and chief executive of Courtaulds (Alabama), Charles Paine, losing his job in the reshuffle of 1962. The I.C.I. bid left its mark both by putting in power in London those disposed to make these changes, and also by bringing home to them the low esteem in which business commentators held Courtaulds' operations in the U.S.A. and Canada. Kearton soon let various executives of Courtaulds North America know about these 'absolutely blistering' comments on a 'decade of fumbling mismanagement' which had made it 'brutally clear to Reg Mathys, Arthur Knight, and myself that the record of our North American interests was regarded as a major blot'. As Table 40 showed there were substantial increases in profits in 1963–5. The development of the polynosic or 'high wet modulus' type of staple fibre[1] added some impetus to improvement, as did rising prices, although the quality of the Alabama product was still the subject of periodic complaint. By the end of 1963, when the rate of profit earned by C.N.A. had moved up at least two bands in the categories of Table 39, a 50 per cent. expansion of staple-fibre capacity was authorized. Meanwhile the 'Celon' project had been authorized in the summer of 1963 and came into production the following year, though in 1964–5 losses were still being made on output, as they were in Canada.

On the other side of the world, Saiccor and Courtaulds (Australia) were presenting contrasting pictures to the Board in London. The former, under continuous pressure from Kearton, was proving its worth and contributing respectably to profits though still presenting one unresolved problem; the latter (not included in Table 39, because at that time only a minority interest of Courtaulds) was proving almost disastrous.

The revised profit forecasts of January 1962 brought a new intensity in Kearton's relentless pressure on Saiccor to make profits and on the group's factories to use its pulp in preference to that from outside sources. A letter of his in May to the Saiccor manager neatly summarizes the position:

> I needn't re-emphasise the vital importance to us of your maximising your profits in the current year. The whole Group stands or falls on the achievement of the £23 million figure that we *had to forecast* during the I.C.I. battle and I am hoping that you will be able to produce for us from SAICCOR an even better figure than you did last year. (My italics.)

[1] Marketed in the U.S.A. at that time as 'Lirelle', though this trade mark was subsequently used for a polyester in the U.K.

Output was stepped up and improved profits came from lower production costs. The buoyant conditions of the mid-1960s kept up the impetus and sales within the group increased. But all the time, pressure had to be maintained to try to solve the problem of how to raise the quality which remained below that of comparable Scandinavian pulp. After the fall in pulp prices in 1958–62, an upward tendency became evident from 1963 onwards.[1] Saiccor was budgeted to provide about 42 per cent. of estimated total group pulp requirements in 1964, the group thereby taking virtually all its output. A sudden sharp drop in quality during 1964 caused much trouble, however, and many complaints from the consuming factories. In 1965, though Saiccor's output had risen so had the group's requirements, and Saiccor's share was only about one-third. So although Saiccor was contributing to the task of keeping down viscose production costs, the problem of quality had still to be solved. The saga of Saiccor as an instance of vertical integration had best be left in 1965 with the then manager being offered a job elsewhere in the group.

If Saiccor was a success with a problem, Courtaulds (Australia) was a failure without a future. In the decade 1952–61 its dismal contributions in the way of dividends—Courtaulds, it will be remembered, held only a minority interest[2]—were as follows:

Year ending 31 March	*Courtaulds (Australia) dividends*
	£000
1952	—
1953	—
1954	—
1955	—
1956	—
1957	24
1958	55
1959	56
1960	83
1961	—

Small wonder that it too was a candidate for 'impending insolvency' in Wilson's memorandum to the chairman in December 1956. Between 1954 and 1960 the price of the company's stock on the Australian market had fallen from 113 to 70. In the summer of 1960 a report on conditions at the

[1] See Fig. 13 below, p. 286. [2] See above, p. 120.

Australian plant and further gloomy forecasts brought a special meeting in London to consider the future of Courtaulds' participation in the enterprise. A special report was commissioned from Barings, to consider what action might be taken, including the possibility of Courtaulds making an offer for the remaining shares of Courtaulds (Australia) Ltd. with a view to exercising much-needed control and improving the management. The Board decided that the shares should not be bought but that an attempt should be made to strengthen the management in consultation with the other shareholders. In 1962, the continuing and vexed question of protection was given a slightly reassuring answer by a small rise in tariffs granted by the Australian Tariff Board. A brief improvement in performance, however, was soon followed by further troubles and in 1964 the conclusion was reached that the Board of the Australian company was so unsatisfactory that if the investment was to be kept at all, and if Courtaulds' name was not to be continuously muddied by a company whose shares were still below par, then Courtaulds U.K. would have to take control. And so, in a burst of optimism about Australian economic prospects in general and in particular Courtaulds' ability to secure effective direction of their enterprise there, some £716,000 was spent in August 1964 on buying shares to give a controlling interest. The consequences within the period of this volume were not greatly encouraging. The ultimate fate was closure as a yarn producer in the mid-1970s.

Closer to home, Courtaulds' European investments received treatment from the new team which varied from liquidation to sizeable injections of capital. In the former category came the joint Courtaulds–V.G.F./A.K.U. enterprise at Cologne. As already mentioned in Chapter VI the Board had on more than one occasion considered trying to dispose of the Courtaulds share;[1] the Board considered it again in 1960 and 1961. Meanwhile, the changing course of relations between the two partners nicely mirrored the changing expectations concerning the future both of viscose rayon and of Britain's participation in the European Common Market. A report by Sheldon early in 1958 had spoken of the 'depressing' state of the German rayon market but in 1959, in the light of the expectations about the European economy, a five-year technical agreement was signed between Courtaulds and A.K.U. with a view to strengthening rayon, and especially tyre yarn, in its struggle with nylon and other competing fibres. The agreement did not, however, extend to what was originally envisaged, i.e. the exchange of information on costs and a possible financial association

[1] See above, p. 107.

between the two groups. The breakdown of the negotiations for the entry of Britain into the Common Market in January 1963 changed the external circumstances; and the internal circumstances were changed by the I.C.I. bid and its aftermath—new men, new policies, the possibility of disengagement from B.N.S., and a stepping-up of nylon 6 production at Spondon, a matter affecting A.K.U. because of its nylon-producing enterprise, British Enkalon. After abortive talks in the course of 1963, the five-year agreement was allowed to lapse in 1964, and in the same year Courtaulds finally sold their 50 per cent. of the business to V.G.F.

The problems of that other pre-war viscose investment, the Calais plant, were tackled in a different way: by using it as a base for new investment, in 'Courtelle' and 'Celon'. Viscose-rayon production at Les Filés de Calais provided, as Table 39 showed, only a very modest return on capital and its contribution to group profits was notably lacking in buoyancy as is evident from Table 41:

TABLE 41

Contribution to pre-tax profits, Courtaulds Group, Les Filés de Calais, 1952–65

£000

Year ending 31 March	*Rayon*	*'Courtelle'*	*'Celon'*
1952	742		
1953	−63		
1954	300		
1955	470		
1956	342		
1957	449		
1958	594		
1959	362		
1960	222	−63	
1961	191	−166	
1962	125	−378	
1963	94	−210	
1964	237	−168	
1965	51	300	−2

So in 1958 the decision was taken to establish acrylic production. In the following years, under Sheldon's direction, a new company was set up, Courtaulds France S.A., with a small participation by French interests, and work started on the construction of a 'Courtelle' plant. Losses continued to 1964; thereafter capacity was increased, and this subsidiary began to contribute respectably to group profits. The possibility of establishing a nylon 6 plant at Calais was being considered in 1963, before disengagement from B.N.S. was assured, and work began on it the following year. At much the same time, appropriately enough, the old name Les Filés de Calais was given up and all operations—viscose, acrylic, and polyamide—came under Courtaulds France S.A. In December 1964, Kearton was writing to Sheldon, in Calais, telling him how he had told Ennemond Bizot[1] that 'the big expenditure we had in mind was progressive expansion of Courtelle, to serve the Common Market'.

The substantial Courtaulds holding in Snia Viscosa had long been viewed by Kearton with distrust, a sentiment which probably owed something to the very favour which Hanbury-Williams (and Davies) had accorded to it and to Marinotti. Between 1956 and 1961 the Board discussed on various occasions whether to participate in increases in Snia's capital and sometimes did so. After a number of purchases and switches, the position in March 1962 was that Courtaulds owned 14·2 per cent. of the share capital and 11·4 per cent. of the total voting rights, together with a holding of privileged shares without normal voting rights. The whole of this Snia investment was then transferred to Courtaulds Investments Ltd. Despite the expressed views in January 1961, of both Wilson and Rendall, that the Snia holding should be maintained, it is difficult to see that it had very much point. As an investment it had an unattractive yield; as a strategy it did not endow Courtaulds with any real ability to control Marinotti's tendency to export yarns and fibres (including nylon) at very low prices. So, with an eye on maintaining reasonable relationships with Snia, as well as on their joint undertaking, Novaceta, Courtaulds Investments proceeded gradually to sell off the Snia shares, a process which by 1965 had left a holding which represented about 5 per cent. of the Snia equity.

Meanwhile, and intertwined with these sales, a long wrangle had continued in 1962–3 about the termination of the caprolactam agreement which, as already shown,[2] was another matter on which Kearton had strong views. At one stage Marinotti himself wished to cancel it; then he changed his mind. Eventually in June 1963 the Board accepted Kearton's

[1] See above, p. 167.
[2] See above, pp. 176–7.

advice to terminate the exclusivity of the rights under the agreement thus avoiding having to pay certain minimum royalties. In August, after a visit to the Snia plant, Courtaulds, contending that the grounds on which they were induced to conclude the original contract were without foundation, notified Snia that they considered compensation was payable and that it would exceed the amount of the £265,626 still due under the contract. After a meeting with Marinotti, Courtaulds paid the amount outstanding —but did so in the form of Snia Viscosa privileged shares. And in 1964 it was agreed by verbal undertaking with Snia that Courtaulds could retain exclusivity rights without charge. On which note can be left the curious relations of Courtaulds and Snia Viscosa.

These varying treatments accorded, under the pressure of the times, to their older continental European investments does not exhaust the catalogue of changing overseas entanglements. Alongside E.E.C. was E.F.T.A. —the European Free Trade Association, 'the Seven' who did not belong to 'the Six'.[1] The 1963 breakdown of negotiations for Britain's entry into E.E.C. turned Courtaulds' eyes, along with many others, towards the E.F.T.A. countries. It was not an entirely new direction, for back in 1946 Courtaulds had entered into a technical agreement with the Swedish producer, Svenska Rayon AB, as a by-product of granting it a licence to work the I.R.C. patents.[2] This agreement lasted until 1955 but further requests for assistance by Svenska were turned down between 1959 and 1962 because of the agreement with A.K.U. By 1962–3, however, sundry influences worked to bring about a change in policy: growing disenchantment both with the A.K.U. agreement and with the various European cellulosic-fibre marketing associations; an increase in imports of staple fibre into the U.K. from producers in E.F.T.A. countries—all with small home markets and excess production capacity—at prices well below Courtaulds'; the collapse of the E.E.C. negotiations; and the changes in the directorate in London. The results were that in 1962 Courtaulds withdrew from all the marketing associations, having decided that they did not work; entered into a series of agreements with rayon producers in E.F.T.A. countries; and supplemented these agreements by buying for £1,517,000 a 49 per cent. interest in Svenska Rayon.[3] The background of this last

[1] E.F.T.A. had been set up in 1960, three years after the Treaty of Rome establishing the European Economic Community.

[2] See above, p. 48.

[3] Details of the imports, the associations, and E.F.T.A. agreements, as well as comments thereupon, will be found in M.C. *Man-made cellulosic fibres*, pp. 18–24, 80–3,

purchase was a report in June 1963 to the effect that Svenska Rayon's 'incursions' into the U.K. market were costing Courtaulds £200,000 per annum in lost profits a figure which it was thought might rise to £1 million by 1966. Courtaulds sought and secured some measure of what was described as 'orderly marketing'.

III

While overseas investments and involvements were thus varyingly re-shaped, the dominant theme of Courtaulds' policies at home was a major sequence of take-over operations. Table 42 is effectively a continuation of Table 25 in Chapter VIII.[1] It sets out in chronological order the main acquisitions during the three years 1962–4 inclusive; as in Table 25, it takes no account of new ventures, minor acquisitions, nor those made by subsidiaries.

Taking Tables 25 and 42 together, they show that between April 1957 and December 1964 Courtaulds spent, in cash or shares at market value, approximately £100 million in taking over other companies. The acquisition of Kirklees belongs to the earlier phase and has already been considered in Chapter VIII. The remaining companies in Table 42 fall roughly into three broad categories: knitters and/or garment makers, e.g. Bairns-Wear or Meridian; 'Lancashire' or 'cotton-type' spinners, e.g. Fine Spinners & Doublers; and miscellaneous textile producers or processors, e.g. Heap (dyers) or Morton Sundour (designers and makers of high-class fabrics). Some spilled over into more than one category; and there were also other and sometimes very different activities acquired, ranging from retail shops to cotton-growing land in the U.S.A. Considered as a whole, however, these acquisitions marked the first phase in a sequence lasting from 1963 to 1971 and almost wholly directed at forward integration into the textile industry. This phase was thus only in part a continuation of the diversifying doings of 1957–61, though it did also build upon some of the acquisitions which came with British Celanese and Gossard. As the whole 1963–71 sequence of constructing a 'vertical fibre-textile group'

106–10. The Monopolies Commission report disapproved of the terms of the agreement with E.F.T.A. producers and recommended its termination in so far as it restricted competition. Ibid., p. 87.

[1] See above, p. 164.

Main acquisitions by Courtaulds, 1962–4

Company	Date of bid	Value put on bid at the time	Direct cost to Courtaulds: Cash	Direct cost to Courtaulds: Ordinary shares	Direct cost to Courtaulds: 2nd preference shares
		£	£	(£1 units)	(£1 units)
Kirklees Ltd.	June 1962	350,000	—	166,667	—
Foister, Clay & Ward Ltd.	May 1963	2,338,000	2,187,900	—	187,500
Bairns-Wear Ltd.	June 1963	1,400,000	345,146	197,255	183,333
Morton Sundour Fabrics Ltd.	Oct. 1963	136,400	136,400	—	—
	Feb. 1965	200,062	200,062	—	—
	Mar. 1966	68,203	68,203	—	—
Susan Small (Holdings) Ltd.	Oct. 1963	2,230,000	1,493,737	225,500	—
Victor Marks Ltd. Berne Silk Manufacturing Co. (England) Ltd. Lester & Cann Ltd.	Oct. 1963	176,000	176,000	—	—
James Nelson Ltd.	Nov. 1963	5,600,000	945,000	1,200,000	378,000
Meridian Ltd.	Nov. 1963	4,100,000	3,626,000	—	51,576
George Brettle & Co. Ltd.	Dec. 1963	550,000	—	120,900	103,661
Barracks Fabrics Printing Co. Ltd.	Feb. 1964	167,000	135,000	—	40,000
Fras. Hinde & Sons Ltd.	Feb. 1964	694,755	—	195,501	—
	Dec. 1964	215,507	215,507	—	—
Premier Dyeing & Finishing (Holdings) Ltd.	May 1964	463,000	412,500	—	62,500
Fine Spinners & Doublers Ltd. (F.S.D.)	July 1964	16,300,000	8,384,968	1,397,495	2,500,000
Lancashire Cotton Corporation Ltd. (L.C.C.)	July 1964	22,400,000	14,162,795	2,023,257	—
Greenhalgh & Shaw Ltd. J. & J. Hayes Ltd.	Sept. 1964	1,327,500	1,327,500	—	—
Spray & Burgass Ltd.	Nov. 1964	1,250,000	800,000	—	—
Joseph Sunderland & Sons Ltd.	Dec. 1964	168,000	168,000	—	—
Samuel Heap & Son Ltd.	Dec. 1964	250,000	250,000	—	—
Total		60,321,224	35,316,965	5,362,908	3,673,237

has been dealt with elsewhere,[1] in broad outline at least, this chapter will concentrate on examining in a rather different way certain limited aspects of the early pursuit of this policy in 1961–4 and some of the problems created thereby.

As this pursuit of vertical integration was concerned overwhelmingly with those yarns and fibres of which the end-uses were predominantly in textiles rather than in some other area of industry, Table 43 tabulates simply the course of output of those yarns, omitting both viscose tyre yarn and acetate cigarette tow.

TABLE 43

Output of textile yarns and fibres, 1961–4

mn. lb.

Calendar year	*Viscose textile yarn*	*Viscose staple fibre*	*Acetate yarns and fibres ('Dicel' and 'Tricel')**	*'Courtelle'**	*B.N.S. nylon (yarn and staple)*
1961	53·6	229·4	57·1	14·0	80·7
1962	59·0	243·5	55·8	15·8	93·7
1963	60·1	279·0	58·0	23·4	113·9
1964	66·4	309·5	73·1	29·8	

* Years are March–March 1961–2, 1962–3, 1963–4, and 1964–5.

The upswing in textile-fibre output is evident in all categories. The prime hope of the policy was to make sure of markets.

Although, as Table 42 made evident, the acquisition of the big spinning combines was preceded by that of the knitters, the earliest moves towards this phase of integration in fact revolved around a big scheme, the 'Northern Project', engineered by Courtaulds for the fusion of a number of 'Lancashire' or cotton-type processors. Although it proved abortive it is worthy of detailed examination. For behind both this project and the ultimate purchase of L.C.C. and F.S.D. lay a number of crucial economic considerations. First, it was the cotton section of the U.K. textile industry, often called the 'Lancashire cotton industry' (not all in Lancashire and not concerned only with cotton but comprising spinners, weavers, etc. using

[1] Arthur Knight, *Private Enterprise and Public Intervention: the Courtaulds Experience* (London, 1974), esp. Chapter 3, and M.C. *Man-made cellulosic fibres*, pp. 25–32.

cotton-type machinery), which provided the largest single market for Courtaulds' big output of viscose staple fibre, taking about 40 per cent. Second, that industry, despite the 1959 Cotton Industry Act, was weak, inefficient, and decaying in face of cheaper imported Asiatic textiles. Third, Courtaulds' investment in viscose staple was both the biggest and the most profitable of its rayon assets. Staple fibre had low costs, owing much to the large scale of the Greenfield plant; was making promising technical advances; and was still responsible for the largest single share of profits. If Lancashire went under who would buy Courtaulds' staple fibre which depended for its profitability on large-scale, full-capacity working?

In 1959 and 1960 there had been some discussions about the possible 'rationalization' of the weaving section of the cotton industry with directors of English Sewing Cotton Ltd. and Carrington & Dewhurst Ltd. It was not, however, until the autumn of 1962 that talks involving Kearton, Mynors, and Koppel and certain officials from the Board of Trade indicated that government policy would apparently welcome a move by one of the big fibre producers, such as I.C.I. or Courtaulds, aimed at the reorganization of the whole Lancashire industry. At Kearton's instigation a study was then made of five companies as potential constituents of a big new grouping to be acquired initially by Courtaulds, with the promise of attracting other shareholdings later. The companies were English Sewing Cotton Ltd., Tootal Ltd., Fine Spinners & Doublers Ltd., the Lancashire Cotton Corporation Ltd., and Combined English Mills Ltd. Their combined net assets stood at £80·5 million and the market valuation of their ordinary shares at £38 million. Between them they took a large quantity of Courtaulds' staple fibre and a small quantity of textile yarn. Barings participated in the ensuing discussions and all five companies agreed to explore the proposed merger/take-over. In a notable memorandum to Dallas Bernard in December 1962, David Eccles, now on the Board, welcomed the project in glowing terms but also saw some snags:

> It is a concept of genius, worthy of England's best days, that the brains of the new fibres should assume the responsibility of putting fresh life into the traditional textiles. I agree with Mr. Kearton that if the rescue is not made now the leading cotton companies will soon become candidates for the knacker's yard.

Making the point that the poor profit performance of the textile companies might not make it an ostensibly easy acquisition to justify and that it was important to know the extent of under-used assets in order to determine to what extent Courtaulds might avoid issuing more shares, he went on to raise a very pertinent issue. How would I.C.I. react? 'Every new share we issue reduces the proportion of the equity they hold—a most desirable objective for us. But men with newly-acquired power in their hands seldom welcome its unilateral reduction.'

So I.C.I. were consulted. Although Mathys reported them as seeming to regard the 'Northern Project' as 'a good thing', Chambers in a letter to Bernard in January 1963 expressed doubts about the wisdom of Courtaulds spending so much money in acquiring the capital of these companies and proposed a scheme whereby the I.C.I. and Courtaulds set up a separate joint company to make offers for the companies in question. I.C.I. had themselves already engaged in talks during 1962 with English Sewing Cotton and were evidently disposed to get into the act on their own terms: 'our interest . . . is not only as a large stockholder of Courtaulds but as suppliers of large quantities of man-made fibres, dyestuffs and other products to the textile industry'. The I.C.I. directors also, not surprisingly in the aftermath of the bid, had qualms about the monopoly aspects of the scheme. Nevertheless, it seems clear that there was government approval for the idea of such firms as Courtaulds acting to create vertically integrated concerns in the Lancashire textile industry. And Courtaulds saw themselves as being in a strong position *vis-à-vis* I.C.I. As Eccles observed to Kearton in February: 'the conjuncture of the national interest that Lancashire must be rationalized and the aftermath of the I.C.I.'s bad showing last summer[1] is not likely to recur'.

With the assistance of the financial advisers, a joint scheme was hatched for a take-over operation of approximately £500 million. In the resulting combine, Courtaulds would have had 55 per cent. and I.C.I. 45 per cent. of the new capital. The scheme was put to the five companies. But valuations could not be agreed; one of the companies wanted a larger share. Agreement proved impossible. In April the Courtaulds Board accepted that the Northern Project had to be regarded as 'in abeyance' and began to consider alternatives. Within weeks some of the firms acted among themselves and got the assistance of the giants. English Sewing Cotton, for example, took over Tootal with the aid of cash from I.C.I. and (with some reluctance by the lender) from Courtaulds; their joint presence was seen as acting as a safeguard against a potential American bidder. Combined English Mills was taken over by Viyella International, the rapidly growing group built up by a passing textile meteorite, Joe

[1] i.e. their poor results in 1962.

Hyman. In June the Board approved the purchase of a shareholding in Carrington & Dewhurst; I.C.I. did likewise.

The Northern Project having been abandoned, Lancashire Cotton Corporation approached Courtaulds in July for funds for a take-over scheme of their own. Courtaulds refused. Nevertheless, whilst Courtaulds' process of acquisition during 1963–4 was mainly following its other paths, i.e. towards the knitting firms and other textile companies, it was also becoming evident that the two big spinning combines, L.C.C. and F.S.D., would not remain independent indefinitely. Could Courtaulds permit this? Each bought around 12 million lb. annually of staple fibre. The Courtaulds/I.C.I. disengagement in 1964 gave greater independence to both parties. I.C.I. were pursuing their own textile integration policy; so were other groups. As Knight put it in a letter to Kearton in July 1964, 'this volume of consumption might be sufficient to encourage somebody to acquire or control them and to set up a staple fibre plant to supply their needs'. A week later the Board formally agreed that offers should be made for each company. As Table 42 shows, the combined value at prevailing market prices was about £38 million, by far the biggest deal of this period. It was soon supplemented by the purchase of J. & J. Hayes Ltd. and Greenhalgh & Shaw Ltd., two spinning subsidiaries of Hayeshaw Ltd. who took most of their man-made fibres from Courtaulds. Here, too, it was important to act rapidly: in August Kearton was reporting to Mathys that Hayeshaw's had had approaches from Hyman, I.C.I., and 'an American fibre company' (possibly Chemstrand). The great project had proved abortive but the result in the end was not so very different. For after these purchases Courtaulds had secured around 30–35 per cent. of the whole 'Lancashire' spinning industry; and, after certain other lesser purchases, had come by the end of 1968 to control about 4 per cent. of total U.K. weaving capacity.

The forward integration into the knitting branch of the industry followed more than one path. The concentration of warp knitting under Furzebrook was designed primarily to render profitable, and expand, the knitting of acetate ('Dicel' and 'Tricel'), nylon 6, and to a lesser extent viscose textile yarns. In this it was successful: the division began to increase its profits and its subsequent expansion, as already mentioned, was aimed at absorbing a planned increase in the output of 'Celon' when this became possible after the disengagement from B.N.S. A different path was that which led into the weft-knitting sector of the textile industry. In this were a number of firms using circular knitting machines to produce knitted fabrics which were proving extremely popular, particularly in women's and children's garments. Some firms in this branch of textiles, as also in warp knitting, had proved very profitable, e.g. N. Corah & Sons, Pasolds Ltd., and the Nottingham Manufacturing Co. They had sailed to success on a wave of fashion for knitted garments. The knitting boom encouraged others to move in, and Courtaulds' entry into this area broadly coincided with other moves in the direction of both vertical and horizontal integration, combining warp and weft knitting, as well as spinning, weaving, dyeing, and converting into garments. Hyman's activities with Viyella International (itself later merged with Carrington & Dewhurst); the absorption of various companies by Pasolds and its subsequent absorption by Coats Paton & Baldwin (itself a product of a 1960 merger): these and several other manœuvres in the 1960s were all part of the general trend in the textile industry at this time.[1] It was a trend transcending the traditional divisions between 'cotton' and 'wool', 'Lancashire' and 'Yorkshire', weaving and knitting, natural fibres and man-made fibres. It owed its momentum to a confluence of various economic, technical, and personal forces. They included the need, recognized by all, to do something about 'Lancashire'; the hope, stimulated by developments in Europe, for economies to be secured by bigger, integrated textile units; the belief, increasingly shared by both Labour and Conservative politicians, that British industry needed bigger units; the rapid growth in the market power of the big chain-store buyers, such as Marks & Spencer; the ambitions of a number of entrepreneurs of whom Kearton was one; and the heavy capital investment demanded by the newer man-made fibres and the consequent urge by their producers to ensure markets for them especially in the face of the relatively falling prices for their products. This last point is worthy of particular emphasis. Fig. 5 in Chapter VII[2] has already demonstrated the long-term fall in the prices of cellulosic fibres relative to the general level of prices, 1940–64. The indexes in Table 44 show how, in the final seven-year period covered by this volume and when the forward integration movement was gathering momentum, the prices of the man-made fibres with which Courtaulds were directly concerned fell, all of them relative to consumer goods and services, some of them absolutely. With price-maintenance schemes increasingly difficult to sustain, the search for control

[1] For general accounts, see Graham Turner, *Business in Britain* (rev. edn. 1971), pp. 439–50; Channon, *Strategy and Structure of British Enterprise*, pp. 173–7; M.C. *Man-made cellulosic fibres*, Chapter 4 (pp. 25–32). [2] See above, p. 148.

TABLE 44

Price indexes: man-made fibres and consumer goods, 1958–64

Year	Consumer goods and services*	Viscose textile yarn	Viscose tyre yarn†	Viscose staple fibre	Acetate 'Dicel'	Acetate 'Tricel'	Acrylic 'Courtelle'	Polyamide Nylon 6
1958	100	100	100	100	100	100	100	100
1959	101	100	91	95	100	100	96	100
1960	101	100	87	95	100	100	96	100
1961	104	103	87	95	99	100	96	97
1962	109	103	91	95	99	100	92	97
1963	110	103	83	95	90	100	84	97
1964	113	104	83	99	103	103	82	91

* Feinstein, Table 61. † T. 105 to 1961; T. 140 from 1962.

of big outlets, as a path to greater sales, became all the more pressing.

When Courtaulds moved into weft knitting they were initially concerned with outlets for the acrylic 'Courtelle' as much as, or more than, acetate or nylon. They started to acquire knitting capacity by buying up companies with falling profit records. Bairns-Wear Ltd., Nottinghamshire-based manufacturers of knitted outerwear for women and children, and George Brettle & Co. Ltd., hosiery and underwear manufacturers of Belper in Derbyshire,[1] provide examples of the type. Both had serious management problems and their profits (pre-tax) were falling thus:

Bairns-Wear		*Brettles*	
	£		£
1960	174,306	1960–1	86,738
1961	171,604	1961–2	73,821
1962	32,854	1962–3	54,010

Such firms as these were already presenting inviting targets for the successful operators seeking to expand. When Courtaulds made their bid

[1] For a full account of Brettle & Co. see N. B. Harte, 'A History of George Brettle & Co. Ltd., 1801–1964' (mimeographed typescript in Courtaulds archives, 1973), and 'The Growth and Decay of a Hosiery Firm in the Nineteenth Century', *Textile History*, VIII (1977), 1–55.

for Bairns-Wear, Kearton soon found himself talking with the Djanogly brothers, who ran Nottingham Manufacturing Co. with a reputation for ruthless efficiency, were major suppliers of knitwear to Marks & Spencers, and who hoped to acquire some of the equity; and with Eric Pasold, creator of the extremely successful knitwear firm of Pasolds Ltd.,[1] who already owned 11 per cent. of the Bairns-Wear equity, and whose booming business was 'terribly short of capacity'. Without going into the details of each firm and the terms of take-over in each case, suffice to say that it was to this end and in this fashion that the main entry into weft knitting was made by the acquisition of Foister, Clay & Ward, Bairns-Wear, Meridian, and Brettles between the spring of 1963 and the beginning of 1964. The absorption of these firms was to pose problems, as we shall see, of a very particular kind. But by the end of 1965, Courtaulds had come to control approximately 27 per cent. of the total U.K. warp-knitting capacity and 6 per cent. of circular knitting, though later it was to increase these percentages.[2]

The third category of take-overs, the miscellaneous group, need not detain us long nor be looked at in detail. Each acquisition in some way, though not always very neatly, fitted into the pattern of vertical integration. The absorption of Morton Sundour was simply the final act in a process which had started in 1934 when the decision had been made to finance the F.N.F. machine.[3] As already mentioned, the F.N.F. company was sold in 1958 and consideration had been given to selling Courtaulds' holding in Morton Sundour Fabrics Ltd.[4] Its profit record continued to be poor—and relations with the family firm not entirely harmonious[5]—but in the circumstances of 1963 it was decided to acquire a majority position (and the advantage of some tax losses). This was done and 100 per cent. secured by two further purchases in 1965 and 1966. The much larger acquisition of Susan Small (Holdings) Ltd. represented in part a further move into the retail-garment trade, entered via Gossards, and partly a further bite into knitting, for it brought in Exquisite Knitwear Ltd. The James Nelson Group contained an important weaving business and were

[1] On Pasolds, see Eric E. Pasold, *Ladybird, Ladybird. A Story of Private Enterprise* (Manchester, 1977).

[2] M.C. *Man-made cellulosic fibres*, p. 29. [3] See Vol. II, pp. 370–2.

[4] See above, pp. 63–4. The holding comprised 25 per cent. of the equity and virtually all the second preference shares.

[5] See Jocelyn Morton, *Three Generations in a Family Textile Firm*, for one view of the relations.

thus consumers of textile yarns, acetate and viscose; so likewise were Fras. Hinde & Sons whose name provided a link, nominal rather than real, with the old days of mourning crape.[1] Some of the various printers, dyers, and finishers testified to the pursuit both of vertical integration and companies ripe for picking. Samuel Heap & Son, for example, a medium-sized, old-established, and family-owned dyeing business, had pre-tax profits which in the last five years of independent existence had this unhappy look:

	£
1960	62,486
1961	9,753
1962	−34,444
1963	−3,062
1964	16,547

It was quite a long way from an average of over £106,000 annually in 1950–4.[2]

As in the earlier, 1957–61, phase of acquiring, new problems of adaptation arose, further pressures were put on management to rejuvenate run-down companies and render them profitable, and new bits had to be fitted in to an organizational structure already under pressure.

The biggest take-over naturally brought the biggest change in structure. The first move in the task of fitting in F.S.D. and L.C.C. was the establishment in September 1964 of a Northern Board with administrative offices in Manchester. Kearton was its chairman and in addition to Mathys, Knight, and Koppel, its other members were Samuel and Drewitt together with the two new directors from the acquired companies, Winterbottom and Whitehead. In October three management groups were set up, under the Northern Board, to cover cotton-type spinning, Lancashire weaving and converting, and Yorkshire woollens and worsteds. The old Arrow and Westcroft mills committee was dissolved and its powers incorporated in the new structure. Then in December these three committees were brought together into a new division, the Northern Textiles Division. The Northern Board was restructured as a divisional Board under the chairmanship of Samuel and including Whitehead, Winterbottom, and Drewitt as its other main Board representatives. Winterbottom was responsible for the 51 cotton-type spinning mills; Whitehead for the woollen

[1] See Vol. I, pp. 164, 168; Vol. II, pp. 72, 369.

[2] For further details of Heaps, see N. B. Harte, 'A History of Samuel Heap & Son Ltd., 1823–1964' (mimeographed typescript in the archives of Courtaulds Ltd., 1967).

and worsted interests and all non-textile activities falling within the aegis of the Northern Division. A substantial programme for the re-equipment and/or rationalization of the spinning and weaving mills was put in train and gathered momentum over the next few years. By May 1966 weekly output per spindle had gone up by 20 per cent. and per operative by 19 per cent. It was necessarily a slow-yielding process. The Northern Textile Division's future had best be left encapsulated, in part at least, in a sentence of a letter from Frank Kearton to George Samuel in July 1965: 'There is no doubt that the overall position is a little disappointing, and the extra drive and bite you are putting in the Division's affairs are very much needed.'

However big the addition to the structure made by the Northern Textile Division, the problems which it brought were not intrinsically different in kind from those familiar to Courtaulds' textile experience. And even Samuel Courtauld & Co., so long a near-blight on group profits in the 1950s, began to prosper in the 1960s. But the problems introduced by the acquisition of the ailing circular-knitting and garment-making companies presented problems of a type not nearly so familiar to those in charge. In spinning as in fibre-making Kearton could, and frequently did, urge increasing output, the fullest utilization of capacity, and hence the lowering of unit costs even if it meant some piling up of stocks. But in the garment-knitting business fashion was directly important, the dictates of the big buyers crucial, the building up of stocks potentially disastrous and a low ratio of stocks to turnover vital. A sequence of letters written by Kearton between September 1964 and November 1965 to those charged with the task of turning Bairns-Wear and Brettles into profitable businesses illustrates both the nature of the problems and Kearton's approach to his managers.

'This garment business requires a lot of expertise we don't have, but it is vital we acquire,' he wrote to Bairns-Wear in December 1964. He repeatedly hammered home the lessons to be learned from the successful companies such as Pasolds or Nottingham Manufacturing as well as Courtaulds own Meridian and Gossard South Africa, viz. high turnover per employee, low ratio of stocks to profits. 'I am most disturbed by the increase in stocks . . . all the successful garment companies have ratios of stocks to profits of something between 1:1 and 2:1. You have a ratio of about 6:1. This is most unhealthy': a rocket for Brettles. There was more to come: 'Our attitude to these garment companies is entirely too complacent . . . What on earth is the point of having 800 people employed by George Brettle if they turn in a loss for one month of £20,000?' As for

Bairns-Wear, even by October 1965, 'progress had been far less than we had fondly hoped'; there were too many small accounts, they must be ruthlessly eliminated. On schemes for computerization, he countered that 'successful people like Pasold have relatively simple systems . . . they rely very much on their own 'eye' and feel for the business, and on simple indices like output per employee'. Garment companies needed such an approach, he insisted, telling one manager that his preoccupation with computers had meant that he couldn't see the wood for the trees. 'Computers are all right for businesses like Celanese, full of good people and honest Johns, but one wants something much more down to earth and easily comprehensible for the garment companies.' Kearton himself was certainly not being incomprehensible when he ended one of his letters in this series—replying to one which had indicated an improvement in performance—with the simple words: 'By Golly, we need the money!'

IV

The great surge of vertical integration must not blind one to all else that was going on in the aftermath of the bid. A few indications must serve further to chart some of the pathways by which those increased profits were secured.

Prinex continued its course of selling plants to distant places though the tasks of erection and operation thereafter were often attended by harassing practical problems. Long and complex negotiations with the Russians preceded Kearton's signing a contract in Moscow in May 1962 for the triacetate ('Tricel') plant, to be erected at Kaunas in Lithuania. It was worth approximately £6 million but it gave rather more favourable credit terms to the U.S.S.R. authorities than had the previous contracts. The second acetate ('Dicel') plant at Kirovakan started up at the end of the year, though reports from the site manager in the ensuing year continued to comment pungently on the deficient performance of the incompetent, haphazard, and ill-disciplined local Armenian labour force. The erection and operation of the tyre-cord unit at Balakovo was likewise the subject of protracted delays and mutual wrangles, productive of numerous fascinating reports from Courtaulds' site managers and technical experts on management–labour relations in the remoter parts of the U.S.S.R., too lengthy to be considered here. Eventually Russian complaints and Courtaulds' counter-complaints reached ambassadorial ears and in January 1965 Kearton departed to attend a crucial high-level meeting in Moscow and also to see the plant at Balakovo. The state of the latter had become 'a major issue in Anglo/Soviet relationships'; the situation, Kearton observed after submitting a long and detailed report, was indeed 'very serious'. A new technical team was sent out. In June, after a further visit to Moscow, Kearton agreed that Courtaulds would accept certain claims by the Russians; conversely the latter agreed on the payment of some of the retention money. Eventually, in 1966, the final instalment of the retention money was paid, despite the fact that Courtaulds' criticism of Soviet management and labour at Balakovo had not, meanwhile, been well received by the Russian authorities. Fortunately, matters went rather better, though certainly not without some difficulties, at Kaunas where the 'Tricel' plant started up towards the end of 1965.

The Polish acrylic plant contract did not run into such stormy waters and a smooth start-up was reported in April 1965. With the Yugoslav authorities sundry negotiations were conducted in response to their requests for tenders (together with substantial credit) for various man-made fibre operations. They came to nothing. The plant was effectively completed in the course of 1963 but, after the devastating earthquake in and around Skopje, its start up was delayed until 1965. The possibilities of China as a market for Courtaulds plant-exporting activities continued to excite interest, and Kearton made another trip there in June 1962. It was not, however, until 1965, after a visit by a Chinese delegation to the 'Courtelle' plant at Grimsby, that a contract was signed for the erection of an acrylic unit.

When Prinex made its report to the Board for 1965 it enumerated contracts signed during the year for just over £5 million. The acrylic factory for China accounted for over £3 million of this, but other items included additions to the Polish acrylic plant, viscose-spinning machinery for Greece, spares for the U.S.S.R., and work on the 'Celon' plants installed in Canada and the U.S.A. Tenders had been submitted during the year to various countries, including Romania, Czechoslovakia, and Greece for plants, machinery, and spares, totalling over £11 million. The real profitability of all these activities is very difficult to assess. The profits (untaxed before the 1962 judgement) from sales of 'know-how' brought in £1,805,000 which, as already shown, were credited to capital reserve and formed part of the capitalization used to create the loan stock during the defence against the I.C.I. bid.[1] In 1963–4 and 1964–5 Prinex recorded pre-tax trading profits of £1,111,000 and £200,000 respectively; as a

[1] See above, p. 228, n. 1.

return on sales this works out at 15·2 per cent. and 10·6 per cent., figures which showed something of an improvement on the 11 per cent. for the two years 1959–61 given earlier.[1] But linked to all these operations was another source of income, actual or potential, which is not taken into account in these figures: the gains from exports of products other than plants to the various countries with which trading relations were expanded as a consequence of these contracts. Heavy emphasis was put in all the negotiations with Communist countries on interesting them in Courtaulds' yarns and fibres, and representatives of Lustre Fibres visited these countries, sometimes accompanying Kearton on his travels thence. Table 45, showing all exports to the U.S.S.R., illustrates how fibre exports increased simply in the period up to 1963.

TABLE 45

Courtaulds' exports to U.S.S.R., 1956–63

Year	*Yarns and fibres*	*Chemicals*	*Machinery*	*Total*	*Total exports**	*Exports to U.S.S.R. as percentage of total exports*
	£ mn.	£ mn.	£ mn.	£ mn.	£ mn.	%
1956	0·04			0·04	13·03	0·03
1957	0·39			0·39	13·04	2·99
1958	—			—	13·50	—
1959	0·55		3·21	3·76	20·64	18·22
1960	0·43		7·13	7·56	26·00	29·08
1961	0·95		8·35	9·30	25·07	37·10
1962	1·62	0·16	0·18	1·96	28·28	6·93
1963	5·16	1·32	4·10	10·58	41·43	25·54

* Year to 31 March following.

Such increases in trade were not confined to the U.S.S.R. Exports of acetate yarn to Poland, for example, rose from 285,461 lb. in 1960 to 1,298,815 lb. in 1962.

Against the gains represented by these export figures, however, there must be set an indirect cost to Courtaulds arising out of the Prinex operation. Was it a suitable activity for the Engineering Division? The burden was very heavy; its resources were not really adequate to do this sort of

[1] See above, p. 200.

job; some of the complaints were justified. Hence costs, both monetary and in terms of prestige, were incurred. On the Balakovo contract, as Kearton admitted in October 1964, 'the Engineering side at Coventry has made a far lower profit . . . than was originally budgeted. This has given me sufficient troubles with my colleagues as it is!' The Courtaulds site experts had at times to admit (privately, at least) that some of the machines sent out by the engineers at Coventry were not up to the standards of established textile-machinery manufacturers—a deficiency which may well have been important in aggravating the troubles caused by their use by an unfamiliar and low-skilled labour force in the remoter parts of Russia. It is possible that a less ambitious and demanding programme of plant sales might have been more profitable.

Whatever the exact balance of real profits and losses on these activities, it remains very unlikely that Courtaulds was in any meaningful sense 'giving away its life-blood', as Wilson had earlier maintained.[1] The dissemination of the techniques of cellulosic-fibre manufacture had been remarkably rapid in the forty years or so up to World War II, and that of all man-made fibres perhaps even more so in the West in the decades thereafter. There was no shortage of firms in the West willing or even eager to sell cellulosic, acrylic, polyamide, or polyester technology to the East. To suppose that by refusing to do so Courtaulds could somehow preserve its position and its profits was wholly illusory.

If Prinex at one extreme and the Northern Textile Division and the garment knitters at another represented activities of the new Courtaulds, there remained at the core the familiar sources of profit: the cellulosic fibres, joined by the acrylics, supplemented by packaging and by paint. There is no point in examining the course of all these in the immediate post-bid years. All received the attentions of the 'new men'; divisions were treated to vigorous demands for profitability; there was much swapping of jobs and some sackings. 'Courtelle' capacity was massively expanded by repeated injections of investment at Grimsby, the Board agreeing another £2·8 million vote in July 1964 to increase capacity from 62 million to 79 million lb. annually. Despite what Kearton admitted to have been 'a most ghastly mess' in attempts to push 'Courtelle' in America, he remained enthusiastic about the potential market there. He planned to set up a production unit there at some date, though admitting in November 1964 that 'to rush into it would be unwise'. In cellulosic yarns and fibres probably the most important overriding achievement was the securing of

[1] See above, p. 193.

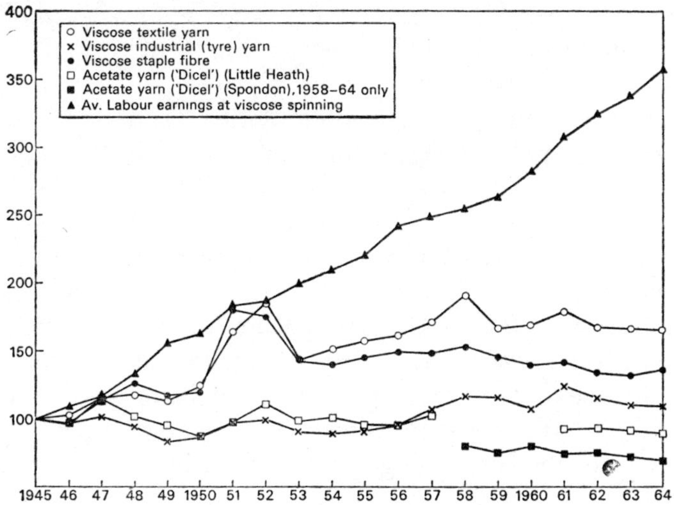

FIG. 11. *Courtaulds, U.K.: indexes of total factory costs and average labour earnings, rayon, 1945–64 (1945 = 100)*

The tyre yarn series is not strictly homogeneous, as there were increases in tenacity in 1956–7 and 1960–1 as well as the introduction of continuous spinning in 1951. There is a gap in the Little Heath acetate yarn series from 1958 to 1960 inclusive.

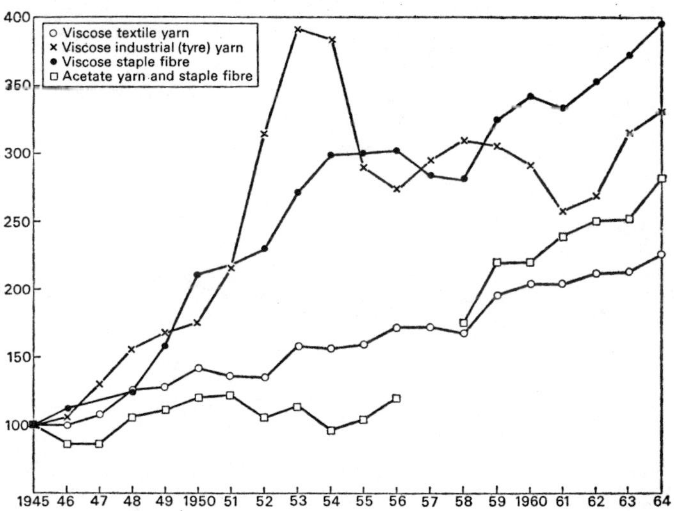

FIG. 12. *Courtaulds, U.K.: index of output per man-hour, rayon, 1945–64 (1945 = 100)*

See note to Fig. 11 on the tyre yarn series. There is a gap in the acetate series in 1957.

productivity increases. Figs. 11 and 12 complete for the whole period 1945–64 what Figs. 2 and 3 did earlier for 1945–54.[1] They show, in the form of indexes, the successful restraint of production costs and the substantial increases in output per man-hour, during a period of continuously rising wage rates and earnings.[2] Amongst the particular products, the gains to Courtaulds from the acquisition of British Celanese are very evident in the improved performance in acetate yarns from 1958 onwards. Viscose staple fibre clearly had the most impressive performance in improving output per man-hour as well as restraining its production costs. As labour accounted for a smaller proportion of total costs in its manufacture, pulp costs were accordingly of greater consequence. Fig. 13 exhibits, also as an index, the steep increase therein during the early 1950s and then the reversal, after 1956, in the trend of pulp costs relative to other production costs, the latter rising slightly whilst the former continued to

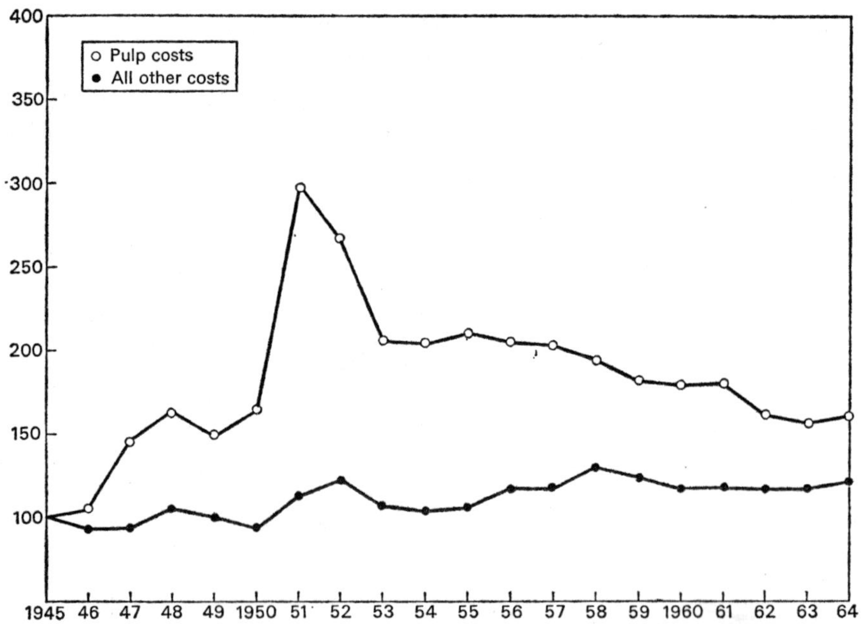

FIG. 13. *Courtaulds, U.K.: indexes of pulp costs and remaining conversion costs, viscose staple fibre, 1945–64 (1945 = 100)*

[1] See above, p. 53.

[2] For further details of rates and earnings, see Chapter XIII, especially, pp. 301–9.

fall. The momentum of improvement was maintained, for example, by the vote in January 1964 of nearly £5½ million for modernization work at the Greenfield plant. Even viscose textile yarn, the subject of a concerted campaign in 1961–5 to step up output and productivity, shared in some of the achievements. But the closure of the former British Enka textile-yarn plant at Aintree in August 1964 was a sign of the times: it was too small to be a viable unit.

V

The consequences of these years of change manifested themselves not only in the absolute level of profits but in the sources of those profits within the group. The first big signs of this shift have already been examined in Part II. Table 46 extends the comparison to reveal the striking differences between the years which mark the beginning of acquiring and diversifying and those which mark the end of the period with which this volume is concerned.

As these figures exclude all investment income, including that from B.N.S. and Novaceta, they slightly underestimate the contributions from non-viscose sources. Even so, the continuing and substantial decline of viscose rayon—yarn, fibres, and associated chemicals—stands out clearly: as trading profits roughly trebled in the course of eight years, its contribution sank from 69 per cent. to 36 per cent. At the same time, acetate products and synthetic fibres increased their joint share from 7 to 26 per cent. Still more striking was the great increase in textile processing and manufacturing activity—after years of neglect—trebling its relative contribution to the total. Packaging, despite that particular flurry of acquiring and diversifying (or indeed perhaps because of its failings), provided a smaller share, whilst paint and engineering contracts, new as profit sources, had come to account for an average of 9 per cent. of trading profits at the end of the period. But the extent of transformation must not be exaggerated. The manufacture, processing, and converting of man-made fibres, in one way or another, provided 80 per cent. of profits, even though this stretched from forests in Africa to dress shops in British high streets. And the remaining 20 per cent. still owed much to viscose and acetate chemicals and technology. A wider and better base for profits had been built, but in the end acquiring had been more important than mere diversifiying. Most of the profits, moreover, came from U.K.-based sources: approximately 85 per cent. of pre-tax trading profits, though slightly less if all investment income is included. A multinational company, but one which had moved a long way from those inter-war years when half Courtaulds' income came from American Viscose Corporation.

TABLE 46

Courtaulds Group: sources of pre-tax trading profit, 1957–8 and 1964–6

Percentages

	average (1956–7) (1957–8)	*average (1963–4) (1964–5) (1965–6)*
Fibres and related activities		
Viscose (yarn, staple, chemicals, etc.)	69	36
Acetate (yarn, tow, plastics, chemicals, etc.)	7	18
Synthetics (incl. 'Courtelle' and 'Celon')	—	8
Yarn processing	1	1
Wood-pulp (Saiccor)	3	5
Total	80	68
Textiles		
Northern Textiles Division		3
Dyeing and finishing		1
Weaving		2
Knitting		3
Garments		3
Total	3	12
Non-textile		
Packaging	16	10
Paint	—	6
Engineering	—	3
Total	16	19
Other	1	1
Total	100	100

Note: as in Tables 6, 19, and 21 these figures are derived from the profit and loss account and exclude deductions for central charges and research and development expenditure.

CHAPTER XIII

Workers, Managers, and Scientists

THE data recorded in the form of graphs in Figs. 2, 3, 11, and 12[1] have already testified to the achievement of higher productivity as well as higher labour earnings in the manufacture of cellulosic yarns and fibres during the two decades after 1945. It is time to look at this achievement from a different angle: the varying size of Courtaulds' labour force, its composition, pay, and management. No attempt will be made here to examine in detail, as was done in earlier volumes, the negotiations with trade unions or the various forms of welfare arrangements provided by the company;[2] the increasing size, diversity, and geographical spread of the group's activities would make this a major investigation in itself. The chapter will simply consider in broad terms certain general characteristics and problems of workers and staff, as they presented themselves to the Board and as they appear in relation to indicators of the company's economic performance as a whole.

I

Because of the frequently changing administrative structure of the group, especially after 1957, a continuous and homogeneous statistical series of the total labour force employed is neither readily available nor easy to construct. Fig. 14 brings together some partial series, giving annual average employment in certain main divisions, as well as some disconnected observations of aggregate employment.

To take the latter first. It would seem that, in round terms, Courtaulds' total U.K. labour force multiplied about three-fold over the whole period, rising from approximately 20,000 to 60,000. Overseas, after the loss of A.V.C., total employment rose from about 3,800 in 1946 to around 12,000 in 1964. Both home and overseas figures exclude associated companies, e.g. Svenska Rayon A.B. If these aggregate figures are compared with profits, it is immediately evident that Courtaulds was earning lower

[1] See above, pp. 53 and 285.

[2] Vol. I, Chapter XI; Vol. II, Chapters VII and XIV.

profits per employee at the end of the period than at the beginning. In rough terms, the relationship works out as shown in Table 47.

TABLE 47

Courtaulds: approximate profit per employee,*
circa *1940, 1960, and 1965*

	(*a*) Pre-tax trading profits	(*b*) U.K. employment	(*c*) U.K. and overseas employment	$\frac{(a)}{(b)}$	$\frac{(a)}{(c)}$
	£ mn.	'000s	'000s	£	£
circa					
1940	8	20	24	400	333
1960	10	48	60	208	167
1965	12	60	72	200	167

* The approximations have all been made in such a way as to minimize the decline in profit/employee over the period. So $\frac{(a)}{(b)}$ and $\frac{(a)}{(c)}$ are probably underestimates even in monetary terms; and no allowance has been made for inflation.

This comparison might be thought unfair because the lower figures for the later dates follow immediately upon the massive acquisitions of those years and thus fail to allow enough time for the requisite adjustments and rationalization to be made and then to show themselves in profits. To some extent this is true. Nevertheless, these figures do underline one of the very real problems of external expansion by merger and take-over: the acquisition, along with productive capacity, of work forces which will add to aggregate costs but contribute little to marginal profits. At one time, massive and ruthless redundancies would have followed; in the 1960s such policies would have been socially and politically out of the question.

An indication of the dependence of these falling profit/employee ratios upon the pursuit of activities outside the traditional core of cellulosic fibres is provided by a comparison of the data in curve A in Fig. 14 with the total output and with the mill profits corresponding to that particular section of Courtaulds' labour force. That section comprises simply the operatives in the yarn mills and processing plants, viscose and acetate, including British Celanese after 1957. Comparison of the weight of output with employment over the two 5-year periods 1939–43 and 1960–4 shows an increase in output per employee of approximately 2·7 fold. Exact comparison of profits per employee is difficult over the whole period partly because of the special circumstances of the war years and partly because of changes in accounting classification. But comparing, as closely as possible, the two 5-year periods 1945–49/50 and 1959/60–1963/4 it would seem as though the profit/employee ratio in that area of the group multiplied by a factor of about 2·4. Both the figures, it must be stressed, are very rough. But, bearing in mind in the case of the latter figure the sluggishness of yarn and fibre prices, they together suggest an order of

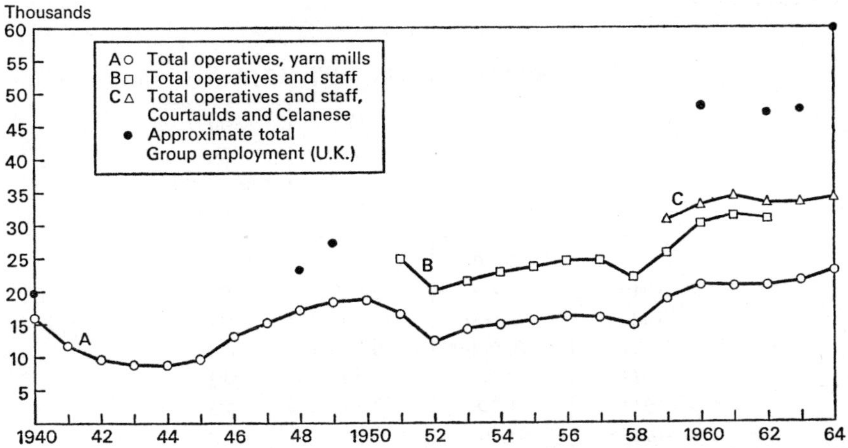

FIG. 14. *Courtaulds, U.K.: employment, 1940–64*

A includes Northern Ireland and covers male and female factory workers. Figures are annual averages.

B covers A plus the 'Courtelle' plants, the textile and chemical divisions, sales and laboratory staffs and the London office. Figures are averages for February, May, August and November.

C covers all Courtaulds/Celanese divisions but excludes the major acquisitions. Figures are averages for January and July.

magnitude of improvement readily compatible with the increases in output per man-hour and the limitations on rises in manufacturing costs exhibited earlier. So within the older, core activities of the business, the increase in numbers employed, after recovery from the war years, was small, and it contributed a more than proportionate increase to output and profits.

In Fig. 14 the continuous series A and the partial series B (which covers both staff and operatives[1]) both clearly reveal the marked fluctuation in employment created by the war and post-war boom (A only) and the recessions of 1951–3 and 1957–9 (A and B). During the war the substantial

[1] For some comments on the meaning of these terms see below, p. 294.

drop in the labour force (both in numbers and in quality) did not, however, result in the fall in output per worker such as occurred at Coventry in 1916–18 during World War I.[1] Indeed aggregate output per worker showed a slight rise partly because of the cuts in the output of both viscose and acetate textile yarns and the concentration on tyre yarn and staple fibre;[2] and partly because of an increase in shift-working and the length of the working week, so that by 1942 the yarn mills were effectively working a 56-hour week.

TABLE 48

Output per worker, yarn mills, 1940–8

	(*a*) Output	(*b*) *Average annual employment*	$\frac{(a)}{(b)}$ *Output per worker*
	mn. lb.		'000 lb.
1940	118,200	15,990	7·4
1941	93,000	11,591	8·0
1942	79,900	9,510	8·4
1943	83,000	8,899	9·3
1944	91,300	8,887	10·3
1945	95,400	9,714	9·8
1946	123,700	13,187	9·4
1947	144,300	15,254	9·3
1948	167,300	17,153	9·8

In 1945, on the cessation of hostilities and the negotiation of new wage agreements, they returned to a 48-hour week and, as Table 48 shows, output per worker went down temporarily. After the post-war boom, which brought a peak in the yarn-mill labour force to reach about double that of the war years, the recession of 1951–3 saw a sharp drop in employment. The slow recovery thereafter reflected the deliberate switch away from the declining textile yarn towards the less labour-intensive staple fibre. By 1954, when total output well exceeded its pre-recession level, numbers employed at Wolverhampton, Preston, Aber, and Castle mills were lower than the 1951 peak; at the Greenfield staple-fibre plant they were higher. The downturn in employment began to show itself after October–November 1951 when, as sales dropped and stocks built up, men and women were laid off. It affected all departments. From a peak of 16,757 at the end of October 1951, yarn-mills employment fell to a low

[1] Vol. II, p. 130. [2] See above, Table 1, p. 6.

point of 9,646 in July 1952; in the Textile Division, the number of staff and operatives at work fell from 2,918 in November 1951 to 2,126 a year later. Even in the London offices, the sort of places normally least affected by such cuts, numbers fell from 422 in November 1951 to 357 in May 1953. The 1957–9 recession brought another drop in employment which though sharp, was not so severe as in 1951–2. In 1951–2 a 24 per cent. fall in output brought a 19 per cent. fall in employment; in 1957–8 the equivalent figures were 18 per cent. and 11 per cent. These figures (curve B in Fig. 14) exclude British Celanese, so they do not fully reflect the changes in Courtaulds' total employment at this time because of the complications arising from the acquisition of British Celanese in the course of 1957 and the redundancies created as a result of the ensuing redeployment of labour, especially at Spondon. In the course of the two years March 1957–March 1959, the numbers working at Spondon were reduced from 8,600 to 4,200. The redeployment affected Courtaulds as well as British Celanese and the figures in Table 49, covering the period March 1957–March 1958, although including reductions due to the recession as well as to rationalization, show how the total net reduction of 7,200 was constituted.

TABLE 49

Changes in total employment, Courtaulds and British Celanese, 1957–8

		Courtaulds		*British Celanese*		*Total*
Mar. 1957	Staff	6,536		3,292		9,828
	Operatives	18,845		9,920		28,765
	Total	25,381		13,212		38,593
Mar. 1958	Staff	6,239		1,988		8,227
	Operatives	16,402		6,764		23,166
	Total	22,641		8,752		31,393
			%		%	
Net reductions	Staff	−297	−4·5	−1,304	−39·6	−1,601
	Operatives	−2,443	−12·9	−3,156	−31·8	−5,599
	Total	−2,740		−4,460		−7,200

Such an operation, clearly affecting employment in the Derby area more than elsewhere, required careful handling. It evoked questions in Parliament but, with the co-operation of the Ministry of Labour, the trade unions involved, and local firms offering alternative employment, the changes seem to have been carried through successfully and with the minimum of friction.

The fluctuations in employment provided occasions for the Board to become concerned about the question of the proportion of staff in the total work force. The distinction between 'staff' and 'operatives' was not merely a matter of monthly or weekly pay (there were weekly-paid 'staff') nor simply of the difference between managers and manual labourers (office cleaners or chauffeurs could appear as 'staff' as well as skilled chemists). 'Operatives' were weekly-paid men and women, receiving wages calculated on a mixed time- and piece-rate system, working on the shop floor in the various mills, plants, or factories and directly engaged in productive processes. 'Staff' covered not only monthly-paid salaried workers in offices and laboratories, but also various grades of supervisors, clerks, and other workers to whom 'staff status' was awarded. Criteria inevitably varied from time to time, so not too much meaning must be read into the varying proportions of staff to operatives. Nevertheless, the growth in what are sometimes unhappily referred to as 'non-productive' workers periodically agitated the Board. In April 1952, for instance, Hanbury-Williams, on calling for a return on staff strength, discovered to his obvious disapproval that staff numbers had doubled since 1939. An economy campaign was launched and contributed to the reductions in staff during the 1952 recession, though some of these simply consisted of demotions from staff to operative status. For example, a decrease in staff of 621 during the first seven months of 1952 consisted of 321 demotions and 300 dismissals. The 1957–9 recession provoked similar reactions and a further set of returns of staff was called for from all divisions. Again, as in 1952, these returns exhibited many increases over the previous few years. Staff, of whatever precise sort, had (and still has) a notable tendency to increase in numbers and further blasts on this theme came from Kearton in 1963–4. In both 1951–3 and 1957–9 the proportionate fall in staff employment was significantly less than that of the numbers of operatives.

It is quite clear therefore that the proportion of 'staff' rose markedly over the period, despite periodic economy campaigns. Exact comparisons are difficult, but the percentage labelled staff probably rose from under 15 per cent. in 1940 to about 20 per cent. in 1948. Thereafter, and despite the reductions during the 1951–3 recession, it moved up to about 20 per cent. in 1954–6 and reached some 28 per cent. in 1957–8. Economies and rationalization pushed it down to 26 per cent. in 1959–60, only to creep up to 27 per cent. in 1962. Efforts to lower this proportion achieved some success in 1963–4, though with the acquisitions of those years, the percentage once again stood at about 27 at the end of our period. Some of this increase was due to changes in the status label; some reflected the greater proportionate demand for men and women with higher educational attainments and professional skills in management, technology, and research; and some testified to the too easy proliferation of bureaucracy.

The proportionate increase in staff employment was especially marked in the research department. In terms of expenditure Courtaulds' research and development effort reached its peak during this period in the later 1950s. The figures in Table 50 are indeed a numerical reflection of Wilson's success in building up the research and development staff, refurbishing the laboratories, and stimulating the varied work which led to improved profits via the route of technical advance.

TABLE 50

Expenditure on research and development, 1945–65

	£000		£000
1945	217	1955–6	2,098
1946–7 (15 months)	490	1956–7	2,248
1947–8	564	1957–8	2,187
1948–9	680	1958–9	1,826
1949–50	837	1959–60	1,810
1950–1	828	1960–1	902
1951–2	1,109	1961–2	1,161
1952–3	1,228	1962–3	978
1953–4	1,359	1963–4	1,329
1954–5	1,695	1964–5	1,479

In terms of staff employment a first peak was likewise reached in the later 1950s although numbers increased again in the 1960s. By the beginning of 1957 the staff employed in the research department accounted for about 14 per cent. of the entire staff strength in Courtaulds. From 125 in 1941, it had risen sixfold to reach 753 in 1954 and then moved up to 908 in 1957. Falling slightly in 1958–60 to an average of about 850, it rose again to around 930 in 1961–3 and to 1,050 in 1964–5.

II

This increase in staff employment and in expenditure on research and development has a double significance in the firm's history in these post-war decades. It meant, directly, a growing need to recruit university graduates in science in order to staff and direct the research and development operations; and, indirectly, as those efforts were translated from laboratory to pilot plant and then to the factory floor, it meant a growing demand for a higher level of education in all levels of management. The Board was undoubtedly aware of these needs; they were made manifest alike in Samuel Courtauld's pre-war strictures upon the company's performance and in the post-war appointment of Wilson.[1] They were likewise evident in some of the reports on staff matters also drawn up just after the war.

Freeman's adverse comments upon the quality of the existing management in Courtaulds have already been quoted in the context of complaints about the Board's excessive concern with departmental matters. Gratwick lamented the 'dangerously low' supply of potential leaders in the company and the need to find 'a better type of candidate than those formerly recruited for senior executive positions'. George Courtauld, as the director in charge of personnel, echoed these sentiments in various memoranda which he sent to the chairman during 1947. The company was 'short of first-class men of a high standard of education, broad outlook, and the qualities of leadership' a fact evident from the difficulties experienced in 'filling from within our own ranks so many jobs which fall vacant'. The shortage was particularly notable in the 25–35 age group; successful staff trainees from outside would have to be paid more (and Courtaulds' rates were then lower than elsewhere) when taken on after their probationary period; and the more conservative departments would have to be willing to promote such people over the heads of long-serving but less able staff. Commenting on the low standard of mill managers, technical managers, mill labour officers, salesmen, and many others, he deplored some specific characteristics of existing policy, notably 'a shortsighted departmental personnel policy'; the unwillingness of existing managers (and directors) to delegate authority; too high a retiring age; past neglect of recruitment; 'a sense of complacency produced by our virtual pre-war monopoly in viscose rayon and by our large past profits' (this earned a question-mark in the margin from Hanbury-Williams); a slow promotion policy because 'we seldom remove people however bad (let alone mediocre) they are'; and a general tendency to 'play over-safe and to accept a fair Civil Service standard as opposed to a first-class commercial standard'. He stressed the need for Courtaulds to do what other companies had found it necessary

[1] Vol. II, pp. 229–42, and above, pp. 17–20.

to do, i.e. externally to adopt an 'intensified and discriminating' recruiting policy, and internally to take vigorous action to discover and encourage 'first-class material of all grades'. A thorough reorganization of salaries was necessary, with the adoption of a policy which would recognize the vital need to improve management at all levels.

In broad terms it can be said these sentiments and intentions informed staff recruitment and promotion policy over the ensuing fifteen years or so. A Personnel Department came into being in 1945; it was speedily enlarged and given greater responsibilities. It operated under the general direction of George Courtauld, as personnel director, who was in turn responsible to the Appointments and Personnel Committee of the Board set up in May 1946. The department evolved a system of grading of staff posts; determined, in co-operation with divisions and operating departments, what staff was needed over the next 5, 10, and 15 years to fill those posts; maintained an inventory of staff of high potential currently employed at middle or junior level but believed to be capable of filling posts at senior level; and planned for the processes of training, promotion, and/or recruitment from outside necessary to fill posts at the required levels. It had come, in 1955, to see its planning tasks as being based on the general assumption that, more than ever before, 'a higher standard of management, scientific, and technical skills at all levels' was needed; and that those requirements were increasing and would continue to increase. To this end suitable candidates were sent on a variety of training courses, internal and external. A company staff-course got under way in 1952; short textile training-courses were operating from 1947 onwards; at various times courses were used at outside bodies, such as the Administrative Staff College at Henley, the Manchester College of Technology, or the Institute of Personnel Management; an internal management course, held at Cambridge, was started in 1959. The universities were scoured for bright young men with science degrees; graduates in law, economics, or arts subjects were taken on as staff trainees. It was all a very long way from the company's policies in the 1930s, typified by the 'practical man' attitude of Harry Johnson and the very occasional appointment of a university graduate.[1]

Just how successful the policy was it is hard to say. In 1949 George Courtauld reported that he thought the company was adequately staffed at 'junior and middling' levels, but that there was 'a material shortage of top grade replacements' in many departments; and if executive standards

[1] Vol. II, pp. 233–5.

were to be raised or new demands made then the position was still 'extremely grave'. In time, the standard of education and of scientific and technical skills in the company's staff unquestionably rose; without that rise Courtaulds could not have maintained such technical momentum as they did. These improvements provide simply a particular example of the general response of successful firms to the more advanced and complex technical demands of manufacturing industry in the mid-twentieth century. Whether, on the other hand, the particular form of the policy was less successful than it might have been or resulted in any specific disadvantages is quite another matter. The standard of management skills presumably rose, in some parts of the company, otherwise the increases in productivity registered in some areas could not readily have been achieved. But might they have been greater or more widespread? Without very detailed investigations such questions cannot be answered at all precisely. It is, however, worth pointing to some criticisms; and to some changes made towards the end of the period.

The pre-war neglect of scientific recruitment in general and of the research laboratories in particular provoked so strong a reaction after the war that it nourished a vigorous new appetite for recruiting scientists. In the years immediately after Wilson's appointment, a big batch of senior scientific staff had to be recruited to re-establish the research laboratories. Competition not only for the recruitment but also for the retention of such skilled manpower was intense in British industry. The turnover of scientists was considerable. In 1950 out of 29 staff requirements in the Engineering and Research departments 4 specified Ph.D. or equivalent qualifications, 12 first or second class honours degrees, and 9 good or good honours degrees in physics, chemistry, chemical, electrical or mechanical engineering, or mathematics. An analysis of 'voluntary wastage' of monthly paid staff during the seven-year period 1949–55 showed that out of 218 persons thus vacating posts, the Research and Engineering departments accounted for the largest single totals, 49 and 47 (22·5 and 21·6 per cent.) respectively, larger than the 44 (20·2 per cent.) of all the yarn mills combined. Because of the increasingly technical nature of the production processes—more synthetic fibres, greater mechanization and automatic control systems, different sorts of chemical plants—the crucial posts of mill manager, production manager, and technical manager were more and more filled by men with scientific qualifications. Consequently, as it came to be admitted within the Personnel Department, science graduates had a better chance of transfer to higher management than did such other specialists as accountants or even engineers. Freeman had already observed this trend in 1953 and protested about it to Wilson: 'I believe there is a feeling that from now on only chemists can achieve advancement.' This remark exactly anticipated a Personnel Department comment made two years later (and after Freeman's death): 'I think that concern and even resentment is detectable among some other groups of specialists, who consider that the scientists of the company have cornered the management market for some years to come.' As the analysis of the Board in Chapter VII has already suggested,[1] there was also a useful route from that market to the Boardroom.

Whatever the merits and demerits of the policy, one member of the Board still found reason in 1957 to complain about precisely that lack of talent for leadership amongst the staff ranks which had exercised his predecessors a dozen or so years earlier. Kearton on the Processing Division:

> within the Divisional staff as a whole we can see few potential leaders in the lower ranks and we are concerned as to how standards are going to be maintained or improved upon. There seems a dearth of people capable of leading or in fact of wanting responsibility in what has become an exacting and difficult industry.

Even though his remarks evidently have a limited application, the comment in the final sentence suggests that he, at least, thought of them as having some relevance to the industry as a whole. There is no *a priori* reason why scientists should make better managers or business leaders than accountants, engineers than salesmen. The need for more educated and technically able staff bears no *necessary* relationship to the need for managerial and decision-making skills. The latter may or may not function better in particular individuals if informed by prior training in physics or chemistry.

In practice, the whole problem of staffing and managerial recruitment within the company was, like so many other matters, pushed into a different shape in the years between 1957 and Kearton's accession to the chairmanship in November 1964. The massive external acquisitions, from British Celanese to Lancashire Cotton Corporation, effectively recruited into the group numerous staff amongst whom could be found managerial skills, actual or potential. The administrative decentralization demanded

[1] See above, p. 132.

by the much more diverse nature of the group changed the role of the old Appointments and Personnel Committee: it was one of those swept away in March 1962. The earlier staffing policies had centred around the yarn mills and the need to find good mill managers. As the group became more diverse these ceased to be the sole centres of productive effort. The policy had to be adjusted accordingly. A deliberate effort was made to promote, train, or recruit with a view to specific needs in the organization as a whole.

This aim had, of course, been the broad intention of the post-war staffing policy for the then much smaller company, but in the course of time it had been frustrated or diverted by a number of developments. The substantial staff turnover had resulted in many of the better recruits leaving the company. The faltering policies, the general lack of leadership at the top, the slipping profits in the 1950s, and the type of aloof paternalism favoured by Hanbury-Williams: these were hardly encouraging to the able and ambitious on their way up the business ladder. Over and above the need to acquire staff with particular scientific qualifications, the pattern of recruitment had been influenced by the cast of mind of Hanbury-Williams and his closer colleagues who tended to be impressed by those describable as in some sort of way as 'the right sort of people' or 'good chaps'. So, under Kearton's direction, the new order began to adopt what it saw as more flexible and less socially restricted policies. What emerged, of course, was something which bore Kearton's personal stamp and particular brand of autocracy. A central department was maintained to look after management training and selection; new courses were introduced. But Kearton had only a limited regard for such formal procedures. Divisions and subsidiaries having been given greater power and responsibility, they were also put under great pressure to make profits. This in turn meant the reality of managers finding themselves under constant pressure from Kearton. In the sacred name of profitability, they were bullied or cajoled, rewarded, transferred, or sacked.[1] In general, and despite some failures, it worked. But, once again, it was the research department (or Division as it had become) which proved to be the major source of talent for top management and the Board.[2] Here again the post-bid policy was not as new as it seemed and was building upon pre-bid developments.

[1] For some examples of his communications with his managers, see below, pp. 318–19.

[2] Knight, op. cit., p. 83, and more generally, pp. 81–6.

III

It is a well-known feature of the British economy in the post-war years that the earnings of labour rose more rapidly than many other economic variables, including prices, output per worker, company profits, and, of course, wage rates. The following figures draw together the general indicators for the U.K. for the first and last years of the period with which this book is concerned.

1940 = 100

	Average weekly earnings	*Average weekly wage rates*	*Retail prices*	*Output per worker*	*Gross trading profits of companies*
1940	100	100	100	100	100
1965	461	343	281	150	434

Source: Feinstein, Tables 1, 20, 65.

So far as wage rates are concerned, Courtaulds' experience did not differ very greatly from that of the economy as a whole. Fig. 15 shows the changes in basic hourly wage rates for the main classes of factory operatives: men and women process workers and tradesmen. Over the period the differentials in rates narrowed to some extent. Expressed as percentages of the men's rates they moved as follows:

	1940	*1965*
Women	53	72
Men	100	100
Tradesmen	131	128

The men's rates rose slightly more than the average for the U.K. as a whole, the women's rates considerably more:

	1940	*1965*
Women	100	529
Men	100	391
Tradesmen	100	381
U.K. average	100	343

This partial closing up of the rate for women reflected, in part at least, the low rates paid pre-war to women in the areas of Courtaulds' yarn mills.[1] The trend, evident before the war,[2] towards the equalization of rates as

[1] Vol. II, pp. 433, 449. [2] Vol. II, pp. 432–3.

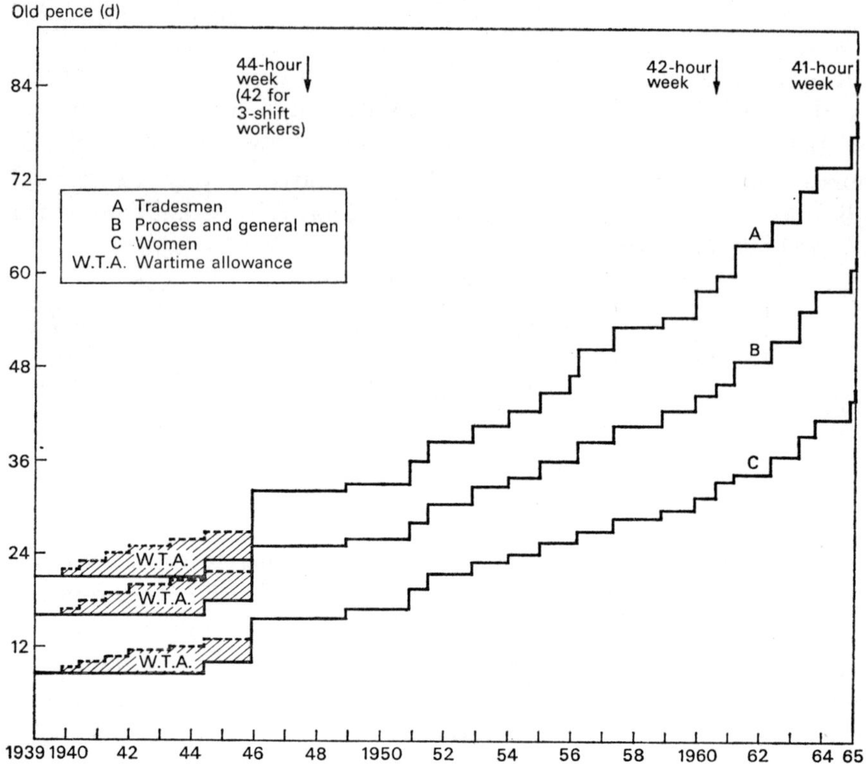

FIG. 15. *Courtaulds, U.K.: hourly wage rates, rayon mills, 1939–65*

between the various mills in different parts of the country was completed; and many of the changes applied both to yarn and textile mills.

The picture presented by the movement of rates in this quarter century stands in very striking contrast to that of the pre-war decades. Although even then the differential between skilled and unskilled was narrowing, the monetary level of male viscose-spinners rates remained the same, despite some intervening fluctuations, in 1939 as in 1919.[1] From 1940 onwards, a combination of rising prices, labour shortages, a lower level of unemployment, and the greatly increased power of the trade unions helped to create the remarkable rising staircase depicted in Fig. 15.

But, of course, these are by no means true indicators of the real increase in the economic return to labour. The constituent elements which made up

[1] Vol. II, p. 432.

the difference between basic money rates and real earnings fall into a number of separate categories. First, chronologically, was a special wartime allowance which is shown by the dotted lines in Fig. 15. This was paid from November 1939 to November 1945 during which period it was raised on five occasions before being combined with the basic rates. Second, and more important, was the shift allowance. At the beginning of the war this was 1½*d.* per hour for 2-shift working, and 4*d.* for 3-shift for male process workers. As continuous 3-shift working was extended to cover the majority of male workers, these increases may be cited as representative. They moved up as follows:

1939–55	4*d.*
1955–60	5*d.*
1960–3	6*d.*
1963–4	6½*d.*
1964–5	8*d.*

Third, there was more than one sort of incentive bonus. A 'time-working bonus' operated until 1963 when it was phased out in a general change in the wage structure. But the more important type was an incentive bonus which functioned by means of a 'bonus calculator'. The latter was an hourly rate set at rather less than the basic rate. To take a simple example: in 1955 the basic (male) rate was 3*s.* per hour and the bonus calculator was 2*s.* 2*d.* If the worker produced a standard output of, say, 100 units, he received 3*s.* but if he produced 150 he received an extra 50 per cent. of the calculator, i.e. 1*s.* 1*d.*, thus earning 4*s.* 1*d.* per hour.

The ratio of the bonus calculator to the basic rate was consequently a matter of considerable importance to earnings. In the 1950s a ratio of about 80 per cent. of the basic rate was thought desirable by management who liked to keep the incentive bonus separate from the basic rate determined by negotiation with the unions. If the basic rate was increased and the ratio allowed to fall, it was clear that the unions might raise objections to the whole principle of the bonus calculator. Largely under Pedder's direction much effort had been put into the work-study necessary for the operation of these incentive schemes. By the mid-1950s over 90 per cent. of the total pay-roll of operatives in the company (textile mills as well as yarn mills) was covered by some form of incentive scheme. The bonus-calculator method was of particular consequence in the rayon plants and management saw it as an important element in the increasing productivity secured therein during the first post-war decade. So, as the figures below illustrate, when, in the 1940s and 1950s, the bonus-calculator slipped significantly below about 80 per cent., it was soon raised.

Date	(*a*) *basic rate* (*men*) *d.*	(*b*) *bonus calculator* *d.*	(*c*) *percentage* (*b*) *to* (*a*)
Aug. 1947	25	20	80
Oct. 1950	28	20	71
Jan. 1951	28	23	82
Oct. 1952	32·5	23	71
June 1953	32·5	26	80
Jan. 1955	36	26	72
Nov. 1955	36	29	81
Oct. 1958	42·5	29	68
July 1960	46	35	76

In the 1960s, however, with strong union pressure for bigger increases in the basic rate, the incentive element in the wage structure was reduced and the ratio between the calculator and basic rate fell.

Apr. 1962	51·5	35	68
Mar. 1963	55·5	37	67
Jan. 1965	62·5	38	61

It is not perhaps wholly unrelated to this initially increasing, and then decreasing, intensity of use of incentive schemes that the indexes of output per man, as shown in Fig. 12,[1] reveal *rates* of improvement notably higher in 1945–54 than in 1955–64.

The fourth element in the increasing return to labour was a series of reductions in hours worked. The pre-war 48-hour week was, as already mentioned, effectively increased to a 56-hour week during the special circumstances of wartime working with a depleted labour force. When the war was over the 48-hour week returned. Thereafter, as shown in Fig. 15, the working week was successively reduced, in 1947, 1960, and to 41 hours in January 1965, itself a prelude to the 40-hour week which came in a year later. Fifth, there were sundry benefits not readily quantifiable or susceptible to easy generalization as they affected different workers in

[1] See above, p. 285.

different ways. They included better entitlements to sickness pay; miscellaneous non-recurrent *ex gratia* payments; longer paid-holidays; supplementary unemployment allowances; the extension of existing staff pensions to include hourly paid workers; and the introduction, in 1955, of a co-partnership scheme designed to provide the opportunity for some extension of share ownership to employees. Vestiges of the long tradition of welfare, which had characterized the firm in the nineteenth century, but had become tarnished under Harry Johnson's rule,[1] persisted in the attitudes of mind of Samuel Courtauld and appealed to the *noblesse oblige* instincts of Hanbury-Williams. In practice, however, the onward march of trade-union power and the welfare state, assisted by the growth in size and diversity of the Courtaulds Group, ensured the disappearance of that world of company dinners, fêtes, reading-rooms, and workers' cottages which had accompanied the power wielded by the nineteenth-century partners over their employees in Bocking, Braintree, and Halstead.[2] One survival provided an opportunity in 1952 for Freeman to dispatch a fine specimen of his acidulous wit which it would be agreeable, though not practicable, to print *in extenso*. His subject was Gatcombe, a large country house which had been bought by Samuel Courtauld, had passed on his death to his son-in-law R. A. Butler, and was used by the company as a convalescent home. A scheme to expand its activities and add further medical services provoked Freeman to derision at the seemingly reverential attitude automatically adopted by certain directors about anything connected with Samuel Courtauld and the company's welfare tradition. Gatcombe, he pointed out, was not an heirloom, having been 'scarcely occupied by Mr. Sam Courtauld . . . and as soon as it is handed back to Mr. Butler, whether now or in ten or twenty years' time, he will sell it'. (The prophecy proved remarkably accurate: it was sold by Lord Butler of Saffron Walden in 1977 to the Queen for the use of Princess Anne and her husband.) The house, said Freeman, performed two functions: it gave employment to the caretaker and his wife; and it made members of Courtaulds' staff 'keep at their jobs with a cheerful countenance when not feeling too fit so that they can avoid the stigma and misery of ten days at Gatcombe'. As for more doctors, his diagnosis had that vigorous simplicity not unfamiliar in H.M. Forces: 'double the doctors in the Company and you will double the sickness. Half a dozen and you will fill Gatcombe to overflowing.'

[1] Vol. I, pp. 247–58; II, pp. 437–49. [2] Vol. I, Chapter XI, *passim*.

In the implementation of the major improvements to labour's rewards, i.e. higher money earnings, shortage of labour combined with growing trade-union strength proved a powerful force. Despite the dismissals and/or short-time during the two brief recessions, despite the redundancies created by the absorption of British Celanese and the closure of old mills such as Aber, and despite improved output per man, the period as a whole was one of relative labour shortage rather than surplus. In 1939 the percentage of the national labour force unemployed still stood at 5·8, less than half the figure for 1934; in 1965 it stood at 1·3; the average for the whole period 1940–65 was 1·4.[1] The post-war boom in rayon output and the recovery after the 1958 recession both provoked comments about labour shortages in areas where other industries were offering competing jobs. In 1950–1, Pedder was reporting on steps taken to relieve labour shortage at Wolverhampton; and on the problems created by the 1,867 foreigners employed in the yarn mills (notably by the 166 Italian girls who complained of English cooking and the absence of *salami* and *pasta* which, Pedder observed, was 'not a British national dish'). And in 1960 Kerr-Muir was telling the chairman that there was still a shortage of labour and likewise reporting on certain problems created by the 1,100 foreign nationals employed. It was, incidentally, a wholly characteristic sign of the changing times that Pedder's letter on the Italian problem was induced by an enquiry which came to Hanbury-Williams from the Duchess Gallarati-Scotti;[2] and that Kerr-Muir's arose from a pending meeting with the Ministry of Labour.

The changing approach to trade unions—and specifically to the Transport and General Workers Union—presented a striking contrast to Harry Johnson's aggressively anti-union sentiments of the 1920s and early 1930s, and marked a continuation of the new attitude adopted by his son and by Pedder in the late 1930s.[3] Samuel Courtauld's suggestion in 1942—publicized in his *Economic Journal* article and elsewhere—that a trade-union representative should be appointed to the Board did not go down at all well with his colleagues; it stimulated Hanbury-Williams to an elaborately

[1] Feinstein, Table 57.

[2] The wife of the then Italian ambassador. It provoked Pedder to observe in a P.S.: 'It is interesting to notice the Duchess's concern for the Italian working people in this country. I had not noticed, after my experience of Italy, that the Italian 'upper classes' take very much thought of the conditions of the working population in their own country.'

[3] Vol. II, pp. 445–9.

diplomatic piece of disagreement. Management was not, moreover, much disposed to adopt a conciliatory attitude to strikers. This was particularly evident in the 1940s. A strike at Castle and Aber mills in 1943, not supported by the union, resulted in a Court of Inquiry and in proceedings for damages by Courtaulds against the strikers. The company was successful, and was awarded £7 damages against each defendant, and by 1952 had finally succeeded in collecting the damages from all but a very few of the 139 strikers involved. But although demands by the union for higher pay or a shorter working week were sometimes firmly resisted, in general they gradually ceased to generate high feelings and Board discussions; instead they came to be treated more prosaically as part and parcel of business life. Much was achieved by improved negotiation procedures with the unions.[1] On more than one occasion vigorously stated intentions to resist claims and go to arbitration ended in compromise offers which proved acceptable to the union. The 'wage restraint' and 'wage freeze' policies of 1947–8 and 1949–50, imposed by Stafford Cripps, the then Chancellor of the Exchequer, were followed, as may be inferred from Fig. 15, by a cascade of wage claims which, as a result of negotiations with the union, resulted in advances in the basic rate in June 1951, October 1952, January 1954, January 1955, and February 1956, as well as some concomitant changes in shift allowances and the bonus calculator. This phase stimulated Board discussions and reiterated intentions to resist demands. Rises were, indeed fewer and less steep in 1956–9. However, the phase of recovery thereafter, the period from 1959 to January 1965, saw no less than eight increases in the basic rate. But although such matters came to the Board, particularly the discussions resulting in a new wage structure in 1963, they no longer evoked the sentiments of outrage which two or three decades or so earlier would have been commonplace.

Finally, the real increase in the return to labour depended upon the relationship of the growth in money earnings to the movement of retail prices. Any comparison on the basis of the 1940 earnings is likely to be imprecise because of the wartime circumstances. The following figures give some estimate of the relative changes which took place over the next quarter-century; and also compare the earnings of Courtaulds' male operatives (mainly spinners in the yarn mills) with general averages and of comparable earnings in the U.K. as a whole:

[1] Notably by George Gibbons, Chief Labour Officer for the company's yarn mills from 1951 (and for Courtaulds as a whole from 1960) until 1967.

	Courtaulds: average hourly earnings*	U.K. average weekly earnings†	U.K. retail prices‡ (a)	U.K. retail prices§ (b)
1940	100	100	100	100
1965	473 (495)	461	262	281

* Average weekly earnings in 1939 were approximately 86*s.* which, for a 48-hour week, is 21·5*d.* per hour. For 1940, after May, the basic rate *plus* wartime allowance *plus* 3-shift allowance equals 22*d.* per hour. In order not to bias the subsequent relative change in favour of Courtaulds, I have assumed 23*d.* as the base-year rate, but give the equivalent figure for the 22*d.* base in parentheses.

† Feinstein, Table 65.

‡ An index of consumer goods and services, ibid., Table 61.

§ A base-weighted index of a collection of consumer goods and services, ibid., Table 65.

TABLE 51

Earnings, prices, and yields, 1945–65

1945 = 100

	Courtaulds' annual average hourly earnings	U.K. average weekly earnings*	U.K. retail prices*	Courtaulds' yield on assets per cent.†
1945	100	100	100	6·1
1946	109	104	104	5·6
1947	116	112	110	9·1
1948	133	122	119	10·5
1949	155	127	122	11·9
1950	162	133	125	21·6
1951	183	146	138	21·5
1952	186	158	150	10·6
1953	199	168	154	16·3
1954	209	179	157	14·6
1955	222	194	164	13·5
1956	241	210	172	10·9
1957	248	221	179	8·2
1958	254	229	184	7·7
1959	263	235	185	10·4
1960	282	248	187	9·0
1961	307	266	193	7·5
1962	324	275	201	9·9
1963	337	287	206	12·7
1964	357	312	212	12·4
1965	387	337	223	12·0

* Feinstein, Table 65. † See above, Tables 5, 18, and 36 (pp. 40, 129 and 256).

The conclusion that in real earnings Courtaulds' workers fared rather better than the average over this whole period is also evident if 1945 is taken as the base period.[1] Accordingly, Table 51 gives the annual average figures in the form of an index, for the period 1945–65, and reveals clearly how Courtaulds' money earnings outstripped the retail price index even more than did average earnings nationally. This increase in the real earnings of Courtaulds' workers became evident as soon as the post-war boom got under way, and was secured much more rapidly than in the economy as a whole. The textile recession of 1952 clearly slowed down Courtaulds' rate of advance relative to both the national indicators. After 1958, however, the gap between prices and earnings widened markedly, and Courtaulds' increase was in this phase largely a reflection of the national trend.

The final column in Table 51 reveals a very different course of change. Up to the mid-1950s profitability had risen more rapidly than labour's earnings. Then came the turning-point. Earnings continued to rise; but yields sagged and fell until the post-bid upswing of 1962–5. The rise took them to around twice the 1945 figure, but earnings were by then well over three times the 1945 level. That the latter had reached this level was a reflection not so much of Courtaulds' particular demand for labour as of the much increased national strength of trade-union bargaining. It meant, for Courtaulds' 'new order', a still greater need to increase economic efficiency via higher productivity.

[1] Statistically safer because a complete earnings series (as used in Fig. 11, above, p. 285) begins in that year.

CHAPTER XIV

Conclusion and Retrospect

I

IN the report, written jointly by Alan Wilson and Arthur Knight in December 1960, which dealt with the troubles of Courtaulds (Canada), there occurred an observation pertinent to Courtaulds' general historical experience since World War II. Having mentioned the drop in the sales of viscose textile yarn at the beginning of the 1950s the report went on:

At that time no one in any part of the Courtaulds Group realised that a fundamental change had taken place in the viscose textile yarn market and that henceforth viscose would be the 'sick-man' of the fibre industry in every part of the world. It was indeed generally felt that this was due partly to a temporary change of fashion and partly to the end of the post-war boom, and that it would be overcome by the classical methods of reduction in price, improvements in quality, and by more aggressive selling to gather in all the business possible. These measures were adopted, but though they arrested the decline, they did not stop it.

Viscose as the '"sick-man" of the fibre industry': here in a nutshell is the main underlying theme in the history of Courtaulds for the whole period covered by this volume. During the post-war boom, just as before the war, viscose products—yarns, fibres, and related chemicals—accounted for 80–90 per cent. of profits; less than two decades later their share had fallen to little more than one-third. The immediate tasks of post-war recovery, the ensuing boom, and then the recession, seen as linked to such external events as the Korean War, had combined to mask the underlying trends in man-made fibres. But when the reality was perceived, when the 'classical methods' were seen to fail, reactions were varied, conflicting, and sometimes extreme.

The reaction which effectively triumphed followed three main routes towards:

(1) new sources of profit internally, either in new products (e.g. 'Courtelle') or modifications to old products (e.g. 'Evlan');

(2) new sources of profit externally by taking over companies which made different but related products (e.g. Celanese or Pinchin Johnson);

(3) new sources of profit and/or greater market power by vertical integration (e.g. Fine Spinners or Meridian).

The result was growth in size: in capital assets, numbers employed, geographical spread; it meant more plants and sometimes bigger plants, a bigger unit to manage and administer. Although large sums were spent under category (1), greater sums were spent under categories (2) and (3). So more of the growth came from merger activities than from internal investment. Until 1957 none had come from such activities. The growth in net assets, exhibited in Fig. 16, had, from 1913 to 1957, been wholly generated within Courtaulds and the subsidiaries which it had itself established.

The large-scale acquisition of companies by other companies has given rise not only to conflicting attitudes and emotional outbursts, such as were evident during the I.C.I. bid, but also to similarly conflicting opinions by the experts. Economists have, as usual, disagreed. About the merits and demerits of mergers they are as split as the politicians whose views they influence. A number of academic studies have considered the question of whether mergers lead to gains in efficiency (as measured by profitability) and have concluded that they do not. A recent such study based on an investigation into a substantial sample of take-overs during the years 1964–72 has reinforced this conclusion, finding that the average profitability of the companies participating in this merging activity fell during the seven years after the mergers.[1]

How does Courtaulds' performance appear in the light of such a finding? Clearly it is not possible in this volume to say anything about the consequences, for the group's profitability of the second, post-bid phase of take-overs, from 1962 onwards. But the results of the first phase, 1957–61, and especially the major acquisition of British Celanese, seem to be wholly at variance with this gloomy conclusion. In a complex, multi-product group, with rapid changes proceeding in organization and finance during the years 1957–64, strict comparability is out of the question. Yet from the evidence already marshalled in Chapters VIII and XII it is abundantly

[1] G. Meeks, *Disappointing Marriage: a study of the gains from merger* (Cambridge, 1977), Chaps. 2 and 3, esp. p. 33. An earlier study—A. Singh, *Take-overs* (Cambridge, 1971), primarily based on an analysis of firms involved in take-overs in the years 1954–60—reached similar conclusions.

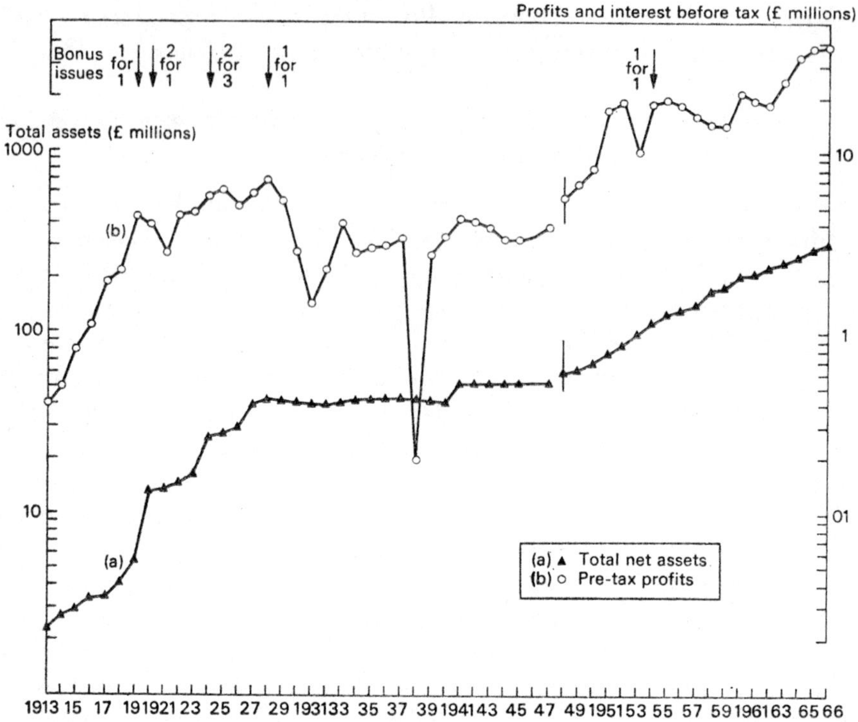

FIG. 16. *Courtaulds Ltd. and Courtaulds Group: net assets and pre-tax profits, 1913–1965/6*

evident that Courtaulds was a more and not a less profitable business in the mid-1960s than in the late 1950s. The course of the trade cycle had certainly helped, as we have seen, but the achievement was real. By 1965–7 the average annual gross pre-tax profits of Courtaulds' acetate activities (yarns, notably 'Tricel', chemicals, and plastics) were much larger than the total profits of British Celanese before take-over plus those of the entire acetate division and plastics manufacture of Courtaulds itself at that time. Likewise, the warp-knitting plants concentrated under Furzebrook had achieved by the mid-1960s a much higher degree of success than had their counterparts in Courtaulds and Celanese before the merger. Even in paint where success by no means attended Courtaulds' efforts to push Pinchin Johnson's sales in the domestic paint market, an equivalent comparison suggests that Courtaulds' profits from paint in 1965–7 averaged about twice those of the combined constituent firms (Pinchin Johnson and Cellon) before take-over.

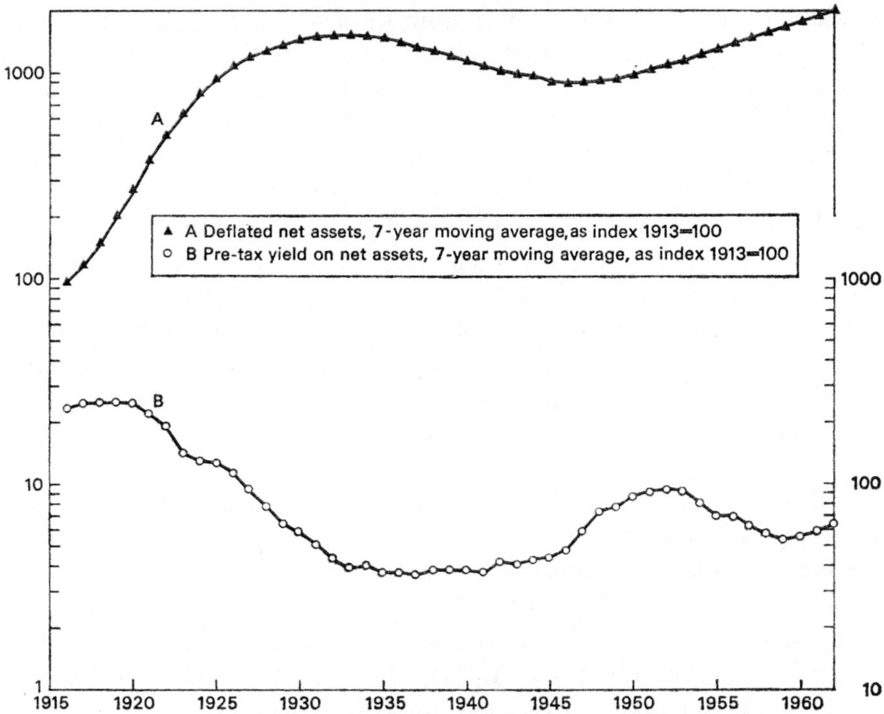

FIG. 17. *Courtaulds Ltd. and Courtaulds Group: indexes of deflated net assets and of pre-tax yield, 1913–1965/6 (1913 = 100)*

Although precise comparison of the yield on assets in particular bits of the business before and after take-over is not possible, it is possible to put the aggregate changes into the context of the long-term historical growth of both assets and the yield thereon. This is done in two stages in Figs. 16 and 17. The former shows simply the two variables which have already been exhibited in several tables in this volume[1] taken forward to 1965–6 and extended back to the beginning of Courtaulds Ltd. in 1913: (a) total net assets and (b) profits plus interest before tax but after deduction of debenture and/or loan interest.[2] The curve (b) does not provide a full indication of the shareholders' gains from the company because it takes no

[1] Tables 5, 18, and 37 on pp. 40, 129, and 257.

[2] The data refer to Courtaulds Ltd. from the calendar year 1913 to the 15-month period January 1946–March 1947 when the company's financial year was changed. Thereafter they refer to Courtaulds Group and the data are plotted according to the calendar year in which the financial year ends, e.g. 1947–8 is plotted as 1948, 1965–6 as 1966.

account of the bonus issues, the timing of which is also shown. Before moving on to Fig. 17 it is worth noting *en passant* that the rate of growth in the monetary value of total net assets is virtually continuous and unchanged for the decades after 1947, i.e. the take-over activities after 1957 merely served to maintain a rate of change already evident rather than drastically altering it. Fig. 17 uses the raw data of Fig. 16 but expresses it in a different form in order to bring out the long-term relationships between (a) and (b) and to allow for changes in monetary values. Between 1913 and 1967 there was a substantial degree of inflation in the British economy, so some part of the growth in Courtaulds' assets simply reflects this. Curve A in Fig. 17 is based on a 7-year moving average of the data of (a), deflated to make allowance for changes in prices of capital goods[1] over the period, and expressed as an index on the base of 1913 = 100. Curve B is simply the yield on assets expressed as a percentage (i.e. (b) as a percentage of (a)) and then likewise smoothed into a 7-year moving average and exhibited as an index on the base of 1913 = 100.

Consideration and comparison of these two curves reveals, first, the failure even to maintain the real value of the net assets during the period from the early 1930s to the end of World War II; second, the notable inverse relationship of rising assets and falling yields during the 1920s and again from about 1952 to 1959; and, third, the correlation of rising assets and rising yields in only two brief periods (apart from the very beginning where the true yield is underestimated by these figures),[2] i.e. in the 1947–53 boom after World War II and then after 1959. The fact that for so much of this whole half-century or so of its existence Courtaulds' financial results should thus have exhibited a picture of falling yields on rising real assets is not of course nearly so surprising as might be thought. According to one's predelictions, the phenomenon may be regarded either as a confirmation of the tendency, commented upon by such early economists as Hume, Ricardo, and Marx, for a falling long-term rate of profit, or as a simple tribute to the effect of competition, albeit imperfect, in rendering impossible the maintenance of the very high returns initially associated with a new product developed in conditions of temporary monopoly. Such a phenomenon could surely be found in many a company's history. Beyond these generalizations, however, it poses questions about the actions and reactions of those who directed the affairs of Courtaulds, or

[1] The relevant price index used was the plant and machinery series (1913 = 100) in Feinstein, Table 63, p. T.136.

[2] As Fig. 16 indicates, it was precisely at this time that three bonus issues were made.

indeed other companies. After the opening bonanza, known to be inevitably short in duration, how does a Board behave in its subsequent policy of reinvesting profits into internal growth? It looks as though, in the circumstances of economic depression and then world war which characterized the 1930s and early 1940s, the Courtaulds Board was in effect content (though its members may not have seen it like that) with a low average yield and assets diminishing in real terms. And, indeed, despite the capital investment in plant improvements and the successful cost-reductions secured, the generally 'safe' policy and accumulation of massive, low-yielding reserves suggests that this was so.[1] When the war ended, vigorous action of some sort seemed urgently to be called for. But of what sort? Answer: the refurbishing of rayon, aided by scientists and higher productivity, together with some investment in new products and much in the recovery of prestige via overseas expansion. When this phase of recovery, borne along by the post-war boom, was seen to be over by the later 1950s, then was posed, far more starkly than ever before in the memories of those then on the Board, the question of what to do now that assets were rising but yields again falling.

If at such junctures radical decisions are not made then businesses do not survive, at least as independent entities or in their existing forms. Amongst the members of the Courtaulds Board there was at least some recognition that crisis was upon them. The historical analogue in the experience of the firm, though not known as such, was the crisis of the early 1890s. But the answer was different. Then, the capital was reduced and the 'new men' were brought in from outside to secure rejuvenation of Courtaulds' fortunes.[2] Now, the capital was increased and 'new men' already inside were given their chance to seek the requisite transformation. In practice one man was to play the dominant role on each occasion. Tetley's energies brought reform in the 1890s followed by his crucial purchase of the viscose patents in 1904; and Kearton's, already active in the 1950s, were liberated by the I.C.I. bid and given full rein thereafter. The bid may appear as a fortuitous event, a chance thunderbolt wreaking havoc with some careers and bestowing unexpected benefits on others. At a personal level this may well have been true. But in the wider context of firms operating in the market economy, it was merely an intervention of the market. It acted upon the relationships of assets and their yield. Courtaulds' directors, as a consequence of previous policy, had made themselves liable to such an intervention. Their reaction, in defence, was crucial to that

[1] Vol. II, Chaps. XII and XVI. [2] Vol. I, Chaps. VIII and IX.

relationship. For by pledging that Courtaulds' stockholders should receive both a substantial share of hitherto undistributed capital profits and a bigger dividend hand-out in the immediate future, the Board committed itself to a concern with the yield on assets which had too often been inadequately heeded in the past.

But why, it may be asked, get bigger when the evidence suggests that bigness puts serious obstacles in the path to higher yields? And why get bigger more by merger and take-over than by internal investment?

To answer these questions it is necessary to ask another one: what were the alternatives? Some possibilities, with varying degrees of realism, may be sketched. First, the Board might have actively sought a purchaser or a merger on not too disadvantageous terms, as did Celanese and the smaller rayon companies. In effect this is what Hanbury-Williams was doing in his 1960 talks with Chambers. But there were only a very few likely candidates as buyers, e.g. I.C.I. or Du Pont. In the event the I.C.I. bid, because of the manner in which it was made and because its price was too low, rallied all the forces hostile to a course which would have lost the company its identity and put many jobs in jeopardy. Second, because it was evident that the 'classical methods'—cost reductions, aggressive selling, etc.—in existing products were not enough, the Board might have pinned its faith to some massive efforts to discover a new product which would reap golden rewards, as viscose had in the past. But this would have been a mirage and was probably never seriously entertained. For all Wilson's efforts in building up the research laboratories Courtaulds was too late in this game to emulate Du Pont and nylon. Polyamides, polyesters, acrylics, like the cellulosics originally, all came from elsewhere; protein fibres were a flop; polypropylene was not the answer to this maiden's prayer; even 'Courtelle' was just a successful search for another acrylic route. A certain level of 'defensive' research was maintained, as in other man-made fibre firms, to prevent competitors stealing a march, and to ensure a continuance of improvements at the margin. But the chances of another bonanza were probably negligible and rightly seen as such. The closure in 1962 of the fundamental research laboratory at Maidenhead was a suitable symbol of the times. Third, the loss-making and low-yielding parts of the business could have been sold off or closed down and any proceeds, together with the still substantial reserves, could have been invested internally in the development of more profitable lines. The backing of 'Courtelle' was just such a development. But what other lines? At one stage Courtaulds might have moved more in the direction of chemicals but it possessed neither the requisite personnel nor the competitive power to tackle the big chemical firms in that market.

In reality, if the company were to retain its independence and identity—and any decision on that score had a strongly emotional content capable of being overcome only by a purchase bid too high to be refusable—then there was no serious economic alternative to a gamble on external expansion. Once Celanese had been offered up and swallowed, the probability of this course was increased, though this act did not in itself necessarily entail the pursuit of diversification, particularly in its wilder and dottier forms. Nor did it dictate the precise direction of growth by external acquisition. But if that policy was to be the chosen path to salvation, it had to be done on a large scale, otherwise there could be no hope of a transformation adequate to improve the yield on assets. Furthermore, such expansion would have to be accompanied by a ruthless concern for profitability, if only because, by definition, acquired firms are likely to be poor and ailing performers.

If a policy for survival means a gamble, risk-taking, ruthlessness, an obsession with profits, it must also entail the right sort of man to carry it out: in brief, that familiar figure of business history, the entrepreneur. The situation does not always produce the man; sometimes the man is already there and manipulates the situation to suit his entrepreneurial fancy; sometimes the man and his policies fail. But what is clear is that such policies are not normally executed by committees, by long-suffering accountants, by patient intellectuals, or by unimaginative bureaucrats. The historical record suggests, instead, that they are carried out by men who combine intelligence with a driving ambition which endows them with an exceptional capacity for hard work; who possess a powerful and restless urge for achievement often attended by a degree of paranoia which makes them uneasy companions; and whose decisions are marked by a certain violence of expression and action which often ensures that, in their business relations at least, they inspire respect rather than affection. Such men create successful new businesses or force radical change in existing businesses. In some business circumstances, these men are a nuisance and their attitudes inappropriate, if not disastrous; with luck, they then depart to seek conquests elsewhere. Sometimes they stay on too long, prove inflexible, and the problem of entrepreneurial capacity proves to be not how to find it but how to get rid of it. No generalizations are adequate; no one entrepreneur is the same as another, in character, experience, or behaviour. But readers of these three volumes, if any there be, will find no difficulty in noticing that Samuel Courtauld III (1793–1881), Henry Greenwood Tetley (1852–1921), and Christopher Frank Kearton (1911–) have shared some, though not all, of these qualities and achievements.

Enough has been said in Vols. I and II about the first two; and much has been said about the last named at various points in the present volume. But as this chapter is primarily concerned to look in a retrospective and concluding fashion at the achievement of profitability it will be appropriate to heed some of his characteristic utterances on this topic. All the following are extracts from letters to managers or directors, mainly the former, within the group. Here, first, is a sample on the general theme of profits in the post-bid Courtaulds:

Courtaulds . . . new look will be vigorous, profit seeking, and very impatient of any inefficiences in any sector of the organisation.

I have quite enjoyed the battle [against I.C.I.] myself. It is all very serious but of intense interest. (February 1962)

this [the presence of I.C.I. as a large shareholder] gives us an additional spur, if one was needed, to do everything we can to maximise profits. We have got to get it realised throughout the whole Company that this is the paramount objective of our work. (March 1962)

I get up in the morning breathing the word 'profits', have it in front of me all day, and go to sleep muttering the same word. Everything depends on profits. (May 1962)

We are desperately anxious to get more profits everywhere . . . the emphasis being on profit, profit, and then profit! (September 1964)

After these statements of the main theme, here are some variations of a slightly more specific character:

It's brutally clear that Bairns-Wear needs not just a wind of change but a gale of change, and I think we should make it absolutely clear we are going to get it, come hell or high water. All our previous experience is that once people know what you want, and have clear ideas of how you are going to achieve things, they will co-operate. (November 1963)

I must say I almost broke down and wept like a baby when I saw the slow build up you now set for me at Furzebrook . . . We must find ways and means of speeding up this Furzebrook side of our production. (December 1963)

Quality being right, we should produce as cheaply as possible, and this always means bulk. (September 1964)

The obvious way is progressively to reduce the overdraft . . . so let's take it as a first target that you will not only not increase the Gossard (Holdings) Ltd. overdraft, but will do your damnedest during the next twelve months to get it down to nothing. (March 1965)

And, finally, some general observations on running the business:

Softness at the top spreads rapidly down an organization. Firmness at the top is its own best example. (March 1962)

A non-stop effort is required to see that exceptional results are obtained, as opposed to what could be described as reasonable results. (January 1964)

Don't get into the habit of relying completely on what the various 'experts' tell you, so that you are reduced in effect to a rubber stamp or dummy. A positive, and indeed a very baleful, personality, is needed to make a success of the tough businesses. One can still remain—I hope—sweetly considerate in private life; business is quite different. (October 1965)

The picture may not be to everyone's taste; and those to whom capitalism is a fashionably dirty word will doubtless find their opinions confirmed. It suggests neither a haven for the complacent nor a recipe for comfort. It also presents an attitude of mind very different from that of the chairman-designate in 1962. Only a few years earlier Alan Wilson, writing about the difficulties which young men experience in settling down in industry, observed of his experience in industry:

I have never found it very different from the academic world. The technical problems are of the same order of difficulty, and human relations are very much the same in a laboratory as in a factory, and at a High Table as at a Board Table, and I am at a loss to understand why so many people find the transition from one to the other so much of a stumbling block.

Perhaps that was the trouble. The contrast between the two men could hardly be more strikingly expressed. There is no shortage of 'baleful personalities' on High Tables, but few, so far as I know, awake breathing the word 'profits'.

Whatever might have been the precise nature of Wilson's route across the crisis years, however different it would have been from Kearton's, it would have represented the fruits of an acute intelligence brought to bear upon a set of problems. By contrast, there is no evidence that Hanbury-Williams had any clear and consistent perception of the crisis, least of all that he had a policy. He was chairman for sixteen of the twenty-five years covered by this book; he was 65 years of age in 1957 when the crisis was becoming apparent and the first of the big acquisitions was made.

Had he retired then, which he should have done, the course of Courtaulds' subsequent history might or might not have been significantly different. That we cannot know. But it would at least have obviated the period of uncertainty between 1959 and 1961 when the Board became too frequently preoccupied with the succession, like some renaissance court busy with intrigue for the Imperial Crown. Thereby was created an atmosphere virtually guaranteed to exacerbate the tension between Kearton and Wilson and highly congenial to the composition of such diversions as George Courtauld's ribald skit upon his own Board. As on other such occasions, an external threat was needed to clear the air. It came in the shape of the I.C.I. bid. It brought a sharp concentration of the corporate mind and much purging of the corporate body.

II

In a review of the first two volumes of this history, Professor Checkland identified four phases in the evolution of the business: 1816–50, 1850–80s, 1880s–1918, and 1918–41. Noting the adjustment or lack of it to external stimuli in each phase, e.g. the decline in the crape market in the 1880s and 1890s or the depression of the 1930s, he posed this general question: 'is it inherent in the growth of a firm, and indeed of all great organizations, that they cannot adjust to change continuously, but must reach some critical level of vulnerability before a response is forthcoming?'[1]

The arrival of a take-over bid must stand as one of the clearest indications of having reached a 'critical level of vulnerability'. So it might be tempting to answer Professor Checkland's question in terms of the events of 1961–2, providing thereby a suitable closing date for a phase starting from the loss of A.V.C. and ending with, say, the unscrambling of the I.C.I.–B.N.S. muddle and the purchase of The Lancashire Cotton Corporation Limited and Fine Spinners & Doublers Limited. But, as this volume has tried to show, there was perception well before the I.C.I. bid of putative crisis; of vulnerability, if not to a take-over, at least to falling profits and the possible bankruptcy of subsidiaries. A strategy of remedial action was being evolved and put into operation. Even the 1964 move to a new London head office, a matter of symbolic significance, had been planned and agreed well before the bid. If in retrospect action seems to have been slow in gestation, this slowness probably owed something to the

[1] S. G. Checkland in *Economic History Review*, XXIII (1970), 559–60.

very organizational structure of the company which, for all the attempts to change it, still ensured that the Board spent too much time on minutiae and not enough on strategic policy. This view of action, or rather inaction, provides some support for Dr. Alford's attempted inversion of Chandler's 'strategy and structure' argument,[1] by thus allowing the organizational structure of Courtaulds an influential role in hampering the earlier emergence of new policies.

Nevertheless, looked at as a longer term phenomenon, the pattern of Courtaulds' experience can be made to fit in a rough sort of way into the Chandler model. The impact of market forces and changing technology, by putting rayon into a disadvantageous position, forced the adoption of an alternative strategy: internally in the development of new products, externally by diversification and acquisition. The pursuit of this strategy created in turn the need for a new structure, as a consequence of vertical integration, geographical spread, diversity of products. Thereby decentralized divisions were multiplied or created, turned into profit centres with a degree of autonomy, though under the ultimate sanction of a newly streamlined Board system. The pre-1957 tinkering can be represented in Schumpeterian terms, as 'adaptive response'; the more draconian post-bid changes as 'creative innovation'.[2] If the result was something of a hybrid—neither quite multi-divisional nor quite a holding company—the route and the pattern can be made to fit into the picture of 'acquisitive diversifiers', depicted by Dr. Channon,[3] itself merely a local variant of the Chandler model.

But it is not evident that this categorization of change according to the longer term model helps in answering Professor Checkland's question. For who is to judge the 'critical level of vulnerability' and how is the judgement made? In the economists' jargon, *ex post* a number of feasible answers can be found; *ex ante*, it is quite another matter, with forecasts and budgets, theories and hunches all deployed in an effort to determine whether continuous adjustment is taking place and that adaptive response is all that is needed or, instead, whether some new and gloomy vista just opened up indeed marks the threshold, the critically vulnerable level, the beginning of the end rather than the end of the beginning. And if the judgement which emerges is such as to imply recognition that the critical level of

[1] Bernard W. E. Alford, 'The Chandler Thesis—some general observations', in Leslie Hannah (ed.), *Management Strategy and Business development* (London, 1976).

[2] Chandler, op. cit., p. 284.

[3] Channon, op. cit., Chapter 6, esp. pp. 176–8.

vulnerability has in fact been reached; and if the resulting new strategy of action is such as to qualify, *ex post*, for the title of creative innovation, then by definition it has been made by an entrepreneur. And, as I have suggested earlier in this chapter, crucial decisions of this sort are often made and executed by men who have historically carried in common a number of roughly recognizable characteristics. The entrepreneur, it will be observed, having been exorcized by abstractions, has reappeared through the back-door. He is not everywhere accorded favour in the explanatory pecking-order: 'the role of top executives is almost certainly somewhat less than might be gauged from much business history . . . Discussion of . . . major crises involving so-called key individuals should be treated, if not with scepticism, then with great caution'.[1] Salutory advice no doubt, when confronted with soap operas about the boardroom or business journalists with an eye for a good story about the latest whizz-kid. But the entrepreneur, the crucial change-maker, the radical decision-taker—call him what you like—will not lie down. He insists upon intruding into the model. And in so doing he is necessarily unpredictable. The alternative is to take refuge in the determinist notion that the new strategy or the perception of crisis will throw up the requisite entrepreneurial talent if not sooner than later, if not X then Y. It may or it may not. Some circumstances or environments, cultures or conjunctures, are probably more entrepreneurially fruitful than others. Given accurate knowledge of a large number of variables, a scale of probabilities could doubtless be constructed. Somewhere on that scale a man would come from Yorkshire via Essex to buy viscose patents from a workshop in Kew, and a chemistry graduate from Oxford would eventually unseat the Courtaulds within Courtaulds and take over from the old brigade. In the short run, such men are as essential a part of business history as are the economics of the context in which they operate and the circumstances that present them with the opportunities which they seize. In the long run they fade into the mists of impersonality in which thrive those models and theories that will exercise their mite of influence upon future generations whence in turn will emerge tomorrow's entrepreneurs—if any there be.

[1] Alford, loc. cit., p. 57.

APPENDIX I

A Note on Sources

As explained in Volumes I and II,[1] no footnote source references were given there to those internal business records of Courtaulds Ltd. which were retained by the company and were not available for public use; but certain early records were deposited at the Essex County Record Office. Since then a further instalment of records relating to the Essex mills has been deposited at Essex County Record Office; and a Group Archives Department has been set up at Courtaulds' Coventry premises. A substantial part of the records used for Volumes II and III has now been, or is in the process of being, deposited at Coventry and consideration will be given to making such records available for the use of bona fide students on written application to the company.[2] Because, however, certain records have to be excluded therefrom and cannot as yet be made available for public use, the same reference policy has been adopted in the present volume as was used in Volume II, i.e. detailed references are given only to external sources.

For those who may wish to consult the records to be preserved at the Group Archives Department, the following notes may be of some assistance.

Much use has been made in both Volumes II and III of the surviving papers of certain directors. Amongst those to be deposited at Coventry are the papers of three successive chairmen, Samuel Courtauld (1921–46), Sir John Hanbury-Williams (1946–62), and Sir Dallas Bernard (1962–64); and of several directors, for example, those of E. L. Lunge (1927–31), Sir Wilfrid Freeman (1945–53), and Sir Alan Wilson (1945–62). Detailed calendars and/or indexes (which were prepared for the purposes of this history) to the Samuel Courtauld, Hanbury-Williams, Bernard, Lunge, and Freeman papers will accompany these deposits. The Hanbury-Williams files, running from 1930 to 1962 and occupying some 400 storage files, provide a particularly detailed and wide-ranging coverage of the company's business, especially from 1940 onwards. Other examples of papers used in Volumes II and III and which have been deposited at Coventry include numerous volumes of statistics prepared for the Board, files relating to the history of A.V.C., to the international consortia before World War I, and to labour and working conditions at Coventry, as well as some of the papers of H. L. Johnson. Amongst the papers which have been used for this volume but which, because of its very recent coverage, have had for the time being to be excluded from deposit at the Coventry archives, are those of Lord Kearton.

Both the Preface to Volumes I and II and the Introduction to the present volume make it clear that I have throughout collected oral evidence to supplement the written sources. The following alphabetical lists include, under three categories, all those who, in the course of interviews at various times between 1962 and 1978, have kindly given me

[1] Vol. I, p. xxi; Vol. II, p. xix.

[2] Any applications should be addressed to the company secretary.

information, views, or impressions which I have noted and drawn upon for this history, be it for Volumes I, II, or III.

Directors of Courtaulds

Sir Dallas Bernard	J. P. Koppel
Lord Butler	Sir Reginald Mathys
G. Courtauld	D. R. B. Mynors
W. P. Courtauld	W. H. Nankivell
J. H. Givens	P. S. Rendall
H. L. Johnson	Lord Rennell
Lord Kearton	C. W. Sheldon
R. J. Kerr-Muir	J. G. Smith
Sir Arthur Knight	G. T. Verrall

Sir Alan Wilson

Other staff of Courtaulds

H. L. Bingham	H. L. Light
E. H. Boas	S. Pearson
J. Elliott	M. W. Pitts-Tucker
G. Gibbons	D. W. Rawlinson
C. St. J. C. Harland	G. Steele-Morgan
H. Hegan	W. H. Stokes

C. H. Ward-Jackson

Outside Courtaulds

Sir Andrew Carnwath	Lady Menzies (*née* Latham)
Miss M. R. Courtauld	Sir Peter Menzies
A. R. French	Sir Basil Smallpiece
G. Goyder	Miss T. Tetley

My notes relating to these interviews will also be excluded from the records to be deposited at Coventry.

APPENDIX 2

Biographical Notes on Directors 1913–1965

Addison, James Stanley (1881–1943): educated New College, Oxford. Entered cotton industry; became managing director of Calico Printers Association. Director, Courtaulds Ltd., 1922–32; managing director, 1932–43. Mainly concerned with textiles.

Bell, George James (1878–1940): joined Samuel Courtauld & Co. Ltd., 1898. Became fabric sales manager. Director, Courtaulds Ltd., 1916–20; managing director, 1920–35. Retired 1936.

Bernard, Dallas Gerald Mercer (1888–1975): educated HMS *Britannia*. After being invalided out of the Royal Navy, joined Jardine Matheson & Co. Ltd. in Hong Kong. Chairman, Hong Kong and Shanghai Bank. Director, Bank of England, 1936–49; deputy-governor, 1949–54. Director, Courtaulds Ltd., 1954–64; deputy chairman, 1954–62; chairman, 1962–4. Bart. 1954. Lieutenant, City of London; Sheriff, County of London.

Bourne, Stanley (1876–1942): educated Rugby and Cambridge; classics. Joined family cotton doubling business. Director, S. Bourne & Co. Ltd. and of Nottingham Manufacturing Co. at various dates between 1924 and 1941. Director, Courtaulds Ltd., 1920–1; deputy chairman 1921–42. JP; Sheriff, Nottinghamshire.

Butler, Richard Austen (1902–): educated Marlborough and Pembroke College, Cambridge; modern languages and history. m.(i), 1926, Sydney, dau. of Samuel Courtauld IV (q.v.); m.(ii), 1959, Mollie Courtauld, widow of Augustine Courtauld, eldest son of Samuel Augustine Courtauld II (q.v.). M.P. (Conservative), Saffron Walden, 1929–65. Minister of Education, 1941–5; Chancellor of the Exchequer, 1951–5; Home Secretary, 1957–62; Secretary of State for Foreign Affairs, 1963–4. Director, Courtaulds Ltd., 1946–51 and 1966–9. P.C. (1939); C.H. (1954); life peer (1965).

Colton, Cyril Hadlow (1902–): educated Reigate Grammar School. Joined British Celanese, 1923; largely concerned with marketing; managing director, 1956; chairman, 1964. Director, Courtaulds Ltd., 1962–7. CBE.

Courtauld, George III[1] (1830–1920): educated Hove House School, Brighton, and London University. Partner, Samuel Courtauld & Co., 1866–91; director, Samuel Courtauld & Co. Ltd., 1891–1920, and of Courtaulds Ltd., 1913–20. M.P. (Liberal), Maldon, 1878–85. J.P.; Sheriff, Essex. Eldest son of George Courtauld II.

Courtauld, George V (1903–): educated Malvern and Pembroke College, Cambridge. Joined Courtaulds Ltd., 1925, on textile side. Director, Courtaulds Ltd. 1938–66; personnel director, 1945–63. Served Army (S.O.E.), World War II. Grandson of George Courtauld III (q.v.).

Courtauld, Samuel IV (1876–1947): educated Rugby and at textile colleges in Germany.

[1] For family trees of the Courtauld family, see Vol. I, Fig. 25, and Vol. II, Fig. 17.

Joined Samuel Courtauld & Co. Ltd., 1898. Mill manager, Halstead, 1901; general manager, textile mills, 1908. Director, Courtaulds Ltd., 1915–17; managing director, 1917–20; chairman, 1921–46. Art collector and founder of the Courtauld Institute of Art. Nephew of George Courtauld III (q.v.).

Courtauld, Samuel Augustine II (1865–1953): educated Charterhouse. Joined Samuel Courtauld & Co., 1884; director, Samuel Courtauld & Co. Ltd., 1894–1913. Director Courtaulds Ltd., 1913–50. J.P.; Deputy Lieutenant and Sheriff, Essex. Eldest son of George Courtauld III (q.v.).

Courtauld, Walter Pierre (1910–): educated Charterhouse. Joined Courtaulds Ltd., 1928, on textile side. Director, Courtaulds Ltd., 1938–65 (non-executive, 1959–62); deputy chairman, 1962–5. Served Army (Welsh Guards), World War II. Second son of Samuel Augustine Courtauld II (q.v.).

Davies, Francis Thomas (1906–): educated Eton. Joined Courtaulds, 1929. Director, Courtaulds Ltd., 1937–54; mainly concerned with overseas trade. After leaving Courtaulds, became a director of Gulf Oil (G.B.) and later chairman British Enkalon. Served Army (Grenadier Guards and S.O.E.), World War II.

Drewitt, James Gordon Napier (1914–): educated Kendal School and Keble College, Oxford; chemistry. Joined British Celanese, 1936; head, chemical research laboratory, 1947; personnel manager, 1960. Director, Courtaulds Ltd., 1962–70.

Eccles, David McAdam (1904–): educated Winchester and New College, Oxford. M.P. (Conservative), Chippenham, 1943–62. Minister of Works, 1951–4; Minister of Education, 1954–7 and 1959–62; President, Board of Trade, 1957–9. Various business interests. Director, Courtaulds Ltd., 1962–70. P.C. (1951); K.C.V.O. (1953); Baron (1962); Viscount (1964).

Freeman, Wilfrid Rhodes (1888–1953): educated Rugby and Sandhurst. R.F.C.–R.A.F., 1914–42; Air Marshal, 1937; Air Chief Marshal, 1940. Chief Executive, Ministry of Aircraft Production, 1942–5. Director, Courtaulds Ltd., 1945–50; deputy chairman, 1949–53. M.C., D.S.O. (1916); G.C.B. (1942); Bart. (1945).

Givens, John Harrison (1904–69): educated Bablake School, Coventry Technical College, and Birmingham University to read chemistry after having already joined Courtaulds in 1922. Patented (with others) high-tenacity viscose yarn, 1935. Head, viscose research laboratory, Coventry, 1949. Director, Courtaulds Ltd. 1962–4.

Glover, Walter Hamis (1883–1963): educated City and Guilds Technical College, London, and Universities of Würzburg and Leipzig; chemistry. Joined Samuel Courtauld & Co. Ltd., 1910; in charge of research laboratory, Clapham and later of No. 1 laboratory, Coventry. Director, Courtaulds Ltd., 1937–45.

Gratwick, Percival John (1885–1954): after apprenticeship to a firm of maltsters, took a part-time degree at London University; chemistry. Joined Pawsons and Leafs Ltd. (textile wholesalers), 1907, and Samuel Courtauld & Co. Ltd., 1911, as salesman. Director, Courtaulds Ltd., 1935–7; managing director, 1937–44; deputy chairman, 1944–54.

Hanbury-Williams, John Coldbrook (1892–1965): educated Wellington. Joined Reiss Bros. (eastern merchants). Served in Army (Hussars), World War I. Joined Courtaulds, 1926. Director, Courtaulds Ltd., 1930–5; managing director, 1935–43; deputy chairman, 1943–6; chairman, 1946–62. Director, Bank of England, 1936–63. Kt. (1950); C.V.O. (1956). Lieutenant, City of London; Sheriff, County of London. Gentleman

Usher successively to George V, Edward VIII, George VI, and Elizabeth II; and Extra-Gentleman Usher to George VI and Elizabeth II.

Johnson, Frederick (1878–1950): educated elementary school, Preston, and evening school while employed in engineering works. Assistant engineer, Samuel Courtauld & Co., 1901; chief engineer, Courtaulds Ltd., 1919. Director, Courtaulds Ltd., 1924–47.

Johnson, Henry (1866–1938): educated elementary school, Macclesfield. Joined his father's local silk-throwing business. Went to Samuel Courtauld & Co., as mill manager, Braintree, 1896; manager Coventry works, 1907. Director, Courtaulds Ltd., 1914–38; managing director, 1917–35. Active in running yarn mills in U.K., and in reorganizing A.V.C. in 1920s.

Johnson, Henry Leslie (1904–): educated Rugby. Joined Courtaulds, 1922. Director, Courtaulds Ltd., 1933–5; managing director 1935–48; non-executive director, 1948–68. Almost entirely concerned with yarn mills. Son of Henry Johnson (q.v.).

Jones, Aubrey (1911–): educated Cyfarthfa Castle Secondary School and London School of Economics, London University. On staff of *The Times*, 1937–9, 1947–8. Joined British Iron and Steel Federation, 1949. M.P. (Conservative), Birmingham, 1950–65. Minister of Fuel and Power, 1955–7, Minister of Supply, 1957–9. Director, Courtaulds Ltd., 1960–3. Chairman, National Board for Prices and Income, 1965–70. P.C. (1955). Served Army, World War II.

Kearton, Christopher Frank (1911–): educated Hanley High School and St. John's College, Oxford; chemistry. Joined I.C.I., 1933. U.K. atomic energy project, U.K. and U.S.A., 1940–5. Joined Courtaulds 1946. Director, Courtaulds Ltd., 1952–7; managing director, 1957–61; deputy chairman, 1961–4; chairman, 1964–75. Chairman and chief executive, British National Oil Corporation, 1976–9. O.B.E. (1945); F.R.S. (1961); Kt. (1966); life peer (1970).

Kerr-Muir, Ronald John (1910–74): educated King Edward VI School, Southampton, and Queen's College, Oxford; science. Schoolmaster. After service in Army (Royal Engineers) in World War II, joined Courtaulds Ltd., 1946. Manager, chemical works, 1951–4. Director, Courtaulds Ltd., 1958–71. O.B.E.

Kilner, Arthur Hugoe (1877–1949): educated City of London School. Chartered accountant. Joined Courtaulds as chief accountant, 1913. Active in Federation of British Industries: vice-president, 1936. Director, Courtaulds Ltd., 1935–46.

Kinnes, Roy Anderson (1892–1959): educated Edinburgh University; law and economics. Chartered accountant; joined Price Waterhouse & Co., 1921. Joined Courtaulds as chief accountant, 1935; director, Courtaulds Ltd., 1939–57 (part-time director, 1950–7). Served Army, World War I.

Knight, Arthur William (1917–): educated Tottenham County School and London School of Economics, University of London (as evening student). Joined Courtaulds, 1938. Active in overseas investment matters, especially concentrating on Europe and North America. Director, Courtaulds Ltd., 1958–70 (finance director, 1961–70); deputy chairman, 1970–5; chairman, 1975–9. Served Army (Royal Berkshire Regiment, S.O.E., and Allied Commission for Austria), World War II. Kt. (1975).

Koppel, John Patrick (1913–): educated Rugby, University of Freiburg, and Magdalen College, Oxford; chemistry and P.P.E. (philosophy, politics, and economics). Joined Courtaulds, 1935. After service in Army (Welsh Guards), World War II, returned to Courtaulds and was concerned with Cologne and Australia project.

Deputy chairman and managing director, British Cellophane Ltd., 1956–61. Director, Courtaulds Ltd., 1961–70; deputy chairman, 1970–6.

Latham, Thomas Paul (1855–1931): educated Manchester Grammar School. Textile salesman. Joined Samuel Courtauld & Co. Ltd., 1894, as sales manager; director, 1898–1904; managing director, 1904–13. Managing director, Courtaulds Ltd., 1913–17; deputy chairman, 1917–21; director, 1921–31. Bart. (1919).

Lunge, Ernest (1870–1931): son of rector of Zurich University; of German Swiss origin, born in England. Called to the English Bar, 1906. Joined Courtaulds, 1916. Director, Courtaulds Ltd., 1927–31. Active in continental European matter; helped to form, in 1928, BISFA (Bureau international pour la standardisation des fibres artificielles) and was its first president.

Mathys, Herbert Reginald (1908–77): educated Cranleigh School and Birkbeck College, University of London. Chartered patent agent. Joined Courtaulds as head of patent department, 1946. Chairman, British Cellophane Ltd., 1956–65. Director, Courtaulds Ltd., 1954–61; deputy chairman, 1961–73. Kt. (1974). Served Army (Royal Engineers), World War II.

Mynors, David Rickards Baskerville (1915–): educated Eton and Oxford. Joined Courtaulds, 1937. Initially concerned with textile side, later with overseas interests; chairman, Marglass Ltd. Director, Courtaulds Ltd., 1955–67. Served Army (Scots Guards), World War II.

Nankivell, William Henry (1897–1975): educated Braintree County High School. Joined Courtaulds 1914. Studied textile technology at Leeds University after service in Royal Navy in World War I. General manager, textile mills, 1946. Director, Courtaulds Ltd., 1947–62. O.B.E. (1946).

Nettlefold, Frederick John (1867–1949): educated Eastbourne College and Universities of Oxford, Heidelberg, and Berlin. Director, Samuel Courtauld & Co. Ltd., 1904–31. Chairman, Courtaulds Ltd., 1913–17; director, 1917–42. Son of Frederick Nettlefold, chairman of Samuel Courtauld & Co. Ltd., 1904–13. Had outside business interests.

Pedder, John Evelyn (1902–59): educated Shrewsbury and Worcester College, Oxford; law. Joined Courtaulds, 1924. Director, Courtaulds Ltd., 1935–59 (general manager, yarn mills); managing director, 1954–9. Cousin of Samuel Courtauld IV (q.v.). J.P.

Rendall, Philip Stanley (1895–): educated Shrewsbury. Joined Courtaulds, 1921, after service in World War I. Sales manager, 1930. Director, Courtaulds Ltd., 1937–43; managing director, 1943–9; deputy chairman, 1949–61. Active in formation of British Man-made Fibres Federation. Sheriff, Warwickshire.

Rodd, Francis James Rennell (1895–1978): educated Eton and Balliol College, Oxford. After service in World War I, entered diplomatic service, then did exploration work in Sahara. Merchant banker: partner, Morgan Grenfell & Co., 1932–67. Director, Courtaulds Ltd., 1935–44. Succeeded father as second Lord Rennell of Rodd, 1941.

Samuel, George Arthur (1904–): educated King's School, Chester. Entered textile industry. Chairman and managing director, North British Rayon Ltd., 1954; director, Harbens Ltd. Joined Courtaulds Ltd., 1959, on acquisition of Harbens. Director, Courtaulds Ltd., 1963–71.

Sheldon, Cecil Wilfred (1905–71): Bank of England, 1924–36. Joined Courtaulds Ltd., 1936; secretary, 1938; director, Courtaulds Ltd., 1948–70. Mainly concerned with overseas interests, especially in continental Europe.

Smith, James Grimshaw (1900–): educated Sedbergh School. Joined Lancashire Cotton Corporation, 1928. Joined Courtaulds, 1932; sales manager for rayon staple fibre, 1944; general sales manager, yarns and fibres, 1950. Director, Courtaulds Ltd., 1952–62.

Stanier, William Arthur (1876–1965): educated Wycliffe College, Gloucestershire. Apprenticed Great Western Railway workshops, Swindon; works manager, Great Western Railway, 1920–2; chief mechanical engineer, London Midland and Scottish Railway, 1932–44. Scientific adviser, Ministry of Production, 1942–8. Director, Courtaulds Ltd., 1947–58. Kt. (1943); F.R.S. (1944).

Tetley, Henry Greenwood (1851–1921): joined Lister & Co. in early 1870s; head of silk manufacturing department, Manningham Mills. Joined Samuel Courtauld & Co. Ltd., 1893; director, 1895–1904; managing director, 1904–13. Managing director, Courtaulds Ltd., 1913–17; chairman, 1917–21. Responsible for Courtaulds' purchase of viscose rayon patents.

Verrall, Godfrey Thomas (1898–): educated Eton and King's College, Cambridge; engineering. Joint managing director, Lagonda Ltd. Joined Courtaulds Ltd., 1948; director and chief engineer, 1949–63.

Whitehead, James Buckley (1898–): educated Oldham High School. Entered textile spinning industry, 1914. Director Lancashire Cotton Corporation Ltd., 1941–64. Director, Courtaulds Ltd. (after acquisition of Lancashire Cotton Corporation), 1964–7. C.B.E.; M.C.: Deputy Lieutenant, Lancashire. J.P. Served in both World Wars I and II.

Whittaker, Croyden Meredith (1878–1960): educated Leeds University; chemistry. Joined Read, Holliday & Sons (dye manufacturers) and became head of their dyeing laboratory. Joined Courtaulds, 1920. Established Courtaulds' yarn dyehouse, Droylsden. Expert on dyeing; awarded Gold Medal of the Society of Dyers and Colourists, 1943; president of that Society, 1946 and 1947. Director, Courtaulds Ltd., 1944–50.

Wilson, Alan Herries (1906–): educated Wallasey Grammar School and Emmanuel College, Cambridge; natural sciences. Fellow, Emmanuel College, 1929–33; Fellow, Trinity College, and university lecturer in mathematics, 1933–45. Author of two standard books on physics; did important research work on semi-conductors. Worked on radio communications and atomic energy during World War II. Joined Courtaulds, 1945, as director in charge of research. Director, Courtaulds Ltd., 1945–54; managing director, 1954–7; deputy chairman, 1957–62; chairman-designate, 1961; resigned 1962. Subsequently chairman, Glaxo Ltd., 1963–76. F.R.S. (1942); Kt. (1961).

Winterbottom, William Travis (1904–): educated Hulme Grammar School, Oldham. Entered cotton industry after World War I. Director Fine Spinners and Doublers Ltd., 1946; chairman, 1950. Director, Courtaulds Ltd. (after acquisition of Fine Spinners and Doublers), 1964–70. C.B.E. (1946).

APPENDIX 3

Glossary of man-made yarns and fibres mentioned in the text

Acrilan	acrylic fibre marketed by Chemstrand
Ardil	protein fibre marketed by I.C.I.
Cellophane	viscose film marketed by British Cellophane Ltd.
Celon	polyamide yarn or fibre of nylon 6 marketed by British Celanese and later Courtaulds
Courlene	polyethylene (polythene) yarn marketed by Courtaulds
Courtelle	acrylic fibre marketed by Courtaulds
Dicel	diacetate textile yarn or fibre marketed by British Celanese and later Courtaulds
Evlan	modified viscose staple fibre marketed by Courtaulds
Fibro	viscose staple fibre marketed by Courtaulds
Fibrolane	casein fibre marketed by Courtaulds
Nylon	polyamide yarn or fibre; generic term, though originally used by Du Pont for nylon 66
Orlon	acrylic fibre marketed by Du Pont
Seraceta	diacetate textile yarn or fibre marketed by Courtaulds
Terylene	polyester yarn or fibre marketed by I.C.I.
Tricel	triacetate textile yarn or fibre marketed by British Celanese and later Courtaulds
Vincel	polynosic viscose staple fibre marketed by Courtaulds

INDEX

60645

Miss Seccatore

6 Cromwell Road

- Ashmolean 765527

- Farquharson 762555

- Prudential 766669

- Pyper 61693